Rediscovering
PAUL

An Introduction to His
World, Letters and Theology

David B. Capes
Rodney Reeves *and*
E. Randolph Richards

IVP Academic
An imprint of InterVarsity Press
Downers Grove, Illinois

Apollos
Nottingham, England

InterVarsity Press, USA
P.O. Box 1400, Downers Grove, IL 60515-1426, USA
World Wide Web: www.ivpress.com
Email: email@ivpress.com

APOLLOS (an imprint of Inter-Varsity Press, England)
Norton Street, Nottingham NG7 3HR, England
Website: www.ivpbooks.com
Email: ivp@ivpbooks.com

InterVarsity Press®, USA, is the book-publishing division of InterVarsity Christian Fellowship/USA®, a student movement active on campus at hundreds of universities, colleges and schools of nursing in the United States of America, and a member movement of the International Fellowship of Evangelical Students. For information about local and regional activities, write Public Relations Dept., InterVarsity Christian Fellowship/USA, 6400 Schroeder Rd., P.O. Box 7895, Madison, WI 53707-7895, or visit the IVCF website at <www.intervarsity.org>.

Inter-Varsity Press, England, is closely linked with the Universities and Colleges Christian Fellowship, a student movement connecting Christian Unions throughout Great Britain, and a member movement of the International Fellowship of Evangelical Students. Website: www.uccf.org.uk.

Scripture quotations, unless otherwise noted, are from the New Revised Standard Version of the Bible, *copyright 1989 by the Division of Christian Education of the National Council of the Churches of Christ in the USA. Used by permission. All rights reserved.*

Design: Cindy Kiple
Images: Scala/Art Resource

USA ISBN 978-0-8308-2598-1
UK ISBN 978-1-84474-242-4

Printed in the United States of America

Library of Congress Cataloging-in-Publication Data

Capes, David B.
  Rediscovering Paul: an introduction to his world, letters, and
theology / David B. Capes, Rodney Reeves, E. Randolph Richards.
      p. cm.
  Includes bibliographical references (p.   ) and indexes.
  ISBN-13: 978-0-8308-2598-1 (cloth: alk. paper)
  1. Paul, the Apostle, Saint. 2. Bible. N.T. Epistles of
Paul—Criticism, interpretation, etc. 3. Bible. N.T. Epistles of
Paul—Theology. I. Reeves, Rodney, 1957- II. Richards, E. Randolph
(Ernest Randolph) III. Title.
  BS2506.3C37 2007
  225.9'2—dc22

                                                                    2007026760

British Library Cataloguing in Publication Data

A catalogue record for this book is available from the British Library.

P	21	20	19	18	17	16	15	14	13	12	11	10	9	8	7	6	5	4	3	2	1
Y	25	24	23	22	21	20	19	18	17	16	15	14	13	12	11	10	09	08	07		

To our professors who taught us about Paul

Bruce Corley

W. D. Davies

E. Earle Ellis

E. P. Sanders

Robert B. Sloan

Contents

Outline

Introduction

The Challenges of Rediscovering Paul

I (RANDOLPH RICHARDS) HAD A NICE, modern Paul, properly trained from centuries in Europe. I liked him. More importantly, I felt comfortable with him. He thought the way I thought. He felt passionately about the same things I did. We shared the same hopes, beliefs and convictions. I was at ease with my Paul. He was a well-domesticated, Western, conservative Paul—one who did not mind that black and white Christians met in separate churches or that I owned an iPod and an Xbox while other Christians lacked basic school supplies. Such inequities should not cause me to lose sleep, my Paul assured me. His commands about wealthier Christians helping to meet the needs of poorer Christians did not apply to my situation. His attempts to get Jews and Gentiles to worship together had no application to the racial problems of today. I was glad that my Paul did not overly challenge me. Some things Paul said did not fit well, but we were able to work it out. Usually I just ignored those statements. My own denomination helped. It printed Scripture passages in our Sunday school booklet (so we would not have to use our Bibles). The assigned passage might be 1 Corinthians 12:1-7, 12-26, nicely avoiding those troubling verses on tongues, healings and miracles.

But then I moved to Borneo and discovered they had a different Paul. I learned this one day when some church elders came to seek my advice about a difficult church issue. A couple wanted to join the church. They had committed a "grievous sin." Afterward they had moved to this village and had been living wonderful, godly lives ever since. Ten years later they asked to join the local church. Should the church accept them? "Well," I diplomatically asked, "how serious was the sin?"

The elders looked pained to have to repeat it, but they told me, "The couple married on the run."

In America we call this an "elopement." I said, "What's the sin?"

They looked at me in shock. Had I never read Paul? I thought I had. They reminded me, "Paul clearly states, 'Children, obey your parents in the Lord'" (Eph 6:1). Of course, children do not always obey their parents, the elders conceded, but surely in what is probably the most important decision of their lives, they should obey. "As Christians," they argued, "should we allow other Christians just to flout the word of God?"

My Indonesian church elders were taking Paul's words very seriously. As an American who believes that individual rights are guaranteed "somewhere in the Bible," I had watered Paul's command down to mean that children should obey their parents while they are minors, or when it was not important, or when they wanted to do it anyway. When my Paul said, "Children, obey your parents," he did not mean to the point of denying oneself, and he certainly did not mean giving up my individual right to choose a spouse. I began to wonder if my Paul was the real Paul.

My college students were stunned when they first watched Mel Gibson's *The Passion of the Christ*. What most stunned them was how "Jesus just took it" when he was abused. They commented, "Steven Segal wouldn't have done that." My American heroes defeat the bad guys and ride off into the sunset. Yet Paul argued that Christians should stay put, raise families, build communities, "lead quiet lives" and take whatever persecution comes their way (1 Thess 2:14; 4:11). I began to question if my Western, domesticated, middle-class perception of Paul was the real Paul. Had my culture superimposed its values over the biblical Paul? Yet don't other cultures do the same? How do we rediscover the Paul of the New Testament?

Perhaps you are reading this book or taking a class in the hope of finding a better understanding of Paul. How will reading another book help us rediscover Paul? There are already plenty of books on Paul out there, and more are written every year. Many of the books are very good. Why another one? As authors, we do not believe that this book offers some new paradigm for understanding Paul, although we do hope to contribute a little to the ongoing discussion. Rather, we see a different problem. Most senior college or beginning seminary courses on Paul try to handle this very broad topic in a single semester or quarter. Most instructors hope to cover a little on the background of Paul, an overview of his life and ministry, a little on Greco-Roman letter writing, perhaps a little exegesis of some select sections of his letters and a survey of Paul's theology. For sources, the instructor has a plethora of options—some of them incredibly detailed. For instance, Martin

Hengel has an entire book just on the life of Paul before his conversion. Then there is Rainer Riesner's comprehensive book on the first years of Paul's ministry. Ben Witherington, John McRay, Jerome Murphy-O'Connor, J. Christiaan Beker, Thomas Schreiner and Michael Gorman each have a useful presentation on the person of Paul, most of them arguing for a particular way of reading his letters. Should an instructor require a student to read several of these to provide a balanced view? To cover Paul's theology, a student could read James D. G. Dunn's 740 pages or the much shorter volume by N. T. Wright. And what about the ministry of Paul, particularly where his experiences connect to his letters, providing context for our exegesis? I (Richards) have written a new introduction to Paul as a letter writer. So, how many books are we up to now? An instructor might well be burned in effigy if he required the purchase of a dozen heavyweight books in a course, especially if he expected the student to actually read them. We are not above challenging our students, but most of these books are intended for a level above an introductory course on Paul.

We wanted a single textbook that covered, in a manageable size, several key aspects of Paul: his background, an introduction to his letters, a survey of his ministry surrounding his letters[1] and an integrated survey of his theology. A little mention of how Paul came to be so important to us in the West would be nice as well. Such a book would reach across multiple fields of study. While there are scholars who excel in all of these disciplines at once, they normally do not write introductory textbooks. Those of us who teach Paul on the introductory level usually feel competent to address one or two of these areas but ill-equipped to deal with the others. One day as we three authors sipped our coffee and bemoaned the problems of teaching an introductory course on Paul, we came to realize that a solution might be a textbook covering multiple facets of Paul written

---

[1]In our reconstruction of Paul's life and career we rely on the Acts of the Apostles and the letters of Paul. Scholarship in the nineteenth and twentieth centuries rightly rejected an uncritical harmony of Acts and the letters of Paul. Unfortunately there arose afterwards a great skepticism of Luke's reliability. Hence books on Paul were written independently of Acts or using only those sections of Acts that the particular author deemed "accurate." More recent studies on Acts, particularly those of Martin Hengel, Luke Timothy Johnson, Ben Witherington, Stanley Porter, Colin Hemer and the six-volume collection of essays, *The Book of Acts in Its First-Century Setting*, ed. Bruce Winter (Grand Rapids: Eerdmans, 1993-), have convinced many that Luke is a reliable interpreter of Paul. My colleagues' description of me will differ from how I describe myself; yet I hesitate to assert which description is more accurate. Both can be reliable, when we understand the nature of each. E. E. Ellis draws another analogy: "Which would give the better historical perspective of, say, Field Marshall B. Montgomery's career in World War II, a dozen of his letters written in the heat of his campaigns in North Africa and Normandy or a considered historical survey written afterwards by a contemporary admirer, say, the historian, A. J. P. Taylor?" (E. E. Ellis, *Pauline Theology* [Grand Rapids: Eerdmans, 1989], p. 134).

by multiple authors. Yet we did not want a collection of disconnected essays. We wanted a finished product that was relatively seamless, speaking with one voice while still drawing on the expertise of each author. So we assigned chapters to each of us and then met regularly to hash and rehash each chapter until we were each satisfied. Our goal was to present an overview of Paul that gathers together context, content and theology with the goal of answering that perennial question of students: "So what?"

We are convinced that the aspects of Paul covered in this book do affect how we understand his letters and ultimately how all of this applies to our lives as followers of Jesus. The Paul discovered by readers and interpreters in America should not be so utterly different from the Paul discovered in Africa or Asia. And since Paul exhorts Christians to imitate Christ by imitating him, we need to find Paul and follow him.

To help us rediscover Paul, we will begin by describing the Mediterranean world in which he lived and worked. We do not present a full description of cities, rivers, mountains and such things—though there would be great value in this—rather, we want to look at how someone in the first-century Mediterranean saw his or her world. For example, it is impossible to understand Paul's world without recognizing the role of honor and shame. Students new to biblical studies often struggle to see how it could be so important, and yet "honor contests" were probably instrumental in leading Jewish authorities to crucify Jesus. It certainly was not his sermon on loving one another. Most of us are aware that Jews were concerned with purity, which American Christians have largely reduced to "sexual purity." The ancient world saw virtually everything in terms of purity. Related concepts of economics and social relationships must also be explored if we wish to understand the Mediterranean world of Paul. In America we see economic factors as disconnected from social relationships: business is business. In the ancient world no one doubted their interconnectedness. For this reason Paul could write, "Whatever was profit to me, I count as loss in view of the surpassing value of knowing Christ Jesus my Lord, for whom I have suffered the loss of all things" (Phil 3:7-8, our paraphrase).

The Mediterranean world of the first century had recently been restructured under the Greeks and then the Romans. According to Luke, Paul was a citizen of the Roman Empire. More than that, Paul was a dislocated member of a conquered race within this empire. He was a Jew, born outside Palestine. Diaspora Jews, as we refer to those who were not living in the land of promise, could not go up to the temple every day for the hours of prayer. They did not routinely offer sacrifices on the Jewish holidays. What did it mean to be Jewish for these people? Moreover,

Paul was not just a Jew living in the Roman Empire. He was a Pharisee. Living as a Pharisee in a Gentile empire shaped Paul's view of law (Torah), his social identity, his values, his mission in life—his worldview.

Once we have a general understanding of Paul's world and how he viewed it, we will look for Paul through his letters. Paul left us no autobiography. Luke did not intend Acts to be a biography of Paul. The best way to find Paul is to examine his letters. We cannot, however, simply read Paul's letters in the same way we read letters today. Two millennia and a vast cultural gap separate us as letter readers from Paul. To help bridge this gap, we must first look at typical letters of Paul's day. This will help us to see how Paul was like other writers of his day. We cannot stop there though, for Paul was also quite different from other writers. It is in his similarities and differences from other first-century letter writers that we begin to rediscover Paul the letter writer.

After describing Paul's world and looking into how he wrote letters, we will place his letters into the context of his ministry. When we do, immediately we are faced with the challenges of the continuities and the discontinuities between the epistolary Paul (the Paul seen through his letters) and the Lukan Paul (the Paul described in Acts). Neither is, of course, the real flesh-and-blood Paul. This, and nearly every other aspect of Paul's life, is debated, and students can become quickly lost in the quagmire of scholarly arguments. Two common approaches to discovering the "historical Paul" are used. Some scholars will begin with a more skeptical approach, questioning the historical accuracy of Acts. This approach centers on the letters, the so-called epistolary Paul, relegating Acts to the status of "secondary source material." Paul's letters, it is argued, are more reliable since they come from his pen. Luke's stories about Paul, on the other hand, cannot be trusted since they are biased secondhand accounts. For example, some question if Paul really was a student of Gamaliel in Jerusalem (Acts 22:3), since he makes no mention of it in Philippians 3:4-6.

The other approach takes Acts to be as reliable as the letters of Paul. Even though the debate over the accuracy of Acts still rages among New Testament scholars, in this book we accept Luke's account of the early church as a useful source for understanding Paul and his world.

Without a general framework on which to hang the various discussions, students often finish well versed in the details of Paul's life but lacking any big picture. In order to establish a context for his letters—why did Paul write this letter to that church?—we shall present an overview of the ministry of Paul, drawing upon commonly agreed reconstructions. His life and ministry will be presented in three general stages: his conversion and call, his itinerant ministry and finally his ministry from prison. While general frameworks can always be critiqued for being inaccurate in the details, we have found it helpful for beginning students of Paul to have such a broad outline.

Looking at Paul's world, his letter-writing practices and his ministry is fruitless if it does not affect how we understand his letters. Paul had his reasons for writing letters. Therefore, we must interpret Paul's letters in light of their historical context, identifying the major themes and theological contributions of the apostle to the Gentiles. Thus we must also pay careful attention to Paul's own situation. The itinerant letters will be examined separately from the prison and personal letters. What was written in his letters had as much to do with what Paul himself was experiencing as the problems he was trying to address. These letters say as much about him as his converts.

But there is one more problem. Not all scholars think that every letter attributed to Paul actually came from him. In fact, only Romans, 1 and 2 Corinthians, Galatians, Philippians, 1 Thessalonians and Philemon are "uncontested" Pauline letters. Doubts persist about the authenticity of Ephesians, Colossians, 2 Thessalonians, 1 and 2 Timothy and Titus. Was it really Paul who wrote these other letters? Prior to the nineteenth century most biblical scholars assumed Paul either wrote his letters or dictated them to a secretary verbatim. This meant that the vocabulary, style and kinds of theological expressions in his letters should reflect a single author's mind. Letters were compared and those noticeably different in vocabulary and style were declared inauthentic: Paul did not write them. For a number of reasons, some scholars decided that Romans, 1 Corinthians, 2 Corinthians and Galatians were the genuine letters of Paul. Letters that shared the same style, manner of argument and themes—particularly justification by faith—were also deemed authentic. Comparing some of the other letters (e.g., Ephesians, 1 Timothy and Titus) with the "genuine letters," these scholars concluded that these other letters are so different in style and theological themes that they could not have been penned by the apostle Paul. Instead, anonymous Christians, inspired by Paul, wrote them in honor of their hero in the faith. Such letters are called pseudonymous, because they were written falsely under the name of another. This practice, it was claimed, was so common in the culture that early Christians did it as well. In the end many scholars pronounced only the undisputed letters to be useful in understanding the apostle to the Gentiles.

Our own research, however, has called into question these assumptions and conclusions at several levels. First, as we will show, Paul's letters were communal products, not the work of a single mind. Secretaries and co-authors exercised an influence over the composition of these letters. So the kinds of stylistic analyses done by previous generations of scholars do not prove whether a letter is genuinely Pauline. Second, Paul's letters contain a significant amount of preformed traditions (quoted material that was formed prior to the letter), including confessions, hymns, Scripture and scriptural interpretations, lists of virtues and vices, and so on. Although the amount of preformed material in the thirteen letters is debated, it is clear that any such preformed materials could differ from Paul in language, style and even theological emphases. Still, the fact that Paul included preformed materials in his letters means that he accepted what they were teaching. Third, Paul's letters were written to address various audiences on various occasions. This alone can account for certain differences in language, style and theological argument. Stylistic analysis is useful only when two distinct documents have (roughly) the same audience and subject in view. Finally, Paul's letters were written over a period of years, while the apostle himself and the churches he served were changing. Paul was no static leader. His was a dynamic church. Although development is hard to track and one must be careful not to draw too many hard-and-fast conclusions, we should at least recognize that twenty years of church planting, struggles against opponents, imprisonments and near-death experiences, as well as just growing older, do change a man. We should expect that these changes would show up in his letters.

We do not find the arguments against the authenticity of the disputed letters convincing. The presence of Pauline features in all of the questionable letters and the early church's witness to their authenticity suggest to us that Paul is at the core of every letter in the New Testament that bears his name. It is hard for us to set aside the claims of those who lived in Paul's culture, who were fluent in his language and were conversant in all the theological problems he faced.[2] If the church fathers were fully convinced these letters came from Paul, we must be careful not to override their voices too quickly in favor of modern, flawed assumptions regarding letter composition in the ancient world.

The final part of the book steps beyond the life and ministry of Paul and considers the importance of his legacy. Paul started churches to extend his gospel ministry, and yet it was his letters that ended up preserving his influence for the ages. His letters were collected, copied and used by the early church because they proved to be helpful to Christians other than the Galatians, Corinthians, Thessalonians and Romans. His timely advice came to be recognized as the timeless Word of

---

[2]See Irenaeus *Against Heresies* 2.17.7; 3.3.3; Polycarp *Philippians* 4.1; also Tertullian *Against Marcion* 2.21.

God. His ideas about Christ, about salvation, about the church and about God extended the reach of his influence far beyond the geography of the Mediterranean and the time of the first century. So we end our study of the apostle's life and ministry by highlighting how Paul has influenced Christians, from the early church fathers in the east to our postmodern world in the west. Since he was known for addressing issues head-on, perhaps Paul can help us with some of the problems we face today.

Paul claimed he was commandeered by Christ and, because of this, the Philippians should join in imitating him, Paul (Phil 3:12-17). We, the authors, want to imitate Paul and have committed our lives to this task. Yet we do not want to follow a Western, middle-class Paul who is so removed from the biblical Paul that children can freely disobey their parents and church members can justify racism. Our personal quest is to redisover Paul so that we can imitate him as he imitates Christ. We hope you will do the same.

SPECIAL FEATURES
Two types of text boxes will appear in most chapters.

SO WHAT?
Several times in each chapter, we will seek to show the "So what?"—the "why it matters"—for the topic we are discussing, whether it be background or letter-writing customs. Why does it matter where and how Paul ministered? How does this help *us* understand his letters? Moreover, why does it matter how *we* read and exegete his letters when we are extracting his gospel—his theology—from the letters? Likewise, why does it matter if *we* study Paul at all? How does his theology impact *us*? What difference has it made in our lives as twentieth-first-century Christians?

WHAT'S MORE . . .
These "What's more . . ." boxes present additional information that supplements our discussion, gives further background or explores related issues we hope will help you rediscover Paul.

Most chapters will end with "Read More About It," a brief list of recommended readings. Among other books, you will find a list of relevant articles from the *DPL: Dictionary of Paul and His Letters,* edited by Gerald F. Hawthorne, Ralph P. Martin and Daniel G. Reid (Downers Grove, Ill.: InterVarsity Press, 1993).

A glossary at the back of this book defines key terms you will encounter in your reading of *Rediscovering Paul.*

1

Rediscovering Paul in His World

PAUL DID NOT THINK LIKE A twenty-first-century Western Christian. His ways were not our ways. His priorities were quite different. For example, he did not share our "family values" that hold up marriage as the ultimate goal for everyone. Instead, Paul contended that believers should try to remain single. To him, a celibate convert was more devoted to Christ than a married person (1 Cor 7:8, 29-35). Paul did not operate with the assumption that all churches should think for themselves either. The apostle to the Gentiles did not believe in freedom of speech. Instead, he required his converts to conform to his directives, to keep his instructions, to think like him, to imitate him (1 Cor 11:1, 2, 16; 14:28, 38; Gal 5:10). And Paul, like his contemporaries, did not maintain that all people are created equal, born with "inalienable rights." Paul was convinced God made some people superior to others (Rom 3:1, 2; 9:20, 21). These convictions offend our sensibilities, tempting some of us to rehabilitate Paul to our way of thinking. The verses we like, we teach. The parts of his letters that do not support our convictions, we ignore, or we try to convince others that "Paul did not really mean that." But before we argue for our convictions, perhaps we should let Paul argue his. Rather than trying to understand Paul on our terms, we should try to figure out what he meant on his terms. Paul belonged to his world, not to ours. His letters were addressed to his converts, not to us. So before we can understand Paul and his letters, we need to study his world.

This is going to require much effort on our part. It is difficult enough to make sense of the beliefs and ways of peoples who live around the Mediterranean today. How much more work will it take to describe the peoples who lived in the same region two thousand years ago? How are we supposed to rediscover the first-century world of Paul and his neighbors?

Resources for a scholarly study of the first-century Mediterranean world are three: texts, artifacts and case studies. Historians study literature from the period—religious writings, political histories, letters, novels, plays, inscriptions—in hopes of getting a first-hand description of life in the first century. The problem with relying exclusively upon literary evidence is that it reveals primarily what the literary elite had to say about their world. Most Mediterranean people were functionally illiterate. Therefore, in order to reconstruct a picture of the everyday life of the common man or woman of the first century, archaeologists excavate sites where Mediterranean peoples used to live. The artifacts they uncover can tell us much about the languages, diet, religious practices, housing conditions, domestic chores, trade labor, infrastructure and economy of certain villages, towns and cities. Finally, anthropologists study rural communities in modern Greece, Turkey, Lebanon, Israel and Saudi Arabia in order to describe the current, shared social convictions of these different ethnic groups. Biblical scholars take these field studies and compare them with observations gleaned from literary texts and archaeological reconstructions and correlate the evidence. Cultural anthropologists show how Mediterranean peoples of the last fifty years share similar social convictions with first-century inhabitants of Achaia, Asia Minor, Syria, Judea and Arabia. Put it all together and students can get a general picture of what life was like in the first-century Mediterranean world.

LIVING IN THE MEDITERRANEAN WORLD

The peoples who lived around the Mediterranean basin in the first century negotiated a multicultural world, as indeed they do today. It was a pluralistic world of various religions, languages, foods, fashions, currencies, schools, houses, shrines and nations. Different ethnic groups sought to preserve their social identity by resisting cultural conformity. Old ways, ancestral customs and family traditions were more easily preserved in rural areas than in the high-traffic urban centers connected by Roman roads. Greeks differed from barbarians as much as Jews distinguished themselves from Gentiles. And yet, despite the diversity, these different peoples had similar religious experiences, shared social customs and possessed a common Mediterranean worldview (also called "symbolic universe"). In certain respects, they looked at life the same way. They shared similar priorities. Their social networks operated according to the same general rules. Consequently, scholars can speak, in the broadest context, about the culture of first-century Mediterranean people. So, what did first-century Mediterranean peoples believe?

All things come from God/gods. In Paul's day, people did not think in terms of "natural resources." Every nation, every trade, every territory was given, governed and controlled by divine powers. Israel believed that Judea was given by YHWH to the Hebrews in order to take care of his people (Judg 11:24). All Mediterranean peoples believed the same about their gods. God sent rain in order to bring crops to maturation to feed his people (Ps 65:9). His blessing would mean abundance.

SO WHAT?
Don't We Also Believe That God Is in Charge of Our Lives?

Actually, we believe in the power of choice. We create our own destinies. We believe in choosing our own lifestyle. To the Mediterranean peoples, a person's destiny was already determined by God's choice. Wealth, status, power and privilege belonged to those who were born into the right family. No one could choose to be a priest or a king or a father or a man. A proper pedigree was required to serve God in the temple or reign over his people. For example, the people of Israel recognized Levites as priests and hoped for a "son of David" to be their king. God is the potter; we are merely the clay. Paul pointedly asked, "Will the one who is molded say to the one who molds it, 'Why have you made me like this?'" (Rom 9:20, author's trans.)

His curse would bring limited goods. Since the great majority of the population dealt with meager resources, most people were convinced they were living under God's curse. In order to placate divine powers, then, devotees would do whatever the priests told them to do without question. Worshiping God was not a matter of choice; it was a requirement of communal life. All were dependent upon God's care and protection. To promote God's honor, then, was to promote the welfare of the community (Prov 3:9-10). Sinners were deviants who jeopardized the favor of God for all. Compliance, therefore, was the mark of a faithful devotee.

God is the source of life—the power that opens the womb of a woman. Fertility drugs were empowered by fertility gods. God created male and female. Men were built for the outdoors; women sought domestication. The rich were born into wealthy families. Landowners inherited their domain. Power belonged to nobility because they owned the land that fed the people. All of this was by divine design (Sirach 33:10-13). God made certain people superior to others—some to rule, some to govern, some to manage, some to labor, some to farm, some to beg. The circumstances of people's birth, their station in life, the place of their birth and even the trade they learned from their fathers were predetermined by God. People were born into their religion and their vocation. If you were born to a king, a king you would be. If you were born to a farmer, a farmer you would be. If you were born poor, you were meant to be poor. If you were born into the retainer class, God intended for you to manage the land and its resources. The Romans, for example, were convinced that the gods gave them dominion over their subjects in order that they could become the world's benefactors. They maintained that the benefit of Roman rule was a gift from their gods.

Herein lies the irony. We know our "natural resources" will eventually run out. We are developing alternative energy sources because one day there will be no oil. Yet we are as wasteful as though we lived in a world of unlimited goods. The Med-

---

WHAT'S MORE . . .
Paul and Predestination

Like his Mediterranean neighbors, Paul believed that God destined certain individuals for certain tasks: "Let each of you lead the life that the Lord has assigned, to which God called you. This is my rule in all the churches" (1 Cor 7:17). Spiritual gifts were assigned by God (1 Cor 12:4-11). God gave certain persons more honorable gifts than others (1 Cor 12:24); he made different persons for different tasks (1 Cor 12:17-18). To object to God's purpose was analogous to a clay pot questioning the design of its maker (Rom 9:20-21). Indeed, to Paul "the gifts and the calling of God are irrevocable" (Rom 11:29). Paul knew that all too well. God made him an apostle (Gal 1:1, 15-16). God assigned him the field of his work: the Gentiles (2 Cor 10:13; Gal 2:8). Yet Paul was no determinist. Did he believe God could change a man's destiny? Quoting Hosea, Paul argued that his Gentile converts were sons of Abraham even though they were born pagans, because God said: "Those who were not my people I will call 'my people'" (Rom 9:25). According to Paul, God added the law to the covenant because of sin (Gal 3:19). Describing the ever-changing ways of God, Paul warned his readers that God could graft in and break off branches of Abraham's family tree (Rom 11:17-21). Indeed, God could change the destiny of a person's birth (Eph 2:11-13). And according to Paul, this was good news indeed.

---

iterranean peoples believed, on the other hand, that all things come from God/
gods—powers of everlasting supply. And yet the gods seemed to parcel out their
blessings in limited supply, making their subjects totally dependent. There was
only so much rain, so much land, so much food, so much wealth, so much power,
so much influence and so much honor to go around in a subsistence society. If
someone had more than they needed, someone else had less. Theirs was an agonistic world, that is, a world where competition for limited goods required alliances among social equals.

This was especially evident in rural areas, where villagers relied upon each other
to maintain their standard of living. They shared their goods and services with
each other. Their children married each other. There was no room (or need!) for
upward mobility. Limited supplies required thrifty lifestyles and occasional forays
into the big cities to sell their wares. Living in towns without gates, villagers did
not take kindly to outsiders. Walled cities, on the other hand, were urban centers
that welcomed travelers because city dwellers needed merchants, day-laborers,
messengers and even itinerant teachers like Paul.

It takes a village to raise a child. In the Mediterranean world, individual accomplishments did not define the significance of a person. Instead, a person's identity
was wrapped up in the reputation of his or her family, community and people
group. Scholars call this a "dyadic personality." Self-discovery came from the opinion of others, not from self-reflection. The family you were born into, the village
of your nativity and the alliances you maintained with other groups established
your individual identity. When Paul was in trouble in Jerusalem, he did not identify himself as "the apostle to the Gentiles" or "slave of Christ" or any other favorite self-designation that we find in his letters. Instead, he relied upon the conventional social markers of his day, "I am a Jew, born in Tarsus in Cilicia, but brought
up in this city at the feet of Gamaliel" (Acts 22:3). First, when Paul identified
himself he was quick to point to his membership within an honorable covenant
community. He was essentially saying, "I am one of you." Second, he saw himself
as a citizen of Tarsus, "an important city" (Acts 21:39). And last, he was the disciple of a prominent Pharisee, raised in Jerusalem, the holy city. These were not
claims of individual accomplishments. Paul was a product of his family, his city,
his people and his traditions.

Those who knew their place in society always promoted the welfare of their
own family in order to maintain their collective social influence in their hometown
(see how Paul applied the same idea in Phil 2:3-4). Fathers kept children in line.
Tribal elders governed family clans. This social hierarchy required individuals to

comply with societal demands, confirming divinely appointed roles and class distinctions. Women submitted to men. Children obeyed parents. Kings ruled over subjects. Priests required sacrifices. To subvert the social order was to disobey God (Sirach 3:16). Individualists, then, were social pariahs bent on destroying themselves and their communities. They committed social suicide when they "left home to make their fortune." Prodigal sons always failed.

Everyone needs a friend in high places. In a world without pension plans and insurance companies, the Mediterranean peoples relied upon each other to weather hard times. Living in an unpredictable, risky world of limited goods made family relations and tribal networks indispensable to maintaining the welfare of any community. Arranged marriages kept economic resources close to

---

SO WHAT?
Isn't Everyone an Individual Deep Down Inside?

Well, we think in active terms. We believe we are the sum of our choices. Who we are is what we make of ourselves. We want to be unique. We want to make our mark on the world. To rise above humble beginnings, to overcome the challenges of a poor neighborhood, to become who we want to be by the sheer force of our will, this is the American dream. For Paul and his contemporaries, however, the drive to "be somebody" would be a Mediterranean nightmare. Self-promotion jeopardized the welfare of the community. Rebels were considered selfish individuals, looking out for their own interests at the expense of others.

---

home. Kinship was the most reliable means of keeping what you had or, more desirably, improving your (and your village's) economic power and social status. Friendships were also used to create some opportunities for upward mobility even though most relations were formed among social equals; that is, the elite kept to themselves, the retainer class had their own clubs, merchants lived in the same part of town. Trade guilds formed to insure shared economic prosperity and protect commercial turf. Religious societies, dining clubs and schools of philosophers and sophists maintained networks among members of equal status. These social groups operated much like families, where shared interests were protected by members swearing the same allegiances.

Whether in kinship or in friendship, persons of low status had a hard time improving their situation in life. Yet not all friendships were social alliances created among equals. Since the only way for most people to get ahead in the Mediterranean world was to become the beneficiary of a wealthy person, everyone wanted to be known as a "friend" of powerful, rich people. Gift-giving was the primary means for social inferiors to form alliances with the aristocracy (Prov 18:16). Magistrates received all kinds of gifts (bribes?) from friends as preventative maintenance, insuring future favorable rulings of the courts. Cities vied for Caesar's affections by erecting monuments and declaring special days in his honor. Ironically, those who had the least gave generously to those who had the most in hopes of garnering favors for an uncertain future. Benefactors, therefore, were constantly greeted by strangers bearing gifts. Patrons had to be careful because once the gift was accepted, the friendship was sealed, and the patron was bound by honor to reciprocate with favors only a wealthy, powerful man could bestow. Why would any patron accept such gifts, since strings were attached? Patrons secured the praise of their clients who would boast of the generosity of their benefactors. Indeed, such boasting was expected; clients were more than willing to comply since ingrates were considered shameful persons. So clients needed money; patrons sought honor. Everyone had to give in order to get. The Mediterranean world operated exclusively on quid pro quo arrangements.

Honor is the only game in town. The quest for honor made everyone play by the rules. Roman law may have prevented chaos. But the universal desire for honor, from the richest to the poorest, made the world orderly. Honor was the highest good. The approval of a man's social group meant more than the acquiring of wealth or the wielding of unquestioned power: "A good name is to be chosen rather than great riches" (Prov 22:1). Honor defined success. Since a person's worth was determined by their social group, honorable recognition established an individual's significance. A man without a country, a woman without a family and a stranger without friends would have no chance of claiming honor. To us, love is the greatest good, a universal need that defines a person's self-worth. Love can be given by anyone and received by all. In the Mediterranean world, honor could only be received by those worthy of recognition. Honor was deserved. It was owed. A man could not claim honor by himself. He had to receive it from those who had it. Honor could only be given by honorable people. Therefore, honor was a social commodity of collective interest. An individual's honor depended upon a group's approval, and a group's honor depended upon the behavior of its members.

All honor came ultimately from God (Sirach 3:2). He endowed certain persons with unquestioned honor: kings, priests and fathers. All subjects honored the king.

All worshipers offered sacrifices required by the priests. All children obeyed their fathers. To honor these whom God had chosen to be kings, priests and fathers was to honor God. By giving honor to whom honor was due, members of a social group preserved their own honor as well. In other words, when children honored their parents, they were bringing honor to their family and, consequently, to themselves (Sirach 3:11). It was up to the members of a social group, therefore, to preserve the honor of their honorable head. Any member that dishonored their head brought shame to their group. This is why, for Paul, church discipline was a corporate reality: "Is it not those who are inside that you are to judge? God will judge those out-

---

WHAT'S MORE . . .
Paul's Gift

During his third mission trip, Paul collected a monetary gift for the mother church in Jerusalem. He required his converts to gather a relief offering for the "poor among the saints at Jerusalem" (Rom 15:26). From Galatia to Corinth, Paul instructed the churches to prepare the offering in anticipation of his visit, collecting the money every time they met for worship (1 Cor 16:1-4). Then he, along with representatives from each church, would carry the gift to Jerusalem, "for the rendering of this ministry not only supplies the needs of the saints but also overflows with many thanksgivings to God" (2 Cor 9:12). Paul counted on a joyous celebration when the poor Jewish Christians in Jerusalem would welcome the gift of his generous Gentile converts. Apparently that did not happen. Luke never mentioned the gift. Would he purposefully exclude such a unifying moment in early church history? In fact Paul's arrival in Jerusalem was greeted with hostility rather than praise (Acts 21:28). It seems the gift meant more than simply a sincere expression of Christian charity. Even Paul admitted that, by accepting the relief offering, the mother church would be putting their stamp of approval on his mission to the Gentiles (Rom 15:31). According to Paul, his converts were paying back materially what they had received from the first Christians spiritually (Rom 15:27). By accepting the gift, the Jerusalem church would have signaled their acceptance of the role of benefactor, with Paul's churches as clients. But more than that, they would then be obliged to repay honor for honor, giving their spiritual blessing to Paul's converts and his ministry. Did Jerusalem accept Paul's gift, perhaps without fanfare? We will never know. But we do know that, in Paul's day, gifts came with strings attached.

---

side. 'Drive out the wicked person from among you'" (1 Cor 5:12-13). Since the social identity of a person's group revealed his or her own significance, members disciplined malcontents, shaming them into submission (see 2 Cor 2:6-11, where the Corinthians had gone too far in shunning a rebel). Sometimes disapproving looks or mocking sounds sufficed, such as turning heads or "separating the lip" (what Americans call giving someone "a raspberry," see Ps 22:6-7). Public beatings or menial tasks were given to those who persisted in their rebellion (Acts 5:40-41; Lk 15:15). People shunned disobedient members of their group to make them ashamed of their socially unacceptable behavior and bring them back into conformity. Peer pressure, then, was considered a good thing (Sirach 4:21).

All males sought esteem and therefore competed for recognition within their social group. These social contests for honor were constant; the honor game was on at all times. As a man you were either trying to get honor from someone or protecting your honor from someone else. Sometimes the quest for honor involved friendly competition. In these cases, honorable men gave honor to noble members to encourage loyalty. Oftentimes the contest for honor was an act of aggression in which one man challenged the manhood of another. These challenges were always made in the public arena, requiring the offended party to defend himself in the presence of his social group, such as when Paul opposed Peter "to his face" (Gal 2:11). If he believed that the challenge was insignificant or that it came from an insignificant man, he would ignore the challenger's demands—it would be beneath him to dignify his inferior with a response (did Peter respond to Paul's challenge?).

If his social group agreed (showing signs of contempt), then the challenger would be shamed by the hubris of his "shameless attempt" to steal the man's honor. If, however, the challenge threatened the offended, then he would be required to make riposte, defending his honor. This could be done by threatening the offender with retaliation, making him back down, by giving one's own version of the events that led to the challenge or by simply appealing to the support of his group. Regardless of the tactics employed by the offended party, the outcome of the contest was determined by the members. A successful challenge or defense would mean the loss of one man's honor to another.

Boasting and jealousy were necessary defense mechanisms for a man trying to maintain his honorable status. In order to make potential challengers think twice before attempting to take another man's honor, members constantly boasted of their significance in their community. To us boasting is bragging, blatant self-promotion. For the Mediterranean peoples, boasting was the surest way to keep social order. Everyone had their place; everyone knew their role. So boasting was the acceptable means of reminding everyone of a man's claim to honor—his status within the group. In fact, members expected their honorable leader to boast of his pedigree, his accomplishments and his importance in order to preserve the honor of the entire group. Members would often join in, adding their claims to his boasting (Acts 12:22). By doing so, they were promoting their own honor.[1] To look out for your own honor was the same as guarding the honor of your group and your honorable head.

Paul believed God gave him the honor of being the apostle to the Gentiles (see Gal 1:1, 15-16). James, Peter and John recognized his apostleship (Gal 2:7-9). His converts were supposed to defend his honor as their apostle (2 Cor 12:11). Paul claimed he was a true apostle because he had seen the resurrected Messiah, just as

---

SO WHAT?
What About Ordinary Questions?

In the world of Jesus and Paul, private conversations were considered "friendly" (see Jn 3:1-2). Public confrontations were always intended as a challenge to a man's honor. Public questions, therefore, were never asked for the sake of gaining information. When the disciples did not understand Jesus' parable, they asked in private (Mk 4:10). If they asked in public, it was a challenge to Jesus' honor. When the lawyer asked Jesus, "What must I do to inherit eternal life?" he was not looking for information (Lk 10:25). When Matthew said no one dared to ask Jesus any more questions (Mt 22:46), he meant public questions. They were tired of losing honor to Jesus. They needed another way to get back their lost honor (Mt 26:3-5).

---

all the other apostles had (1 Cor 15:7-10). Despite the fact that many questioned Paul's claim to honor, he argued that his converts proved his apostleship; they believed the message he delivered as Christ's emissary (1 Cor 9:2). What better proof did he need (2 Cor 3:2)? Yet even his own converts questioned his authority as their apostle (2 Cor 13:3). After all, Paul refused apostolic privileges, such as receiving payment for preaching. He refused to boast in his strengths and would only boast in his weaknesses (2 Cor 11:30). He admitted that he should be considered the least honorable of the apostles (1 Cor 15:9). All of this invited chal-

---

[1]See 2 Corinthians 12:11-13, where Paul is annoyed with his converts because they *did not* protect his honor, thereby also compromising theirs.

lengers to question his honor as an apostle. Therefore in most of his letters Paul had to defend his honor. To us it looks excessive—a man constantly setting before his readers his claims and putting down his opponents. Perhaps Paul was vulnerable to these challenges since he did not measure up to the conventional requirements of an apostle, such as those laid out by Luke in Acts 1:21-22. Furthermore, this constant challenge and riposte was typical of an agonistic culture, in which those who claimed honor were required to defend it all the time.

Rituals preserve the sacred. Even though Mediterranean societies believed that God shared his honor only with certain people, they were convinced he lent his power to all creation. Behind every power was a divine initiative. Rain, wind, fire, disease, life, death—these uncontrollable forces could prove to be benevolent or malevolent, depending upon the purity of the devotees. Reckless living invited chaotic powers to wreak havoc. So all religions had their own ideas about how they could placate malevolent powers and invoke the blessings of good gods. Typically these rules not only governed how priests and temples were to function in the presence of the holy but also what rituals were to be performed outside the bounds of "sacred space" in hopes of creating order and controlling the powers. We would call such rituals "superstitions," because we presume to know why it rains, or how viruses invade bodies, or why infections cause fevers.

We understand the microscopic world. But to people of the first century, fevers were not a good sign. Instead, when a child suffered a fever, they believed evil powers were attacking. Indeed, children seemed to be the most vulnerable to evil powers; they were always getting sick. According to our best estimates, in the first-century world only one out of five children lived to the age of thirty.[2] To the inhabitants of that world, the survival of the fittest was not a function of natural selection. Healthy persons were favored by the gods. When Jesus was asked to bless the children, it certainly included the hope that they would not die.

Since first-century people did not know about bacteria, why did they care so much about cleansing and purity? They seemed to be obsessed with cleanliness; all religions had purification rites. Why all the fuss? Every power, every divine gift was a dangerous blessing—a prickly pear that must be handled with care. The ability to give birth, for example, was a sacred event, a sharing of divine power with humans. Therefore, sacrifices were required and purification rites were followed in order to show proper homage to the God who made it all possible. To share in the execution of divine powers rendered humans unclean, unworthy to partake of the

---

[2]T. F. Carney, *The Shape of the Past: Models and Antiquity* (Lawrence, Kans.: Coronado Press, 1975), p. 88.

sacred. Being "clean" had nothing to do with being sterile. Instead, devotees kept certain taboos in order to ward off any hostile spiritual power that would harm them. These rituals were not ethical instructions based on a moral rationale, such as "we must give thanks to God because he is good." Purity rites were required to protect the unclean from a holy God. Those who did not observe these rituals polluted their community with their uncleanness. Sickness, disease and death were the result (see 1 Cor 11:29-30). Uncleanness begat more uncleanness, making matters worse, which is why those who were cursed by God were segregated from the clean, the purified, the blessed.[3]

A holy God could only be worshiped by a holy people in a holy place. The first-century Mediterranean people divided the world into sacred and profane (or

---

WHAT'S MORE . . .
Chronological Snobbery

It is good to live in the modern era where infectious diseases are conquered by antibiotics (sort of), weapons of war are sophisticated (we have "smart" bombs), and people are not oppressed by demons (at least my friends aren't). Are we kidding ourselves? We know "how" flu viruses invade bodies, but "why" did this person get it and not that person? Bad luck and poor hygiene? Should Christians even believe in "luck"? Could God (or worse, a malevolent spirit) be behind it? Not in our worldview. We are convinced spiritual forces have nothing to do with the microscopic world. We look at people one hundred years ago and say, "Bless their hearts; they didn't really understand the world. They just did the best they knew how." A hundred years from now, will others say the same about us?

"common") space. Territory that was sacred was clearly marked out and dedicated in purity to a holy God. Everywhere else was considered profane since it was traversed by unclean as well as clean persons. Those who served in the presence of the holy—priests—needed to be "clean" by observing special restrictive regulations regarding dress, diet, sexual intercourse and purification rites. Entrances to shrines warned visitors about violating sacred space. To enter the temple with unclean

---

[3]In his book *Honor, Patronage, Kinship and Purity: Unlocking New Testament Culture* (Downers Grove, Ill.: InterVarsity Press, 2000), David A. deSilva gives a number of examples from Greco-Roman literature of the problem of purity and pollution in religious life, pp. 249-53.

hands, offer an unfit sacrifice or partake of a sacred meal in an unworthy fashion would pollute the sanctuary and defile fellow worshipers, inviting holy wrath ("Whoever, therefore, eats the bread or drinks the cup of the Lord in an unworthy manner . . . eat[s] and drink[s] judgment against themselves," 1 Cor 11:27, 29). Uncleanness was a contagion, contaminating the whole community ("For this reason many of you are weak and ill, and some have died," 1 Cor 11:30). On the other hand, obedient members curried the favor of God by maintaining holiness, that is, keeping themselves clean (via purification rites, observing taboos, offering sacrifices) and avoiding impurity (observing social boundaries determined by the sacred). This would mean God's blessing upon a man's family, his clan, his village and even his land ("For the unbelieving husband is made holy through his wife, and the unbelieving wife is made holy through her husband. Otherwise, your children would be unclean, but as it is, they are holy," 1 Cor 7:14). So worshiping the right gods in the right place and in the right way was important to all Mediterranean peoples. Even foreigners were expected to pay their respects to local gods.

Exclusive devotion to their God created problems for the Jews of the Diaspora, those Jewish people who did not live in Palestine. They refused to pay homage to local gods. They kept strict purity codes (diet, purification rites, dress). Indeed, since purity codes established social boundaries for all peoples, the holiness code of Judaism made the Jewish people appear to be isolationists. Their nonconformist ways created social problems that sometimes led to political confrontations.[4] For example, the imperial cult (the worship of Caesar) brought political favors to devoted subjects of any particular city. The Jewish people, of course, refused to promote the worship of Caesar, either by offering the obligatory annual sacrifices at imperial shrines, by contributing to funds for the construction of imperial shrines, or by participating in civic events that deified emperors past or present (birthday memorials, pagan festivals, etc.).[5] Even though Judaism was recognized by Rome as an official religion, in certain regions hostilities persisted against the Jewish people for their noncompliance (especially in Egypt and parts of Asia Minor). Sometimes Jews of the Diaspora were able to mollify their pagan neighbors by supporting other public works projects or by adopting Gentile habits that did not

---

[4]See one of the many examples found in Josephus *Antiquities of the Jews* 12.3.2, where the people of Ionia complained to Marcus Agrippa that "if the Jews were to be their fellows, they should worship the Ionians' gods" (*Josephus*, ed. H. St. J. Thackeray et al., vol. 9, trans. Ralph Marcus, LCL (London and Cambridge, Mass.: Harvard University Press, 1943).

[5]Augustus allowed the exception: Jewish priests offered sacrifices in their own temple on Caesar's behalf; they were not required to "burn the ashes" to Caesar at one of the imperial altars. See Philo's justification: *Legatio* 317, 356.

threaten their religious convictions. Some Jews abandoned their traditions and lived like Gentiles. The question, however, for most Jews trying to maintain holiness was: "How much is too much, and how far is too far?" To dress like the Romans, to speak like the Greeks, or to eat like a pagan was not living like a Jew, regardless of where he or she may have lived in the Mediterranean world. So this makes our task of rediscovering Paul harder still when we recognize that there were significant differences between Greeks, Romans and Jews, for it seems as though Paul belonged to all three.

LIVING IN THE GRECO-ROMAN WORLD

By his own admission, Paul was a crafty fellow (2 Cor 12:16). Paul claimed: "I have become all things to all people, that I might by all means save some" (1 Cor 9:22). He saw his cultural dexterity as a necessary function of sharing the gospel. Incarnation required accommodation. To be a servant of Christ, Paul had to become a slave to all peoples (1 Cor 9:19). To his detractors, however, Paul was acting more like a "man pleaser" than a "God pleaser" (see Gal 1:10). His chameleon-like behavior looked more like hypocrisy and apostasy than unquestioning obedience to God, for no child of Abraham had the right to question Moses or set aside even the least of the commandments (see Mt 5:19). To his opponents, then, it seemed as though Paul was justifying his duplicity, using the modus operandi "Let us do evil so that good may come" (Rom 3:8). Paul took issue with such a "slanderous charge." And yet even the apostle to the Gentiles knew that he had given up his ancestral ways when he adopted the pagan ways of his converts (Gal 2:11-18; 4:12). In fact, toward the end of his life, Paul came to consider his Jewish past as "rubbish" compared to gaining Christ (Phil 3:8).

This is why we have a difficult time figuring out Paul. Who was he? He claimed to be a "Hebrew of Hebrews," but he preferred the Greek translation of the Hebrew Scriptures. He was from Tarsus but claimed that he was "brought up" in Jerusalem. He preached a "law-free" gospel yet relied upon the law to make his argument.[6] He claimed to be an apostle of Christ but rarely referred to what Jesus

---

[6]"Law-free" is a loaded expression. It appears that Paul released his converts from obeying part of law, but not all of it. Scholars have tried to discern the difference, i.e., why Paul required his Gentile converts to keep parts of the law. Some have argued Paul dismissed the "ceremonial" laws and accepted the "moral" laws of the Torah. Others maintain that Paul set aside those laws that operated as social boundary markers, i.e., circumcision, sabbath and purity codes (food, washings, festivals). Therefore, Paul did not preach a "law-free" gospel but a "circumcision-free" gospel, i.e., a "non-Jewish" gospel. Yet, there seems to be more to it than that for Paul. Paul's view of the law will be discussed more fully later.

taught. He ridiculed idols but ate their sacrifices. He opposed circumcision for his converts but had one of his coworkers circumcised. His mission trips were sponsored by the Antioch church, but he collected money for the Jerusalem church. Paul claimed Roman citizenship but was beaten and imprisoned like an imperial subject. Paul argued like a rabbi but quoted Greek philosophers. Paul's versatility makes him a difficult person to pin down historically. At times he behaved like a devout Jew, obeying the Torah. At other times, under different circumstances, he acted as if he were a Gentile, ignoring Jewish purity codes. Sometimes he sounded like a Jew of the Diaspora: "you turned to God from idols, to serve a living and true God" (1 Thess 1:9). At other times, he read more like a Stoic philosopher: "do not be conformed to this world, but be transformed by the renewing of your minds" (Rom 12:2). Finding Paul is a challenge most historians relish. What kind of man was he? What were the influences that shaped Paul's thought? How did he live? Or, even more to the point, how did he appear to his contemporaries—as a Jewish man trying to fit into a pagan culture, or, as a Hellenist who once lived like a Jew?

To put the question before us in such binary fashion is misleading. Typically scholars have set the influences that shaped Paul's world on a continuum. At one end there is Paul's Judaism—a religion known for its provincialism and obscurantism. At the other end is the cultural matrix called the "Greco-Roman world," with all of its social peculiarities and syncretistic religious tendencies. Then arguments are put forward as to where Paul belongs on the line of social identity. Is he more Jewish or Hellenistic? One sector of Pauline scholarship prefers to describe Paul in his Hellenistic context.[7] Another contends that he was thoroughly Jewish.[8] However, the question "Jewish or Hellenistic?" is far more complex.[9]

First, the binary division places Judaism at odds with Hellenism, as if one were the cultural opposite of the other. Despite current references to "culture wars," there is no such thing as cultural purity—even though the authors of 1 and 2 Maccabees would have us think Hellenism was to blame for the degeneration of Judaism (see 1 Maccabees 1:41-53; 2 Maccabees 4:10-17). The Greek way of life and Judaism were not necessarily mutually exclusive. Second, placing Judaism at odds with Hel-

---

[7]Troels Engberg-Pedersen, ed., *Paul in His Hellenistic Context* (Minneapolis: Fortress, 1995).

[8]See, for example, Martin Hengel, *The Pre-Christian Paul,* trans. John Bowden (Philadelphia: Trinity Press International, 1991); E. E. Ellis, *Paul's Use of the Old Testament* (Edinburgh: Oliver & Boyd, 1957); and the standard, W. D. Davies, *Paul and Rabbinic Judaism: Some Rabbinic Elements in Pauline Theology* (London: SPCK, 1948).

[9]See the discussion in J. Paul Sampley, *Paul in the Greco-Roman World: A Handbook* (Harrisburg, Penn.: Trinity Press International, 2003), pp. 4-15.

lenism assumes a singular expression of the Jewish faith of the first century. Most scholars, on the other hand, prefer to speak of Judaism(s), emphasizing the diverse background of Paul's faith. Was Paul's Judaism mystical, apocalyptic, prophetic or rabbinical? Finally, we cannot speak of first-century Judaism apart from the influence of the Greeks as well as the Romans. Indeed, a study of the Greco-Roman world would be incomplete without a description of Judaism. Living in the Greco-Roman world meant living with Jewish people and their Jewish ways. Despite their attempts to live separate lives, Diaspora Jews influenced their neighbors and pagan influences changed how Jewish people practiced their religion.

Paul was a Jew of the Diaspora. He spent his early years in Tarsus. He devoted most of his adult life to traveling around the world, building a gospel ministry to Gentiles. A world of opportunity brought to Paul a lifetime of experiences that shaped his beliefs, his lifestyle, his work and his gospel. When scholars find a unique contribution to the gospel in Paul's letters, they want to know, "Where did Paul get that idea?" When the apostle to the Gentiles gives an unconventional explanation of the Hebrew Scriptures, scholars want to know, "How did Paul arrive at that interpretation?" Where Paul gives varied advice to different churches in different parts of the world, scholars try to determine, "Why did Paul do that?" Since Paul was a man of his time, context is the key. To study Paul in his context, then, means we have to go beyond his life in Tarsus, or his study of Torah under Gamaliel in Jerusalem, and to follow him on all of his journeys in the Greco-Roman world. We must identify the distinctive religious, social and political customs of first-century Greeks, Romans and Jews, so that we can locate Paul in his world.

Greek living. Long before the Romans ruled the Mediterranean world, the Greeks had exported their way of life to all the peoples of that region. More than two hundred years before the Roman Empire, Alexander the Great brought the social reform called Hellenism to his conquered subjects. This is why historians refer to the first-century Mediterranean world as Greco-Roman. The Romans may have controlled the economic resources of the Mediterranean at the time, but the Greeks had already captured the minds of its subjects—including the Romans. The influence of Greek language, mythology, philosophy, literature, art, education, architecture, fashion, polity and leisure can be traced throughout the Mediterranean world, extending even to the remote corners of the empire. By the first century, to be Hellene was no longer a matter of descent but of disposition. Greece taught the world how to live.

The extent to which Greek culture infiltrated different regions—especially rural areas—of the Mediterranean world is difficult to determine (see 2 Maccabees

WHAT'S MORE . . .
Greek Spoken Here

Alexander founded cities that would govern themselves. Each Greek *polis* ("city") had its own governing council, housed in public buildings where policies were forged and political debates were heard. Temples were built for local deities as well as the Greek gods. The hub of the city was the *agora* (forum)—a large, open plaza often lined with Greek columns that served as a market for merchants. Huge theaters were built to accommodate massive crowds who would gather to watch Greek tragedies and comedies. These ornate cities attracted every walk of life—from the literary elite to the common tradesman. Whether to work or to listen or to watch, everyone had to learn the Greek language to join in the commerce of city life. For this and many other reasons, by the first century Koine (common) Greek had become the universal language of the Mediterranean world, especially east of Rome. Alexander's conquest had resulted in nearly everyone speaking the same language, something comparable to English in today's world.

4:9-16). If Hellenism's reach extended to rural as well as urban regions of the Mediterranean world, among the uneducated as well as the educated, then scholars are more justified in speaking of Paul as one who was "thoroughly Hellenized." Did Paul come from a wealthy family? Those who believe so insist that a formal Greek education is the only way to explain how Paul could have written such powerful letters, for the style of his argument betrays rhetorical techniques taught in the schools known as gymnasia. Tarsus of Cilicia, where Paul was born and probably lived for several years, was known as a major center for Greek education. Or did Paul pick up some rhetorical training as a rabbinical student in Jerusalem, as some scholars maintain? It seems some Greek-speaking Jews read Homer as well as the Torah in Jerusalem schools.[10] On the other hand, is it more probable, given his trade as a craftsman, that Paul belonged to a family of modest means? In this case, scholars make him out to be a Hellene hack, a pseudo-intellectual who learned a little rhetoric by listening to orators (a common pastime for the curious).

---

[10]In the Mishnah the Sadducees leveled a charge of inconsistency: "We complain against you, Pharisees. For you say, 'Holy Scriptures impart uncleanness to hands, but the books of Homer do not impart uncleanness to hands,'" *Yadayim* 4.6.

SO WHAT?
Why Does It Matter If Paul Was Hellenized?

Scholars who maintain that Paul was thoroughly Hellenized tend to attribute Paul's theology to Greek ideas, for example, universalism, determinism or immortality of the soul. Take, for example, Paul's comments about life after death in 2 Corinthians 5:1-4. All of this talk about not being "found naked" at death and being "absent from the body" (as a disembodied spirit?) sounds very similar to the way Greek philosophers described life after death—a soul separated from the body. Soul sleep, or sleeping with their ancestors, or being gathered to their ancestors, seems to be the more common Jewish way of describing the postmortem state before the resurrection of the body (see 1 Thess 4:13 NRSV footnote; 1 Cor 15:51 KJV, NASB). Since the Greeks held to the preexistence of the soul, a dualism of body and spirit, they denied the resurrection and believed the soul was released from its terrestrial prison at death. Therefore, some maintain Paul left behind Jewish ideas of soul sleep and adopted Greek categories in order to speculate on what happens to believers after they die but before they are raised—a question that Paul was far more interested in personally. Earlier he believed that he would be in the company of the living and witness the parousia ("appearance") of Christ (1 Thess 4:17). A few years later, when he was writing 2 Corinthians, Paul was convinced that he would not live till the parousia (2 Cor 4:14). So some think that Paul injected Greek thinking into his Jewish eschatology in order to fill in the gaps of his "already/not yet" schema. Is this an indication of Paul's cultural adaptability, becoming all things to all men, accommodating the Greek mindset in Corinth? Are these ideas attributable only to Hellenistic thinking? Those who see Paul using Greek ideas concerning life after death (whether his own or the convictions of his readers) argue for a Pauline anthropology that includes a "spiritual," embodied existence between death and resurrection. Those who think not, tend to deny a Pauline doctrine of the intermediate state. Determining the sources of Paul's thought, then, may define outcomes of Pauline theology as well as help us answer the difficult question, "Where do Christians go when they die?"

Paul spoke and wrote Greek. But was it his primary tongue? And, even it if was, does it necessarily mean that Paul "thought like a Greek"? Was he, therefore, more readily able to embrace a Gentile mission? Did it make it easier for Paul to subscribe to the "law-free" gospel that got him in trouble with his Jewish brothers? In other words, to what extent was Paul Hellenized?

Currently the debate regarding the degree to which Paul assimilated to Greek culture hangs in the balance. There seems to be little doubt that, to some extent, even uneducated citizens adopted the Greek way of life. Common people attended the games, enjoyed the festivals, watched Greek plays from the cheap seats and were entertained by public speeches. They wore Greek styles. They gave their children Greek names (Philip, Andrew, Nicodemus). In some regions local shrines allowed shared altars for sacrifices to Greek gods. Whether he was a product of Greek schools or not, Paul probably watched the athletic contests and may have attended the theater now and then (1 Cor 9:24-27; 4:9). We know he quoted common aphorisms coined by Greek poets (1 Cor 15:32-33). And he showed some rhetorical skills—in writing if not in public speaking (2 Cor 10:10). Isn't this conclusive evidence that Paul ascribed to Greek ways?

According to John Barclay, we may never know the answer to that question.[11] He maintains that Diaspora Jews in different regions of the Mediterranean world assimilated to Greek culture to different degrees and in different ways. Most Jews in Alexandria lived together in separate districts—segregated from the Gentiles— yet some sent their sons to Greek schools. Without apology, the Bible of Egyptian Jews was written in Greek. In Asia Minor, Jews held public office, contributed to the military and supported civic projects. At the same time, however, most refused to participate in local festivals and engage in business on the sabbath, despite the angry protests of their fellow citizens. Certain social climbers married non-Jews and joined in the pagan festivities. Others, like Philo and Josephus, maintained their Jewish ways while trying to build bridges of mutual respect and trust with pagan rulers. To some, men like Philo and Josephus were apostates—too worldly to maintain proper standards of holiness.[12] To others, they were heroes—leaders

---

[11]See John Barclay, *Jews in the Mediterranean Diaspora: From Alexander to Trajan* (Berkeley: University of California Press, 1996), pp. 381-95.

[12]Hear Josephus's justification in his prayer to God: "I willingly give them [the Romans] my hands, and am content to live. And I protest openly, that I do not go over to the Romans as a deserter of the Jews, but as a minister from thee," *A History of the Jewish War* 3.354. See also Philo's defense of his relationship with the procurator Flaccus: "I am not mad, my friend, nor am I a downright fool, so as to be unable to see the consequences of connection of things. I praise Flaccus, not because it is right to praise an enemy, but in order to make his wickedness more conspicuous," *In Flaccum* 6-7.

who tried to preserve Jewish identity in the face of hostile powers who threatened their existence. Many Jews wanted to be left alone, keeping their sacred traditions without harm. Others took to the streets, forcing local leaders to recognize Jewish claims to sacred privilege. Whatever the level of assimilation or resistance to Greek culture, Jewish men and women earned a reputation as a peculiar people, keeping their own customs despite being heckled by their neighbors and maligned by pagan rulers. At the same time, it must be said that by the first century all Jews lived like the Greeks to varying degrees.

Rome rules. The Roman general Octavian took the imperial title "Caesar Augustus" when he was confirmed by the Senate as the leader of the conquered world (27 B.C.). He was the last man standing after the infamous civil war that gave birth to an empire. The adopted son of Julius Caesar, Octavian attributed his rise to power to the gods who wanted him to bring the benefit of Roman rule to the imperial provinces. He left domestic policy to the Senate, focusing his attention on establishing order among the conquered peoples of Egypt, Illyricum, Galatia, Raetia, Noricum, Judea and Pannonia. Augustus's "foreign policy" was supposed to bring peace through the strength of his army, justice by way of Roman law and economic prosperity by connecting major cities with new roads. Legions of soldiers occupied urban centers and patrolled Roman highways. Roman procurators governed imperial provinces and held court over civil matters. Chain gangs of exiled prisoners and slaves laid down roads to connect east and west, increasing trade traffic. Of course, all of these benefits cost money, and Caesar laid the burden on the shoulders of his subjects. Roman tribute was heavy; in some places production taxes reached 33 percent. Sometimes social unrest, economic hardship and ethnic pride would incite subjects of the empire to rebel against their sovereign overlords. In every case, however, the revolution would be put down by the heavy hand of the Roman rulers. No insurgent army could stand against Roman soldiers. Resistance was futile. Most subjects, therefore, learned to seek the advantages of Roman benefaction rather than tempt fate by rebelling against Roman supremacy.

Trouble spots in the empire (like Jerusalem) invited direct Roman rule via Roman procurators. Occasionally among conquered peoples, certain local rulers would gain the trust of the emperor and govern their own people on Rome's behalf as "client kings." Yet even in those cases, Roman governors were looking over the shoulders of these ethnarchs (literally, "ruler of the people"), ready to step in at any moment to guard Roman interests. Cities that proved to be compliant (like Tarsus) tried to earn status as "free cities." As the term implies, these cities were free to govern themselves and to issue their own currency, and were exempt from the heavy tribute paid by imperial provinces. Most free cities were located in the well-established senatorial provinces—regions where Rome had ruled for quite some time, for example, Italy, Macedonia, Achaia and Asia Minor. Senatorial provinces were governed by high-ranking officials called proconsuls, that is, former senators and equestrians. Citizens of Roman colonies, however, had the greatest advantage. Colonists in these Roman outposts paid little or no taxes, governed themselves, promoted the state religion (with all its lucrative benefits) and were not required to offer any support to the military. Most colonies, like Corinth, were populated by former soldiers and freedmen from Italy. They were the cities most often selected to host imperial festivals and athletic games. Of course, Roman colonies and free cities were the major economic markets of the empire, connected by common trade routes. Not surprisingly, Paul the tent maker and Roman citizen conducted most of his mission work in free cities (Ephesus, Thessalonica, Athens), and colonies (Pisidian Antioch, Iconium, Lystra, Derbe, Troas, Philippi, Corinth), where pro-Roman sentiment was strong. So when Paul got in trouble during his missions trips, he appeared before proconsuls of senatorial provinces and magistrates in free cities and colonies. Since he was a Roman citizen, Paul was afforded rights of legal privilege. Even though Roman justice was supposed to extend to any subject of the empire, governors were more careful with citizens, knowing they could appeal to Caesar for the final verdict.

Augustus extended the reach of Roman rule beyond cities and provinces to the *familia* (household). Laws were passed to make sure men and women married by a particular age, produced children during a particular age span and managed their households according to Roman customs of divorce, inheritance, adoption, abandonment, treatment of slaves and property rights. The head of the household was the *paterfamilias*. Like the emperor, he had absolute power over the subjects and resources of his household. As long as he lived, the "family father" controlled the interests of his wife, sons (and their wives), daughters, grandchildren, servants, slaves and clients. He was the master of his domain. All property belonged to him. All decisions were made by him: when and whom his children, servants and slaves would marry, the kind of living his sons would earn and the jobs his clients would take.

Household servants and slaves were considered part of the family—in the east as well as the west. But the Romans often freed their slaves, making the "freedmen" members of the household. In fact membership in the family extended beyond those who actually lived in the family home. Freedmen who lived in their own houses, as well as clients of the family father, were considered part of the

WHAT'S MORE . . .
Roman Wives

The only person a Roman man did not have complete control over was his wife. Roman women enjoyed a level of independence unparalleled in the Greco-Roman world. They could divorce their husbands. They remained in the power of their fathers, sharing in his inheritance. If they came from wealthy families, they could own property and maintain economic resources outside the charge of their husbands. That is not to say, however, that Roman wives equaled their husbands in power and status. Indeed, the Roman family was a patriarchal system. Men ruled the household. Yet the social structures of Roman patriarchy operated differently from those of the rest of the world.

household: receiving an allowance, obeying the commands of their "father" and extolling the virtue of their honorable head. Clients joined the household by offering their services to their patron, such as brokering business opportunities in "unseemly" vocations, overseeing distant farming operations and keeping watch over political developments that would affect the patron's social and economic interests. Clients were expected to pay their respects every day. They would appear at their patron's house early in the morning, lined up in the street dressed in their togas, prepared to report on the family business, to dine with the ruling father, to accompany him around town and to receive their assignments for the day.[13] In return, the family father was responsible for the social and economic welfare of all his clients as well as the entire household. He was their social security.

Every member of a Roman household worshiped the god of the family father. Part of the ritual of paying respects to the paterfamilias included the veneration of the household gods. To us it may seem opportunistic for a client to worship the gods of his patron—we might even call it "lip service." But to all peoples (except the Jews) it was considered apropos to honor all gods. In fact, the Romans accused the Jewish people of atheism since they did not acknowledge the existence of gods. If a god had been around for a long time, worshiped by many peoples (especially by a man's ancestors), then he deserved veneration. This is why Roman mythology

---

[13]The culture reflected in movies like *The Godfather* stands in the tradition stretching back to the *paterfamilias*. We can still see some similarities.

was built on Greek mythology. The older the religion the better; ancestral worship was sacred because it was not "new." To us, for the Romans to adopt Greek mythology, simply changing the names of the gods (from Zeus to Jupiter, from Artemis to Diana) smacks of unoriginality; syncretism looks like compromise. To the Romans, it was a matter of recognizing what had been true for centuries.

It was commonplace for a man to worship at the shrine of several gods, to belong to several "religions." We find the practice fickle—a man should choose a religion and stick with it. Yet there were many pagans who embraced local gods, imperial gods and even the Jewish God. This was not unusual; this was the way it was supposed to be. These "god-fearers" believed all gods deserved veneration, especially since there were certain religious ideas everyone believed, for example,

---

WHAT'S MORE . . .
Paul as Family Father

Paul loved to think of himself as the father of his converts. He did not refer to them as his disciples; they were his children (1 Cor 4:14-15). And, as their father, he would require their obedience to him and his ways—his gospel. Since Paul was the head of his household, all members were supposed to imitate him: "I appeal to you, then, be imitators of me. For this reason I sent you Timothy, who is my beloved and faithful child in the Lord, to remind you of my ways in Christ Jesus" (1 Cor 4:16-17). In his household, Paul was the ruling father who was supposed to keep his children in line with their new ancestral traditions: "I commend you because you remember me in everything and maintain the traditions just as I handed them on to you" (1 Cor 11:2). When his converts disobeyed, he was quick to reprimand their noncompliance (Gal 1:6). All his churches were subject to his direction (1 Cor 4:17). Paul was their unquestioned gospel source: "anyone who claims to be a prophet, or to have spiritual powers, must acknowledge that what I am writing to you is a command of the Lord. Anyone who does not recognize this is not to be recognized" (1 Cor 14:37-38). Rebel children threatened his authority, disrupted social order and required proper discipline (1 Cor 5:1-13). Trouble in his churches was most often attributed to outsiders trespassing on his sacred turf (Gal 3:1; 4:17; 5:7-8; 2 Cor 11:3-15; Phil 3:2, 17-19). Paul had to write letters because his children did not listen only to him (Gal 1:9; 5:10).

---

that sacrifices were required to placate the divine, gods inhabited shrines dedicated
for worship, dreams and oracles were means of divine communication, divine
blessing meant abundance on earth, and gods delighted in iconic worship. This is
how deities lived among humanity. Idols were everywhere. That more than anything else would have impressed a twenty-first-century visitor to the Greco-
Roman world. Devotees erected idols in their homes, in shrines, in bathhouses, in
schools, in shops, on the sides of roads, in cities, in the villages, in prominent public places, in the middle of nowhere. Shrines cropped up everywhere at the hands
of dedicated worshipers (often by divine command received in a dream). Greco-
Roman religion meant iconic worship; it seems a person could not worship a god
without an idol.

In addition to the preservation of ancestral traditions, veneration of local gods
had political and social significance. Civic pride welled up in the hearts of dedicated worshipers who offered sacrifices to the gods for protecting their city, their
interests, their citizens. Competing for divine favors meant building bigger shrines
than other devotees who worshiped the same gods in other cities and villages. In
this religious environment the imperial cult took root and grew throughout the
empire. Many cities competed for permission to establish a shrine to Caesar and
so become an outpost for Roman religion. Rather than "kick against the goads" of
their imperial overlords, conquered subjects welcomed the opportunity to worship
the powerful gods of Rome. It may have even been in the best interest of the
wealthy to promote the imperial cult—better to placate the powers that can help
keep the poor under their thumb than to risk social anarchy. Since the wealthy
funded these projects, the rich got richer still. Indeed, the veneration of Caesar
had its rewards: political, social and economic. Becoming a "free city" and a "friend
of Caesar" was a lucrative deal. For example, Pergamon distinguished itself as the
first city of Asia Minor to build a temple to Augustus. An insignificant town under
Greek rule, Pergamon became a major city during the empire, housing a library
that rivaled the collection in Alexandria.

Not everyone played along. Jewish communities refused to promote the imperial cult, even withholding funds for city projects like building shrines to dead
Caesars. Synagogues preferred sending their money to their own temple in Jerusalem. To us, this seems perfectly reasonable. To Greco-Roman city officials, however, when Jews sent heavy tribute to a foreign temple (Jerusalem), it was an economic drain on local religious business. Supporting local shrines was
indispensable to the economy. Therefore, it should not surprise us that magistrates
sometimes tried to prevent synagogues from carrying their temple tax to Jerusa-

---

SO WHAT?
What's the Big Deal with Idols?

Idols were everywhere, but couldn't you just ignore them? Worship of the gods was woven into the fabric of life. When your ship arrived at Ephesus, it stopped at the entrance to the harbor to make an offering to the goddess Diana who guarded the harbor. Should a Christian captain pay for the offering? This was how harbor operations were paid for. We might call it a harbor fee. Yet the custom was not so benign. The offering was also a request for Diana to guard the ships from storms. When you entered the pubic bath, you made an offering to the god/goddess to whom the bath was dedicated. Should Christians be allowed to use the bath for free? What of the public restroom off Curetis Street? Every shop and restaurant in Ephesus would have had an idol. Today when you purchase an item from a street vendor in Bangkok, if you are the first customer, he will likely slap your dollar bills on his other items for sale, to ward off evil spirits and bring good luck (more sales). Are you contributing to a pagan ritual? When you visit Schwe Dagon, the massive Buddhist temple in Yangon (Rangoon), you must "pay an entrance fee" or "make an offering," depending upon how you want to spin it. The problem is not just an ancient one.

---

lem—one governor confiscated a Jewish offering sent to the temple (a hundred pounds of gold), redirecting it for Rome's purposes.[14] Eventually, Augustus settled the matter. Jews would be allowed to support their temple without Roman intervention.

Nevertheless, occasional hostilities persisted against Diaspora Jews. Even though Caesar gave them the freedom to worship their God according to their traditions, it was quite apparent that the religious devotion of the Jews could not be practiced in isolation from their neighbors. There was no separation of religion and politics in the Greco-Roman world. To worship the gods of the community was politically expedient. And yet for Jews to be devoted to their God meant a denial of the gods of their neighbors. They did not go about tearing down pagan altars and destroying idols. But Diaspora Jews refused to acknowledge the existence

---

[14]Cicero *Pro Flacco* 28.68.

of patron gods who protected the cities and villages of their residence. Therefore, Jewish noncompliance was seen as civil disobedience, putting their neighbors at risk from jealous gods. Gentiles could adopt Jewish ways, but for Diaspora Jews holiness meant refusing to join in the pagan ways of the world. A holy people, the Jews worshiped a holy God.

Jewish holiness. Like all ethnic groups, the Jews were recognized as a peculiar people—but for reasons different from their neighbors. The Romans were known for their voracious appetite for violence, entertained by gladiator contests. Greeks earned reputations as smooth talkers, undisciplined men given to the baser appetites of food, wine and sex. The Jewish people, on the other hand, were known for their religion. They observed a weekly day of rest from their work to attend synagogue, they despised idols, they supported only one temple, and they circumcised their sons. The very things Jews found objectionable about pagans—iconic worship and sexual immorality—are what distinguished the Jews from all other peoples. Other gods had many temples; the God of the Jews had one. Other gods required iconic worship; the God of the Jews hated idols. Other gods encouraged fertility rites and sexual promiscuity; the God of the Jews required circumcision and fidelity in marriage. Any day was a holy day for other gods; one day a week was set aside as holy for the God of the Jews. The Jewish people distinguished themselves by their religion. They saw themselves as the only people who worshiped the one, true God. Either an irritant to their neighbors or a light to the Gentiles, the Jews marked sacred space by holy living.

The most sacred space of them all, of course, was the Holy of Holies: the place where God lived. The temple in Jerusalem was a sanctuary of concentric walls. The Holy of Holies was the inner sanctuary of the temple, a building entered only by priests. A wall surrounding the temple separated the men from the women and children. Beyond that barrier, another wall separated holy people from unholy people, that is, the circumcised from the uncircumcised, the healthy from the diseased, the whole from the maimed. Like all temples, the Jewish temple was primarily a place of sacrifice. Even though prayers were offered along with songs of praise, the worship of God required the slaughter of animals. Therefore, in a world without refrigeration, the bulk of fresh meat would be found near temples.

Holiness radiated out beyond the precincts of the temple. Synagogues were satellites of Jewish worship—a place where holy people could mark out holy time. Although no animal sacrifices were offered in the synagogue, both the Jews and their pagan neighbors saw the sabbath as a day of worship for Jews who gathered together for prayer and Scripture readings ("synagogue" derives from the Greek *synagōgē* or "gathering"). Synagogues were called "prayer houses" by many Diaspora Jews, even though they were also used for community meetings during the

---

SO WHAT?
Aren't Hedges Good?

What's wrong with explaining what commandments mean or elaborating on how to apply them? Putting "a hedge around a law" was designed to make it easier to keep the law. It made holiness and righteousness more accessible to the average person. "Do not commit adultery" (Ex 20:14) is hedged with the wise advice: "Do not go near the door of her house" (Prov 5:8). Building hedges was an old practice. Adam apparently did it for Eve, telling her not even to touch the fruit that God said not to eat (Gen 3:3). What's wrong with that? Jeremiah said not to carry things on the sabbath (Jer 17:21-22). But Jesus commanded a man to do that very thing (Jn 5:8-9). Following the instructions of Jeremiah, the man (and later Jesus) was accused of being a sabbath-breaker (Jn 5:10, 18). As each generation added a new row of hedges, Jesus believed they had lost sight of the law itself. The teachers were so busy ruling that the lame man and Jesus were lawbreakers that they never rejoiced over the healing. Peter denounced the hedges as a heavy yoke that no one should bear (Acts 15:10). Paul left these traditions behind when he was called to preach the gospel of Christ (Gal 1:14-24). He believed the whole law was summed up in one commandment: "You shall love your neighbor as yourself" (Gal 5:14).

---

week. It was during this weekly worship that most Jews would be able to hear the Scriptures read in their language. Very few could afford to own their own copies. Teachers who studied under rabbis of the Pharisees recited oral traditions they had been taught, quoting how different rabbis applied different Scriptures to different situations. Also, those in attendance, especially important guests, would be invited to offer comments on the Scriptures (see Acts 13:15). Indeed, the Jews were a people of the book. All religious activities—prayers, recitations, expositions—seemed to revolve around texts. To outsiders, then, synagogue worship must have looked more like a gathering of philosophers and their students, with men poring over writings and teachers passing on the instruction of their mentors.[15]

Lessons learned in the synagogues taught the Jewish people how to live holy lives. "Remember the sabbath and keep it holy" is a rather vague commandment. Of course, the law goes on to say what it means to keep the sabbath holy: no labor. And yet devotees wanting to obey God had to know: does every kind of work violate the holy day? After all, priests worked on the sabbath. Babies were born and people died on the sabbath. Obviously, the commandment prohibited preparing food (Ex 16:23), so Jews refused to cook on the sabbath, leading their neighbors to think that the seventh day was a day of fasting. Over time, other prophets and teachers added their interpretations of sabbath observance, for example, Jeremiah contended that no one should carry anything on the sabbath—either in and out of the city or even their own homes (Jer 17:21-22); Nehemiah commanded that the gates of Jerusalem be closed, preventing merchants from selling on the sabbath (Neh 13:19-20); Mattathias ruled that acts of self-defense during war were not in violation of the sabbath laws (1 Maccabees 2:41).

In the same way, rabbis added conditions to protect the sanctity of the day of rest. The Pharisees memorized these teachings—oral traditions passed down from generation to generation—in order to help their kinsmen keep the sabbath day holy, as well as to obey all of the commandments of God. As a matter of fact, the Pharisees believed these traditions were part of the living word of God—a body of divine instruction that started with Moses, handed down to every generation. So they took it upon themselves to teach the people what God required according to the traditions of their forefathers.[16]

This is where the Pharisees seemed to have exerted their influence, that is, how to obey Jewish law when extenuating circumstances made maintaining holiness less obvious. There was no "in-between" category of purity; God could not be ambivalent about holiness. The Jews believed they lived in a binary world; all things were either clean or unclean. Therefore, the Mishnah[17] is filled with rabbinical instructions that deal with "gray" areas of purity as black and white realities—how to be holy in an unclean world.

---

[15]Philo referred to sabbath deliberations over the Scriptures as "philosophizing." See *De opificio mundi* 128.

[16]There is no solid evidence any Pharisees lived among the Diaspora in Paul's day. They did, however, travel to visit synagogues and make converts of those living outside of the holy land (see Mt 23:15; Acts 9:2; Josephus *Antiquities of the Jews* 20.43). Therefore, it is hard to believe their oral traditions never made it beyond the borders of Palestine.

[17]The Mishnah is a second-century collection of rabbinical teachings that claim to go back to the time prior to the destruction of Jerusalem.

WHAT'S MORE . . .
The Rabbi in the Bathhouse

One of our favorite examples of rabbinic instruction regarding gray areas is when a pagan confronts a well-known Pharisee about his apparent hypocrisy:

A. Peroqlos b[en] Pelosepos asked Rabban Gamaliel in Akko, when he was washing in Aphrodite's bathhouse, saying to him, "It is written in your Torah, *And there shall cleave nothing of a devoted thing to your hand* (Deut 13:18). How is it that you're taking a bath in Aphrodite's bathhouse?"

B. He said to him, "They do not give answers in a bathhouse."

C. When he went out, he said to him, "I never came into her domain. She came into mine. They don't say, 'Let's make a bathhouse as an ornament for Aphrodite.' But they say, 'Let's make Aphrodite as an ornament for the bathhouse.'

D. Another matter: Even if someone gave you a lot of money, you would never walk into your temple of idolatry naked or suffering a flux, nor would you piss in its presence.

E. Yet this thing is standing there at the head of the gutter and everybody pisses right in front of her."

It is said only, ". . . *their gods*" (Deut 12:3)—that which one treats as a god is prohibited, but that which one treats not as a god is permitted. (*Abodah Zarah* 3.4)[a]

---

[a] See Paul's similar teaching in 1 Corinthians 8:5-7. Jacob Neusner, ed., *The Mishnah*, trans. Jacob Neusner et al. (New Haven, Conn.: Yale University Press, 1988), p. 665.

The Pharisees maintained that complete obedience would be a sign of covenant faithfulness and would bring a light of righteousness to the Gentiles. Even though the Jewish people ultimately maintained their distinctiveness by the rite of circumcision—the essential marker that separated insiders from outsiders—social boundaries were more clearly drawn in the way Pharisees defined holiness. Indeed, circumcision was a private affair; holiness was a public matter. And this is how the Pharisees distinguished themselves among their kinsmen: to them the quest for holiness extended beyond "kosher" food, holy days and ritual washings. Purity touched every facet of life: not just clean food, but clean pots. It meant not only eating with clean hands but also sharing the table with clean guests. It meant not only keeping the sabbath but also avoiding defilement. The Pharisees taught the people how to live holy lives, meaning separate lives. And this was indeed a noble goal; when it came to obeying the law of God, they wanted to be found blameless (see Phil 3:6). No one could exceed the righteousness of the Pharisees. In their zeal, they went above and beyond the letter of the law. How many common Jews followed their example, we'll never know. But, one thing is certain: the Pharisees established the benchmark of holiness among the people.

Zeal for the law and the pursuit of holiness helped create divisions within Judaism, separating the holy from the unclean, the righteous from the sinners, the blessed from the cursed. It comes as no surprise that a Pharisee named Saul was "breathing threats and murder against the disciples of the Lord" (Acts 9:1). That he did so against the advice of his mentor (Acts 5:34-39) may reveal a righteous indignation that went beyond the desire to maintain holiness for the sake of purification. Since Jesus died a cursed death according to the law, his crucifixion would have been seen by Saul the Pharisee as the just punishment of God. By persecuting followers of Christ, Saul was not only preserving the sanctity of the law and the purity of God's elect, he was extending the judgment of God. Jewish Christians, on the other hand, preached that the cross of Jesus was a divine act of apocalyptic rectification—the cursed had become blessed. After his "conversion," Paul professed the same (Gal 3:13). In fact, Paul eventually preached a gospel of Gentile inclusion that would lead to a denial of Jewish exclusivism. In a complete reversal, he claimed his kinsmen were the ones who were cursed, like branches broken off the covenant tree, and needing salvation (Rom 9:3; 10:1; 11:17-21). Ironically, Paul's gospel of inclusion was also a message of exclusion, turning Jews against Jews—which was nothing new for Abraham's descendents (in the Mishnah, Samaritans are treated as if they were Gentiles). Maintaining holiness was a divisive pursuit; removing the unclean was an act of divine judgment. Paul applied the same standard to his churches. For example, he used Deuteronomy 17:7 to encourage the church in Corinth to remove an immoral member (1 Cor 5:13). Indeed, the pursuit of holiness drew lines dividing outsiders and insiders, marking out the evil and the good.

So it should not surprise us that Judaism could not contain the splinter group whose members were known as Christians. Even though Jewish members of "the way" may have seen their zeal for the gospel as part and parcel of their Jewish heritage, eventually their kinsmen found their message and their ways blasphemous. The temple, the Torah, circumcision, the dietary code, even the sabbath—everything distinctively Jewish was compromised by early Christianity. It is no wonder, then, that the Jesus movement eventually broke away from its Jewish moorings (Paul made sure of that). So, with the influx of Gentile Christians and the steady erosion of Jewish traditions, imagine how hard it was for early Christians to distinguish themselves in the marketplace of religions. Christians had no temple, no sacred space. That must have put them at a disadvantage in attracting devotees. Where does one go to worship the Christian God? What are the holy days of sacrifice? Which animals must be slaughtered for divine purpose? Among pagans it was common for temples to host sacred meals. Christians had sacred meals without temples. Was it possible to have sacred meals in an ordinary house? Christians read Jewish Scripture but did not observe Jewish law. They had no prayer houses, only house churches. In certain respects, these people had no definable, distinctive features other than the fact that they proclaimed the resurrection of their leader, baptized their novitiates in his name, shared a common table and gathered on the first day of the week to sing, pray, prophesy and occasionally listen to the reading of letters written by a man whose name was Paul.

READ MORE ABOUT IT

DPL Articles

"Diaspora," pp. 211-13, by W. R. Stegner.

"Emperors, Roman," pp. 233-35, by D. E. Aune.

"Hellenism," pp. 383-88, by E. M. Yamauchi.

"Philosophy," pp. 713-18, by T. Paige.

"Political Systems," pp. 718-23, by M. Reasoner.

"Religions, Greco-Roman," pp. 786-96, by D. E. Aune.

"Revolutionary Movements," pp. 812-19, by P. W. Barnett.

"Social-Scientific Approaches to Paul," pp. 892-900, by S. C. Barton.

"Social Setting of Mission Churches," pp. 883-92, by D. J. Tidball.

2

Paul, the Letter Writer

IT IS AMAZING HOW MODERN CHRISTIANS put so much stock in reading old letters. These letters from Paul were not written to us. When we read them, we are initially prying into someone else's business. Yet we also believe that God continues to speak to us through these old letters. This is our business too. Since we take ancient letters so seriously, it is surprising most of us have never read any other letters from that place and time. Looking at some other ancient letters from the Mediterranean world can help us to understand and appreciate the letters of Paul better. We can see which parts of his letters were normal, expected and routine, and which parts were innovative, unusual and even striking. These other letters give us some context for understanding Paul's.[1]

RUMMAGING THROUGH ANCIENT MEDITERRANEAN MAIL

How do we know so much about ancient Mediterranean letters? Basically, our information comes from two quite different sources. Famed rhetoricians of antiquity like Seneca wrote letters. Collections of these letters were published. In antiquity this meant paying for a few dozen copies to be prepared by hand. Over the centuries, these editions continued to be copied and recopied, and were eventually published in modern critical editions. The other major source of information about ancient Mediterranean letters is some actual, original let-

---

[1]For a fuller discussion, see E. Randolph Richards, *Paul and First-Century Letter Writing: Secretaries, Composition and Collection* (Downers Grove, Ill.: InterVarsity Press, 2004).

ters uncovered by archaeologists. Sometimes old letters were thrown away; others were flipped over and reused, eventually ending in the trash. Still other letters were stored and treasured by the recipient, to be found in the ruins of the home or buried with the deceased. Archaeologists in the last hundred years or so have uncovered thousands of letters from ordinary people, writing about ordinary things.

A generation before Paul, the great Roman orator Cicero began to use the letters of everyday correspondence for more lofty purposes. Cicero began to write letters to an individual that he knew would also be read by many others. Rhetoric, reserved usually for public speaking, was finding expression in letters. Topics such as philosophy were being discussed in letters. The very brief, artless private letter grew more like the rhetorical letters, longer and more complex.

In the time of Paul (the generation after Cicero), another Roman orator, Seneca, developed this pattern further. In supposedly private casual letters to Lucilius, his disciple and friend, Seneca described his philosophical ideas, further blurring the lines between the bare everyday letter and the published rhetorical letters. Paul, it appears, belonged in the middle of this stream of gradual transformation. Like the skilled writers of the previous generation, Paul was aware others were reading his letters; in fact, he encouraged it (Col 4:16). Also like those before him, Paul wrote with spontaneous vitality. In fact, Paul's wording and phraseology often resembled what we find in the everyday letters uncovered in the ruins. Yet Paul's letters were too long and complex to be compared to the simple letters. Like several talented letter writers of his generation, Paul intended his letters to convey his deeper thoughts and not just routine matters.

Peeking at Greco-Roman Letters

Most of the inhabitants of the Roman Empire were at least bilingual. They spoke their local language and then the language of the empire. In the West, this meant Latin, the official language of government. However, in the East, the language of trade and commerce was Greek. As a Jew studying in Jerusalem, Paul spoke Aramaic. As a trained rabbi, he also spoke Hebrew, which was related to Aramaic. He probably also had some ability in Latin. For example, when Paul was tried by Roman authorities, he spoke in his own defense and this likely was in Latin. Nevertheless, in Paul's world, the language that tied regions together was Greek. For this reason, Paul wrote his letters in Greek.

Because of the unifying force of the Roman Empire (and of the Greeks previ-

---

WHAT'S MORE . . .
The Beginning and Conclusion of a Greek and a Latin Letter.

The following excerpts are from an ancient letter written in Greek (*PMich.* 8.491):

> Apollinarius to Taesis, his mother and lady, many greetings. Before all else, I pray for your health . . . I wish you to know, mother, that I arrived in Rome in good health.
>
> I salute all your friends, each by name. I pray for your health.

These next excerpts are from a letter written in Latin (*PMich.* 8.468):

> Claudius Terentianus to Claudius Tiberianus, his father and lord, very many greetings. Before all else, I pray for your health. . . . Know, father, that I have received the things you sent me. . . .
>
> Salute all our comrades. Farewell.

---

ously), there was a great deal of commonality in letter-writing customs.[2] From England to Egypt, we find Greco-Roman letters following the same format and using the same language, and even generally the same diction and rhetoric. Even while the Jews (and some other cultures) stubbornly held on to their local languages, they still followed the general format of the Greco-Roman letter. When we compare Greek and Latin papyrus letters, we find them strikingly similar, even though the languages were different. Because of the similarities, scholars speak of Greco-Roman letters.

"Dear . . . , Sincerely . . ." The form of ancient letters. Greco-Roman letters had a general three-part structure: opening, body and closing. The simpler, briefer papyrus letters tended to follow this format more diligently. The more rhetorically complex the letter, the more it varied. Nonetheless, across the range of ancient Greco-Roman letters, there was amazing conformity.

For example, a papyrus letter (*PZen.*10) begins: "Antimenes to Zenon, greetings." Most letters included some qualifying description of the recipient; much less commonly the sender was described more fully, as in *Michigan Papyrus*

---

[2]Abraham Malherbe argues that the uniformity of the Greco-Roman letter may indicate that it was a standard part of elementary education: see "Ancient Epistolary Theorists," *Ohio Journal of Religious Studies* 5 (1977): 4-5; see also Ronald Hock, "Writing in the Greco-Roman World," *SBL Forum*, May 10, 2004 <www.sbl-site.org/Article.aspx?ArticleID=264>.

WHAT'S MORE . . .
A Standard Letter Outline from the Time of Paul[a]

Opening

  Prescript

    Sender (in the nominative case)

    Recipient (in the dative case)

    Greeting (in the infinitive)

  Prooimion

    Health-wishes

    Thanksgiving

    Prayer or statement of remembering

Body

  Opening

    Rejoice formula

    Disclosure or petition formula

    Recommendation or self-recommendation

  Middle

    Information

    Command or admonition

    Admonition, recommendation

    Request formula

    Stereotyped expressions

  End

    Possible request or admonition

    Plans for visiting or traveling

Closing

  Epilogue

    End-admonitions

    Reflections on the act of writing the letter

    A wish to visit

  Postscript

    Greetings

    First person

    Second person

    Third person

    Wishes, such as "Farewell"

    Remark about a personal signature

    Date

---

[a]Adapted from Hans-Josef Klauck, *Ancient Letters and the New Testament*, (Waco, Tex.: Baylor University Press, 2006).

(PMich.) 8.486: "Sempronius Clemens to his most esteemed Apollinarius, greeting." Paul's letters began in similar fashion, as we can see in Romans 1:1, 7: "Paul, a servant of Jesus Christ, called to be an apostle. . . to all God's beloved in Rome. . . . Grace to you and peace." Although Paul's opening follows the pattern, he expands all three parts of the address. Paul described himself in greater detail than what was typical for his day. When he identified himself, as in his letter to the Romans, he did not use his full name (his old household) and his town. Paul was a member of a new household, that of Jesus Christ. In Paul's view, it was better (more honorable) to be a servant in the household of Christ than to receive any honor he was due from his previous household (Phil 3:4-8). Paul also describes his recipients more fully than was normal and he used an expanded, Christianized greeting. Instead of *chairein* (greetings), he used *charis* (grace). Jewish letters often began with variations of the traditional Jewish greeting: "Peace to you" *(shalom)*. Paul combined the two greetings, producing what becomes his characteristic opening: "Grace and peace to you."

Immediately after the opening, it was quite common to find a statement that the sender has been wishing for or praying for the recipient's good health. In the ancient world with its high mortality rates, disease and death were constant threats.

While Paul did, on occasion, mention in a letter that he was praying for the recipients (Eph 1:17 and Col 1:3), he adopted a much less common opening: a thanksgiving. Occasionally a writer opened his letter with an expression of thanks to the gods.

WHAT'S MORE . . .
Examples of Opening Prayers

PMich. 8.466: "Before all else I pray for your good health, which is my wish, since I revere you next to the gods."

PMich. 8.477: "Before all else I pray for your health and success, which are my wish, and I make obeisance for you . . . daily in the presence of our lord Sarapis [*sic*] and the gods who share his temple."

PMich. 8.491: "Before all else I wish you good health and make obeisance on your behalf to all the gods."

We have found no other ancient letter writer who had such elaborate and extended thanksgivings. More than that, though, Paul often used his thanksgiving as a preview of what he was going to discuss in the letter. From the example below in 1 Corinthians, we see that the items mentioned in the thanksgiving were then discussed at length in the letter. He thanked God for their knowledge but then warned them not to be "puffed up" (1 Cor 1—4). Paul spent several chapters discussing the proper use and abuse of "speech," especially in light of spiritual gifts (1 Cor 12—14). He then discussed their misunderstanding of the return of Christ (1 Cor 15).

After the opening prayer/thanksgiving/health-wish, the typical letter writer usually began what we call the body of the letter. We should be careful about say-

---

WHAT'S MORE . . .
Comparing *PMich.* 8.465 and 1 Corinthians 1:4-7

Apollinarius to Tasoucharion *(PMich.):*
I give thanks to Sarapis [*sic*] and Good Fortune that while all are laboring the whole day through at cutting stones I as an officer move about doing nothing.[a]

1 Corinthians 1:4-7
I give thanks to my God always for you because of the grace of God that has been given you in Christ Jesus, for in every way you have been enriched in him, in speech and knowledge of every kind . . . so that you are not lacking in any spiritual gift as you wait for the revealing of our Lord Jesus Christ.

---

[a]See also *POxy.* 1299, 1070, 1481. Thanksgivings were not common in the papyrus letters.

---

ing the letter body contains the "reasons" for writing the letter. Ancients often wrote to let the recipient know they were alive and well and to maintain friendships (*PMich.* 8.495; *POxy.* 1666). Nonetheless, most letters addressed at least some items of business or news and this was usually done in the body of the letter.

Most Greco-Roman letters ended with a series of greetings.[3] The sender sent greetings to others, as in "I greet your father" (*PTebt.* 415), or asked the recipient

---

[3]Closing greetings are rare in Aramaic letters and none are found in extent Hebrew letters.

to pass on a word of greeting, as in "Greet your mother" (*PTebt.* 412). Sometimes a third party sent greetings, such as in "Apollos greets you" (*PMich.* 8.514). Usually the list of greetings is relatively short, a line or two. However, long lists of greetings are not unknown.[4] Paul included words of greeting in most of his letters. He used generic greetings, such as "Greet every saint in Christ Jesus" (Phil 4:21) or "Greet all the brothers and sisters with a holy kiss" (1 Thess 5:26), as well as named ones, as in "Aristarchus my fellow prisoner greets you, as does Mark the cousin of Barnabas" (Col 4:10). In fact, his letter to the Romans includes all three types of greetings: first person, "I Tertius, the writer of this letter, greet you" (Rom 16:22); second person, "Greet Prisca and Aquila" (Rom 16:3); and third person, "All the churches of Christ greet you" (Rom 16:16).

After closing greetings, ancient letter writings often included another brief health-wish and an authenticating subscription. Today we end our letters with a closing phrase, like "Sincerely" or "Yours truly," and then we write our name below it in cursive script. This "signature" functions as a sign of authenticity. Ancient Greco-Roman letters had a similar custom. They often ended their letters with a common phrase, such as "I pray for your good health" and/or "farewell." As today, the personal handwriting of the sender was the most common sign of authenticity. Ancients, however, did not "sign" their names. Rather, they wrote the final phrase in their own handwriting. Since the Thessalonians may not have known Paul's handwriting, when he signed his final greeting in his own handwriting, he specifically noted it, so they could learn his handwriting: "I, Paul, write this greeting with my own hand. This is the mark in every letter of mine; it is the way I write." Paul then writes the closing greeting: "The grace of our Lord Jesus Christ be with all of you" (2 Thess 3:17-18).

"I'm fine. How are you?" Letter formulas and rhetoric. Even today, letters have certain standard ways of saying things. Letters open with "Dear So-and-So," even if we do not think of "So-and-So" all that dearly. We have standard ways of phrasing some thoughts. Ancient letters were far more standardized, both in the content of the phrases (stereotyped formulas) and in the ways of saying it (epistolary rhetoric).

Stereotyped formulas. Although the Greek language has great flexibility in the word order of a sentence, the word order was rather fixed for these standardized phrases or stereotyped formulas. The familiar wording helped to alert the recipient. When a writer said, "I want you to know, Clemens, that . . ." then Clemens knew information was coming and was likely an important reason for the letter.

---

[4]In *POxy.* 533 the final 10 percent of the letter is greetings. Thus the long list of greetings in Romans 16, while quite striking, was not unprecedented.

These set phrases also let the recipient know if the writer was in a friendly mindset or was displeased. The most common formulas found in letters were disclosure, appeal (petition), joy (rejoice), astonishment, compliance, report, rebuke, thanksgiving, greeting and transitions.[5]

WHAT'S MORE . . .

Examples of Stereotyped Formulas

The "Disclosure Formula" generally used this format: "I want you to know, [name], that . . ." (followed by the information to be disclosed).

> *POxy.* 1493 reads: "I want you to know, brother, that . . ." or *POslo.* 50: "I want you to know that we arrived in the city."

> Philippians 1:12 reads: "I want you to know, beloved, that what has happened to me has actually helped to spread the gospel."

The "Appeal (Petition) Formula" generally used this arrangement: "I appeal to you, [name], to . . ." (usually followed by an [aorist] infinitive).

> *PGiss.* 17 reads: "I appeal to you, sir, to send to us . . ."

> Romans 12:1-2 reads: "I appeal to you therefore, brothers . . . to present your bodies as a living sacrifice."

The "Rejoice Formula" was: "I rejoiced (usually followed by an adverb like "greatly") when (usually the arrival of a letter or some news) that . . ." (the reason for the rejoicing).

> *PGiss.* 21 reads: "I rejoiced exceedingly to hear that . . ."

> 1 Corinthians 16:17 reads: "I rejoice at the coming of Stephanus and . . . because they have . . ."

The "Astonishment Formula" was: "I am astonished that/how . . ." (followed by the object of astonishment, usually that the recipient has failed to write).

> *PMich.* 8.479 reads: "I am astonished how you have not replied to me."

> Galatians 1:6 reads: "I am astonished that you are so quickly deserting the one who called you . . ."

---

[5]The best discussions of these formulas are in John Lee White, "Introductory Formulae in the Body of the Pauline Letter," *Journal of Biblical Literature* 90 (1971): 91-97; and Terence Y. Mullins, "Formulas in New Testament Epistles," *Journal of Biblical Literature* 91 (1972): 380-90. Both sources provide ample examples of the various formulas.

Epistolary rhetoric. In antiquity, saying something well was a valued and honored skill. Paul also took care to state his points eloquently. He was a skilled rhetorician. While Paul was not trained to the same level as the aristocratic orators of Rome, he stood many levels above the typical man of the streets. In antiquity, a speaker's physical appearance was considered an important element of his message. Ancients expected a good speaker to have a sound, symmetrical, "attractive" body and a pleasing voice.[6] We modern folk tend to dismiss such matters since they are "genetically determined." Ancients considered it part of the rhetorical equation and part of the gifts of the gods. This is where Paul probably lost ground. Paul's opponents criticized him, saying, "His bodily presence is weak, and his speech contemptible" (2 Cor 10:10). In their eyes, God made Paul that way. Perhaps Paul's appearance was rather ordinary; he may have shaken with fear when speaking. He could have been poor at on-the-spot dialogue. Quintilian emphasized great speakers could respond quickly and deliver the goods on the fly.[7] Paul clearly excelled, however, when he had time to prepare a carefully crafted, well-reasoned argument. His opponents granted Paul that point: "his letters are weighty and strong" (2 Cor 10:10). In the Lukan examples of Pauline eloquence (Athens, Paul's trials), Paul had time to prepare in advance. Cicero also admitted

---

SO WHAT?
Why Does It Matter If Paul Used Stereotyped Phrases?

How does this help us read Paul's letters better? We should not focus our attention upon the formulas. These were set phrases in Paul's day; these were the parts to skim over to get to "the good stuff." We should notice the content of the formula. For example, when Paul wrote that he rejoiced at some news (1 Cor 16:17), we should not launch into a discussion of how Paul was always rejoicing. When Paul wrote that he was astonished, we should not discuss how Paul was completely unprepared for the news. Rather, we should explore what types of things caused Paul to rejoice or be astonished, and how Paul was using these statements to have a rhetorical effect.

---

[6] See Aristotle's description in *On Rhetoric* 1361a (mid-350s B.C.) and Cicero *On the Orator* 30 (55 B.C.).

[7] Orators often had stock, memorized responses *(topoi)* to common questions, not unlike politicians' "talking points."

WHAT'S MORE . . .
What Then?

Epictetus

"What then *(ti oun)*, would anybody have you dress out to the utmost? By no means *(mē genoito)*, except . . ." (*Arrian Epicteti Dissertationes* 4.11.5)

Paul

"What then *(ti oun)*, should we sin because we are not under the law but under grace? By no means *(mē genoito)*, do you not know . . ." (Rom 6:15)

By using this question-and-answer structure, Paul prepared his readers to hear his response to something they were likely pondering. This rapid-fire dialogue form makes Paul's letter to the Romans all the more engaging to read (and trickier to follow).

---

that he could be more impressive in a letter than in person:

> Often when I have attempted to discuss this topic with you face to face, I have been deterred by a sort of almost boorish bashfulness; but now that I am away from you I shall bring it all out with greater boldness; *for a letter does not blush.*[8]

Paul probably learned rhetorical devices by listening to effective speakers in the marketplace, or agora. The Greek agora or Roman forum was not merely a place to buy and sell goods. Paul likely dialogued with hearers in the marketplace. We have the writings of another famous marketplace preacher-philosopher, Epictetus.[9] Both Paul and Epictetus used a rhetorical device that has been termed "an imaginary interlocutor." The speaker asks an abrupt question as if interrupted by someone. There is no actual person interrupting; the speaker interjects a question that he assumes his hearers are thinking. This gives him the chance to answer the question. The use of an imaginary interlocutor (or interrupting questioner) has become popular in American culture. During a history lecture, the professor might

---

[8] Cicero *Letters to Friends* 5.12, emphasis added. Cicero's comments may be mere rhetoric; however, Plutarch notes it was said of Cicero he was weak in his delivery and he often trembled and shook with fear as he spoke (Plutarch *Cicero* 5.3-4; 35.3).

[9] The writings of Epictetus were "written down" by his disciple Arrian. W. A. Oldfather, the LCL translator of Epictetus, concludes: "That Arrian's report is a stenographic record of the ipsissima verba of the master there can be no doubt" *Epictetus*, LCL, 1:xiii. For a discussion of the use of Greek shorthand in the time of Paul, see E. Randolph Richards, *The Secretary in the Letters of Paul*, Wissenschaftliche Untersuchungen zum Neuen Testament 2/42 (Tübingen: Mohr/Siebeck, 1991), pp. 26-43.

say: "The tribal leaders killed the Soviet magistrate in their village. Could the Soviet Union ignore that? Absolutely not." *Romans!*

Paul and Epictetus both used a similar format and vocabulary to express their ideas.[10] They interrupted themselves with a short question: "What then *(ti oun),* shall we . . . ?" The response also had a standardized beginning: "By no means! *(mē genoito),*" followed by an explanation.

Another common rhetorical device in Paul is chiasm. This device had been more popular in previous generations, but Paul appears to use chiasm more than most of his contemporaries. When we modern writers wish to make a point, we often build toward it. Thus, our "point" is often near the end of our argument. Sometimes, it is stated as a "zinger" at the end. (Most American jokes are told this way.) In chiasm, a writer builds several statements toward his main point, states his main point and then backs away from it, restating each build-up point in reverse order. A classic chiasm is found in a familiar passage from Paul, Romans 10:9-10 (see textbox on p. 65). To our modern ears, chiastic passages may seem to ramble; they sound redundant. To an ancient, it was clever poetry.

A final example of epistolary rhetoric in Paul is his inordinately large amount of paranesis (Greek for "advice" or "exhortation"). In Paul's world, paranesis (also spelled paraenesis) is material that exhorts the reader to socially acceptable behavior. Catechesis instructs a believer in the proper content of the faith (what to be-

---

SO WHAT?
Are Imaginary Interlocutors Real?

Why does it matter if Paul was using an "imaginary interlocutor"? Let's ask this: Were those questions from real opponents in Rome or merely rhetorical? Was Paul answering questions he thought important (and thus his questions provide a window into the core of Paul's theology or common objections to the gospel he preached), or was he answering their questions (and thus the questions provide a window into the church and their particular problems)? Who was really asking those questions?

---

[10]It is debated if this was a well-known pattern since it is found only in these two writers and not in the rhetorical handbooks. This was probably a more "low-brow" method of argumentation, better suited for the agora than the Senate. We should note neither Paul nor Epictetus (a freed slave) were trained aristocrats.

WHAT'S MORE . . .
A Chiasm of Phrases in Romans 10:9-10

A = confess with your mouth
  B = believe in your heart
    C = you will be saved
  B' = with the heart, one believes
A' = with the mouth, one confesses

---

lieve); paranesis exhorts a believer into proper behavior (how to behave). Paranesis applies instruction to the practical problems of daily living. Not all writers then or now concerned themselves with paranesis. Paul's letters on the other hand contain more paranesis than those of any other ancient writer. In fact, Paul's letters tended to flow from catechesis to paranesis, from "the indicative to the imperative," from the "you are" to the "you ought." The transition is often marked by "therefore." The old cliché has some truth to it: "whenever you see a therefore in Paul, you should ask 'what is it there for?'"

Paranesis took several common forms. For example, lists of virtues to be imitated and vices to be avoided were common (often as a list of five virtues or vices). Paul also has virtue and vice lists. Codes for the conduct of a household were common, usually indicating lines of submission to the head of the household: wives to husbands, children to fathers, slaves to masters.   ORDER!

Since Paul was at least a reasonably skilled rhetorician, how did he use his "power to persuade"? He did not consider rhetoric the key to his success (1 Cor 2:4), but it was one of his tools, for he states, "we try to persuade others" (2 Cor

---

SO WHAT?
What Good Is a Chiasm?

Chiasm gives us a wonderful insight into what the writer considered the "main point." For chiasm, find the "center" of the chiasm to find the point the writer wished to stress. In the example in Romans 10:9-10, the simple chiasm centers upon the phrase "you will be saved," clueing us in on what Paul wanted to emphasize. Find the ABCDE chiasm in Ephesians 2:18-22 and you will see what Paul was emphasizing.

5:11). Where and how did he use this skill to open doors for the gospel? Traveling philosophers often preached their views in the agora. If they were persuasive—or at least entertaining—they were often invited to stay in the large home of a wealthier person. This person, a patron or patroness, provided food and lodging. It was honorable, and thus expected, for a wealthy person "to patronize" (to support) the arts, such as philosophy. After Paul spoke in Philippi, a wealthy woman,

---

WHAT'S MORE . . .
Virtue and Vice Lists in Colossians 3 (in Sets of Five)

- "fornication, impurity, passion, evil desire, and greed . . . these are the ways you also once followed" (Col 3:5-7)
- "now you must get rid of . . . anger, wrath, malice, slander, and abusive language" (Col 3:9)
- "clothe yourselves with compassion, kindness, humility, meekness, and patience" (Col 3:12)

Lydia, invited Paul and his team to stay in her home. When a speaker such as Paul was invited into a home, he would often be expected to provide "entertainment" to the patron's guests after dinner. Philosophers would speak about their ideas or poets would recite poems, reciprocating the honor (hospitality) given by the patron. Such occasions provided Paul with a wonderful opportunity to share his ideas, that is, the gospel. Paul probably used these opportunities to read new material he had been composing, to expound Old Testament texts and to hone his arguments that Jesus was the Christ.

Glancing at Jewish Letters

How Greco-Roman items like rhetoric and stereotyped phrases impact Paul's letters are fairly easy to point out. Jewish influences on Paul's letters are more difficult to determine. Yet Paul's letters reflect his Jewish subculture both in the stories he tells and the words he uses.

Signs of a Jewish subculture: Stories. When Paul argues for the universality of sin, he adds, "Death exercised dominion from Adam to Moses" (Rom 5:14). He does not explain who Adam and Moses were. He assumes his readers know those stories. Paul refers to Old Testament accounts not only as illustration but also as authority (1 Cor 9). He feels free to refer to Abraham, Hagar and Isaac (Gal 4)

SO WHAT?
What's the Virtue in a Virtue?

When Paul lists virtues and vices, we should not try to find theological significance in the fact that he lists five of each, or that he even lists them at all. Rather, we should look at what Paul considered virtues and vices compared to what his society commonly listed. Stoics typically listed folly, intemperance, cowardice and injustice as vices. Humility was not a virtue stressed by the Stoics. Virtues and vices for the Greek philosopher were for one's personal purification. Paul spoke of virtues and vices that affected the community. Knowing the standard form helps us to see how Paul altered it to make his particular point. Much today is made of the fact that Paul tells wives to submit to their husbands (Eph 5:22). All household codes had that; to say otherwise would have been viewed as subversive of traditional family values. Rather, we should note that unlike other household codes, Paul's code gives reciprocal duties to the head of the household. In fact, he begins the entire code by insisting that everyone submit to one another (Eph 5:21).[a]

---

[a]Translations commonly fail to show the connection between Ephesians 5:22 and 5:21. In fact, they usually fail to show the larger picture. Paul argues, "Be filled with the Spirit, by singing, . . . by making melody, . . . by giving thanks, . . . by submitting to one another" (Eph 5:18-21). For Paul, those are the "keys" to being filled with the Spirit.

---

without needing to elaborate. Paul also refers to Jewish traditions outside the Old Testament, such as Jannes and Jambres (2 Tim 3:8) or the rock that followed Israel in the exodus (1 Cor 10:4). Most Jews and God-fearers would have known these stories, not from reading Tanakh (the Old Testament narratives) but from hearing the stories told in the synagogue. Often, they were more familiar with later versions of the story (like the version of Sarah and Abraham told in *The Testament of Abraham*) than the original story in Genesis.[11]

Sounds of a Jewish accent: Semitisms. Paul sometimes expresses a sentence in a way more common in Hebrew or Aramaic than in Greek. Paul often used the Hebraism "son of" to indicate "of the same quality." For example, in the Greek text he literally speaks of "sons of disobedience" (Eph 2:2), "sons of light" (1 Thess 5:5)

---

[11]E.g., 1 Peter knows the Sarah story from *The Testament of Abraham*, where she calls him "lord" (six times) rather than from Genesis, where she is hardly an example of wifely obedience and submission. Likewise, many of us know the Noah story from children's programs and not from reading Genesis 6.

and "son of destruction" (2 Thess 2:3). Paul speak of a woman "being" with a man as a reference to marriage (Rom 7:3, literal translation). Far more telling is Paul's use of "walk" as a symbol for living; Paul instructs us to walk by faith, to walk in the Spirit, not to walk in darkness and not to walk in disobedience. To apply these conclusions to letter writing, we must consider Paul's exegetical training as a rabbi, while not neglecting his considerable abilities in Greco-Roman rhetoric. Paul may have reached his conclusions using rabbinic exegesis, but he expressed them eloquently using Greco-Roman epistolary rhetoric in letters that conformed at least in some ways to prevailing customs.

WHO'S THE LETTER WRITER?

When we speak of Paul's letters, we commonly use the expression "Paul wrote." This phrase is accurate, but we must take care not to read our situation back into Paul's.[12] Paul was the "author" and he "wrote" the letters, but in the first century, this process was different from our own. Letter writing involved a secretary as well as input from coworkers, and in Paul's case often a cosender, all of whom could and did contribute to the final product.

Secretaries

Many people did not have the ability to write. Obviously, a secretary was essential if they needed to send a letter. Typically, one located the secretaries' shops in the market and contracted to have a letter sent. The secretary took down a rough draft of what the letter was to say, usually writing it on a wax tablet. The sender and the secretary might then discuss any modifications to the draft. The sender would arrange to return later when a nice draft of the letter was prepared. The letter was finished and ready to be "signed" and folded. In the case of official correspondence, if the sender was completely illiterate, he would arrange for another to "sign" the letter with a formula like, "Eumelus the son of Hermas wrote for him because he does not know letters."[13] Otherwise, the sender would scratch a brief greeting at the end of the letter in his own handwriting, the ancient equivalent of our signature.

When archaeologists find original letters, it is customary to see different handwriting at the end of the letter. In such a letter, the original recipient could actually see the change in handwriting and know the sender was now writing in his own

---

[12]For a more thorough discussion, see Richards, *First-Century Letter Writing*, pp. 19-26.

[13]See Adolph Deissmann, *Light from the Ancient East: The New Testament Illustrated by Recently Discovered Texts of the Graeco-Roman World*, trans. Lionel R. M. Strachan (London: Hodder & Stoughton, 1912), pp. 166-67.

hand. More famous writers realized copies of their letters often circulated around. Copies obviously had no change in handwriting. In these cases, the writer often referred to a change in handwriting. For example, "Greetings to Pilia and Atticus . . . The rest I write to you in my own hand" or "Let my secretary's handwriting be an indication to you that my eyes are inflamed."[14] Paul was aware and even encouraged the sharing of copies of his letters and thus we see him making similar comments when he himself picked up the pen at the end of his letters: "I, Paul, write this greeting with my own hand" (1 Cor 16:21; see also Gal 6:11; Col 4:18; 2 Thess 3:17; Philem 19). Paul's secretary for his letter to the Romans apparently was known to the recipients, for he even sends his own greeting: "I Tertius, the writer of this letter, greet you in the Lord" (Rom 16:22). The fact Paul, like virtually all other ancient letter writers, used a secretary is not disputed.[15]

Why would a literate author want to use a secretary? Evidence is clear that highly literate people like Cicero, Atticus and Paul used a secretary. In the modern world, we equate "literacy" with the ability to write. Ancients equated it with the ability to read. Ancient writing was a craft that required skill. Secretaries had to cut their own paper into sheets, measure and score the lines, mix their own ink, cut their own reed pens and write on the rough fibrous paper (papyrus) of antiquity. Furthermore, ancients valued beautiful handwriting—more what we would call "calligraphy." While an ancient might be able to scratch out the lines, he would not want to send such an ugly letter. Archaeologists who study ancient letters often comment on the difference between the secretary's writing ("an upright flowing cursive of fine appearance") and the sender's handwriting ("coarse," "large").[16]

The various ways to use a secretary. Not all writers used secretaries the same way. In fact, there was a range of uses. Secretaries were used commonly as composers for routine, brief correspondence. The letter sender described what he

---

[14]Cicero *Letters to Atticus* 12.32.1 and 8.13.1.

[15]For a comprehensive argument, see E. Randolph Richards, *The Secretary in the Letters of Paul*, Wissenschaftliche Untersuchungen zum Neuen Testament 2/42 (Tübingen: Mohr/Siebeck, 1991).

[16]Herbert Chayyim Youtie and John Garrett Winter, eds., *Papyri and Ostraca from Karanis*, Michigan Papyri (Ann Arbor: University of Michigan, 1951), 8:74, 41, respectively. In actuality, even when the sender could write quite elegantly, he often still used a secretary. We should not assume Cicero or Paul were poorly skilled at handling a pen. Among preserved papyrus letters from Egypt, we find some examples where the sender writes closing comments in his own handwriting and the handwriting, grammar and style are equal to the earlier part from the secretary; e.g., *PMich.* 8. 500: "The farewell formula and the postscript were added by a second, more delicate and more rapid, hand" (ibid., p. 117). *PMich.* 8. 495 ends with comments written by the sender in colloquial but quite fluent Greek (p. 105). In *PMich.* 8. 513, the sender's handwriting is in a "large, fluent and elegant hand" (ibid., p. 147). Evidently, some letter writers were quite capable of writing personally; yet, as a general practice, letter writers of Paul's day used secretaries.

wanted the letter to say, such as "I arrived safely on the third of the month. I sold the goods for the price we wanted. I am remaining here for the festival and then will return. Greet my father and mother." The secretary made notes and then prepared a nice address, health wish and so on. He used the appropriate formulas, like "disclosure." He even added personal greetings. The letter was ready to sign when the sender returned. On the opposite end of the spectrum, a secretary could be merely a transcriber. The author dictated every word to the secretary. Skilled authors did this when they wanted the document precisely as they intended. When Cicero fretted over a composition he was sending to a respected colleague, he chose to dictate it carefully, "syllable-by-syllable" (Cicero *Letters to Atticus* 13.25.3).

Why didn't everybody dictate? Well, secretaries were better trained to write letters than most senders. It was best to leave such details to the experts. However, even those who were better trained than a secretary often did not dictate the letter. It was too laborious to dictate at such a slow rate. Imagine dictating 1 Corinthians: "Paul . . . [pause]. . . called . . . [pause]. . . an apostle . . . [pause] . . . of Christ Jesus . . . [pause]. . ." At that rate, it would likely take two days to dictate 1 Corinthians.[17]

Aside from brief letters, most letter writers did not relinquish the letter's contents over to the secretary nor did they dictate the entire letter. The typical process was somewhere in between these extremes. The sender gave the secretary detailed instructions, perhaps even dictating the exact wording of some key passages. The secretary then prepared a rough draft. Such drafts were usually written on stacks of wax tablets or on parchment notebooks, a recent innovation of Paul's time. These notebooks, called *membranae,* were specially prepared so that the ink could be washed off. In 2 Timothy 4:13, Paul asks Timothy to bring Paul's books (scrolls) and his *membranae* (parchment notebooks).

After a rough draft was ready, the author of the letter read the draft (or more probably, listened to the draft read aloud). He then made corrections and additions. This process continued until the author was completely satisfied. The less

---

[17]Secretaries wrote about eighty-five lines per hour when copying. Taking dictation would be slower. For a fuller discussion, see Richards, *First-Century Letter Writing,* pp. 163-65. In Paul's time there were secretaries trained to take shorthand in Latin or Greek. Since such specialists are mentioned as in use in Rome and in provincial governments, we would be unwise to assume that every place had such tachygraphists ("rapid writers") and that the average person could afford them. With the possible exception of his letter to the Romans, we find no evidence that Paul's secretaries could take shorthand. It is very unlikely Paul dictated his letters word-for-word to his secretary, whether rapidly to a tachygraphist or painfully slowly to a transcriber; see Richards, *Secretary,* pp. 26-42, 189-98.

literate the writer (or the less important the letter), the more was left up to the secretary. Since Paul was literate and considered his letters important, it is wise to assume that Paul did not give his secretary any freedom to compose. Paul spent a great deal of energy and expense on letters. He was better educated than a secretary, particularly in the Scriptures. Paul crafted his letters rhetorically to make them more powerful (2 Cor 10:10), and there seems to be no case where he allowed a secretary to compose freely for him.

Possible effects of using a secretary. If Paul did not give his secretary latitude to compose, then were there any effects from using a secretary? Unless it was very slow dictation, using a secretary introduced minor variations. When the secretary fleshed out his notes, he might use a different word or might phrase an expression slightly differently that Paul had.[18] The question we face, however, is not if such variations could occur, but what were the effects since they did occur. Let us consider two letters from outside Paul. *Michigan Papyri* 8.490 and 8.491 are letters from the same man, Apollinarius. The handwriting is markedly different because he used different secretaries. What is more striking is that the letters also differ considerably in style and spelling.[19] Secretaries caused variations. The amount of variation was not fixed. Some secretaries were more skilled and reproduced the author's verbal draft more literally. Some authors were less concerned and allowed the secretary more latitude. In any event, the secretary was a factor in the letter's composition. Now, let's take this to Paul. Many Christians presuppose the words coming from Paul's mouth are "the inspired word" and therefore are predisposed to reject anything that could muddle the transition of the word uttered from Paul's lips to the written word on the page. In light of ancient letter writing practice (and better theology), the written letter rather than an earlier oral draft is better considered the inspired word. Thus, for example, 1 Corinthians is inspired, or to be more precise, 1 Corinthians, which claims for itself to be from Paul and Sosthenes (1 Cor 1:1), written through the hand of a secretary (1 Cor 16:21), is inspired.

Apollonarius's secretaries clearly accounted for the considerable stylistic differences in his letters. Scholars of Cicero indicate that Cicero's letters varied considerably in vocabulary and style. In fact, some of his letters are more similar to the letters of others than to his own.[20] Since secretaries often caused such minor differences in the letters of other writers, we should allow for this in the Pauline cor-

---

[18]For a description of how inspiration and even inerrancy can be maintained in such a scenario, see Richards, *First-Century Letter Writing*, pp. 224-29.

[19]So also the conclusions of the editors, ibid., pp. 94-95.

[20]See R. Y. Tyrrell and L. C. Purser, *The Correspondance of M. Tullius Cicero* (Dublin: Hodges & Figgis, 1915), 2:lxix-lxx.

SO WHAT?
Do Secretaries Matter?

In a letter, where the author retained tight control over the content, using a secretary still introduced minor differences. For example, when the secretary read back a draft, Paul hears *dōron* (gift) when he usually used *dōrea* (also meaning gift).[a] Yet the synonym was fine and it was certainly not worth interrupting the secretary to make the alteration. From the point of view of most readers today, this is rather insignificant. However, some scholars have pointed out that certain letters attributed to Paul use vocabulary or expressions that are not typical of Paul. This, they argue, is an indication that Paul did not write that letter—it was written by someone else and is a pseudonymous letter or perhaps even a forgery. Clearly, given the practice of using secretaries, variations in style and vocabulary should not be determinative as a criterion for authenticity.

---

[a]*Dōrea* occurs five times (Rom 5:15, 17; 2 Cor 9:15; Eph 3:7; 4:7) and *dōron* only once (Eph 2:8).

---

pus.[21] Some letters of Paul may have more variations because the secretary for that letter was less adept at reproducing every word. Some scholars have criticized the idea that we should allow for such secretarial influence. They suggest it takes authorship from Paul's hand and gives it to the secretary. But are we implying Paul relinquished control of his letter to some unnamed, perhaps non-Christian, secretary? To allow minor shifts in vocabulary and style is not to abandon the letter. The image of Paul we glean from his letters and from Luke[22] is not that of a man who would allow anything in his letters that he did not approve.

The secretary, and other aspects of first-century letter writing, can explain other features of Paul's letters. It was quite customary for the author to summarize a letter's main point when he personally signed the letter. This is clearest perhaps in Philemon 19-25. We notice two things about Paul's autographed postscript

---

[21]Classical scholars have long noted significant stylistic variations between, for example, some of Cicero's letters; yet they do not look to pseudonymity for the solution. They ascribe it to secretarial mediation. See the very insightful analysis by T. Zieliński, summarized by Tyrrell and Purser, *Cicero*, 2:lxvii n.

[22]The differences between the Paul seen in his letters (the epistolary Paul) and the Paul described in Acts (the Lukan Paul) should not be overstated since no self-description is objective.

here in Philemon. First, there seems to be no convention requiring a postscript to be brief. In one of his letters Cicero writes a postscript in his own hand that is five times longer than the original letter written by the secretary![23] It has long been suggested that perhaps 2 Corinthians 10—13 was a postscript in Paul's own hand.[24] This is not clear, but its length does not preclude this. The second thing we notice about the Philemon postscript is that it seems to be more abrupt or stern. In fact, one could argue this seems true whenever Paul personally picked up the pen (1 Cor 16:22-24; Gal 6:11-18; Col 4:18). Did the secretary and his co-authors tend to moderate Paul somewhat? The Paul of the postscripts does match more closely the Paul described in Acts.

Are we suggesting Paul was diluted or distorted in the earlier "secretarial" sections of his letter? Are we suggesting the "pure Paul" is found only in his post-scripts? No, *mē genoito*. More significantly, we suggest it is an error to seek the "pure Paul." The earlier discussion of Mediterranean culture versus Western in-dividuality comes into focus here. Many imagine an unmediated Paul (the indi-vidual) is the closest to the inspired word. Yet the letter is what is inspired. Moreover, Paul was not struggling to free himself from his coworkers' influence. He was part of a team. Paul was, though, the dominant figure. He was the clear leader, the overwhelming force of the team. Things went his way. An author was held responsible for everything in a letter. An author could not blame a secretary for poor wording or grammar. For Paul, the letter was not finished until he agreed with all of its content, because Paul was accountable for it. His name was on the line.

Writing as a Community Enterprise

So if Paul were part of a contributing team but accountable for the content, how would the writing process take place? Paul or a colleague would find the secretar-ies' stall in the market and contract for a secretary to prepare a letter. Most secre-taries were paid per standard line of writing (a *stichos*). On an agreed date, the sec-retary would arrive with stacks of wax tablets or leaf-books, although he might be using those newfangled parchment notebooks. Paul had already been discussing with his team members what needed to be said. He would have his notebooks there with some material he had already worked up and excerpts from Scripture,

---

[23]Cicero *Letters to Atticus* 12.32.1.

[24]So has argued Dibelius (and others), perhaps caused by Paul receiving new information after chapters 1—9 were written (so Munck and others) or perhaps by a sleepless night (so Lietzmann) or by a sud-den doubt over the genuineness of the Corinthians' repentance (so Guthrie).

collections of early Christian hymns and sayings, Jesus tradition and other material gathered over the years. Paul would already have a clear agenda for what he
wanted to cover in the letter.[25]

Preformed traditions. A sign of a particularly gifted speaker was the ability to
ad lib an answer to an unexpected question. This gift was praised because the average speaker was expected to prepare ahead of time to address the expected questions. Paul's letters were his answers to their questions, even though he was absent
from them in body (Col 2:4-5). We should not assume Paul thought so little of his
churches that he "winged it," that he did not prepare his answers thoughtfully.
Moreover, speakers and writers even worked up material ahead of time, in anticipation of a need. For example, philosophers of Paul's day used memorized responses to certain situations.[26] Paul also included this type of material in his letters. For example, Romans 13 is a series of three sermonettes that Paul has
included to illustrate his point of overcoming evil with good (Rom 12:21).

This type of material is best termed "preformed," meaning that it was composed on an earlier occasion. It was not composed specifically for the situation addressed in that letter. Paul himself may have composed the preformed material for
another situation and simply found it useful for this letter also, or he may have
been using material he had heard and kept. Regardless of who "wrote" it, the fact
that Paul decided to include a particular preformed tradition in his letter meant he
stood in full agreement with its teaching. Other types of preformed material were
well-known hymns and sayings.

Paul exhorts his friends in Philippi to have humility, like Jesus. He then quotes
a section of a hymn they knew, emphasizing Christ's humble nature (Phil 2:6-11).[27]
When Paul used something preformed, whether an Old Testament quotation, early
Christian hymn or creed, or clever chiasm, we should not assume he had to dictate
it to the secretary. If Paul had previously composed a piece on a subject, why would
he then read it to the secretary for the secretary to scribble into his notes? He would
hand it to the secretary to be copied into the next draft. The secretary would make

---

[25]Paul usually previewed a letter's main themes in his opening thanksgiving. We are assuming he did
not compose the thanksgiving *after* the letter but rather at the beginning, thus indicating that he had
certain topics he intended to cover. The fact that his letters often have other topics not previewed in
the opening thanksgiving is merely an indication that the letter developed and expanded as it was
created and edited.

[26]Ancients called such a response a *topos* (place), because it was a familiar "place" for the speaker to
return to when faced with a common question.

[27]Since archaeologists have not yet uncovered the Philippian Christian Hymnal, we can only deduce
which passages appear to be quotations of hymns based on certain, reasonable criteria. Thus, such
passages are often disputed by some scholars.

SO WHAT?
Why Does It Matter If Paul Is Quoting?

Isn't it all just Scripture? Quoting familiar material from hymns or sayings helped solidify Paul's ethos (character) for his audience. We use the same technique. For example, if I were speaking to a senior adult group, it could be very effective to say, "My life was changed by what happened on a hill far away." All the listeners would recognize the allusion to a beloved hymn.[a] In fact, the allusion has the added benefit of conjuring up the positive feelings associated with that hymn. For this to work, the hearers have to recognize the allusion. Many young people today (and most foreigners) would not catch the reference and could be confused. All of us have the same problem when we read Paul. We often do not catch when he is quoting something. Paul tells the Ephesians that every deed will be exposed in the light of Christ. He then continues, "Sleeper, awake!" (Eph 5:14). It strikes us as an odd thing to say. Many scholars think Paul is quoting a baptismal saying, and that he is doing so for the same reason that we might use the quotation "on a hill far away."

---

[a]"On a hill far away stood an old rugged cross" are the opening words to George Bennard's beloved hymn "The Old Rugged Cross," written in 1913.

---

a sign in his notes of where to place it when he wrote out the draft. Paul would then move on. For this reason, Paul's text often reads rather smoothly if such preformed material is pulled out.[28] Our point here is to note the composition of a letter was not merely an oral process, nor was it necessarily a singular process.

Input from team members. In the West, individuals "make up their own minds" quite independently (supposedly) of others. Individuals cast their votes and the "majority" decides. In a dictatorship, one individual imposes his or her will upon other individuals. The first-century Mediterranean world was dyadic—as is most of the non-Western world today. Dyadic cultures think in terms of "we" more than

---

[28]There are significant implications for the process of detecting interpolations in Paul's letters; see Richards, *First-Century Letter Writing*, pp. 109-21. Careful study will sometimes reveal telltale signs of this interpolation (insertion of "foreign" material). Scholars need to distinguish between pre-dispatch interpolations (foreign material inserted into the letter during composition and with Paul's approval) and post-dispatch interpolations (material added by others after Paul's time, and thus needing extraction). For a full discussion, see Richards, *First-Century Letter Writing*, pp. 99-121.

"I." Decisions were reached by consensus. The problem was discussed—usually at great length—with everyone having a chance to speak. Then the Patriarchal Voice, the recognized (usually male) leader, expressed the consensus. We can see this in Acts 15. The church leaders convened (Acts 15:6) to decide if Gentile Christians

---

WHAT'S MORE . . .
Decision by Consensus

College students often ask, "What's to keep the leader from saying what he wanted?" Indeed, for us the "I" must always come before the "we." This is not to say that a leader in an honor culture did not on occasion stretch consensus in his direction. But it was up to the group to decide if his decision would be acceptable. Let us consider a recent experience one of us had.

In some parts of Indonesia, the leading male in a girl's clan determines her bride price. The family of her fiancé must provide the requested gift. On one occasion a young couple was planning to marry and enter ministry in a remote village. His family was very poor. Her family was excusing the bride price because the couple was "going to serve the Lord." When her father's oldest brother, the head of the clan, arrived, he set a bride price of four oxen, because "no niece of his is a cheap woman." This effectively canceled the wedding. The clan called a meeting. They discussed the situation at great length, with everyone except the uncle urging that the bride price be dropped. After about four hours—which seemed even longer—the uncle announced that he had decided what to do. He stated, "I think it best that no bride price be required, but they cannot marry until next summer."

From where did this extra stipulation come? We can only suspect the uncle was "saving face." The group sat silently for a moment. The others were deciding if this was acceptable or if they should reopen the discussion, with the risk of a different consensus. Finally, the bride's father agreed, "They shall marry next summer." The group had reached a decision and no votes had been taken. When James appears to add extra rules (Noachian Laws?) to the group decision (Acts 15:20), was he taking some license as the Patriarchal Voice? Did these extra stipulations sour Paul to the decree? At least not entirely, for Luke tells us that when Paul and Barnabas returned to Antioch with the letter from Jerusalem, everyone received the news with joy (Acts 15:31). Culture helps us to understand what happened.

had to become Jews first (be circumcised). There was much discussion (Acts 15:7). Luke records two of the most prominent speakers, Peter and Paul (Acts 15:8-12). After this, James spoke and expressed the consensus (Acts 15:13-21).

First-century folks preferred not to work or travel alone. The image we have of Paul, both from his letters and from Luke, shows a man who led a team. When his original partner, Barnabas, left him, Paul found a new partner, Silas, before he began a new project. It was not that Paul had decided a team approach was best for ministry; it would not have occurred to him to do otherwise. If a team member interjected a comment while Paul was talking, would Paul have snapped, "Mind your own business"? We should assume dialogue was a regular part of the letter-writing process. While we would hesitate to interrupt or question "Saint Paul, the beloved apostle to the Gentiles," his team members had not read the press releases. He was their leader, but they felt free to voice alternative or even dissenting opinions.[29] Their input would not have been ignored.

Input woven into Paul's argumentation would be thoroughly "Paulinized" and would be difficult for us to detect, except perhaps by comparing several letters. On the other hand, input from a co-author that was prewritten would be more discernible. Elsewhere, we have suggested that 1 Corinthians 10:1-22 was a midrash by Sosthenes against idols and that 2 Corinthians 6:14—7:1 was from Timothy.[30] The verdict on any particular passage is not important here. It is necessary, though, to note it is meaningless to name a co-author who does not actually contribute anything. We have no reason to assume that Paul would silence his team members. We should allow room for a complementary, although secondary, voice in Paul's letters.

Rough drafts and the public reading of excerpts. We should recognize that Paul, as a creative missionary and theologian, was composing even when he was not writing a letter. Refining an argument probably occurred during the process of writing a letter. Some refinement no doubt also happened in the months or years between writing one letter and another. When Paul had to write follow-up letters to clarify confusion (1 Cor 5:9; 2 Thess 2), surely he also altered how he presented the same material on other occasions.

Paul hammered out material as he theologized. If Galatians was written early, as we think, then Paul did not have a lot of time to float his argument concerning

---

[29]We see two examples in Luke's account. In both cases, Luke picks a topic where his readers would know right away that Paul was wrong: Paul's poor opinion of Mark (Acts 15:37-39) and Paul's confidence that his trip to Jerusalem carrying the relief offering would be successful (Acts 21:4, 11-14).

[30]Richards, *First-Century Letter Writing*, pp. 115-18.

the law. As he heard rebuttals and confusion, Paul honed his argument. He realized his argument for the law being given after Abraham could be muddled by his opponents, for they could point out that circumcision was before the offering of Isaac (as the example of faith). As he defended his position, Paul refined his argument to avoid giving his opponents opportunity to muddy the water. His earlier argument in Galatians was not wrong, but Paul worked out a more effective way to present his point. Thus, in Romans we find Paul using the example of Abraham differently (see below, chapter 4, footnote 11). It was not that Paul changed his mind; rather, he refined his argument in light of his experiences interacting with opponents. Likewise, today the crucible of ministry often causes us to refine our approaches.

THE COST OF PAUL'S LETTERS

The process of writing and rewriting was not free. A secretary charged by the line. Like anyone whose living depends on billing customers, the secretary kept up with how many lines he wrote each time. Although we do not know the exact charges for making drafts and producing a letter, we can make some educated guesses. A rough, and very conservative, estimate of what it cost in today's dollars to prepare a letter like 1 Corinthians would be $2100, $700 for Galatians, and $500 for 1 Thessalonians.[31] Why were Paul's letters so expensive to write? Paul's letters were inordinately long. The initial shock in the church at Corinth was not over the contents of Paul's letter but over its length! It is no doubt a double-edged jab at Paul when his opponents said Paul's letters were "weighty" (2 Cor 10:10).[32] His letter to Philemon was not short, as we often think. If anything, the letter was a trifle longer than a typical letter of Paul's day. Yet, a letter like Philemon was a reasonable enough expense ($100).[33] But Paul wrote some letters so long that they had to be rolled like a book (scroll)!

MAILING PAUL'S LETTERS

Although many modern Christians have not really thought about it, they probably

---

[31]Estimates include the labor for one rough draft, and papyrus and labor for the finished letter and a copy for Paul. Estimates were based upon the lowest figures any time there was data. After estimating, an additional 10 percent was removed in the hope of avoiding any inflationary errors. The resulting estimate seems plausible and matches the little hard data currently available. For an explanation of how the estimates were made as well as the costs of other letters, see Richards, *First-Century Letter Writing*, pp. 165-69.

[32]The pun works well in both Greek and English: "weighty" as "heavy" as well as "influential."

[33]We are accustomed to the idea that letters represent an insignificant expense. We think, "I would not pay a hundred dollars to write a letter home." Yet nowadays American soldiers abroad may spend a hundred dollars on a phone call to let their loved ones know they are safe and sound.

envision Paul dictating his letter. When he had pronounced the last word, he then took the sheet from the secretary, wrote some final words and sent off that copy. We have tried to show that Paul invested much more time and effort into his letters. After finishing his last revision, he ordered the secretary to prepare a polished draft for dispatch. When that draft was returned—and checked!—Paul would append his postscript. Then that copy was ready for dispatch.[34]

Many ancient letters ended with merely a word of farewell and often a date. (How we wish that Paul had written the date at the end of his letters!) More official letters tended to summarize the key point or points of the letter.[35] Paul sometimes summarized. In the postscript of his letter to the Galatians, he returns to the problem of circumcision (Gal 6:11-18). In his letter to Philemon, Paul reminds Philemon of his own debt to Paul (Philem 19-21). Other times Paul ends with a closing benediction in his handwriting.

Once the dispatched copy was prepared, was it too late at this point to "correct" something? No. Before a wedding invitation was ready to be dispatched, the date of the wedding could be changed.[36] What if news arrived that altered something already written in the letter? Ancients understood this. Letters did not always leave as soon as expected.[37] During the delay, situations could change. For example, the situation had changed enough so that in one of his letters Cicero needed to modify what he had said earlier: "I wrote to you above that Curio was very cold; well, he is warm enough now; . . . he had not done so before I wrote the first part of this letter."[38] It was not uncommon for an author's tone to change or his opinion to shift in a postscript. Something happened, news arrived, the situation shifted, and the author needed to clarify, modify or change his view on the matter. A writer needed to soften (or stiffen) his tone in light of some new information. Scholars have long noted the shift in tone near the end of 2 Corinthians, beginning in 10:1. The shift is sufficient that some have suggested 2 Corinthians 10—13 was originally a separate letter. We have no manuscript evidence to support this. Furthermore, it is unnecessary. Abrupt shifts in tone were not uncommon in letters.

---

[34]An interesting question is raised as to which is the "autograph," the dispatched copy or the copy Paul retained for himself.

[35]The main point of summarization was to show the author (writing in his own hand) was fully in accord with the sale or whatever business the letter was handling.

[36]*POxy.* 1487.

[37]"When he [Oppius] has decided to send letter carriers and has received a letter from me, something unexpected hinders him, and he is unavoidably later than he intended in sending the carriers; while I [Cicero], when once the letter has been handed to him [the carrier], do not trouble about having the date altered" Cicero *Letters to Quintus* 3.1.8.

[38]Cicero *Letters to Friends* 8.6.5.

Moreover, the repetition of the author's name ("I, Paul") at the beginning is not uncommon for a postscript.[39] The shift in tone near the end of Philippians could have a similar explanation.

Sealing a Letter

When the author had personally written any closing remarks and was completely satisfied with the letter, it was time to fold and seal it. The purpose was the same as today. We seal envelopes to keep out prying eyes. Also, as today, it had mixed success. Cicero complained, "There are very few who can carry a letter of weight without lightening it by a perusal."[40] To reduce this chance, typical letters were folded accordion-style, as we do when making a paper fan. The result was then folded double. A sliver of the papyrus was pulled off the edge and used to tie around the letter. A piece of clay was pressed over the knot. If the writer had a seal (most did not), he pressed it into the clay. Secretaries commonly pre-wrote the address on the back of the sheet at right angles in the proper place so that when the letter was folded, the address was on the outside. Most of Paul's letters, however, were much too long to fold in the normal fashion. They were rolled into a scroll and tied.

Sending a Letter

Having invested so much time and money in writing a letter, Paul now had to consider how the letter was to be sent to wherever he intended it to go. The Romans had set up an imperial postal service, operating much like the Pony Express of the American West. The Roman post, however, was only for official government business. Paul did not have access to it. Like everyone else, he had two choices of letter carrier: the happenstance carrier and the private carrier. The happenstance carrier was someone who happened to be traveling to that locale or in that general direction. If you were traveling to Ephesus, for instance, you expected people to drop by and leave letters with you to be delivered in Ephesus. Most people did not engage in spur-of-the-moment travel. Traveling season was generally from March to November, because winter provided too many dangers at sea and on the road. Arrangements needed to be made and funds gathered. Folks would find out where and when you were going. Part of being a responsible member of a community was a willingness to carry letters with you in your satchel.

There was another option. If you wanted to send a letter and by chance no one

---

[39] *POxy.* 264. For a fuller discussion, see Richards, *First-Century Letter Writing*, pp. 81-90, 176-81.
[40] Cicero *Letters to Atticus* 1.13.

was going that way, then you personally had to send someone there: a private carrier. The advantage of a private carrier was that the letter was safer and more likely to arrive. Also, since Paul could likely choose whom to send, he may well have picked someone who could read the letter publicly. The ancients had long known (and we are rediscovering) that body language, intonation, gestures, facial expressions and so on are vital aspects of communication. A reader who knew Paul's letter and intent could much more effectively read (perform) the letter. Since much effort was expended on writing the letter, it is reasonable that Paul would consider who could best deliver it. In at least some situations, Paul deliberately picked someone to carry the letter who could give a trustworthy elaboration. It was expected for the carrier to share additional information if he had any: "Tychicus will tell you all the news about me. . . . I have sent him to you for this very purpose so that you may know how we are" (Col 4:7-8).

It is possible, even likely, that Paul used happenstance carriers to deliver his early letters. The cities of southern Galatia were stops along the main road between Antioch and the West. Paul would have no trouble finding reliable people traveling that way to deliver his letters to the Galatians. The same is possibly true for the Thessalonian letters and possibly the so-called previous letter to the Corinthians (1 Cor 5:9). Paul probably saw no reason to send a private carrier. However, his situation was changing, especially concerning his letters. Some opponents may have been forging letters in Paul's name (2 Thess 2:2). The need arose to authenticate his letters (2 Thess 3:17), which could be done by a known and trusted associate. More significantly, Paul's earlier letters were often marked by misunderstanding on the part of the recipients. In 1 Corinthians 5:9-13, Paul notes they had misunderstood something he had written previously. A trusted carrier, particularly one who could read publicly the letter, could easily have corrected this misunderstanding. These problems (forgeries, opponents, misunderstandings) may have prompted Paul to begin to use private carriers. The advantages of these carriers quickly commended their use as well. A private carrier could clarify Paul's meaning and also provide additional information or admonition, as Tychicus was clearly expected to do: "so that you may know how we are and that he may encourage your hearts" (Col 4:8).

Conclusion

Rediscovering Paul amid the piles of Mediterranean mail has helped us to understand his letters better. In many ways, Paul was a typical first-century Greco-Roman letter writer and thus studying letters from his day is helpful. We learned that Paul often used routine phrases (such as our "How are you?"). We probably should not make too much of these typical phrases. We saw some styles of argumentation used by Paul were common enough and had particular purposes. We should read Paul's arguments with these in mind. We also encountered some common aspects of first-century letter writing we might not have known before. Paul used a secretary. Paul was probably less individualistic than most of us. Modern readers have probably unfairly excluded the influence and contribution of Paul's teammates, particularly those who co-sent the letter, and his secretaries. Finally, readers of Paul should major on the points Paul was emphasizing rather than the ones that stand out to modern Westerners. One way to do this is by studying Paul's use of common letter-writing customs like stereotyped phrases and epistolary rhetoric.

Having said that in many ways Paul was a typical letter writer, we must also say Paul was unusual—if not unique—in other aspects. In fact, it is often in his divergence from custom that we see Paul more clearly. Paul wrote very long letters of theological complexity and depth. While he did not have the rarified vocabulary and syntax of the orators—his letters tended to use common speech—Paul wrote of difficult concepts and ideas, as others complained (2 Pet 3:16). Paul used some letter elements that were not particularly common: thanksgivings and paranesis. In fact, Paul used both of these more than any other writer of his time. Since Paul is the common thread through all of his letters, we conclude that Paul's letters are unique because of Paul. For that reason, we need to look more closely at this Saul of Tarsus who was conscripted by Jesus (Phil 3:12) on the road to Damascus, becoming the slave of Christ.

READ MORE ABOUT IT

DPL Articles:

"Diatribe," pp. 213-14, by D. F. Watson.

"Letters, Letter Forms," pp. 550-53, by P. T. O'Brien.

"Rhetorical Criticism," pp. 822-26, by G. W. Hansen.

"Teaching, Paraenesis," pp. 922-23, by M. B. Thompson.

"Thanksgiving," pp. 69-71, by P. T. O'Brien.

Richards, E. Randolph. *Paul and First-Century Letter Writing.* Downers Grove, Ill.: InterVarsity Press, 2004.

3

Paul's Conversion, Call and Chronology

THE TRANSFORMATION OF SAUL THE PHARISEE from persecutor of the church to Paul the apostle, the architect of the Gentile mission, is one of the best-known stories in the New Testament. What actually happened to Saul-Paul is the subject of a debate based in large part on different interpretations of the evidence from Acts and Paul's letters. We will begin with a discussion of Saul's zeal and persecution of Jesus' followers. Then we will turn to Paul's account of his conversion or call in his letters before considering the account in Acts. Afterward we will show how scholarly discussions have something to offer in locating Paul's experience within his world. In the last part of this chapter we will attempt to construct a coherent chronology of Paul's life.

PAUL AND ZEAL

Paul refers to himself as "zealous for the traditions of my ancestors" (Gal 1:14) and indicates that "zeal" caused him to persecute the church (Phil 3:6). *Zeal* is a technical term for a particular approach to God and a specific attitude toward those who dishonored him. Zeal and persecution went hand in hand. When it came to zeal, everyone's hero was Phineas. In Numbers 25 Israelite men were engaging in sexual relations with Moabite women. They attended their feasts and bowed down to foreign gods. God became angry and instructed Moses to kill all the chiefs of the people. When an Israelite stepped forward to take a Midianite wife, Phineas killed them both. Although thousands died in an associated plague, God's wrath

SO WHAT?
Conversion or Call?

Why does it matter if we describe Paul's Damascus-road experience as a "conversion" or a "call"? Traditionally, the dramatic change in Paul's life is seen as a "conversion" from Judaism: frustrated by his failure to meet the standards of the law, Paul inwardly struggled under a guilty conscience. On the way to Damascus, Paul "saw the light" and "converted to Christianity" with its promise of forgiveness. Saul the Jew changed religion and became Paul the apostle. The problem with this view is that Paul never says any of those things. After meeting Christ, he still describes himself as a Jew (Rom 9:3), undergoes Jewish purification rituals (Acts 21:24); he never implies he struggled with guilt (Phil 3:4-6). Paul says he is a new creation (2 Cor 5:17), not that he converted to a new religion.

---

was satisfied by Phineas's action and many were saved through his zeal. Nearer the time of the New Testament, the hero was Mattathias. During the madness of Antiochus IV's reign, Mattathias and his family moved to Modein, Judea. He grieved when he saw the blasphemies performed by the Syrians and apostate Jews (1 Maccabees 2:1-14). When King Antiochus's representative, a Syrian, arrived in Modein to force Jews to sacrifice to the Greek gods, Mattathias refused despite the promise of great reward. Another Jew stepped forward to offer the sacrifice and Mattathias, burning with zeal, killed both the Jew and the Syrian. This is how the Maccabean revolt began. Mattathias is celebrated in this way (1 Maccabees 2:26): "thus he burned with zeal for the law, just as Phineas did against Zimri son of Salu." On his deathbed Mattathias urged his sons to have zeal for the law and to give themselves completely to God's covenant. In reciting the great deeds of his ancestors, Mattathias included Phineas along with Abraham, Joseph, David, Elijah and Daniel.

Zeal, then, as Paul uses it, refers to firm resolve and forceful resistance against anyone who in any way appears to compromise God's unique covenant with Israel.[1] Although zeal could be expressed toward Gentiles, more often zeal meant confrontation with Jews who flagrantly fouled God's honor and people. The goals of zeal were: (1) to maintain the purity of God's people—an issue of honor—

---

[1] James D. G. Dunn, *The Theology of Paul's Letter to the Galatians* (Cambridge: Cambridge University Press, 1993), p. 68.

against a world demanding assimilation and (2) to avert God's displeasure and punishment against his people.

Saul (Paul) lived during a time when God's people hoped for the missing blessings of the first covenant. They longed for deliverance, for God's enemies to be destroyed, for Israel to be restored, and for the exile to come to an end.[2] They believed that one day the word of the prophets would come to pass. Then Jerusalem would be the center of the world, and the entire world would recognize Israel's God as God. But, many thought, God would not act as long as his people lived in disobedience. Saul envisaged himself as a key player in Israel's unfulfilled story. He had a part to play in readying Israel for God's visitation and judgment. Zeal compelled the pre-Christian Paul to protect the covenant by punishing the disobedient so the path to Israel's glorious future could be realized and the covenantal blessings restored.

PAUL'S CONVERSION/CALL

Apparently, Saul considered the followers of Jesus a clear and present danger to Israel's future. He was compelled to persecute them to preserve the purity of God's people. Yet neither the letters nor Acts give a clear picture of why he considered them dangerous. Some scholars think Saul's persecution stemmed from the early Christians' opposition to temple and Torah.[3] Others point out the dangerous political overtones associated with calling Jesus the Messiah. *Messiah* meant, among other things, king, and Rome took a dim view of any royal claim. Saul and the Judean power brokers likely feared the reprisal of Rome if these Nazarenes[4] did not silence their seditious preaching.[5] Perhaps Saul looked at the Jesus movement as a threat to Israel's uniqueness because it opened the door for Gentiles to enter without circumcision, dietary rules or Torah observance.[6] Or maybe the primary reason Saul persecuted the church had to do with its religious practice, namely, its Christ devotion. Early Christians worshiped the crucified Jesus. This was an offense to Israel's God, on a par with idolatry.[7] Indeed, Paul's preconversion view of

---

[2]N. T. Wright, *What Saint Paul Really Said: Was Paul of Tarsus the Rebel Founder of Christianity?* (Grand Rapids: Eerdmans, 1997), pp. 30-31.

[3]See Martin Hengel, *The Pre-Christian Paul*, trans. John Bowden (Philadephia: Trinity Press International, 1991), pp. 72-86.

[4]One of the earliest names for the followers of Jesus was the Nazarenes.

[5]Paula Frederiksen, "Judaism, the Circumcision of Gentiles, and Apocalyptic Hope: Another Look at Galatians 1 and 2," *Journal of Theological Studies* 42 (1991): 556.

[6]Dunn, *Theology of Paul's Letter to the Galatians*, pp. 67-68.

[7]Larry Hurtado, *Lord Jesus Christ: Devotion to Jesus in Earliest Christianity* (Grand Rapids: Eerdmans, 2003), p. 94. Zeal was considered appropriate for offenses like perjury, sorcery, dietary violations, sexual or marital relations, and idolatry.

the matter may be reflected in Galatians 3:13: the crucifixion proved that Jesus was under God's curse and thus not the Messiah. To worship him was blasphemy. If Christology, both in belief and practice, was the catalyst for Saul's zeal against the Jesus movement, it took a revelation of the true identity of Christ to reverse his campaign of violence and terror.

The evidence of Paul's letters: The epistolary Paul. Paul never relates the story of his conversion in detail in his letters. Conversion stories generally lie at a more foundational level and would have been shared during those first days when the apostle was establishing the church. Letters function differently. In his letters Paul addresses problems and challenges in the church. So he does not relate the details of his conversion in his letters; yet on a few occasions, when it serves his purposes, he does remind the church of the revelations he received and how they have redirected his life.

Paul refers to his conversion in Galatians, a letter with more autobiography than any other. Yet it occurs as Paul is adopting a defensive posture against detractors who have attacked his apostleship and his gospel. In Galatians 1:11-12 Paul responds by claiming his gospel did not originate with men; he says "I received it through a revelation *(apokalypsis)* of Jesus Christ." He describes the transformational event of his life as an "unveiling" *(apokalypsis)* of Jesus as Messiah, in other words, a Christophany. By Christophany we mean a manifestation of the risen Christ.[8] Although the phrase "revelation of Jesus Christ" can be interpreted to mean either "a revelation about Jesus" or "a revelation from Jesus," it is best taken to indicate that Jesus the Messiah is the object of revelation. In other words, the true identity of Jesus the Messiah was revealed to Paul and in Paul. But who revealed Jesus to him and through him? Paul continues (Gal 1:13-17):

> You have heard, no doubt, of my earlier life in Judaism. I was violently persecuting the church of God and was trying to destroy it. I advanced in Judaism beyond many among my people of the same age, for I was far more zealous for the traditions of my ancestors. But when God, who had set me apart before I was born and called me through his grace, was pleased to reveal his Son to me [or "in me"], so that I might proclaim him among the Gentiles, I did not confer with any human being, nor did I go up to Jerusalem to those who were already apostles before me, but I went away at once into Arabia, and afterwards I returned to Damascus.

The language Paul uses to describe his revelation is a deliberate echo of the call narratives of Isaiah's servant (Is 49:1-6) and the prophet Jeremiah (Jer 1:4-9).

---

[8]Those who experience a "Christophany" describe the event in visionary terms with verbs of *seeing*.

WHAT'S MORE . . .

Types of Christophanies

Paul was not the only first-century Jew to experience a Christophany. Apparently the risen Jesus appeared to hundreds of men and women at different times and places (Lk 24; 1 Cor 15:1-9).

The New Testament contains two types of Christophanies. Recognition Christophanies (a revelation about Jesus) demonstrated to Jesus' followers that he had conquered death (Mt 28:9-10; Lk 24:13-42; Jn 20:11-16). Commission Christophanies (a revelation from Jesus) enlisted a disciple into missionary service (e.g., Mt 28:16-20; Jn 20:19-23). In Paul's case a single Christophany may have served both functions. First, the Christophany convinced Saul the persecutor that Jesus is the Messiah. Second, the same Christophany served to call Saul to be the apostle to the Gentiles. Since Paul claimed to have had frequent "visions and revelations of the Lord [Jesus]" (2 Cor 12:1-9), we do not know whether his conversion and call derived from a single or multiple Christophanies.

In each "report" given by Isaiah and Jeremiah, God knows his servant and sets him apart from the womb. In each the mission is the same: to proclaim God's salvation to the Gentiles. Paul's revelation report has been informed by, if not fashioned after, these prophetic call narratives. The revelation of the risen Messiah to Paul even while he zealously persecutes the church establishes him as God's prophet. This may explain why the apostle considers prophecy as the greatest gift (1 Cor 14:1-5). Clearly, he sees his mission as linked with the destiny of the Lord's Servant.[9]

Paul's description of his Christophany in Galatians 1:11-17 appears as a call to a new vocation, not as a conversion to a new religion. He was transformed from someone willing to use force to destroy the church to the one who adopted its mission as his own.

Philippians 3 provides a very different kind of Pauline autobiography. The context, however, appears similar. References to mutilating the flesh (Phil 3:2) and the true circumcision (Phil 3:3) suggest Paul is facing some threat by Jewish oppo-

---

[9]Paul may well have considered himself the end-time figure described in Isaiah 49:1-6. If so, he is interpreting Scripture in a manner similar to the authors of the Dead Sea Scrolls. Like Paul they saw their stories and destinies written hundreds of years before in the prophets.

nents. He responds by contrasting his pre-Christian and Christian life: "If anyone else has reason to be confident in the flesh, I have more; circumcised on the eighth day, a member of the people of Israel, of the tribe of Benjamin, a Hebrew born of Hebrews; as to the law, a Pharisee; as to zeal, a persecutor of the church; as to righteousness under the law, blameless" (Phil 3:4-6). These are not the words of someone who felt: "I'm a lousy Jew" or "I sure hope God is pleased with me." Paul stood before God with confidence.

Paul's self-portrait presumes his Christophany (Phil 3:7: "because of Christ"). His experience causes him to reassess his entire life. Everything of which he used to boast he now counts as loss compared to knowing Jesus. In fact Paul willingly suffers the loss of all things and counts them as "dung" so he can gain Christ Jesus and be found in him (Phil 3:7-9). Paul's new desire is "to know Christ and the power of his resurrection and the sharing of his sufferings by becoming like him in his death, if somehow I may attain the resurrection from the dead" (Phil 3:10-11). His experience of Jesus effects a total transformation of his life. His allegiance shifts from Torah to Christ because the arrival of the Messiah has always been the goal of the Torah (e.g., Rom 10:4; Gal 3:23-26).

Other references to Paul's Christophany are found in 1 Corinthians. In 1 Corinthians 9:1 he asks, "Am I not free? Am I not an apostle? Have I not seen Jesus our Lord?" Later, in handing on the gospel tradition of Christ's death, burial and resurrection appearances, he concludes: "Last of all, as to one untimely born, he appeared also to me. For I am the least of the apostles, unfit to be called an apostle, because I persecuted the church of God" (1 Cor 15:8-9).[10] Because he had persecuted the church, Paul felt out of step with the rest of the apostles. In both texts he links apostleship and Christophany because for him his apostolic office is part and parcel of the Christophany. The risen Christ called the persecutor to be his emissary to the Gentiles. The zeal with which Saul had persecuted the church is now redirected to extend the gospel to the ends of the earth.

For Paul the language of transformation provided a compelling way to describe conversion. In 2 Corinthians 3:15-18, Paul uses the Moses story (Ex 33—34) to unveil his own apocalyptic, mystical experiences. His reference to visions and revelations in 2 Corinthians 12:1-9 discloses the extent of his mystical experiences. For Paul, salvation is a process involving transformation into God's and/or Christ's

---

[10]As a result of his Christophany, Paul discovers the zeal that led to his persecution of the church was misdirected. He was actually opposing God and his Messiah, not honoring him. Paul never seems to forgive himself completely for what he had done. Fortunately, through Jesus he learned God's grace and forgiveness is greater than all our sin.

image (e.g., Rom 8:29; 2 Cor 3:18; Phil 3:21). Only at the parousia is it fully realized (Phil 3:21).[11] Also in 2 Corinthians 3:15—4:4 Paul presses the language of spiritual transformation into service to describe his own experience and the experiences he expects others will have. When a person turns to the Lord Jesus, he writes, the veil is removed and he experiences the "glory of the Lord." This phrase

SO WHAT?
Does this Qualify for Apostleship?

What difference does it make that Paul worked to link his apostleship to his Christophany experience? Paul had to defend his apostleship constantly. Obviously, many of his opponents (and even some of his converts) questioned his right to be called an apostle. He certainly failed to meet the criteria for apostleship established by the early church when they were seeking a replacement for Judas Iscariot (Acts 1:21-22). Paul didn't "walk" with Jesus when he was on earth. Yet Paul believed he was no less of an apostle than the twelve because he, too, was commissioned by Jesus to preach the gospel. What about others who are called to preach the gospel? Does that mean there are apostles today?

is best understood as a reference to Christ and interpreted as a technical term for the *kavōd* (Hebrew, meaning "heavy weight" or "glory"), the manlike appearances of God in the biblical story (especially Daniel 7 and Ezekiel 1). Experiencing the *kavōd* transforms a person into the likeness of the divine image. As a result of the Christophany, Paul identifies Jesus with the image and glory of God (2 Cor 4:4).

The evidence of Acts: The Lukan Paul. Luke records Paul's conversion and call three times. Each serves a different purpose in the overall story. In Acts 9 the account functions as part of the plot line. In Acts 22 it is part of Paul's justification before an angry mob. In Acts 26 it serves as the centerpiece to Paul's defense before Agrippa. Although the three accounts differ in detail, they agree in the essentials: (1) Saul is authorized by Jerusalem authorities to go to Damascus to persecute the followers of Jesus. (2) Suddenly a light from heaven flashes, and Saul hears a voice say, "Saul, Saul, why are you persecuting me?" (3) He answers, "Who are you, Lord?" (4) Jesus answers, "I am Jesus, whom you are persecuting." (5) Saul

---

[11]Alan F. Segal, *Paul the Convert: The Apostolate and Apostasy of Saul the Pharisee* (New Haven, Conn.: Yale University Press, 1990), pp. 20, 34-47, 60-61.

is subsequently appointed to be Jesus' witness.[12] Obviously, Luke did not seem concerned with the variations in the accounts.

According to some interpreters, Luke's account is suspect both because it comes later in the first Christian century and because it has a theological agenda. We should, however, recognize that Luke's historical distance provides a perspective not available in Paul's letters. Also, an agenda does not necessarily invalidate a report. If it did, then we couldn't trust any news story. "Total objectivity" is a myth. Paul's own accounts are not unbiased historical reports. Besides, there is coherence between Luke's and Paul's accounts including: (1) the violent backdrop of his conversion and call; (2) the catalytic event of the Christophany; (3) the new call to be Christ's apostle to the Gentiles; and (4) the new community he joins. In Acts Paul is clearly a person of heroic stature and his conversion is a crucial chapter in the progress of the gospel to the ends of the earth.

What happened to Saul? Traditionally, the dramatic change in Paul's life is seen as a "conversion" from Judaism. Martin Luther believed Saul the Pharisee converted to Christianity because he was frustrated by his inability to keep the Jewish law and was therefore overwhelmed by a sense of sin and guilt. Luther based his interpretation in part on Paul's despairing remarks regarding his former manner of life (e.g., Rom 7 and Phil 3). Following a dramatic encounter with the risen Jesus on the Damascus road, Saul left behind Judaism with its emphasis upon a works-based righteousness and converted to Christianity with its promise of a righteousness based on faith in Christ. This is why Paul objected to the law: it offered salvation based on human merit. Paul came to believe no one could keep the law entirely. So he left the religion of his ancestors when he traded "a righteousness of my own that comes from the law" for the righteousness that comes through "faith in Christ" (Phil 3:9).

The "New Perspective on Paul" challenges this take on Paul's conversion. First, the pre-Christian Paul does not seem to have been plagued with guilt nor to have been dissatisfied with his religion. On the contrary, Paul lived confidently before God and guiltless before the law (Phil 3:4-6). In a pivotal article Krister Stendahl exposes the misconceptions of the traditional understanding of Paul.[13] Stendahl

---

[12]Cf. Ben Witherington, *New Testament History: A Narrative Account* (Grand Rapids: Baker, 2001), pp. 203-5. In Acts 9 and 22 Ananias plays a pivotal role in spelling out the implications of Saul's encounter. He is not mentioned explicitly at Paul's defense before Agrippa (Acts 26). Paul credits the risen Jesus with exhortations to be a witness. We need to remember the tenet: the action of the agent is the action of the principal. In other words, when Ananias speaks prophetically, it is as if the risen Christ speaks.

[13]Krister Stendahl, "The Apostle Paul and the Introspective Conscience of the West," in *Paul Among Jews and Gentiles* (Philadelphia: Fortress, 1976), pp. 78-80.

charges that Western culture has been influenced by the psychological misgivings of Luther, who had a rather robust "introspective conscience" and felt a load of guilt and shame because of his sins. Luther interpreted Paul's Damascus road experience in light of his own dramatic conversion and believed that Paul must have felt the same relief as Luther did when his burdens were lifted. Until the Christophany, there is no evidence to suggest the persecutor was anything but perfectly content with his faith. He was not looking for salvation, because he believed himself to be already a part of God's redeemed, chosen people.

SO WHAT?
Why Ask What Paul Was Feeling on His Way to Damascus?

We need to de-Westernize our understanding of Paul. We have often interpreted Paul through our Western introspective grid. For example, we believe "feeling guilty" must precede conversion, like it did for Luther. So when we share the gospel with someone, we must first make sure they "feel guilty on the inside." This approach seems to limit the work of the Spirit to Western ways of thinking. Indonesians have a powerful sense of "shame"—something we often lack—but the Indonesian language, for example, does not even have a phrase for "feeling guilty." The Spirit seems to lead them to repentance by "being shamed" by their sins—a feeling that begins on the "outside" as their community points out their sin. Can Indonesians become Christians without ever "feeling guilty on the inside"? Paul did. He encouraged the Christian community to shame members to repentance (1 Cor 5:11), just as Jesus did (Mt 18:16-17). A preoccupation with inner feelings of guilt is more our problem than it was Paul's.

Second, when Paul discusses the impossibility of observing God's law perfectly (Rom 2:17—3:30; Gal 3:10-12), it is in a context where grace and forgiveness are operative within the old covenant, and it is written from the point of view that the righteousness of God has been revealed in a new covenant apart from the law. When Paul was arguing against the works of the law as the means of salvation, his objections appear in a letter for Christ-believers written by a Christ-believer. In other words, Paul's polemic against the law was not directed against Judaism per se, but against a Christian misuse of the law. E. P. Sanders, who is credited with initiating the New Perspective on Paul, emphasized that Luther's take on Paul was based on a faulty description of first-century Judaism as well as a misunderstanding of why Paul objected to the law.[14] Jews did not believe that they earned their salvation via human merit. Instead, Jews in Paul's day believed they were saved by grace, that is, they "got in" a right relationship with God because they are the "elect of God," and they "stayed in" a right relationship with God by obeying his law. But, what if a child of Israel "broke covenant" and disobeyed God by not keeping his law? As all Jews believed, the law not only provided the standard of correct behavior, it also offered the remedy when somebody stepped over the line (according to the law, repentance, restitution and/or sacrifice covered a multitude of sins). When the pre-Christian Paul sinned, the law prescribed a course of action so that the sin could be forgiven. So Saul considered himself blameless, not because he never sinned, but because when he sinned, he followed the directives in the law to maintain his right relationship with God. If we are to understand Saul's transformation, we must lay aside the notion he was a frustrated Jew who couldn't keep the law, plagued by guilt and searching for a Savior.

So what was the problem with the law? According to Sanders, it was because righteousness according to the law automatically excluded Gentiles. God gave the law to Israel. But, if God is the God of Gentiles as well as Jews, then righteousness must come apart from the law. In other words, Paul worked from the "solution" (of faith in Christ for all peoples, Jews and Gentiles) to the "problem" (of the exclusivity of the law). Paul objected to righteousness via the law because his Gentile converts had already obtained the righteousness of God via faith in Christ—both for "getting in" and "staying in." But, didn't Paul use the law, quoting it in his letters when he was correcting his converts? James Dunn argues that Paul objected to the parts of the law that distinguished Jews from Gentiles. In other words, Paul only set aside the social boundary markers within the Law—circumcision, dietary code, sabbath regulations—not the moral code that would apply to Gentiles and Jews.[15] J. Louis Martyn goes even further. He maintains Paul assigned the law to the "present evil age" that is passing away. Because of the cross of Christ—the apocalyptic event that changed everything—the law had come under the power of sin; it could not bring blessing, only a curse. It could only convict sinners of their sin. Martyn points to Galatians 3:19—4:11, where Paul argues the law was inferior because it was given through angels (see Acts 7:38) and it led to slavery. Since the new age of the gospel had broken into history via the cross of Christ, the law

[14]See E. P. Sanders, *Paul and Palestinian Judaism* (Philadelphia: Fortress, 1977), pp. 419-28, 474-518.
[15]See James D. G. Dunn, *Romans 1-8*, Word Biblical Commentary (Dallas: Word Publishers, 1988), pp. 185-94.

was now being used by malevolent powers (bad angels) against humanity, enslaving adherents to its decrees.[16] But Paul's gospel set believers free. Indeed, old things (the law!) had passed away; everything was becoming new through the gospel according to Paul. Whether Sanders, Dunn and Martyn have identified the reasons Paul objected to the law, they all agree that human merit had nothing to do with its ineffectiveness.[17]

A final problem with Luther's understanding of Paul's conversion involves the relationship between Judaism and the followers of Jesus at that time. The Jesus movement began as a reform movement within Judaism. The parting of the ways between Judaism and what would later become Christianity did not occur until many years later, over an extended period of time. It's not like one day there was Judaism and the next there was an identifiable religion called "Christianity." For Paul there was no religion to convert to, in the modern sense. Besides, Saul did not see himself as leaving his ancestral faith. He continued to identify with the Jews. But there is a difference. Now he believed Jesus to be God's Messiah. Now, because of the resurrection, he understood that he was living in the final, decisive era of God's work in the world. Now he saw himself as God's apostle called and gifted to extend salvation to all nations. Yet this was not a new religion; it was the fulfillment of God's promises to Abraham and the completion of Israel's destiny.

Still, from our perspective, good reasons exist to describe Saul's transformation as a conversion. First, the dramatic nature of the event and the extent of his life's redirection make this an appropriate way to speak of what happened to him. Second, as sociological studies of conversion have shown, conversion results in a change of community and a reevaluation of one's past based upon the values and beliefs of the new group.[18] For Paul this was surely the case. He began to affiliate with those he formerly persecuted and describe his former life using the new outlook of the followers of Jesus. This reevaluation was comprehensive and eventually addressed his entire theology and practice. For Paul everything changed, including the most important symbols of his faith: the Torah, the temple, the people and the land. Seyoon Kim argues convincingly that the lion's share of Paul's theology came directly from his Christophany and conversion. In a relatively short time, the apostle unpacked the significance of the revelation for every area of his faith and

---

[16]See J. Louis Martyn, *Galatians*, The Anchor Bible (New York: Doubleday, 1997), pp. 354-408.

[17]Otherwise, God would have given the law only to set up Israel for failure—a notion Paul finds offensive (Rom 11:11-12).

[18]Segal, *Paul the Convert*, pp. 72-75.

practice.[19] Though there were other forces and factors at work in reformulating Paul's theology,[20] the Christophany holds a prominent place as the catalytic force in his spiritual transformation. Third, prior to his Christophany, Saul saw the Jesus movement as an unacceptable way of being Jewish. Although he considered the followers of Jesus to be Jews, he judged their theology and practice to be incompatible with the true faith. They were the target of his zeal. They had not joined a new faith, but they had exceeded the limits of what genuine Jewishness meant. By joining this movement and becoming its chief missionary, Saul adopted a way of being Jewish that he had initially rejected. Furthermore, he became an object of scorn because now his Jewishness was rejected by others; he became the target of others' zeal. The parting of the ways[21] has already begun.

So Paul "converted" from one kind of Judaism to another—from a Judaism of Torah and temple to a Judaism centered in the crucified and risen Christ. It is clear Paul did not simply add Jesus to his former way of life. His encounter with Jesus changed his manner of devotion to God, his observance of the law and his understanding of how Gentiles could become part of the Israel of God. He describes this change as a spiritual transformation that began when he saw the light of God's glory in the face of Jesus (2 Cor 3:16—4:4). As he continued to behold the glory, the transformation continued. One day, at the parousia, the change would be complete. In the language of a prophetic call (according to the order of Isaiah and Jeremiah) Paul describes his experience as a radical redirection, not to a new god or a new religion, but to a new mission for his life.

PAUL'S CHRONOLOGY—PULLING TOGETHER THE PIECES

From the significant turning point of Paul's Christophany, we consider the rest of his life. His conversion and call set a new course, a course that continues to influence the world through his legacy left in letters. Since Paul used letters, we need to understand the context of those letters, which requires us to attempt at least to reconstruct Paul's ministry in order to understand the "who," the "where," and the "why" of each letter. Any modern reconstruction of Paul's life should begin with

---

[19]Seyoon Kim, *The Origin of Paul's Gospel* (Grand Rapids: Eerdmans, 1982), pp. 330-35; for example, Paul's favorite metaphor for the church, the "body of Christ," was inspired by the words of the resurrected Messiah: "Saul, Saul, why are you persecuting me?"

[20]See chapter 10.

[21]Scholars use the phrase "the parting of the ways" to refer to the eventual break between Judaism and Christianity that took place in the last decades of the first century. Initially, the Jesus movement appeared to be a reform movement within Judaism. Ultimately, however, the faith and practice of the Christ-believers was judged completely incompatible with life in the synagogue. External pressures, like those exerted at the destruction of the temple in A.D. 70, likely accelerated the breach.

humility. Using the meager evidence provided inside and outside the New Testament, entire books have been written with the sole purpose of tracking the apostle. Interpreters offer methods and schemes that vary significantly. In the final analysis a big question mark stands over the enterprise because the internal and external sources do not provide the kind of evidence we need to construct a watertight chronology. Nonetheless, we do not believe the task impossible. Our goal here is modest. We will first consider the evidence in Paul and Acts. Then we will examine briefly the evidence external to the New Testament. This evidence from "secular" sources helps to anchor Paul's life in dates we recognize on our calendar. Finally we will offer a chronology of Paul's life, noting at key points where there is more disagreement.

Sequences and time designations in the letters. Paul's letters seldom give up much in the way of autobiography. When they do, scholars mine them to extract every tiny, elusive nugget to fashion a chronology. One of the mother lodes is Galatians 1:16—2:14 because it provides a sequence of important events:

Gal 1:16	Paul's call and conversion
Gal 1:16-17	A period of time in Arabia and Damascus
Gal 1:18-20	"After three years" he visits Jerusalem for fifteen days
Gal 1:21	A period of time in Syria and Cilicia
Gal 2:1-10	"After fourteen years" he visits Jerusalem with Barnabas and Titus
Gal 2:11-14	The incident in Antioch with Cephas (Peter)

This passage still leaves unanswered questions, despite its seemingly straightforward sequence of events and time indicators. First, is Paul in Syria and Cilicia the entire time between his first and second visits to Jerusalem, or are there travels and stops along the way outside the Galatian chronology? Second, how are the time designations "three years" and "fourteen years" to be understood? Should we take them consecutively (three years and then fourteen more years, thus seventeen total years) or concurrently (three years and then eleven years, for a total of fourteen years)? Third and more generally, why does Paul bother telling this sequence of events to the Galatians? Is he giving them his complete itinerary or has he selected only certain events relevant for their situation? If we knew the answer to these questions, our results would be more certain.

Other event sequences can be gleaned from reading Paul's letters. For example, 1 Thessalonians 2:2; 3:1-5 and Philippians 4:15-16 discuss his travels to Philippi then Thessalonica then Athens. This is consistent with the move from east to west and is similar to Luke's report (Acts 16—18). But the length of each stay and the connection with other missionary endeavors remain vague.

Sequences and time designations in Acts. As a narrative, Acts arranges Paul's life sequentially. To get a handle on it, some scholars emphasize his trips to Jerusalem as an organizing principle. This makes sense given Luke's interest in Jerusalem. But the most common convention for organizing Luke's portrait of Paul revolves around the apostle's missionary journeys. According to this scheme, Antioch serves as his home base; from here Paul and his coworkers go on three missionary journeys, sometimes stopping off in Jerusalem on the way back to Antioch. There are problems with this sort of scheme. First, it is unclear whether Paul regarded Antioch as a home base to which he occasionally returned. Given his frequent trips—often perhaps out of the way—to Jerusalem, it may be that the holy city served that function. Second, it is unlikely that Paul thought of his Gentile mission in terms of missionary journeys. Rather Paul's letters demonstrate a constant flurry of missionary activity, interrupted by the occasional imprisonment, shipwreck or longer stays. Once Paul begins his Gentile mission, he seems to be in perpetual motion. Although the missionary journey schema is artificial and not entirely accurate, it is nevertheless well known and provides a useful way to get at some of the details of his missionary travels (see maps of journeys, pp. 317-19).

Luke does not typically provide exact times for Paul's itinerary. He reports that Paul and Barnabas spent "a long time" in Iconium (Acts 14:3) and "some time" in Antioch of Syria (Acts 14:28). These stays could be winter layovers or deliberate periods of ministry. Following the Jerusalem conference, Luke says that "after some days" Paul and Barnabas decided to go back to visit churches they founded (Acts 15:36). This is Luke's custom. Nonetheless he occasionally provides more precise lengths of time for Paul's stays and imprisonments. When he does, we take note:

Acts 11:26	a year in Antioch
Acts 18:11	a year and six months in Corinth
Acts 19:8-22	two years and three months in Ephesus
Acts 20:3	three months in Greece
Acts 24:27	two years in Caesarea
Acts 28:30	two years in Rome

As expected, statements like these provide considerable help in constructing a chronology for Paul. Still, these reports account for only about 30 percent of his time on mission. To anchor these relative dates in history, we need a fixed point.

External evidence. To anchor the event sequences and relative time frames found in Paul's letters and Acts, we need to connect the accounts in Acts and the letters to datable events.[22] Fortunately, there are places where Paul's story comes into contact with recorded accounts of officials in Arabia and the Roman Empire. These "secular" events can often be dated reliably to within a few years. More than anything, this data provides a way to connect the internal sequences and time frames found in the New Testament to known people and events in external sources. They are of immense significance in locating Paul in his world. We note here the key examples:

1. In 2 Corinthians 11:32 Paul reports that he escaped from Damascus when the governor under King Aretas (IV) was trying to seize him. External sources fix the beginning of Aretas's reign in Damascus to A.D. 37 and his death to A.D. 38-40. So it is likely the apostle's escape took place between A.D. 37 and 39.[23]

2. In Acts 11:27-30 Luke refers to a famine that affected much of the world during the reign of Claudius (A.D. 41-54). Although the time frame for any famine is by its very nature hard to calculate, it is reasonable to date this famine to A.D. 46-48.[24]

3. In Acts 18:2 Paul meets Aquila and Priscilla in Corinth after the Emperor Claudius ordered all the Jews to leave Rome. Suetonius (*Claudius* 25.4) reports that Jews were constantly disturbing the peace at the instigation of a certain "Chrestus" (perhaps a reference to Christ) and that Claudius expelled Jews from Rome. Most scholars date this to A.D. 49.[25]

4. By far the most significant datable event in Acts is the reference to Gallio (Acts 18:12-17). In the first part of the twentieth century archaeologists uncovered nine fragments of an inscription at Delphi. The Gallio inscription, as it came later to be known, contains a letter written from the emperor to the people of Delphi. In it he refers to his "friend and proconsul L. Iunius Gallio." The letter is dated to April or May A.D. 52. Other sources indicate his reign was brief, perhaps only a year (Seneca *Epistle morales* 104.1). Using this and other evidence, scholars date the beginning of Gallio's brief term of

---

[22]To illustrate: one of the authors was married six years before his first child was born. Two years later, he graduated with his Ph.D. These details are of little use without a solid date to anchor it. But knowing one date (e.g., his first child was born in 1986) helps us figure out the rest. Working backward and forward from the fixed date, the other dates can be determined within an acceptable margin (plus or minus a year or two). This is how we figure out Paul's chronology.

[23]Robert Jewett, *A Chronology of Paul's Life* (Philadephia: Fortress, 1971), pp. 30-33.

[24]F. F. Bruce, *Paul: Apostle of the Heart Set Free* (Grand Rapids: Eerdmans, 1971), pp. 276-77.

[25]For a description of other Roman conflicts with Jews see Charles H. Talbert, *Reading Acts: A Literary and Theological Commentary on the Acts of the Apostles* (New York: Crossroad, 1997) pp. 166-67.

office to July A.D. 51. Luke reports that Gallio heard charges against Paul by local opposition leaders in Corinth (Acts 18:12). The inscription and the account in Acts locate Paul in Gallio's Corinth in A.D. 51 and/or 52 at the latest.[26] Working forward and backward from this date, scholars are able to date much of the apostle's career. It is the "linchpin of Pauline chronology."[27]

5. Less than two weeks after the new procurator Festus arrived in Caesarea, Paul appears before him to answer the charges of his Jewish accusers (Acts 25). Most scholars date Festus's succession to power to A.D. 58-60.

These are the primary anchor points for chronology of Paul. With these external dates it is possible to construct a coherent chronology, recognizing the limits of our sources.

PAUL'S CHRONOLOGY: MAPPING IT OUT

The following chronology is approximate and interdependent, that is, one date relies on another. Space does not allow us to justify each date, sequence or connection.[28] We must acknowledge some dates (such as his birth) may be off by as much as three to five years. Others, particularly those that can be corroborated in secular history, may be right on target. Still, it is remarkable that we have any evidence at all, given Paul's social situation. Further, because of the coherence of Acts and the letters at many points, we can speak with more confidence regarding Paul than we can for most other people of ancient history. Indeed, historians of the ancient world are thrilled to have this level of detail.

A.D. 5-10	Saul is born in Tarsus (Acts 22:3).
A.D. 15	Saul moves to Jerusalem where he is "brought up" and trained by Gamaliel (Acts 22:3).
A.D. 30	Pilate crucifies Jesus in Jerusalem (Mark 14—16 and par.).
A.D. 31-34	Saul persecutes "the Way" in Jerusalem and surrounding regions (Gal 1:13-14; Acts 7:58—8:3; 22:4). At Stephen's stoning, Saul is said to be a "young man" (Acts 7:58), likely in his twenties.
A.D. 34	The risen Jesus appears to Saul on the Damascus road (Acts 9:1-19 and par.; Gal 1:16); Ananias baptizes and instructs Saul in Damascus.

---

[26]Jerome Murphy-O'Connor, "Paul and Gallio," *Journal of Biblical Literature* 112 (1993): 315-17.

[27]Jerome Murphy-O'Connor, *Paul the Letter Writer: His World, His Options, His Skills* (Collegeville, Minn.: Liturgical, 1995), p. 15.

[28]For rationale and further argumentation see Ben Witherington III, *The Acts of the Apostles: A Socio-Rhetorical Commentary* (Grand Rapids: Eerdmans, 1997).

A.D. 34-37	Saul preaches in Arabia and Damascus (Gal 1:17; Acts 9:19-22).
A.D. 37	Saul escapes from Damascus during the reign of Aretas IV of Nabatea (2 Cor 11:32-33; Acts 9:23-25). He "goes up" to Jerusalem ("after three years" Gal 1:18) to visit Cephas (Peter) for fifteen days.
A.D. 37-46	Saul preaches in Syria and Cilicia (Gal 1:21; cf. Acts 11:25).
A.D. 47	Barnabas locates Saul in Tarsus and brings him to Antioch (Acts 11:25-26); they meet and teach the church for a "whole year."
A.D. 48	Saul's second visit to Jerusalem ("after fourteen years" Gal 2:1-10)[29] with Barnabas and Titus; they hold a private meeting among the leadership ("the pillars"); the Jerusalem leaders affirm Paul's gospel and recognize his apostolic call to the Gentiles.

In Acts 11:27 Saul and Barnabas "go up" to Jerusalem following a prophetic revelation by Agabus. They carry a famine offering from Antioch to the "elders" ("pillars" perhaps) of Jerusalem. We take this to be the same visit (Gal 2 = Acts 11).[30] Nonetheless, many scholars identify Galatians 2 with Acts 15.[31] This may well be the most debated topic in Paul's chronology.

---

[29]We take the "after fourteen years" (Gal 2:1) as concurrent with the "after three years" (Gal 1:18) because it appears to be Paul's habit to reckon time from visions and revelations (cf. 2 Cor 12:1-9) not Jerusalem visits. Therefore, "fourteen years" means fourteen years after the Christophany.

[30]In the end the visit had two purposes: (1) to provide relief for Jerusalem's poor during the famine and (2) to affirm Saul's law-free gospel to the Gentiles. It is interesting Luke never tells how either this offering or the later offering (2 Cor 8—9; Rom 15) are received.

[31]Many are convinced Galatians 2:1-10 and Acts 15:1-30 refer to the same Jerusalem visit. The reason is the correlation between the two accounts. First, both refer to the same issue, i.e., whether Gentiles are required to keep the law. Second, both meetings involve the same participants, Paul, Barnabas, Peter and James. Third, both arrive at the same decision, i.e., Gentiles are not required to keep the Law. But there are difficulties with equating Galatians 2 and Acts 15: (1) if the question of how Gentiles are included was resolved, it is difficult to understand how the situation in Galatia spiraled so out of control that a letter like Galatians was needed; (2) it is hard to explain the withdrawal of Peter from table fellowship with the Gentile Christ-believers in Antioch (Gal 2:11-14) if the decision of the Jerusalem Conference is in the past (Acts 15); (3) despite their similarities, Galatians 2 and Acts 15 may represent different meetings with the same principals dealing with a single problem. For example, the cause of the Jerusalem visit in Galatians 2 is a revelation; in Acts 15 it is an appointed task by the church at Antioch. The Galatians 2 meeting appears small and private, like an executive session, compared to the Acts 15 conference. The resulting request to remember the poor (Gal 2) does not parallel the four requests made by the Jerusalem leaders (Acts 15).

Given everything we know, it appears that the question of Gentile inclusion was not resolved overnight. It likely took a series of meetings, agreements and handshakes between the movers and shakers in Jerusalem, Antioch and the other Gentile congregations. Even with that, the peace was easily shattered. Paul writes from the midst of the fray (Gal 2). Luke writes (Acts 15) from hindsight after the issue has been resolved, perhaps prompting him not to mention the earlier preliminary attempts (such as that of Gal 2) to resolve the matter.

A.D. 48-49   Paul and Barnabas travel to Cyprus and southern Galatia with the gospel (Acts 13-14). This is called the First Missionary Journey.

A.D. 49   Paul arrives in Antioch. It is reported that Judaizers were troubling the Galatians, persuading them to be circumcised. Paul responds with a fiery letter (Galatians), rebuking them for abandoning the gospel so quickly (Gal 1:6). The church at Antioch sends Paul and Barnabas to Jerusalem because Pharisaic Christians were insisting that Gentile believers had to be circumcised and to observe Torah to be "saved." The Jerusalem Conference convenes to decide the matter (Acts 15).

A.D. 50-52   Paul and Silas revisit the Galatian churches and establish churches in Macedonia and Achaia (Acts 15:36—18:21; cf. 1 Thess 2:2; 3:1-5; Phil 4:15-16).[32] Paul meets Aquila and Priscilla in Corinth after Claudius had expelled the Jews from Rome (A.D. 49). He remains in Corinth for eighteen months. He writes 1 Thessalonians from Achaia (Corinth?) after commending their faithfulness (1 Thess 1:7-8) and writes 2 Thessalonians soon after.[33]

A.D. 51   Gallio (proconsul of Achaia) dismisses charges against Paul in Corinth (Acts 18:12-18).

A.D. 52   Paul visits the Jerusalem church before journeying to Antioch (Acts 18:22). End of Second Missionary Journey.

A.D. 53-56   Paul revisits churches and has a lengthy stay of more than two years and three months in Ephesus (Acts 18:23—19:41; A.D. 53-55). During this time he writes several letters to the Corinthians and makes two visits. He writes 1 Corinthians from Ephesus (1 Cor 16:8-9). He makes a "painful visit" to Corinth from Ephesus (2 Cor 2:1). He writes 2 Corinthians from Macedonia.

A.D. 56   Paul works in Greece for three months (Acts 20:1-6). He writes Romans from Corinth (Rom 15:25-27; cf. 1 Cor 16:3-5 and Acts 20:2-3) and then heads back to Antioch. End of Third Missionary Journey.

A.D. 57   Paul travels to Jerusalem "to take aid to the saints" (Rom 15:25; cf. 2 Corinthians 8—9).

---

[32]Macedonia (northern Greece) contained the cities of Philippi, Thessalonica, Beroea and others. Achaia (southern Greece) had Athens and Corinth, among others.

[33]When collected together, New Testament letters to the same recipient were listed according to length. Thus, 1 Thessalonians was called "first" because it was longer than 2 Thessalonians, not because it was written first.

A.D. 57-59	Paul is arrested and imprisoned in Jerusalem initially; then he is moved to Caesarea where he remains two years. Felix and Agrippa hear Paul's defense. Eventually a new governor is installed and the apostle appeals to Rome (Acts 21:27—26:32).
A.D. 59	Paul sails for Rome but is shipwrecked on Malta (Acts 27:1—28:10).
A.D. 60-62	Paul arrives in Rome, where he lives for two years under house arrest. He writes Philemon, Colossians, Ephesians and Philippians (Acts 28:10-31).[34] Luke's story ends here. Some believe Paul is executed at this time. Others, relying on early church writings, believe he is released and engages in further missionary activity.
A.D. 62?	Paul is released from Roman imprisonment.
A.D. 62-64?	Paul travels to the limits of the west (perhaps Spain); other missionary travels cannot be ruled out. He writes Titus and 1 Timothy.
A.D. 64	A catastrophic fire in Rome (July 64) precipitates increased persecutions of Christians under Nero.
A.D. 65?	Paul is arrested and imprisoned a second time. He writes 2 Timothy.
A.D. 66-68?	Paul is executed (by beheading) during Nero's reign.

CONCLUSION

The end of Paul's life extends beyond the New Testament writings. Luke leaves him in prison awaiting trial (Acts 28). Tradition has it that he was beheaded under Nero in Rome (A.D. 64-68). This tradition has some merit. In any case, Clement pays Paul a fitting tribute (*1 Clement* 5:5-7):

> Through jealousy and strife Paul showed the way to the prize of endurance; seven times he was in bonds, he was exiled, he was stoned, he was a herald both in the East and in the West, he gained the noble fame of his faith, he taught righteousness to all the world, and when he had reached the limits of the West he gave his testimony before the rulers, and thus passed from the world and was taken up into the Holy Place—the greatest example of endurance.

READ MORE ABOUT IT

DPL Articles:
"Call, Calling," pp. 84-85, by C. G. Kruse.

---

[34]This order is more likely the sequence in which the letters were written. Again, our Bible arranges them by length, and thus Romans is first and Philemon is last.

"Chronology of Paul," pp. 115-23, by L. C. A. Alexander.

"Conversion and Call of Paul," pp. 156-63, by J. M. Everts.

"Itineraries, Travel Plans, Journeys, Apostolic Parousia," pp. 446-56, by P. Trebilco, esp. "Galatians 2:1-10 and the Visits of Acts," pp. 453-54.

"Jealousy, Zeal," pp. 461-63, by A. B. Luter.

4

The Itinerant Paul

Galatians

WHETHER PAUL MADE TENTS OR SIMPLY REPAIRED THEM, his trade was given to travel. The apostle was constantly on the move. Annual festivals (religious functions, athletic games, political events) throughout the empire drew all kinds of merchants and craftsmen to cities and even villages. The constant need of shelter for temporary residents and merchants probably overwhelmed local trade guilds during these "peak" seasons, giving men like Paul opportunities to offer their services. There were always soldiers needing a tent repaired or replaced. Paul seemed to find work wherever he wanted (Acts 18:3; 1 Thess 2:9). And yet it was not economic interests that compelled Paul to move from one region to the next. He probably could have settled in one place and made a decent living. Paul was commissioned by God to take the good news of Jesus Christ to Gentiles throughout the world. At first the church in Antioch of Syria supported his missionary operations (Acts 13:1-3). Then his own converts in Philippi added their help to his ministry (Phil 4:15-16). Finally Paul made an appeal to the church in Rome to help finish what had been started: to continue to take the gospel as far as land would take him, Spain (Rom 15:24-28). Acts tells the story of this westward push.

That Paul spent most of his time in urban centers rather than rural areas makes sense: more people meant better possibilities for the gospel and more opportunities to ply his trade. And cities were more open to foreign travelers. The question that remains unanswered is why Paul seemed bent on heading west to fulfill his calling. Why not south, spreading the good news in Egypt? Or why didn't Paul take his message eastward, gathering converts in Mesopotamia or Armenia?

Paul doesn't say, but there are a number of possible reasons why Paul went west. Moving westward kept Paul within the borders of the Roman Empire. Practically speaking, it was risky to travel into the hinterlands of northern Europe, or east into the Parthian Empire, or south beyond the regions of Rome's imperial presence in northern Africa. Roman roads were popular routes. More travelers meant better protection from bandits. And the rights of Roman citizenship would have been lost outside the confines of Roman rule. Even Paul's movement west within the empire, from imperial territories to senatorial provinces, was a movement toward a better chance at law and order. Remember, Paul was stoned in the more remote regions of the imperial province of Galatia (Acts 14:5, 19). But when he got in trouble in the more established free cities and colonies in the senatorial provinces of Macedonia or Achaia, a riotous mob did not lead to a public lynching. Instead, magistrates and proconsuls intervened, bringing the troublemaker before the courts. In Athens, accusations that Paul acted illegally were handled in an orderly manner (Acts 17:19-33). No riot there. Indeed, the arrest that led to Paul's lengthy imprisonment happened on the eastern edge of Roman sovereignty, in Jerusalem—the explosive, tumultuous city of the imperial province of Judea.

In addition to practical reasons, Paul may have had theological designs in the geography of his mission. If Paul saw himself as the servant of the Lord (from Is 49), then his attempt to gather Gentile converts from east to west may have been guided by Isaiah's vision of the salvation of the world:

> I am coming to gather all nations and tongues; and they shall come and shall see my glory, and I will set a sign among them. From them I will send survivors to the nations, to Tarshish, Put, and Lud—which draw the bow—to Tubal and Javan, to the coastlands far away that have not heard of my fame or seen my glory. (Is 66:18-19)

Whether Tarshish refers to Tartessus in Spain or Tarsus in Cilicia, the regions represented by these cities correspond roughly to Paul's westward mission of the gospel: from Asia Minor to the coastlands.[1] Indeed, Paul may have believed his mission efforts "to gather all nations" would bring about the end of the world. The faster Paul reached the "ends of the earth," bringing with him the "full number of the Gentiles" (Rom 11:25), the sooner Jesus would return to establish his kingdom on earth. The relief offering Paul collected from his Gentile converts and delivered to the church in Jerusalem, then, was part of Isaiah's grand design (Is 60:5-6, 9-

---

[1] See Rainer Riesner, *Paul's Early Period: Chronology, Mission Strategy, Theology*, trans. Doug Stott (Grand Rapids: Eerdmans, 1998), pp. 245-53.

11), sealing the apostle's effort to "win obedience from the Gentiles, by word and deed" (Rom 15:18). Paul looked forward to the day when he would be able to present all of his converts "blameless before our God and Father at the coming of our Lord Jesus with all his saints" (1 Thess 3:13).[2] On that day Paul would finally be vindicated as the apostle to the Gentiles, justified for taking his gospel to the ends of the earth.

PAUL, THE ITINERANT APOSTLE

From the time of his conversion, Paul was a man who couldn't stay in one place. Like his master, Paul had no home. There was no place to which he could return. At first he spent some time in Arabia and Damascus (Gal 1:17). After visiting Jerusalem, he tried to return "home" for a while, spending the so-called silent years of his missionary activity in and around Tarsus. Then, according to Acts, Paul was invited to join the work in Antioch, eventually launching the first missionary effort.

Yet Paul was a man of his culture and understood the importance of community. Likely Paul and Barnabas first traveled to Cyprus because Barnabas was from Cyprus (Acts 4:36). They moved on to Anatolia (the Romans called it "Galatia") because this moved back toward Paul's home. Derbe was approximately 150 miles from Tarsus on the Via Sebaste (the road that connected the cities Paul and Barnabas visited in southern Galatia). These men were covering familiar territory, walking roads they had traveled before. Furthermore, some have suggested Paul and Barnabas concentrated their mission work in South Galatia where there was a substantial Jewish population, having a better chance of hospitality among their own people. The proconsul Sergius Paulus, a convert from Cyprus (Acts 13:7), may also have followed kinship lines, sending Paul and Barnabas to his homeland, where he had family living in Pamphylia and Pisidia.[3] Paul left familiar regions, crossing the Aegean Sea, only after a vision from God (Acts 16:9-10). Perhaps it was never Paul's intention to take the gospel beyond Anatolia and Asia Minor; this seems implied by Acts 16:6-7. It is possible the westward march of his mission was an unfolding drama Paul didn't see until hindsight, the end of his ministry (Rom 15:19-23). Paul had no map of the Mediterranean world. He did not survey the terrain, plot his course from here to there (did he even see the world in such visual

---

[2]See Johannes Munck, *Paul and the Salvation of Mankind*, trans. Frank Clarke (Richmond, Va.: John Knox, 1959), pp. 297-305.

[3]Was Paul a member of the clan of Sergius Paulus? Was he evangelizing distant cousins? They share the same clan name, Paulus, and Paul does gain a hearing with a proconsul, but there is not sufficient evidence to be sure.

terms?)[4]. The apostle to the Gentiles went where the Spirit led him (2 Cor 1:15-22). A homeless man, Paul had no place to go except where God would take him—the necessary life of a tent maker who preached the gospel of Jesus Christ.

Acts gives the dramatic details of Paul and Barnabas's earliest experiences of sharing the gospel with their Jewish brethren and pagans outside of Antioch (read Acts 13:4—14:28). At first, Paul and Barnabas seemed to find a hearing among those who attended the synagogue—both Jews and God-fearers. Then trouble would begin. One minute Paul and Barnabas were worshiped as divine messengers, the next minute the locals gathered stones and ran the missionaries out of town (Acts 14:11-19). After reporting to the Corinthians that he had been beaten several times by Jewish leaders and Roman authorities (once even stoned), Paul summed up his trials and tribulations as "danger from my own people, danger from the Gentiles, danger in the city, danger in the wilderness, danger at sea, danger from false brothers and sisters" (2 Cor 11:26). Yet all of these perils notwithstanding, Paul claimed the gnawing problems of the churches troubled him more than anything else (2 Cor 11:28). That is obvious when we read his letters. He never complained much about his difficulties (see the brief references in 1 Thess 2:2 or Gal 6:17). Most of the time Paul was more concerned about his apostleship, his gospel, his converts. Paul jealously guarded both his calling as an apostle of Jesus and the evidence of his calling, the faithful obedience of his churches. Mainly on the defensive in most of his letters, Paul was either apologizing for his itinerary or protecting his apostleship or correcting those who misunderstood his gospel. Sometimes the problems came from within—his own converts questioned his credibility, challenged his teaching or ignored his instructions. Sometimes outsiders made a mess of things, trespassing on his apostolic turf, preaching "another gospel." Sometimes it seemed like problems came from within and without. This is what we find in Paul's letter to the Galatians.

A DEFENSE OF THE "GOSPEL ACCORDING TO PAUL"

Paul didn't want his converts to be circumcised, because they already belonged to Christ. That is the essence of Paul's argument in his letter to the Galatian Chris-

---

[4]One of us was quite lost among a cluster of islands in the South Pacific. I had a map. I asked a local where I was. He looked confused and then pointed to the ground. "No," I said, "where am I on this?" pointing to the map. He looked confused and said I was holding it not standing on it. I explained it was a picture of this island. He wondered where the trees and rocks so clearly around us were in the picture. "If you were a bird flying high in the sky," I explained, "and you looked down, which of these islands would you see?" "I have never been a bird," he replied in disgust and walked off. Maps and other visual representations of the world are not as natural and self-explanatory as we often assume.

tians. Evidently some of the Galatians had already submitted to the Jewish rite and others were contemplating the same decision. Paul was angry when he found out what had happened to these, his first converts. Some of his most vitriolic language is found in this letter: "You foolish Galatians! Who has bewitched you?" (Gal 3:1), or "if anyone proclaims to you a gospel contrary to what you received, let that one be accursed!" (Gal 1:9), or "[you] have cut yourselves off from Christ; you have fallen away from grace" (Gal 5:4), or "I wish those who unsettle you would castrate themselves!" (Gal 5:12). Obviously, Paul didn't preach a gospel that included circumcision. So where did the Galatians get the idea that they should submit to circumcision? Who was promoting this "other gospel"? Were they insiders or outsiders, opponents of the gospel or teachers of another version, Jews or Gentiles? How we answer this question will be a determining factor in how we read the letter and will also reveal what we think about the conflicts that existed within the early church.

SO WHAT?
Is There Any Good in Airing This Dirty Laundry?

The early church was not the utopia that we sometimes imagine. The evidence is clear that there were many ways of following Jesus, some of which came into serious conflict with others. Diversity characterized the churches of Paul's time. We need to set aside any romantic notion that the early church was completely unified and that all the divisions and denominations we see today are the inevitable result of time and distance from the ideal. The church has not been coasting downhill since the first century. There is no way to make a modern church into a New Testament church. And if we could, we'd find divisions and problems had not gone away.

Identifying Paul's opponents in Galatians leads to one of three possibilities. First, many argue the troublemakers in Galatia were Jewish Christians who believed that circumcision was necessary for salvation. These were the Judaizers who appeared at the Jerusalem conference (Acts 15:1-5). They were outsiders, dogging Paul's trail, coming to these newly established churches once the apostle left the area. The Judaizers were Pauline antagonists, trying to correct Paul's incomplete gospel by encouraging Gentile believers to obey the whole law. Scholars who subscribe to this description of Paul's opponents typically argue that Paul wrote his

letter to the Galatians after the first mission trip but before the Jerusalem conference. In this scenario, Paul thought he had an arrangement with the Jerusalem
church: he would evangelize Gentiles and Peter would evangelize Jews. But the
Judaizers were unsatisfied with this division of labor. They were suspicious of the
Antioch church and Paul's mission to the Gentiles. So they went to Antioch to
argue for their lawful gospel and traced the steps of Paul and Barnabas, sneaking
into the churches and preaching the "other gospel."[5] Therefore, it was the incident
at Antioch (Gal 2:11-14) that led to the meeting in Jerusalem described by Luke
in Acts 15. This Jerusalem conference was convened to settle the matter. The Judaizers lost and Paul won. The gospel for Gentiles, it was decided, did not include
circumcision (see Acts 15:6-35).

Second, some scholars argue that Paul's opponents were not antagonists trying
to steal the apostle's sheep. Although they were also outsiders—Jewish Christian
"missionaries" visiting Pauline territory—they were not necessarily looking to
make converts among Paul's churches. They were "teachers" of the faith, leading a
law-observant mission to the Gentiles, sponsored by the mother church in Jerusalem. They preached faith in Jesus *and* obedience to the law:[6] a circumcision gospel. Scholars who hold this position typically assign Paul's mission activity—and
that of the teachers—to north Galatia, where there seemed to be little or no Jewish
presence. These ethnic Galatians were descendants of the Celts (Gauls), who
would have been unfamiliar with Hebrew Scripture and Jewish ways. In this scenario, Paul founded the church after the Jerusalem conference, during his second
mission trip, and the teachers arrived shortly after Paul had moved on. Preaching
a law*ful* gospel, they founded a separate church of newly converted pagans who
followed Jewish ways. Yet they also convinced Paul's converts to observe holy days
and to submit to circumcision. This meant, of course, that the Jerusalem conference had settled nothing; Luke paints too rosy a picture. Paul and Antioch were
at odds with James and Jerusalem, especially after the conference (in this scenario
Galatians 2 is another description of the events of Acts 15). To Jerusalem's way of
thinking, Paul had gone too far in requiring Jews to give up their Jewish ways in
order to maintain unity in a mixed congregation. Therefore, it is argued that
James, the Jerusalem church, and their commissioned teachers believed Gentiles
had to give up their Gentile ways and live according to Jewish law in order to belong to the faith—meaning Paul's "law-free" gospel mission was not the only game
in town.

---

[5]F. F. Bruce, *Paul: Apostle of the Heart Set Free* (Grand Rapids: Eerdmans, 1977), p. 179.
[6]See J. Louis Martyn, *Theological Issues in the Letters of Paul* (Nashville: Abingdon, 1977), pp. 7-24.

Finally, some scholars have argued Paul's opponents were not outsiders but insiders. That is to say, those who were preaching "another gospel" were the Galatians themselves, not intruding Jewish Christian missionaries. Johannes Munck argued some of Paul's converts began to read more carefully the Scriptures the apostle referenced when he preached the gospel. In his absence, their desire to obey God's word led them to circumcision—the sign of covenant faith.[7] These Gentile Judaizers, then, began campaigning in the other churches of Galatia, convincing their brothers in Christ of the importance of circumcision. Mark Nanos also argues the Judaizers were insiders, but that the issue over circumcision was not a problem caused by Christians. Nanos believes native Galatians who had converted to Judaism were convincing Paul's converts of the *social* advantages of circumcision. The "good news," according to these Gentile converts to Judaism, consisted of the benefits of belonging to a synagogue, that is, social identity, something Paul's converts lacked. As Christians, they weren't pagans, they weren't Jewish, what were they?[8] Becoming a Jew would provide membership in a community, social recognition and political protection (Gal 6:12?). When Paul's converts left their old religion (for instance, when a Christian baker removed the idol of the "baker god" from his shop), to what group did he belong? Ancients thought in terms of "we," but who was "we"? There was no "Christianity." Paul identified himself as a Jew. In any event, Munck and Nanos argue that the problems Paul confronted in Galatia had nothing to do with Antioch, Jerusalem or the results of the conference.

We maintain that the identity of Paul's opponents lies somewhere between the first two options. From Acts we might assume Antioch was the only "missional" church and Paul the only apostle founding churches (who started the Roman church? Acts 28:14-15). Did Paul feel like he was the only apostle to the Gentiles? It is quite apparent others did not share that opinion. There were many teachers/preachers/missionaries moving from one city to the next, from one assembly of Christ to the next (they came not only to the regions of Galatia, but also to Corinth, Ephesus and Rome). More than likely, then, not all Jewish Christian missionaries from Jerusalem were hostile to Paul's intent. After Paul and Barnabas had returned to Antioch at the end of their first mission trip, some Christians passing through Galatia—it was the major road—may have preached circumcision as part of the gospel. Others, preaching the gospel of Jesus Christ from the He-

---

[7]Munck, *Salvation of Mankind*, pp. 130-34.
[8]Mark D. Nanos, *The Irony of Galatians: Paul's Letter in First-Century Context* (Minneapolis: Fortress, 2002), pp. 217-44.

brew Scriptures, may not have believed circumcision was required for salvation but probably encouraged Gentile believers who wanted to submit to circumcision and keep dietary codes and holy days. Who could object to the zeal of those who wanted to obey the Word of God? Paul could. Since he didn't preach circumcision, he became furious with those who did. If his converts submitted to circumcision, then it made Paul look like he had not given them the "whole gospel." It made his converts appear as though they had come to realize Paul's gospel—not to mention his apostleship—was deficient. In fact, Paul may have been accused of preaching an "easy" gospel. The apostle felt betrayed. "I am astonished that you are so quickly deserting the one [Paul? God?] who called you in the grace of Christ and are turning to a different gospel" (Gal 1:6). This is what led to the missive we call "Galatians."

PAUL'S LETTER TO THE GALATIANS

Galatians is one of the easiest letters to outline; the flow of Paul's argument is not difficult to follow. In the first two chapters, Paul lays out the narrative of his gospel experience as a model for his converts. After threatening with a curse those who preach another gospel,[9] Paul protested he was not a "man pleaser" but a "God pleaser." Then he describes how God made him an apostle of Jesus Christ; he received his gospel from God. Indeed, a key verse in this passage is when Paul claimed God was "well pleased to reveal his Son in me" (Gal 1:16, author's trans.).[10] For Paul, the gospel was more than a set of beliefs; it was a way of life, his way of life (1 Cor 4:17). The Jerusalem church concurred. As a matter of fact, it was Peter and James who were spreading the news that the one who used to persecute the church had become one of them (Gal 1:18-24). When Paul visited Jerusalem the second time, some "false believers" tried to get the "pillars of the church" in Jerusalem (Peter, James and John) to require Paul to preach circumcision (Gal 2:1-6). It didn't work. The pillars honored Paul as their equal, and he returned to Antioch, taking Titus the Gentile out of Jerusalem unscathed (or, should we say, uncut). For Paul, Titus was the poster boy of his circumcision-less gospel. A Gentile didn't have to become a Jew to be a Christian. But neither did a Jew have to become a Gentile to follow Christ. James would make sure of that. He sent a delegation to Antioch, where Peter and other Jewish Christians were sharing table with Gentiles. Evidently, the party from James got Peter and the rest of

---

[9]Modern Westerners rarely take curses seriously, although we often pronounce blessings, the flip side. Yet Old Testament and New Testament characters did, as did God (Deut 28).

[10]The NRSV reads "to me." We take the preposition along with the word translated "reveal" (*apokalypsai*, "apocalypse") to mean that Paul believed that his life was a revelation of the gospel.

SO WHAT?
Um, Why So Much About Circumcision?

Why does it matter if a Christian is circumcised? (Some of you probably are.) In Paul's day, circumcision was a sign of commitment to keep the Old Testament law. The question is: "Are we saved by faith plus doing a few things or keeping a few commandments?" We often say "no" but then live like we mean "yes." The general practice in many Western churches is to reject the parts of the law we don't like (prohibition on bacon, shrimp and pepperoni pizza) but keep the parts we like (tithing, sabbath), and some of Paul's opponents accused him of the same thing. Yet should we have the right to pick and choose parts of the law? Paul argued we are no longer under the law (Gal 3:25). He believed the power of the Spirit would lead his converts to live holy lives (Gal 5:18). After all, Jewish law didn't apply to his Gentile converts. As a result, we want to know: What about tithing? Should Christians be under an Old Testament system of tithing? Some say, "10 percent belongs to the Lord." Others say, "100 percent belongs to the Lord." Paul concluded: "Each of you must give as you have made up your mind, not reluctantly or under compulsion" (2 Cor 9:7). But what about the sabbath? Some say, "Isn't Sunday a Christian sabbath, the Lord's Day"? Still others say, "Every day is the Lord's Day." Paul concluded: "Some judge one day to be better than another, while others judge all days to be alike. Let all be fully convinced in their own minds" (Rom 14:5). Paul refused to allow the law to become a requirement for salvation or a standard for holiness. Instead, he maintained Christ is our salvation and his Spirit will guide us in all holiness.

the Jewish Christians to withdraw table fellowship from their Gentile brothers in Christ. That left Paul as the only Jew at the table of the "unclean." Paul may have won the argument up in Jerusalem, but the more devastating challenge to his gospel happened in his own backyard, in Antioch and Galatia. The honor game was on.

This is why Paul was so angry with the Galatians, with Peter and Barnabas, and with his Jewish brothers in Antioch. At this point in the letter Paul confronts all of them, claiming he was the only one staying true to the gospel of Jesus. He accused Peter of trying to proselytize Gentile believers to the Jewish

---

WHAT'S MORE . . .
The Honor Game in Galatia

Paul had claimed honor	"Paul, an apostle—sent neither by human commission nor from human authorities, but through Jesus Christ and God the Father" (Gal 1:1)
His opponents challenged that claim	He got his gospel from the disciples and not directly from Jesus (Gal 1:6—2:8)
Paul defended his claim	"when God, who had set me apart before I was born and called me through his grace, was pleased to reveal his Son to [or, in] me" (Gal 1:15-16); "the one who formerly was persecuting us is now proclaiming the faith he once tried to destroy. And they glorified God because of me" (Gal 1:23-24); "for he who worked through Peter making him an apostle to the circumcised also worked through me" (Gal 2:8)

The crowds who would decide the verdict were the Galatians themselves. Did the Galatians decide Paul was honorable (and thus accept his gospel message)?

---

way of life (Gal 2:14). Paul claimed that he was "crucified with Christ," that the law brought death in his life just as it did for Jesus (Gal 2:19-20). Then he quickly turned to address his converts straight on: "You foolish Galatians! Who has bewitched you? It was before your eyes that Jesus Christ was publicly exhibited as crucified!" (Gal 3:1). It was Paul's cruciform life before the Galatians that had already revealed the truth of the gospel. According to Paul, his death to the law was another public portrayal of the crucifixion of Jesus. Indeed, Paul had moved beyond the law to embrace faith in Christ via the Spirit. Why would his converts want anything else? The Spirit was all they needed. They didn't "get in" via works of law (the argument of Gal 3:6—5:1); and they wouldn't "stay in" by finishing in the flesh (the argument of Gal 5:2—6:10). For Paul, then, works of law and living according to the flesh were synonymous, as seen especially in the rite of circumcision. Why couldn't they see the Spirit supplied every spiritual blessing (Gal 3:5)? It was as if the Galatians were living under a hex. Paul's argument would break the spell.

A theology of the cross. As even a casual reading demonstrates, Galatians is an epistle of the cross. Paul writes: "[Jesus] gave himself for our sins to set us free from the present evil age, according to the will of our God and Father" (Gal 1:4). On the cross Jesus "gave himself" and dealt finally and completely with human sin. For Paul the cross marks the way to freedom from law, sin and spiritual powers in the world. Through faith in Jesus, Jews and Gentiles alike experience deliverance from the "present evil age."

WHAT'S MORE . . .
What About the Law?

Paul gives several reasons why circumcision is unnecessary, even dangerous. First, in an argument he would eventually develop more fully in his letter to the Romans, Paul maintained that children of Abraham are blessed by God because they believe—Gentiles are children of Abraham because they act like Abraham, that is, they are justified by faith (Gal 3:6-9). Second, Paul lists several reasons why the law is inferior to faith: because it led to a curse (Gal 3:10-14); because it came along after the covenant between Abraham and God was established (Gal 3:15-17);[a] and because it was given through angels (Gal 3:19-20). Third, Paul speaks of the subservient role of the law in regards to faith. That is to say, the law works like a tutor, leading those who keep it to faith in Christ. Once it serves its purpose, children are freed from it, especially Gentile believers who become children of Abraham by faith. That which the law divided, Jew from Greek, male from female, slave from free, is now united in Christ. Sharing in the inheritance of Christ, Gentile believers are adopted sons because they possess the Spirit of Jesus (Gal 3:23—4:7). The end of the age (law, death, powers, slavery) comes for those who believe Paul's gospel (see Gal 1:4).[b]

---

[a]This is where Paul's argument could be muddied by his opponents. He uses circumcision as a cipher for the law of Moses. Although it is true that the Sinai law was given after the covenant was made with Abraham, circumcision marked the covenant between God and Abraham, long before the law of Moses. So, what Paul said of the Mosaic law, that it is temporally later and therefore inferior to the covenant of Abraham, was true but technically could not be applied to circumcision. (Notice how this part of the argument does not appear in his later argument in Romans 4.)

[b]Martyn, *Theological Issues*, p. 408.

Paul asserts that his cross-centered gospel, like his apostleship, is not some human invention (Gal 1:11). The message he proclaims came "through a revelation of Jesus Christ" apart from human agency. Paul's own place in the drama of redemption began before the risen Jesus appeared to him. Like the prophets of old, God set him apart from the womb. The Father called him and chose him to be the one through whom God's Son would be revealed among the nations (Gal 1:15-16). After that turning point, Paul's identity is lost in the crucified Messiah. His life is to epitomize the gospel. His body is to bear the marks of Jesus' suffering (Gal 6:17). The cross is to take shape in his life (Gal 2:20).

Justified by faith. Paul insists all people, Jews and Gentiles, are "justified" by faith in Christ alone. No one is "justified" by doing the "works of the law" (Gal 2:16). Justification is a soteriological[11] metaphor borrowed from the courtroom. It means to acquit or pronounce a verdict of "not guilty." The apostle uses this image as one way of expressing his understanding of what Jesus accomplished on the cross. The word *justified* comes from a root that means "righteous" or "just." To be justified is to have one's wrongs forgiven and to be accepted as righteous by God (cf. Rom 3:21-26). God's righteousness makes possible the justification of sinners.[12] Because of what Jesus did on the cross, God declares the guilty "not guilty" and simultaneously begins transforming their character.[13] It is not enough to leave a sinner a sinner; God's righteousness transforms the character of sinners to make them saints. Justification, Paul insists, does not happen because Gentiles submit to circumcision, dietary rules and sabbath observance ("the works of the law"); it happens because they trust in the finished work of Christ and thus are united with him (baptism).

Abraham: Father of faith, exemplar of righteousness. In one sense, justification by faith is nothing new. Paul finds it in Scripture related to his ancestor, Abraham. In another sense it is brand new because of what Jesus had accomplished on the cross. Much of Galatians 3—4 is an extended argument from Scripture on the (continuing) validity of justification by faith.

"Abraham 'believed God, and it was reckoned to him as righteousness,'" writes Paul (Gal 3:6; quoting Gen 15:6). For the apostle, the patriarch was the prototype of righteousness or justification by faith. God declared him righteous before he

---

[11]The term *soteriology* comes from a Greek word meaning salvation. *Soteriological* then means referring to or relating to salvation.

[12]The use of two English terms *(righteousness* and *justification)* blurs the fact that both words come from the same Greek root.

[13]I. Howard Marshall, *New Testament Theology: Many Witnesses, One Gospel* (Downers Grove, Ill.: InterVarsity Press, 2004), pp. 221-25.

WHAT'S MORE . . .
"By Faith in Jesus" or "By the Faithfulness of Jesus"?

Galatians 2:16 presents us with a significant interpretive question. Paul writes: "we know that a person is justified not by the works of the law but through faith of Jesus Christ [faith in Jesus Christ or the faithfulness of Jesus Christ?]. And we have come to believe in Christ Jesus, so that we might be justified by faith of Christ [faith in Christ or the faithfulness of Christ?], and not by doing the works of the law, because no one will be justified by the works of the law." The brackets tell the story. When Paul writes "faith of Christ/Jesus Christ" does he mean that a person is justified by faith in Christ (objective genitive) or by the faithfulness of Christ (subjective genitive)? The Greek genitive and the word for faith/faithfulness could be translated either way. While many modern translations render the phrase "faith in Christ," Richard Hays and others have argued convincingly that in some passages the apostle has "the faithfulness of Christ" in view (e.g., Gal 2:16, 20; 3:22).[a] The import of Hays's interpretation is that it highlights Jesus' faithfulness to God the Father. It makes salvation depend squarely on the work of the cross. This is not to say that Paul did not advocate faith in Jesus. Clearly there are places in Paul's letters where he wishes to underscore that (even in Gal 2:16). He intends, however, in Galatians to distance justification as far as possible from any human achievements under the law. Justification depends totally and completely, for Paul, on the faithfulness of Christ, demonstrated primarily in Jesus' self-giving on the cross.

---

[a]Richard Hays, *Faith of Jesus Christ: An Investigation of the Narrative Substructure of Galatians 3:1—4:11*, Society of Biblical Literature Dissertation Series 56 (Chico, Calif.: Scholars, 1983). James D. G. Dunn, *Romans*, Word Biblical Commentary (Dallas: Word, 1988), 1:116, continues to prefer the traditional "faith in Christ."

---

was circumcised. Furthermore, God declared him righteous hundreds of years before he gave the law to Israel. According to Paul, the story of Abraham demonstrated that from the beginning God's people were characterized by faith and reckoned as righteous. Since then, the true sons and daughters of Abraham have lived by faith. Paul continues: "And the scripture, foreseeing that God would justify the Gentiles by faith, declared the gospel beforehand to Abraham, saying 'All the Gentiles shall be blessed in you'" (Gal 3:8; quoting Gen 12:3). God's purpose all

WHAT'S MORE . . .

A Passionate Paul

Paul's opponents insisted that Gentiles must be circumcised and observe the law to be put right with God. Paul found in Scripture, however, that faith is what God reckons as righteousness. So what then is the role of the law? No issue in Pauline studies is more hotly debated. For Paul himself, however, the question of law was not merely academic. It threatened to divide the body of Christ. After Paul makes his argument that we are no longer under the law, Paul changes his tone and gets personal (and a little rough at times). Throughout the rest of the letter, the apostle alternates between harsh warnings and gentle reminders. He begins by questioning his converts' affection for him, wondering aloud if his gospel efforts were a waste of time (Gal 4:8-20). Then, Paul calmly reminds the Galatians of their spiritual heritage— that they were meant to live as freedmen not slaves (Gal 4:21—5:1). Next, the dire consequences of submitting to circumcision are put in graphic terms of being "cut off" from Christ, of "falling away from grace" (Gal 5:2-4). But then the apostle appears to change tactics, acting as if circumcision were irrelevant, for "neither circumcision nor uncircumcision counts for anything" (Gal 5:6). No big deal. Yet when he thinks about the intruders who disturbed his converts, Paul pronounces his own vicious curse: castration for those who wield the knife (Gal 5:7-12). Then, he switches back to a more moderate tone, claiming the law is fulfilled by those who keep one commandment: love thy neighbor (Gal 5:13-15). The Spirit-filled life reveals it (Gal 5:16-26); the law of Christ completes it (bearing each other's burdens, Gal 6:1-6); the eschatological harvest will confirm it (Gal 6:7-10). Finally, when Paul picks up the pen himself, the caustic tone returns, and with short, pithy statements the apostle fires a parting shot at his opponents (Gal 6:11-16) and his converts (Gal 6:17). It is quite obvious that the question of requiring circumcision was as much about him as it was about them. He didn't preach it, so they shouldn't have believed it.

---

along has been to bless the nations through Abraham. This blessing was to come to all nations through Abraham's kind of faith-reckoned righteousness. Paul expands and interprets Abraham's story to include those who come to God through faith in Jesus. They enter into the blessing of Abraham and become children of promise apart from keeping the law. But, if righteousness is found apart from the law, why did God give the law?

Paul had some things to say about the law. It has had an important role in salvation history, but in God's purpose it has never resulted in justification. To the contrary, the law pronounces a curse upon those who do not observe all its precepts (Gal 3:10; quoting Deut 27:26). Eventually all Jews and Gentiles run afoul of the law. But the Scripture teaches that faith, not law observance, brings life and justifies a person before God (Hab 2:4). But what about the curse? Paul continues: "Christ redeemed us from the curse of the law by becoming a curse for us—for it is written, 'Cursed is everyone who hangs on a tree'" (Gal 3:13; quoting Deut 27:26). Some wrongly interpret Paul here to be saying that the law itself is a curse. Nothing could be further from the truth. By "curse of the law" he does not mean the whole law; he means that part of the law that pronounces curses (see the list of curses in Deut 27—28). Effectively, all Jews and Gentiles stand under those curses. For Paul, however, Christ's death upon the cross nullifies the curses so that Abraham's blessing might extend to Jew and Gentile alike through Christ Jesus (Gal 3:14). How did this happen? When Jesus was crucified, he became sin and a curse for us (cf. 2 Cor 5:21). But when God raised the cursed one from the dead, he vindicated him and released him from the curse. From then on, all who identify with Jesus through faith share in his vindication and are released from their curses as well. By his death on the cross the power of the law to pronounce curses has come to an end. But there is more to the law than its power to curse!

Four hundred and thirty years after God established the covenant with Abraham, he gave the law to Abraham's children at Mount Sinai. Now we must remember that in the ancient world antiquity trumped novelty. So the promise inherited by faith (the old) was not set aside because of the law (the new). Instead, the law became a servant of the promise. According to Paul, the law had a temporary and mediating role in the promise-fulfillment story: (1) to name and try to curb sin and (2) to prepare the way for the Messiah (Gal 3:15-20). So the law is not contrary to the promises of God. Rather, the promise and the law perform different functions. Faith and promise are the basis for life and righteousness. Law defines sin and leads to faith in God's Messiah. Paul pictures the law as a pedagogue (tutor?) in a well-to-do Greek or Roman family. This slave's job was to provide protection, discipline and some education for a minor boy until the day when the child became an adult. It was a powerful but temporary position. The temporary duty of the law, according to Paul, was to ready the people for the coming of the Messiah and to prompt faith (Gal 3:24). But now that Christ has come, the custodial role of the law is no longer needed.

Scripture then, particularly the story of Abraham, provided Paul with the basis for understanding justification by faith and Gentile inclusion. Because of what Christ accomplished, all Jews and Gentiles, all slave and free, all male and female may enjoy the status as "sons of God" through faith. All are one in Christ Jesus (Gal 3:26-28). Through his experience of Christ and rereading of Scripture, Paul discovered that monotheism demands monolatry. In other words, the oneness of God requires the (eventual) oneness and unity of all God's people. For Paul that day of unity had arrived and baptism was its sign. Baptism, properly understood, creates unity out of diversity, so that the ethnic, social and gender barriers that define our societies are eclipsed once and for all by what Christ has done. Those who belong to Christ, no matter what their pedigree, enter into Abraham's true family of faith; they are heirs to God's eternal promise (Gal 3:29).

For freedom Christ sets us free. The universal human predicament, according to the apostle, is slavery. Whether it is slavery to sin, to law or to spiritual powers, humans are in bondage and long for liberty. To a significant degree Paul's language about salvation in Christ is couched in language of liberation from the governing powers. In the first age the human race was like a child enslaved to the "elemental spirits of the world" (Gal 4:3). These were the spiritual powers or tribal gods that people thought ruled over specific races or territories. Much of Gentile Galatia lived in fear of these deities and felt their fate intertwined with these capricious powers (Gal 4:8-9). But in the fullness of time "God sent his Son, born of a woman, born under the law, in order to redeem those who were under the law, so that we might receive adoption as children" (Gal 4:4-5). Redemption is a soteriological metaphor found frequently in the Old Testament in relation to the exodus. When God delivered the Hebrews from slavery in Egypt, it is said that he redeemed them. Redemption assumes a prior state of bondage. Paul believed this bondage amounted to servitude to the spiritual powers that rule the world and constantly threaten human existence. The answer to our plight: God sent his Son to redeem us. According to some interpreters,[14] the sending of the Son implies his preexistence, that is, the Son existed with God prior to his entrance into the world. For Paul, the sending of the Son into the world is the pivotal event of the ages.

---

[14]Simon Gathercole, *The Preexistent Son: Recovering the Christologies of Matthew, Mark, and Luke* (Grand Rapids: Eerdmans, 2006), pp. 28-29; Douglas McCready, *He Came Down from Heaven: The Preexistence of Christ and the Christian Faith* (Downers Grove, Ill.: InterVarsity Press, 2005), pp. 92-94.

WHAT'S MORE . . .
The Allegory of Hagar and Sarah (Gal 4:21-31)

Hagar (the slave)	Sarah (the free woman)
[Ishmael], son of the slave	Isaac, son of the free woman
born according to the flesh	born according to the promise/Spirit
covenant of Mt. Sinai	[new covenant in Christ]
bearing children of slavery	[bearing children of freedom]
present Jerusalem (seeking justification by works of the law)	Jerusalem above (seeking justification by faith in Christ)
persecuted the child of promise	persecuted by the child of the flesh
covenant of circumcision and law observance	covenant of promise, freedom and Spirit

---

His coming offers the solution to our plight.

Redemption from bondage to the malevolent spiritual powers is only part of salvation. According to Paul, God liberates humans from slavery in order to adopt them into his eternal family. "Adoption as sons"[15] *(huiothesia)* is a soteriological metaphor drawn from family life in the Roman world, where adoption was common. Paul uses it in his letter to the Galatians (cf. Rom 8:15) to contrast the former life of slavery to the present experience of liberty and privilege in the Spirit. Although complete redemption and adoption will be realized only at the parousia[16] (Rom 8:23), the adopted children of God enjoy a unique relationship with their heavenly Father: "because you are children, God has sent the Spirit of his Son into our hearts, crying, 'Abba! Father!'" (Gal 4:6). The sending of the Spirit into the hearts of the children of God provides yet another perspective on Paul's picture of salvation. "Abba" is an Aramaic term of endearment for "father"; it implies a close bond between a child and its "daddy."[17] It recalls the intimacy with which Jesus addressed God and recollects the way Jesus told his disciples to pray ("our Father"; Mt 6:9).

---

[15]The new status enjoyed by the redeemed is that of a son because in that day sons enjoyed privileges not shared by daughters, particularly inheritance rights. The language is not intended to be sexist and limiting but rather inclusive and liberating.

[16]*Parousia* is a technical term for the second coming of Jesus.

[17]For lack of a better translation in English, "Daddy" is usually chosen. "Abba" implied the same intimacy as "Daddy" but in Jesus' day grown men called their father "Abba," while in America "Daddy" is usually only a child's term. Paul's use of "children" should not be misread as "toddlers."

Abraham's two wives. The apostle concludes his argument with an allegory[18] drawn once again from the story of Abraham and his descendents. He finds the crisis confronting Gentile believers prefigured in the story of Abraham's wives and children. For those who wished to live under the law (Gal 4:21), the law itself (Gen 16—18) provided the needed corrective. The allegory compares the two women and thereby two covenants.

Paul's perspective is informed by an apocalyptic understanding of the ages. Now that the new covenant has arrived, life under the old epoch looks like slavery (cf. 2 Cor 3—4). The punchline of the allegory comes in Galatians 4:30: "Drive out the slave and her child; for the child of the slave will not share the inheritance with the child of the free woman" (quoting Gen 21:10). Paul directed this mandate to the Galatians so they would throw out his opponents and appropriate the freedom of Christ by not submitting to "a yoke of slavery" (Gal 5:1). For Paul, this yoke is epitomized in the rite of circumcision. Any Gentile who receives this mark in order to improve his standing with God, according to Paul, finds he is ultimately severed from Christ (Gal 5:2). Anyone who seeks justification through the law discovers he is fallen from grace (Gal 5:4). In the final analysis what matters is "faith working through love," not whether one has sworn to uphold the law (Gal 5:6). For the apostle to the Gentiles, this salvation comes by the work of the Spirit, not by the works of the flesh, especially the rite of circumcision.

The ethics of justification. Throughout the letter Paul deconstructs the false claims of the Judaizers while fashioning a new identity for those who remain faithful to his gospel. This new identity demands a new behavior (ethics). So he moves back and forth between the indicative (what to believe) and the imperative (how to behave). Every command (what to do) is based on an indicative (what God has done). The imperatives indicate that Christ-believers have an active role to play in living out the gospel.

For Paul, human beings left to their own devices will live in the flesh and inevitably give in to temptation and desire. Fleshly desires are deceptive. They appear to lead a person deeper into life and all it has to offer. In fact, however, fleshly desires lead away from life to destruction and away from freedom to slavery. The deeds of the flesh are evident, as Paul's list of vices demonstrate (Gal 5:19-21). They indicate what life in the new age is not supposed to be. Deceptively, those who seek justification by doing the works of the law will fulfill their sensual desires and not inherit the kingdom of God (Gal 5:21).

---

[18]Allegory was a popular technique for reading ancient texts and applying their lessons to current situations. In allegory the elements of a story are taken to symbolize deeper, spiritual truths.

SO WHAT?
Is This Grammar or Ethics?

Why does it matter that Paul used "indicatives" before "imperatives" rather than vice versa? For Paul, theology leads to ethics; behavior derives from status. (The world tends to do the opposite: "If you want to become vice president of the company, you have to work for it." Paul would say, "You are the vice president. Now, act like it!") So the "we ought" arises from the "we are." Good ethics rarely flow from bad theology. What we teach about the gospel, whether in a Bible study or through the words of a song, will affect how listeners live. Likewise, we are empowered to live rightly because of our new status in Christ. We don't earn status by living rightly.

Paul theologizes in this way: "Live by the Spirit, I say, and do not gratify the desires of the flesh" (Gal 5:16). The Spirit and the flesh are at odds. The flesh reflects human weakness and dependence on the law; it belongs to the age that is passing away. The Spirit is the power that enables the children of God to live according to the divine will; it belongs to the age inaugurated in the coming and resurrection of Jesus. The ethics of the new age can be summed up in the fruit of the Spirit: love, joy, peace, patience, kindness, goodness, faithfulness, gentleness and self-control (Gal 5:22-23). By "fruit of the Spirit" Paul means two things. First, the Spirit produces these traits.[19] Second, these traits reproduce the character of Christ in the life of the believer. For Paul, the goal of the Christian life is conformity to the image and likeness of Jesus (Gal 4:19; cf. Rom 8). The Spirit provides the power to make that so. Paul draws upon his Jewish heritage and language for the metaphor "walk," meaning a way of life. Therefore, to walk in the Spirit is to live by the power of the Spirit that enables believers to bear the fruit of the Spirit.

So the freedom Paul preaches is not an opportunity for the flesh; it is freedom to love and serve one another. In truth the entire law can be summed up in one command: "You shall love your neighbor as yourself" (Gal 5:14; quoting Lev 19:18). Additionally, he admonishes: "Bear one another's burdens, and in this way

---

[19]Paul uses a singular (fruit). He does not mean there are nine different fruits of the Spirit, and thus we can claim to have some and not others. Rather, the fruit of the Spirit is described as a-love-joy-peace-patience-kindness-generosity-faithfulness-gentleness-self-control-kind-of-character.

you will fulfill the law of Christ" (Gal 6:2). By appealing to "the law of Christ," he shows that the Christian life is not a lawless existence. This law is an internal dynamic, written in the language of the Spirit. It is inscribed in the heart, patterned on the example and teaching of Jesus himself who ultimately bears all burdens.

DID GALATIANS WORK?

Did Paul's argument work, or did he lose the Galatians to another gospel? It depends on the question of location. (So "background studies" do matter!) Where were these churches located? Those who subscribe to a South Galatian readership would argue that Paul was able to keep the Galatian sheep in the fold of his gospel ministry. He mentions their participation in the relief offering in a letter written during his third mission trip (1 Cor 16:1). Those who hold to a North Galatian theory say the question is at best unanswerable—the Galatian letter was written about the same time as the Corinthian letters, so the Galatians had not yet decided. Martyn conjectures that Paul was unable to recover the Galatian congregation from the influence of his opponents. Since Paul doesn't list the Galatian churches among those who supported the relief offering (Rom 15:26), it may indicate they were no longer supportive of Paul's mission.[20] But this is an argument from silence. Other churches in Asia Minor probably contributed to the relief offering—especially an important church like Ephesus—and Paul didn't mention their participation to the Romans, either. In fact, Paul wouldn't have told the Corinthians about the instructions he gave to the Galatians for the relief effort for Jerusalem if they weren't supportive of the effort. Paul was using the Galatians as an example of obedience for the Corinthians to follow (1 Cor 16:1). Furthermore, Acts mentions Paul returning to southern Galatia during the second and third mission trips (Acts 16:1-6; 18:23). We think the evidence suggests that the Galatian churches remained loyal to Paul and his gospel.

The importance of Paul's letter to the Galatians letter cannot be overestimated. As James Dunn has noted, it is the "first extant statement of Paul's distinctive theology."[21] Galatians provides considerable insight into Paul's self-understanding as the apostle to the Gentiles. Paul clearly saw his life as a revelation of the gospel. As the Lord's delegate, he was commissioned to carry the message to the nations and to embody the cross. The autobiographical material in Galatians is indispensable in understanding his call and relationship to the other apostles. Indeed, without Galatians it would be difficult to put together a chronology of his life at all.

---

[20]J. Louis Martyn, *Galatians*, Anchor Bible (New York: Doubleday, 1997), pp. 28-30.
[21]Dunn, *Theology of Galatians*, p. 133.

The fiery invectives in this letter demonstrate Paul's passion for the true gospel and the maternal instincts he possessed to protect it. Galatians assumes a particular perspective on the world—its past, present and future—from the mind of an apocalyptic prophet. Spiritual powers and forces have enslaved humanity, corrupting the present age, but God has worked his plan through the patriarch Abraham to set the slaves free and make them part of his family. In this sense redemption comes from the top down, from God who sent his Son and his Spirit in the world to bring salvation.

Galatians is the earliest statement of Paul's understanding of justification by grace through faith, the doctrine that launched the Protestant Reformation in Germany. Paul traced this faith-righteousness from Abraham, through the Sinai covenant, ultimately to the finished work of Christ. The astounding news that God raised Jesus and reversed the curse of a crucified man meant that all people, both Jews and Gentiles, could share in Abraham's blessings and become the true Israel of God. Finally, Galatians gives us one of Paul's earliest attempts to come to grips with the significance of the Law for Jews and Gentiles. The question of how believing Gentiles were included in this faith community along with believing Jews was not answered overnight. Without Galatians it may never have been answered at all.

READ MORE ABOUT IT

DPL Articles:

"Abraham," pp. 1-9, by N. L. Calvert.

"Cross, Theology of," pp. 192-97, by A. E. McGrath.

"Ethics," pp. 269-75, by S. C. Mott.

"Galatians, Letter to the," pp. 323-34, by G. W. Hansen.

"Opponents of Paul," pp. 644-52, by P. W. Barnett.

"Travel in the Roman World," pp. 945-46, by L. J. Kreitzer.

5

The Itinerant Paul

The Thessalonian Letters

PAUL DID NOT WRITE A LETTER to be distributed among the Macedonians as he had in the case of the Galatians. Obviously, one letter for an entire province wouldn't do this time—the Thessalonians were facing different issues than the Philippians or the Beroeans. And, unlike when he wrote to the Galatians, Paul wasn't angry when he wrote these letters. Instead, he addressed his Thessalonian converts in a more pastoral, nurturing tone. Besides the tone, the argumentation and themes of these letters are also different from Galatians. For example, Paul never quotes the Hebrew Scriptures in the Thessalonian letters. The Pauline theme of "justification by faith" is absent. Instead, what was practically missing in Galatians—eschatology—dominates 1-2 Thessalonians. Indeed, these letters are very different, owing as much to the resourcefulness of Paul's gospel as to the variety of problems he encountered in different parts of the Roman Empire.

When Paul crossed the Aegean Sea during his second mission trip, he came into a different world. He had already traveled some six hundred miles from Antioch—a difficult journey involving circuitous roads and steep mountain passes—visiting the churches he founded in Galatia during his first mission trip. After leaving the Galatian province, little is made of Paul's travels through Asia Minor; there is no report in Acts of the success of the apostle's mission work in these regions. Instead, Luke mentions that the Spirit twice prevented Paul from circling northward in

SO WHAT?
Is There a Lesson Here?

Why should we take notice of Luke's story about the Spirit preventing Paul from entering Bithynia (Acts 16:6-10)? These are not incidental details, for we can easily draw three quick lessons. First, it is normal to remain in one's home culture. We doubt Paul deliberately chose to avoid Greece; it may never have occurred to him to visit the Macedonians. Only when the Spirit interfered did Paul move crossculturally. Second, Luke does not tell us how the Spirit hindered them. An angel with a flaming sword is unlikely since Luke does not elaborate. Paul may have been unfamiliar with the occupants of northern Galatia, only moving that direction as a plan to work homeward.[a] Most of the isolated, often hostile, inhabitants there didn't speak Greek. Paul had a painful lesson (literally) in Lydia about what happens when no team member speaks the local language (Acts 14). The Spirit may have "hindered" merely by not providing a translator. The Spirit moves in mundane as well as dramatic ways. Third, when Paul moved into Macedonia and Greece, he ran into local legal trouble almost immediately (and repeatedly). Working crossculturally requires knowledge of the new culture.

---

[a]Without maps, traveling in a loop was a wise method of navigating unknown territory.

---

what was probably an attempt to head back toward home. Luke culminates his brief story of the Spirit's interference with describing Paul's vision of the Macedonian man as the impetus for crossing the Aegean (Acts 16:6-10).[1] Once he arrived in Macedonia, Paul stayed on the main road: the Via Egnatia, the major land route that crossed Macedonia, connecting the Aegean and the Adriatic seas. Next to the Appian Way, this was the most traveled road in the entire Roman Empire. Several major cities were strung along this highway—about a day's walk apart—giving Paul and his companions plenty of opportunity for work and ministry.

Besides possessing level roads and major urban centers, Macedonia was a more established province, run by proconsuls of the praetorian rank and popu-

---

[1]These Lukan stories are probably the source of a modern expression, "When the Spirit closes one door, he opens another," building on Luke's description of how God "had opened a door of faith for the Gentiles" (Acts 14:27).

lated predominantly by Greeks.[2] The women of these cities played more significant roles in society, many owning property and businesses. Paul encountered a
much more progressive, robust economy, since these free cities on the Egnatian
road were also strategically located along the coastline, benefiting from maritime
travel and trade. More trade brought more ethnically diverse populations, which
also meant more religions, gods, shrines and temples. Thessalonica, the capital
city of Macedonia, housed temples and shrines for Serapis and Isis, Dionysus,
Cabirus, Zeus, Aphrodite, Asclepius, Demeter, Roma and Julius Caesar, as well
as a Jewish synagogue.

Most of Paul's converts in Thessalonica were Gentiles who "worked with [their
own] hands" (1 Thess 1:9; 4:11). That is to say, Paul's gospel seems to have been
more successful among the pagan tradesmen in Thessalonica than any other
group. And yet, like other Pauline churches, there were probably a few Jewish
members, a few members of nobility,[3] and a few "God-fearers" among the Thessalonian believers (see Acts 17:1-9; 1 Thess 5:12-14). Evidently, Paul had a rough
time of it in Thessalonica, just as he did in other Macedonian cities (Acts 16:19—
17:14; 1 Thess 2:2, 17-19). In Acts, Paul's countrymen were the source of his conflict; it was the Jews in Thessalonica who were accusing Paul before the local authorities. They were the ones who ran him out of town, dogging his trail all the
way to Beroea. In his letter Paul seems to suggest that Thessalonian Gentiles were
causing Gentile Christians grief in his absence: "you suffered the same things [per-
secution] from your own compatriots" (1 Thess 2:14).

Some scholars try to put the two scenarios together, claiming that reference to
"your own compatriots" doesn't necessarily exclude Thessalonian Jews—Paul was
using the term "compatriots" politically, not ethnically.[4] The difference between
Acts and the Thessalonian letters could be attributed, however, to a sequence of
events: the trouble began between Paul and the Jewish leaders and, once "the Jewish troublemaker" left the area, the conflict evolved into a problem among Thessalonian Gentiles. As evidenced by Acts in other places (Philippi and Ephesus),
Paul's religious activity created economic problems that led to political confronta-

---

[2]Malina and Pilch have recently argued that "Greek" was a term indicating "civilized" (as opposed to
"barbarian") and had not ethnic meaning at all. They argue that for Paul, a "Greek" meant a Jew in
the Diaspora as opposed to a Judean; see *Social-Science Commentary on the Letters of Paul* (Minneapolis:
Fortress, 2006), pp. 371-72. In our work, we understand Paul's use of "Greek" to mean a civilized (vs.
barbarian) *non*-Jew.

[3]The "rulers" were probably patrons (so Jewett, W. Meeks, E. Judge et al.).

[4]See Karl P. Donfried, *Paul, Thessalonians, and Early Christianity* (Grand Rapids: Eerdmans, 2002),
pp. 195-208.

tions. Modern Westerners like to compartmentalize these as if one did not impact the other. Paul's experiences prove otherwise. Paul's converts in Thessalonica left the synagogue, forsook their pagan gods, abandoned their trade guild gods and perhaps even withheld support from the imperial cult. We need to remember it was not just the loss of worship but also of honor and of money. Luke's comment about Paul converting "not a few of the leading women" (patronesses!) may indicate such an economic threat (Acts 17:4)—"you can steal sheep as long as you leave the tithers alone!" Thus, in a free city like Thessalonica, it would have been up to the citizenry to try to bring this renegade group into compliance. It appears, therefore, that trouble surrounded Paul's converts on every front, which would have made the apostle's hasty nighttime exit (Acts 17:10) even more suspicious and his credibility suspect. Ancient cities also had their "snake-oil salesmen" who popped in, collected money and then skipped town (often at night).

HOLY LIVING UNTIL CHRIST COMES AGAIN

Were the Thessalonian believers persecuted to the point of death? Is this why the Thessalonians were grieving "as others do who have no hope" (1 Thess 4:13)? And did their confused eschatology lead to the problems of the "unruly" (1 Thess 5:14; 2 Thess 3:6-13)? Some scholars think that all of these questions are interconnected, that is, that all of the issues addressed by Paul in the Thessalonian correspondence derive from one source: his emphasis on the parousia ("appearing") of Christ. When Paul preached the gospel to the Thessalonians, they latched on to his emphasis of remaining faithful until the Day of the Lord. Paul meant to encourage his converts with the promise that, when Christ appeared, he would reward his loyal saints with kingdom riches. This caused some of the Thessalonians to wonder whether those who died before the coming of Christ would miss out. Paul's apocalyptic gospel may have created other problems as well. Some within the church quit their jobs, relying upon others to meet their needs, believing the return of Christ was imminent. So, according to some scholars, when Paul wrote these letters, he was addressing two symptoms (grieving without hope, leading unruly lives) of one problem: his converts had misunderstood the significance of the parousia of Christ.

But the pieces of the puzzle do not fit together quite so nicely. It must be admitted 2 Thessalonians comports well with the problems associated with the unruly, that is, those who refused to work with their own hands did not heed Paul's advice, so the apostle had to write a more detailed rebuke: if you don't work you don't eat (2 Thess 3:10). Water meant to put out the fires of grief became gasoline that ignited the rebellion of the unruly. Paul was trying to comfort the afflicted (the dead in Christ would get their reward) and afflict the comfortable (the day will come like a thief—get ready!).[5] Since Paul taught that Jesus could come back any day, the unruly asked, "Why work? Why worry?" So, this is why Paul had to devote much of his letter to correcting the rebels in 2 Thessalonians 3. But, given this scenario, the beginning of Paul's second letter to the Thessalonians doesn't make sense. After reading or hearing 1 Thessalonians, some within the congregation began to claim: "the day of the Lord is already here" (2 Thess 2:2). This prompted Paul to offer an eschatological timetable that put off the return of Christ—a delay of sorts (1 Thess 2:3-15). What in 1 Thessalonians could possibly have misled the rebels to claim the day of Christ had already come? And wouldn't their "realized eschatology" work against their purposes, that is, "Since Jesus isn't coming back, I'd better get a job"?

Robert Jewett maintains that the unruly were operating with a realized eschatology from the beginning: "the New Age has already begun." So, Paul's first stab at correcting the false teaching was to emphasize the imminent parousia in 1 Thessalonians;[6] Christ is about to come back (meaning he hasn't yet). But when that teaching didn't solve the problem, Paul took another tack: laying down an eschatological timeline in 2 Thessalonians, that is, no one can claim the Day of the Lord has already come because certain things have not yet happened. While Jewett's approach is creative, it seems 1 Thessalonians was devoted more to encouraging the saints than chastising the sinners (even the "warning" at 1 Thess 5:6 sounds more edifying than correcting). Indeed, if the unruly were such a nefarious problem from the beginning, wouldn't Paul have spent more time addressing the theological and social implications of this dangerous teaching in his first letter? Perhaps Paul did. The canonical order doesn't necessarily preserve the chronological sequence of the letters. It is possible the longer letter (1 Thessalonians) was not written first. Thus, Paul could have written 2 Thessalonians first in order to counter the false teaching and practice surrounding this "realized eschatology." His timetable for the end of the world (2 Thess 2:1-12)—which was supposed to show that the Day of the Lord had not occurred yet—led some church members to believe they wouldn't be around when Christ returned—the Day of the Lord was a long way off. So they grieved without hope, which is why Paul wrote a sec-

---

[5]Michael J. Gorman, *Apostle of the Crucified Lord: A Theological Introduction to Paul and His Letters* (Grand Rapids: Eerdmans, 2004), p. 169.

[6]See Robert Jewett, *The Thessalonian Correspondence: Pauline Rhetoric and Millenarian Piety* (Philadelphia: Fortress, 1986), pp. 168-78.

ond letter about the imminent return of Christ (1 Thessalonians).

Even though it is possible that 2 Thessalonians was written first—the canonical order was not meant to imply chronological order—switching the order of the Thessalonian letters creates problems of its own. For example, Paul's "apology" for his actions—why he was forced to leave Thessalonica and was subsequently unable to return (1 Thess 2:1-20)—makes better sense coming in the first letter after his departure. And in 2 Thessalonians 1:3-12 Paul isn't concerned about how his converts were handling persecution, but in 1 Thessalonians 3:1-10 the apostle expressed relief when he heard that the Thessalonians were persevering. This seems backwards if 2 Thessalonians was written first. Besides, Paul refers to a previous letter in 2 Thessalonians 2:2, 15, which is probably 1 Thessalonians.[7] We maintain, then, that the canonical order happens to reflect the historical sequence of the letters. If so, how should we explain the various problems Paul addresses?

It may make better sense to recognize that these problems (confusion over the Day of the Lord and the rebellion of the unruly) were unrelated. Churches can have more than one problem. Even though our attention may be drawn to (what seems to us) the more dramatic parts of 1 Thessalonians (1 Thess 4:13—5:11), some of the problems may have been social and not "theological." Some scholars have argued Paul was taking on the patron-client relationship in Thessalonica— the unruly were clients spending all their time courting an alliance with patrons in order to keep from working with their own hands.[8] Their undisciplined life had nothing to do with questions regarding the dead and the coming of Christ. As a survey of these letters show, Paul addressed a variety of issues.

FIRST THESSALONIANS

The elect of God. Paul lays down a familiar triad in the letter opening that previews the first half of the letter: "remembering before our God and Father your work of faith and labor of love and steadfastness of hope in our Lord Jesus Christ" (1 Thess 1:3). Throughout the letter, Paul affirmed the Thessalonian believers were, indeed, God's elect because of their faithful work (the gospel came in power, in the Holy Spirit and with full conviction, 1 Thess 1:4-5), their labor of love (they were an imitation of Paul, persecuted for their faith, bearing witness to others, 1 Thess 1:6-8), and their steadfast hope (they left their pagan

---

[7]Jewett, *Thessalonian Correspondence*, pp. 26-30.

[8]See Bruce W. Winter, *Seek the Welfare of the City: Christians as Benefactors and Citizens* (Grand Rapids: Eerdmans, 1994), pp. 42-60, who argues a famine in Macedonia after Paul left Thessalonica contributed to the problem: patrons stockpiled food, doling out their personal surplus to potential clients.

idols to serve God, waiting for his Son to rescue them from wrath, 1 Thess 1:9-10).[9] Paul and his coworkers recognize the Thessalonians as the "elect" of God because of (1) how powerfully the Spirit accompanied the preaching of the gospel and (2) how joyfully they received the word despite growing affliction (1 Thess 1:4-8). By calling them the "elect," Paul underscores God's initiative in salvation over against human claims to superior status. Patrons saw themselves as superior. Clients often earned or courted their own special position with a patron. Paul did not want that model taken into the church. The "elect" are not chosen because they are special; they are chosen because God is gracious. Paul always uses the term "elect" to refer to those who are already members of God's people. He never uses it to prescribe who is going to be saved. Instead he employs it to remind those who have answered God's call that they are members of God's covenant people.[10]

In 1 Thessalonians 2:1—3:13 Paul recounts how this happened. The Thessalonians' work of faith was evidenced by their reception of Paul and his gospel (1 Thess 2:1-8). By imitating Paul and the first Christians—persevering in the midst of persecution—their labor of love emulates the passion of Jesus (1 Thess 2:9-16). And, in light of Paul's absence, their steadfast hope in Christ's return is seen by their faithful anticipation of Paul's return (1 Thess 2:17—3:13). On the last day, Paul will present these Thessalonian believers—his joy, his crown—blameless at the parousia of Christ.

Called to holiness. For Paul, the election of God is a call to holiness for all believers (1 Thess 4:3-8). A person who is holy is one who is set apart for God and who is therefore different from the rest of the world. In the first covenant God had commanded Israel to be holy because he is holy (e.g., Lev 19:1). Human holiness is predicated on the holiness of God, and the pursuit of holiness is a crucial aspect of both old and new covenants. *Sanctification*[11] is a technical theological term for the process by which something or someone becomes holy. According to Paul, people are first made holy by virtue of entering into a covenant with a

---

[9]Here we see that the gospel preached by Paul *(kerygma)* consisted of four elements (1 Thess 1:9-10): (a) the affirmation of the one, true God; (b) the proclamation of the resurrection of Jesus from the dead; (c) the expectation that the Son of God will come again from heaven; and (d) a description of salvation, namely, deliverance from divine wrath. Paul describes the Thessalonians' response as turning to God from idols to serve the living and true God (1 Thess 1:9). *Kerygma* (Greek for "proclamation" or "preaching") is the word commonly used by scholars to refer to the content of the gospel proclaimed in early Christian preaching.

[10]Marshall, *Theology*, 241-43.

[11]Holiness *(hagiasmos)*, sanctification *(hagiadzō)* and saint *(hagios)* are all derived from the same Greek root.

WHAT'S MORE . . .
Apocalyptic Eschatology

With the exception of the Sadducees, most Jews believed in a coming judgment day, life after death and the existence of two worlds: the terrestrial and the celestial. Scholars call this worldview *apocalyptic*, after the kind of literature that was produced almost exclusively by Jewish writers during this period of time. For several centuries Jews had come to believe that the current age would give way to a golden age of God's justice, that good would triumph over evil, that the profane would give way to the sacred, that God's reign would break into history with a cataclysmic event of cosmic proportions. In other words, they believed the world, as they knew it, would come to an end—that heaven would come to earth, that the celestial would overtake the terrestrial, that angelic powers would conquer evil and that God's presence would mean peace and justice on earth. To them there were two ages: the present, evil age and the age to come (temporal dualism). And there were two worlds: heaven and earth (cosmic dualism). Heaven's mysteries were revealed by God in secret to the faithful through visions of and journeys into the other world. They believed that on the last day—the day of God's wrath—these mysteries would be revealed to the whole world, when the old age would give way to the new and heaven's realm would become earth's reality.

To Christians, of course, these matters don't seem novel or inventive. Instead, since much of Christian theology derives from Jewish theology, apocalyptic ideas are considered conventional. Most pagan religions, however, did not espouse such "end-of-the-world" scenarios.[a] The resolution of time, the culmination of the age with a "judgment day," was predominantly a Jewish idea that made the quest for holiness even more crucial. On the last day, God would reward the faithful and pour out his wrath on the unholy, unclean and unrighteous.

---

[a]Some scholars consider the Persian religion Zoroastrianism as one of the primary sources for Jewish apocalyptic thought.

holy God. In Christian terms, to have faith in Jesus and submit to baptism initiates one into a life of ever-growing holiness or sanctification. In the first stage, personal holiness is derived from the holiness of one's covenant partner. Christ is holy and thus those who belong to him are holy as well. In the second stage of sanctification, people grow in holiness by the power of the Holy Spirit (1 Thess 4:7-8). For this to happen, believers must yield to the Holy Spirit, who transforms their character into the image and likeness of the Holy One. As far as Paul was concerned, the only thing his Gentile converts needed to live a holy life was the Holy Spirit. Indeed, sanctification is a process that takes place over the lifetime of those who submit to the power and work of God in their lives. So the first stage of holiness is relational and derivative. The second is transformative; it changes one's nature.

Paul applies the call to holiness in two ways—individually and corporately. For the individual, holiness means that a person abstains from sexual misconduct. The term Paul uses for such misconduct is *porneia*. This is a broad term covering all kinds of se.... , including rape, incest, homosexuality, premarital ... 3). On the positive side, holiness means that each person .... ody, particularly the sexual part (literally "vessel," *skeuos*), as an expression of holiness and honor (1 Thess 4:4). For some, holiness in sexuality may mean celibacy, but for most it means controlling one's body and remaining faithful in marriage (e.g., 1 Cor 7). Corporately, holiness means hospitality, taking care of fellow Christ-believers and not depending on the help of outsiders (1 Thess 4:9-12). Paul didn't want his converts to draw unnecessary attention as troublemakers who lead unruly lives. Instead, Paul directed them to "mind your own affairs, and to work with your hands," behaving properly toward outsiders.

The hope of the resurrection. The occasion that sparked Paul's exhortation in 1 Thessalonians 4:13-18 was a report that some Christ-believers were troubled about the ultimate fate of those who died prior to the parousia. Whether by natural causes or persecution, some had "fallen asleep" and apparently many were concerned that the dead would miss the joyful return and destiny awaiting the living Christ-believers. The apostle sought to comfort them and clear up any confusion they had on the fate of their friends and family members who had died. This is the only passage in the letter where Paul doesn't say, "Excel still more," or "You already know the instructions we gave you," or "You do not need to have anything written to you." In fact, this is where the Thessalonians needed help; they were ignorant of what happened to the dead in Christ. So

WHAT'S MORE . . .
The Rapture

The term *rapture* (from the Latin word *raptus*) is used for the teaching that God will snatch up the living and dead to meet the Lord in the air. Unfortunately, some have distorted Paul's teaching by suggesting that "the rapture" refers to some secret snatching of believers prior to the parousia. There have been eschatological charts and schemes, book series and movies predicated on the notion that Christ comes secretly to snatch away his elect prior to a great tribulation. As millions of people suddenly disappear across the planet, the world is left in chaos. Such is the plot of million-dollar bestsellers—but it is not the stuff of biblical teaching on the end times. There is no evidence Paul believed in a secret rapture; there is no biblical basis to suggest the church will avoid the great tribulation.[a] In fact, tribulation and suffering with Christ is the atmosphere in which the church lives out its entire existence—a very unpopular (and perhaps inconceivable) view among American Christians. Yet many Asian and African Christians would argue they are already experiencing great tribulation. If Christ were to come back today, their suffering would qualify to fulfill Jesus' prediction, but it wouldn't fit into the schema of "last days" charts promoted by "Americentric" preachers. Indeed, the parousia, according to Paul, will be the unexpected ("like a thief in the night") but very public arrival of the crucified and risen Jesus to the earth he died to redeem. The "second coming" of Christ will be an event of such cosmic proportions that no one, not even the dead, could miss it. The language Paul uses to describe this event is wonderfully poetic, powerful and political.

[a]See, e.g., N. T. Wright, "Farewell to the Rapture: Little did Paul Know How His Colorful Metaphors for Jesus' Second Coming Would Be Misunderstood Two Millennia Later," *Bible Review* 17 (2001): 8, 52.

Paul filled in the gaps of their eschatology and told his converts to "encourage one another with these words" (1 Thess 4:18).

Paul based his eschatological hopes, like much of his theology, on the death, burial and resurrection of Jesus. Jesus' experience was the "first fruits" (1 Cor 15:23). His resurrection guarantees the future resurrection when "through Jesus, God will bring with him those who have died" (1 Thess 4:14). Paul claimed to

SO WHAT?
Does Close Attention to Scripture Pay Off?

Jesus talked about "two men in the field"; one was taken away and the other left behind. But which one was "saved"? In the 1960s Larry Norman wrote a song, "I Wish We'd All Been Ready," made popular for this generation by DC Talk. In that song Norman describes being "left behind" as a bad thing. Yet Jesus' story (Mt 24:37-41) compares the end times to the days of Noah when Noah entered the ark. The biblical echo is deliberate: the outsiders were "taken away" by the flood, but Noah and his family were "left behind." Larry Norman's song flipped Jesus' meaning on its head for an entire generation of American Christians, who now pray not to be left behind when Jesus returns!

have a word from the Lord (Jesus) on these matters;[12] he was not shooting from the hip. He taught that those still living when the Lord returns will not arrive ahead of those who have fallen asleep; the dead will rise first. Appealing to apocalyptic and imperial imagery, Paul paints a memorable picture of what will happen on the final day. The Lord Jesus himself will descend from heaven accompanied by a shouted command and the blast of God's trumpet. At his coming, the dead in Christ will be resurrected first; then the living will be transformed, snatched up with the resurrected believers to meet the Lord in the air.

When Paul describes these events with words like *parousia* and *meeting (apantēsin)*, he is using stock phrases borrowed from life in the empire. The first means "arrival" and is a common expression for the visit of an important military or political figure. Likewise, the term *meeting* refers to occasions when the city elders and officials go out to welcome a visiting monarch or general to their city. In that culture, dignitaries did not merely stride into a city; the rules of hospitality required that they be met, welcomed and escorted back to the city.

In Paul's scenario, the resurrected and transformed believers make up the official delegation that will "meet the Lord in the air." But what happens next? Where

---

[12]Although this could be by a special vision, some parable or saying of the earthly Jesus dealing with the Lord's coming and the gathering of the elect may well have been passed on to him. David Wenham, *Paul and Jesus: The True Story* (Grand Rapids: Eerdmans, 2002), pp. 97-100, suggests the following passages from the Gospels as possible sources: Mt 24:30-31; Mk 13:26-27; Lk 21:27-28. He thinks it is most likely that the parable of the wise and foolish virgins (Mt 25:1-13) provided the apostle with his understanding of what happens at the parousia.

do the victorious Lord and his people go? Given the imperial language he employs and other early Christian thought (e.g., Rev 20—21), Paul probably expects the redeemed to welcome Jesus in the air and escort him back to the earth where he will reign eternally as Lord.[13] The imperial language is intended to provide believers with an alternative vision of the world. Kings, even the emperor in Rome, will one day stand aside as the King of kings and Lord of lords takes his rightful place to rule the (new) creation.

The day of the Lord. Paul then reminded the Thessalonians of what they already knew: that the day of the Lord would come suddenly, without warning, so they should stay on the alert (1 Thess 5:1-11). The descent of the Lord Jesus from

---

SO WHAT?
Does It Matter What We Believe About the End Times?

Well, if we believe the Lord is about to return at any moment, how motivated will we be to work to relieve world hunger or evangelize? Some might say, "Why should we work for world peace? Isn't there supposed to be war near the end times? Isn't working toward peace in the Middle East like working against the final plans of God?" Yet Jesus said the children of God would be peacemakers (Mt 5:9, 43-48).

---

heaven initiates "the day of the Lord." This phrase occurs throughout the Hebrew Scriptures in prophetic verse to depict a day when God's vengeance will be spent on his enemies (e.g., Jer 46:10; Amos 5:18-20). For Paul, the day of the Lord has become the day of the Lord Christ (Phil 1:6). When it comes, that day will overtake the world as labor pains come upon a woman.[14] Sudden destruction will sweep up those who chant the mantra of Rome, "peace and security" *(pax et securitas)*, and bow the knee to the emperor.

Some believe the eschatology of 1 Thessalonians is incompatible with that of 2 Thessalonians. In 1 Thessalonians Paul appears to teach that the parousia will come as a surprise and may occur anytime. On the other hand, 2 Thessalonians teaches that the parousia will be preceded by signs in some distant future. According to some, the

---

[13]Gorman, *Apostle of the Crucified Lord*, p. 160.
[14]"Labor pains" is a standard apocalyptic image for the travail that precedes the birth of the new age (e.g., Mk 13:8).

WHAT'S MORE . . .
Paul's Philosophy of History

Like many of his contemporaries Paul operated with a linear view of history. While some religions and philosophies looked at history as an endless series of cycles, the apostle believed history was headed somewhere. He viewed history as constituted in two ages. The first age is ruled by the god of this world (2 Cor 4:4), populated with malevolent spiritual powers, characterized by sin and death, and destined to end when God is good and ready. The second age will be lived under the unquestionable reign of God. It will effectually reverse the curse of the first age and create a world of universal peace, justice and righteousness. Paul believed this new age had already dawned in the life, death and resurrection of Jesus the Messiah—even if it was not completely realized. To his surprise, the two ages were now overlapping. The first had not been brought to a complete end. Both ages existed simultaneously in the world (see Mt 13:24-30). This new reality makes it possible for those living in darkness to be transferred into the kingdom of the beloved Son (Col 1:13).

contradiction is severe enough to conclude that Paul did not write 2 Thessalonians. We argue that the alleged differences in eschatology between 1 and 2 Thessalonians are exaggerated. The predictable-yet-unexpected nature of the parousia characterizes the eschatological hope of most early Christian literature (e.g., Mk 13). To the sons of darkness Jesus will come like a thief in the night; his coming is both surprising and unwelcome because it brings destruction (1 Thess 5:2-3). The sons of light, however, may be "startled" by the Lord's return but will not be surprised because they have been waiting and watching for that day (1 Thess 5:4-11). A pregnant woman is "startled" by the onset of labor but hardly surprised, knowing it was coming.

Two kinds of people have two separate destinies. The sons of darkness/night are headed for wrath and destruction. The sons of light/day, on the other hand, are destined for salvation (1 Thess 5:8-10), predicated on the death of Jesus "for us," a typical Pauline theme. Those who belong to the day are to stay awake, remain sober (in contrast to drunken night-revelry), put on the breastplate of faith and love, and place the hope of salvation on their heads like a helmet (1 Thess 5:8). Ultimately, whether we are awake (are alive) or asleep (the sleep of death), "we will live with him" (1 Thess 5:10).

SECOND THESSALONIANS

Second Thessalonians reveals that everything had gotten worse. Persecution had intensified. Paul intended his teachings on the last day to comfort, but they created more anxiety among some Thessalonians. The unruly had grown in numbers and were threatening the integrity of Paul's gospel mission. As a result, the more moderating, pastoral tone of his first letter gives way to an anxious, edgy response to these growing problems.

First, much like the author of 2 Peter, Paul encourages the faithful to endure severe "persecutions and afflictions" by promising that the wicked will get their due. When Christ comes in his glory, it will mean not only that the righteous will be rewarded but that their oppressors will "suffer the punishment of eternal destruction" (2 Thess 1:5-12). Before Christ comes, there will be rebellion, deception and destruction (2 Thess 2:1-12). But Paul is convinced that his converts will not be deceived in the throes of this apocalyptic, cosmic battle between God and Satan (2 Thess 2:13-17). Their sanctification is assured since they "hold fast to the traditions" Paul taught them, by word or by letter (2 Thess 2:15). Second, Paul saves his harshest rebuke for the unruly. They seem to have been teaching that the end of the world had come, fitting the description of the lawlessness and deception indicated in chapter two. The unruly had given up imitating their apostle: they were not working with their own hands but instead relying upon others to supply daily provisions (2 Thess 3:5-13). Evidently some of the poorer members were taking advantage of the charity of those of greater means, who may have been complaining of the abuse. So Paul lays down two seemingly contradictory rules: those who don't work, don't eat; and those who have the means should help those who don't (2 Thess 3:10-13). Each side had their own instructions and Paul required compliance. Those who disobeyed were to be shunned. And to make sure everyone knew that these were the commands of the apostle, Paul called attention to his signature at the end of the letter (2 Thess 3:14-17).

Eschatological justice. The question of divine justice is never far away when good people suffer. How does the suffering of the righteous square with God's justice? According to Paul, God's justice will become evident at the parousia when the Lord Jesus comes from heaven with powerful angels in flaming fire (2 Thess 1:7-8). His coming will right two wrongs. First, the Christ-believers will experience relief from their anguish. Second, the unbelievers will face the vengeance of God. Their punishment will be "eternal destruction, separated from the presence of the Lord and from the glory of his might" (2 Thess 1:9). The phrase "eternal destruction" can be interpreted in two ways: (1) eternal in duration or (2) eternal in result. By "eternal in duration" we mean that one is destroyed throughout eternity, that is, always being destroyed but never completely consumed. By "eternal in result" we mean that one is destroyed for eternity, that is, punished and then annihilated. However Paul understood the fate of the Thessalonians' afflicters, one thing is clear: their punishment was permanent—separated from God's presence forever. This is only reasonable. If salvation is eternally living in his presence, damnation must be eternal separation from him. In the coming of Jesus the justice of God will be satisfied.

Before the end. Despite what some were claiming, the day of the Lord had not arrived. At this point Paul turns his attention to a movement that declares that day has already come.[15] A forged letter in his name may be one of the causes (2 Thess 2:1-2). The apostle denies the claim and declares that the Lord's Day will not come until (a) there is a great rebellion against God and (b) the man of lawlessness is exposed. The two "signs" before the end are not unrelated; the appearance of the lawless one precipitates the great apostasy. He will set himself up as a god and will enter the temple in Jerusalem to usurp the rightful place of Israel's God. This is a familiar scenario repeated throughout history when arrogant dictators have conquered lands and annexed kingdoms. As a way of subjugating the populations,

---

SO WHAT?
How Will We Recognize the Lawless One?

Some interpret Paul's phrase in 2 Thessalonians 2:4 very literally. The lawless one will enter a rebuilt temple in Jerusalem and declare himself "God." So as long as no one is pouring concrete or laying stone in Jerusalem for another Jewish temple, we don't have to worry about Paul's warnings. The lawless man can't enter a temple if no temple is standing. Others interpret Paul more symbolically. The lawless one is going to seek to replace God in the center of our lives and society. If this is what Paul meant, then even now we should be wary. Consider those who are telling us (as the serpent did in the garden) "You can decide for yourself what is good and evil. You can be like God!" That sounds like what the lawless one would say.

---

[15]In today's world of cable news, it is hard to imagine how someone could believe news the Lord had already returned. Yet in Paul's day it was possible for a new Caesar to be reigning in Rome, declaring new edicts, and the provinces not yet hear of it. Apparently, some were teaching that "signs of the New Age" (manifestations of the Spirit?) were indicating that something had changed; "Jesus must already be reigning in Jerusalem and we should be sharing possessions."

they entered local temples as a symbol indicating that the local god(s) had abandoned the people in favor of the conqueror.[16] Afterward they often set themselves up as gods to be honored and feared. In fact, less than ten years earlier, Emperor Caligula had shipped an idol to be placed in Jerusalem's temple. His untimely death prevented this abomination from happening. So the people Paul addressed knew this routine well.

The arrival of the man of lawlessness, according to the apostle, will be accompanied with miracles and wonders performed by the power of Satan (2 Thess 2:9; cf. 2 Cor 4:3-4). He will deceive many who refuse the offer of salvation through Christ. But the rebellion is short lived. At the parousia the Lord Jesus will slay him "with the breath of his mouth"—as easily as blowing out a candle—and bring the mutiny he inspires to an end (2 Thess 2:8).

If you don't work, you don't eat. The final chapter of 2 Thessalonians confronts

---

WHAT'S MORE . . .
Restraining the Man of Lawlessness

Paul appears to think that the man of lawlessness is already in the world. He writes: "you know what is now restraining him, so that he may be revealed when his time comes. For the mystery of lawlessness is already at work, but only until the one who now restrains it is removed" (2 Thess 2:6-7). Something and/or someone is restraining him, keeping him from disclosing himself for now, but the apostle does not explain what the restraining power and/or person is. Some speculate that it is the Holy Spirit, the gospel or even Paul himself. Others suggest that the might and cruelty of Rome keeps the man of lawlessness in check. But since Paul never discusses this scenario in his other letters, all suggestions are mere guesswork. For the Thessalonians, however, it was not guesswork: Paul shared these teachings when he was with them. Now he calls them to remember what he taught in person. This is one of those times when reading someone else's mail leaves us scratching our head.

---

[16]Invaders often ritually asked the god(s) to abandon their temples before beginning their assault of the city. See the cogent argumentation of John Kloppenberg, "*Evocatio Deorum* and the Date of Mark," *Journal of Biblical Literature* 24, no. 3 (2005): 419-50. Entering the temple "proved" either the local god(s) had abandoned the temple or they were now favoring the conqueror. When the invading general offered a sacrifice in the temple, it was to indicate the latter; when he erected a different idol, it was to indicate the former.

those living in idleness, that is, the unruly. Paul commands them to go to work and to follow the example set by Paul and his coworkers. He writes the famous words "Anyone unwilling to work should not eat" (2 Thess 3:10). In addition, he commands the rest of the church "in the name of our Lord Jesus Christ" to shun—stay away from—those living in idleness. They are not to consider them enemies; they are to think of them as wayward brothers (2 Thess 3:15). The apostle is using social pressure to shame them into compliance, a good technique in a dyadic culture but not so effective in our modern individualistic one. For Paul the idle are not just a nuisance, they are "malformed believers" who burden the church unnecessarily.[17] In a community where Paul's ingenuity and Christ's self-giving are the models, these misshapen saints have a long way to go before they realize the true nature of the Christian life.

The Thessalonian congregation remained loyal to Paul, since the Macedonians were able about five years later to give "according to their means" (2 Cor 8:3) to the relief offering for the poor in Jerusalem. Paul records that, despite their "severe ordeal of affliction, their abundant joy and their extreme poverty have overflowed in a wealth of generosity on their part" (2 Cor 8:2). Paul bragged to the Corinthians that the Macedonians had even given beyond their means, begging to participate in the relief offering (2 Cor 8:3). Apparently, the Thessalonians not only survived their "ordeal of affliction," they were an important part of Paul's worldwide Gentile mission to help the impoverished saints in Jerusalem—a relief offering Paul would spend his entire third mission trip collecting.

READ MORE ABOUT IT

DPL Articles:

>   "Man of Lawlessness and Restraining Power," pp. 592-94, by L. Morris.
>   "Eschatology," pp. 253-69; esp. "3.4 The Awaited Day of the Lord and Final Judgment," pp. 259-60, by L. J. Kreitzer.
>   "Thessalonians, Letters to the," pp. 932-39, by J. W. Simpson.
>   "Holiness, Sanctification," pp. 397-402; esp. "2. Sanctification and Justification," pp. 398-400, by S. E. Porter.

---

[17]Gorman, *Apostle of the Crucified Lord,* p. 178.

6

The Itinerant Paul

The Corinthian Letters

PAUL BELIEVED IN ONE CHURCH. He was adamant that the body of Christ should be united despite the powerful forces threatening the cohesiveness of this new community of faith. Problems inside and outside the church led to divisions even in Paul's day. Paul seemed to devote much of his energy to keeping his converts together—united as one. His letters were meant to seal the cracks, to keep the dykes from rupturing, so that he didn't "labor in vain" among the nations. As a matter of fact, he was convinced his letters would patch up the differences. He would write "nothing other than what you can read and also understand" (2 Cor 1:13). He believed that the gospel of Jesus Christ had the power to make all people brothers and sisters, all sinners righteous, all races children of God. In Christ all were equal. But amid other pressing realities, stress fractures made the reservoir of Paul's gospel ministry vulnerable to a serious breach. For example, patrons needed to overcome their favoring of clients while ignoring poorer members at the Lord's Table. Husbands and wives had to learn how to worship together as brothers and sisters in Christ. Jews had to learn to listen to Gentiles teaching from the Hebrew Scriptures. The illiterate relied upon the elite to make sense of Paul's writings. And the simple fact that Paul's converts had to meet in separate houses no doubt encouraged birds of a feather to flock together—solidifying the social, religious, linguistic[1] and ethnic walls that divided them. When they met as one for com-

---

[1]"I belong to Cephas" boasted some believers in Corinth (1 Cor 1:12). The fact that they refer to this apostle by his Aramaic name (Cephas) rather than by his Greek name (Peter) may indicate it was an Aramaic-speaking congregation. Those following Apollos may have been Jews from Egypt, preferring the exegetical methods of that region. Like today, followers tended to flock to teachers most like them.

munion, divisions were obvious to everyone. Cultures that esteem honor take careful note of where people sit at meals. Paul's converts needed a unity of purpose that would not only bind the churches together but would draw the entire world—Jew and Gentile, rich and poor, nobility and commoners—into one collection of restored humanity. Paul found that purpose not only in the gospel he preached but also in an offering he collected.

The relief offering was supposed to pull it all together—a tangible representation of the body caring for its members. If there were lingering doubts about the legitimacy of the Gentile mission, about the solidarity of Antioch and Jerusalem, about the content of the gospel according to James and Paul, then a gift would seal the alliance once and for all. Paul had already instructed his churches during the second mission trip to begin to put money aside for the Jerusalem church. His third mission trip (except for the new work in Ephesus) looked more like a whistle-stop circuit, visiting all of his churches long enough to pick up the money and head on to the next destination. During this journey, Paul wrote some of his most extensive letters: several letters to the Corinthians and one to the Romans. In these letters Paul seems to be at his theological best, working out the significance of his gospel for a congregation he barely knew (Romans) and a group of converts he knew too well (Corinthians). And in both places it was the unity of the church that was in jeopardy. Ironically, it was not the relief offering that ended up securing the success of his ministry: one body, one gospel. Instead, these letters saved the Pauline mission: sorting out the problems of the past (Corinthians) and establishing the singularity of the gospel for the future (Romans). If Paul had not reeled in the rebellious Corinthians and wooed the prospective Romans, then the history of Christianity may have taken a completely different course.

CHURCH DISCIPLINE

Corinth was one of the few towns Paul was not forced to leave. Even though he got in trouble there—dragged before Gallio the proconsul of Achaia and accused by his kinsmen as a lawbreaker—this time these Jewish problems did not lead to pagan resentment (Acts 18:12-17). It might appear to us that since the Corinthians were tolerant of many different religions and seemed to be a permissive society, Paul had a better chance of not being run out of town. It is true the ancient Greek city had earned the reputation as a place where unbridled sexual passions could find limitless opportunities: "to corinthianize" was a euphemism for fornication. That prostitution and fertility cults prospered in Corinth comes as no surprise. Sex in the city had as much to do with the fact Corinth was a trade city.

WHAT'S MORE . . .
"The New Testament Church"

"Churches today need to be more like the New Testament church" has been a popular admonition. There are two reasons we need to be careful of such a battle cry. First, it is inaccurate to characterize the first-century church as particularly pure or perfect. Paul paints quite a different picture. In Corinth, house churches were meeting separately and probably divisively (1 Cor 2:14—3:1); leaders were filled with arrogance (1 Cor 4:6-7), one member was sleeping with his stepmother (1 Cor 5:1); others were immoral, idolaters, revelers, drunkards, robbers (1 Cor 5:9-12); church members were suing each other (1 Cor 6:1-8); and some were teaching that Old Testament laws against immorality were like the laws against pork—they didn't apply to Christians (1 Cor 6:12-13). Second, to paint such an ideal portrait of the early church maligns the work of the Spirit. Behind such a model is often a perception that Jesus started a perfect church that has ever since been slowly coasting downhill—a sort of "big bang" theory for the church age. Has not the Spirit been working over the last two thousand years? Perhaps the church today has just as many problems and offers the same potential for witness to God's kingdom as the church of the first century.

Corinth connected two harbors, linking east and west, the Adriatic and the Aegean, and bridged two landmasses, joining north and south, the mainland of Achaia and the Peloponnesus. By land or by sea, merchants marched through Corinth like ants seeking their claim. Indeed, Corinth had one of the most diverse populations in the Mediterranean. Archaeological remains give the impression that just about every god in the Greco-Roman world once had a shrine or a temple in Corinth.

Yet this ancient Greek city known for its licentiousness was destroyed by the Romans in 146 B.C. and was eventually replaced by a Roman colony inhabited by Roman citizens, being rebuilt by Julius Caesar in 44 B.C. As the administrative center of Achaia, Roman law and order dominated everyday life. In fact, Latin was nearly as common as Greek. Therefore, when the complaint against Paul the Roman citizen came before Gallio, it was up to the proconsul of this Roman colony to determine if the apostle's actions were criminal according to Roman law—it had little to do with the openness of their society. And, since Gallio dismissed the

charge despite vociferous protests from the synagogue rulers, it is also likely that
the Jewish population in Corinth was not as large or as influential as in the older,
well-established Macedonian cities. Perhaps Paul found it easier to blend into the
citizenry of Corinth, where newcomers and new money were the standard. In certain respects, Paul the Roman citizen, the merchant, the traveler, had found the
perfect place to land for a while. The trouble Paul confronted later among his own
converts, however, may suggest Corinth was among the most difficult places to
start a church.

The modern reader of Paul's letters would be hard pressed to find a church with
more problems than the one in Corinth. Think about it. Here's a church where incest is ignored, believers are taking each other to court, men are serviced by prostitutes, women are refusing their husbands sexual intimacy, men are getting drunk at
the Lord's table, and some are even denying the resurrection of believers. And that's
just the half of it. Why were the Corinthians so corrupt? How could Paul call these
people saints (1 Cor 1:2)? Why did church discipline apply only to the man who
was sleeping with his stepmother? Shouldn't Paul have instructed the church to
kick out the drunks, adulterers and swindlers as well? Most of these problems appear only in Corinth; we don't read of such things in Thessalonica or Ephesus or
the churches of Galatia. Was Corinth Paul's only problem child? How could things
have gotten so out of hand in Corinth? Why was this church so divisive?

Bruce Winter has argued that secular ethics plagued Paul's church plant after he
left Corinth.[2] In other words, once the apostle moved on, Corinthian ways filled in
the gaps of Paul's teaching. When they had no specific word from Paul on how to
deal with certain situations, they handled their problems according to their cultural
inclinations. For example, the Corinthians were enamored with sophistry;[3] teachers of rhetoric were in high demand in this city where movers and shakers had a
better chance at upward mobility than in older, well-established cities built on bed-
rock traditions. This is why Paul spent the first four chapters of 1 Corinthians de-
moting the art of public speaking and promoting the power of a gospel that exalts
the weak and the foolish (Paul!). Getting ahead through the power of public persuasion was contrary to the Pauline message of Christ crucified.

Another example is the head-covering issue. In Roman society men with cov-

---

[2]See Bruce W. Winter, *After Paul Left Corinth: The Influence of Secular Ethics and Social Change* (Grand
Rapids: Eerdmans, 2001).

[3]Sophistry is the art of using clever speech to make a persuasive argument for a wrong conclusion. Thus
some were arguing convincingly that immorality was neutral, building off Paul's argument against
food (1 Cor 6:13): the stomach was meant for food; the body (genitalia) for sex; neither had any effect
on the "soul."

ered heads and women with uncovered heads were signs of high status. A citizen, who wore his toga, parading his vestige of honor, would cover his head during priestly rituals. Unlike all other women, some Roman wives did not cover their hair in public, indicating their high status and freedom. Additionally, prostitutes and fertility cult priestesses also openly displayed their "glory," that is, their hair. And, all women left their heads uncovered in the privacy of the domicile—a woman's domain. These dynamics came into play when Paul's converts gathered for worship in houses.

Was the patron's house public or private space? Were worship services private or public rituals? When the patroness prophesied without a head covering, or when the patron read the Scriptures with a head covering, were they claiming superior status? Was the Lord's Table a private dinner where everyone ate their own food, or was it supposed to be a public affair with equal portions distributed to rich and poor guests? Did the host have the right to distribute the food? (Patrons were

SO WHAT?
Does It Matter How the Corinthian Church Reached Its Conclusions?

So long as they reached the right conclusions (usually we mean the culturally acceptable ones), isn't it okay? The modern Western church faces the same problem. We have no direct word from Paul about such volatile issues as abortion, genetic research or nuclear weapons. Many Christians decide these issues using Western cultural standards. A Christian argues against abortion, appealing to the "right to life" by saying, "these babies are given no choice" (individualism), "these babies haven't done anything wrong" (legal justice), or "one of these babies might grow up to cure cancer" (pragmatism). Western values are the true basis of the argument. Thus, some Christians oppose abortion but still favor capital punishment ("they deserve it") or even euthanasia ("it's what she would have wanted") using other Western values. "Right to life" never really gets beyond the slogan. Or, consider how honoring a donor increases the size and frequency of gifts. Does your church honor donors with plaques? All three authors work at universities with buildings named in honor of big-dollar donors. What's the motivation of those involved? Christian mission or American pragmatism? The Corinthians were making decisions based upon Corinthian values and not Christian ones.

in the habit of giving clients larger or better portions during banquets.) Were claims to honor via status symbols and patronage acceptable in Pauline churches? While he was with them, Paul may have emphasized that in Christ there is neither male nor female, master nor slave, Jew nor Greek. But quite obviously, Paul had not worked out all the details of what this would mean for his converts. Therefore it comes as no surprise that in his absence local customs ended up eclipsing Pauline traditions in a place like Corinth.

The Corinthians pushed Paul's law-free gospel to the limit. What was hypothetical in Romans ("Should we continue in sin in order that grace may abound?" Rom 6:1) was reality in Corinth. But, it wasn't that Paul's converts in Corinth were simply a bunch of miscreants or malcontents. Corinth tested the mettle of Paul's doctrine of grace unlike any other city. The flaming passions of sexual immorality and prideful arrogance could have consumed the church, revealing that Paul's Corinthian labor was little more than wood, hay and straw (1 Cor 3:12). And yet some of the blame for the Corinthians' bad behavior may rest on the shoulders of Paul, or, one should say, on Paul's pen. For all of Paul's talk about the foolishness of rhetoric and the wisdom of preaching the simple message of the gospel, the Corinthians had a hard time understanding what Paul wrote. Indeed, some of his most complicated arguments occur in these letters, and the Corinthians seem to have misunderstood Paul on several points. In fact, it is quite apparent that Paul had to clear up several misunderstandings.

For example, was Paul for or against marriage (1 Cor 7:28-29)? What difference does it make whether Paul's instruction derives from a command of the Lord or was simply his own opinion—especially when he's laying down a rule for all the churches (1 Cor 7:17)? If one's liberty should not be subject to the judgment of someone else's conscience (1 Cor 10:29), then isn't the risk of causing a brother to stumble irrelevant when it comes to eating meat offered to idols (1 Cor 8:9)? And, what about this idol meat? At first Paul writes as if eating idol meat was acceptable (1 Cor 8:4-6). Later he argues that eating idol food is tantamount to consuming deviled meat (1 Cor 10:19-21). So which is it? Finally, was Paul advocating a hierarchy of men and women in worship (1 Cor 11:8-10), or was he arguing for equal status (1 Cor 11:11-12)? Could women speak in church (1 Cor 11:5) or not (1 Cor 14:34)? It's no wonder scholarly commentaries on 1 Corinthians are thick volumes. We have a difficult time understanding what Paul meant. Once again we are reminded that we are reading someone else's mail.

In several respects, Paul's relationship with the Corinthian church was unlike any other. First, there was a greater amount of letter traffic between Paul and the

Corinthians. Paul wrote several letters (at least four) to the Corinthians, only two of which were preserved.[4] In 1 Corinthians 5:9 Paul referred to a previous letter. In 2 Corinthians 2:3 and 7:8, Paul mentioned a "sorrowful letter" that doesn't match the tone of 1 Corinthians (a letter that doesn't sound very sorrowful). And the Corinthians were not the kind of people who simply received letters; they sent them as well! (1 Cor 7:1). Second, Paul made several visits to Corinth during his third mission trip in order to deal with certain problems face to face. Tellingly, when it came to the Corinthians, it seems Paul's pastoral visits made things worse, not better (2 Cor 10:10). His letters appeared to work, however. Indeed, like aerial sorties meant to soften the combatants before his arrival, Paul sent his letters ahead of his visit to Corinth (2 Cor 7:5-13). Most other Pauline letters were written and delivered after he visited his converts. Finally, notice how Paul wasn't reluctant at all to rely upon financial support from other churches (Rom 15:24; Phil 4:15-16; Gal 6:6). But, when it came to the Corinthians, Paul refused their help, much to their chagrin (1 Cor 9:3-18; 2 Cor 12:13-21). Why? Money and gifts were flying around in this "Johnny-come-lately" city where power-broker-wannabes were trying to move up the social ladder. Patrons were gathering clients. New alliances were constantly forming. Paul knew Corinthian gifts would come with puppet strings, and there was no way he would tie himself to the whims of their directives, dancing to their tune. They may employ many tutors of sophistry, but he was their father (1 Cor 4:15). They may have several patrons sponsoring the mission, offering their houses as meeting places, but no one owned Paul; he would never be their client (1 Cor 9:12-19).

FIRST CORINTHIANS

It is hard to find a unifying theme in 1 Corinthians. Instead, what we have is an eclectic response to oral reports and written letters from the Corinthians. For the most part the first six chapters appear to be Paul's response to the report that came from the group that met in Chloe's house (1 Cor 1:11; 5:1)—was this the house group loyal to Paul (1 Cor 1:12)? In the last ten chapters Paul seems to be respond-

---

[4]Some scholars think that both the "previous letter" and the "sorrowful letter" have been interpolated into 2 Corinthians: 2 Corinthians 6:14—7:1 sounds like the content of the previous letter and interrupts the flow of Paul's rhetoric (2 Cor 7:2 seems to pick up where 6:13 leaves off), and 2 Corinthians 10:1—13:13 breaks from the conciliatory tone of the first nine chapters—could these four chapters be the nasty letter that Paul regretted sending? Probably not. Letter-writing practices explain these shifts of style and content better than appealing to interpolations (inserted material), for which there is no manuscript evidence. See chapter two of E. Randolph Richards, *Paul and First-Century Letter Writing: Secretaries, Composition and Collection* (Downers Grove, Ill.: InterVarsity Press, 2004), pp. 94-121.

ing to a letter from all of the Corinthians (see 1 Cor 7:1; the phrase "now concerning" may indicate where Paul is picking up the next topic raised by the Corinthians; see 1 Cor 8:1; 1 Cor 12:1; 1 Cor 16:1), interspersed with other reports (1
Cor 11:18; 15:12).[5] If this observation is correct, it is telling to note which issues
were brought up by the Corinthians and which issues were ignored (or considered
irrelevant or embarrassing) by the converts who did not meet in Chloe's house. Indeed, the gross sin of incest was evidently not considered a big problem by most
of the household churches, while the more tedious questions of marriage, idol
meat and spiritual gifts were of the greatest importance to the larger church community. No wonder Paul dealt first with what he heard. The church was divided
(1 Cor 1:10-17). The gospel message was taking a back seat to sophistry; that is,
how something was said had become more important to the Corinthians than
what was said (1 Cor 1:18—4:7). And the arrogance of the Corinthians led them
to dismiss Paul as a "spectacle to the world" and "rubbish of the world" (1 Cor 4:8-
21) and yet accept what was considered despicable to pagans, incest (1 Cor 5:1-
13).[6] They defamed the body of Christ, the temple of God, by taking up lawsuits
against each other in pagan courts and by having sex with prostitutes (1 Cor 6:1-
20). Claiming to be wise, the Corinthians were fools. Obviously, these converts
did not think they needed Paul's advice or judgment on these matters. And yet,
ironically, they eventually turned to Paul with their own questions about abstain-
ing from sex in marriage, about eating sacrifices in pagan temples and about speaking in a tongue that makes no sense. This was a divided church.

Some of this division may have roots in Paul himself. His opponents had a slogan, "all things are lawful for me" (1 Cor 10:23); was this originally Paul's? It
sounds like the triumphant claim of a Jew who would set aside the law, eating unclean foods, when he shared table with Gentiles (1 Cor 9:19-23). Following Paul's
example, then, some Corinthians ate food sacrificed to idols without any sense of
shame. This put Paul in a difficult spot. His converts were imitating him, just as
he encouraged them to do (1 Cor 11:1). But, Paul was quick to point out his converts were not following his example to the fullest; that is, Paul refused to exercise
his liberties when they offended brothers and sisters in Christ. Paul made himself
a slave to all, especially the Corinthians, when he set aside status and claims of apostolic privileges: refusing to take a wife or getting paid for the gospel like other

---

[5]We have examples of a letter of Cicero similarly using "and now" to answer topic after topic in sequence: Cicero *Letters to Friends* 12.30.
[6]The issues raised by the Corinthians may have had more to do with status and rights of privilege
within the community of faith than with questions regarding immoral practices or theological error.

apostles (1 Cor 9:1-19). Similarly, the Corinthian meat-eaters shouldn't parade their liberties at the expense of weaker members. They should defer to the welfare of the community. But, how does one know when to stick by one's convictions and when to defer? Some had leaders who made seemingly wise arguments: "if our meat-eating offends other Christians and they leave, we didn't need those others anyway." Paul argued, "The eye cannot say to the hand, 'I have no need of you'" (1 Cor 12:21). Paul believed each member must sacrifice the pursuit of individual recognition in order to edify the entire church (1 Cor 12:12-31) and the only way to do that is with love (1 Cor 13:1-13).

The word of the cross and the wisdom of God. The remedy for the schisms in Corinth, according to Paul, is to be found in the common confession of the gospel (1 Cor 1:10-17). If the Corinthians will focus their attention on the cross of Christ rather than on eloquent, human wisdom, the dissonance plaguing the church will resolve into harmony. Though folly to the world, the "word of the cross" is "the power of God" to those being saved (1 Cor 1:18). In a world addicted to signs and wisdom, Paul offered "Christ crucified," not in eloquent wisdom to tickle the ears but in weakness, fear and trembling. Indeed, Paul incarnated the gospel (1 Cor 2:3). His message, though weak by human standards, demonstrated the Spirit and the power of God. To those who have answered God's call, Christ is "the power of God and the wisdom of God" (1 Cor 1:24).

In Proverbs 8 wisdom is personified as a woman whom God made prior to the creation of the world (Prov 8:22-26). As he fashioned the heavens and the earth, Wisdom was beside him as a master worker (Prov 8:27-30). She invites people to follow her path, promising wealth, fame and honor to all who walk with her (Prov 8:1-11).[7] Three aspects of "personified" wisdom are significant for the background of Paul's christological use: (1) wisdom's presence with God from the beginning; (2) wisdom's role in creation; and (3) wisdom's function in bringing salvation to humanity. When early Christians re-read wisdom texts in light of their experiences with the risen Jesus, they quickly found that divine wisdom provided a scriptural way to express the significance of who Jesus was and what he had accom-

---

[7]Similar ideas are found in other "wisdom" passages (Job 28; Sirach 24; Wisdom of Solomon 8—9). Some interpreters take the language about wisdom to refer to a created, intermediary being who works alongside God. Others take it as a vivid, poetic expression of God's nearness to his creation and salvation. We have simplified a complicated subject. For example, in later Jewish writings, Wisdom sought to dwell (tabernacle) among God's people. Sirach (Sirach 24:10-11) argues it came to dwell in the temple. Others (Baruch) claimed Wisdom dwelt in the Torah (Baruch 3:36—4:1). First Enoch 42:1-2 argued Wisdom found no place to pitch her tabernacle and so left and returned to heaven. In the Gospel, John will argue Wisdom did dwell (tabernacled) among us, not in the temple nor the Torah, but in Christ.

plished. By identifying Jesus with Wisdom, early Christians were able to express his divine origin, preexistence, role in creation and salvation, and still maintain the uniqueness of Israel's one God. In 1 Corinthians 1:24, 30 Paul identifies the crucified Messiah with divine Wisdom. Although the title "wisdom of/from God" is not frequent, the unpacking of all the implications from this identification covers a great deal of the landscape in Paul's letters.

Keeping the temple pure. Although the divisions, partisan wrangling and spiritual arrogance in the church at Corinth were a major source of problems, they had a secondary effect: immorality that threatened the well-being of the young Corinthian church. When the apostle hears about a case of incest, he chastises them for letting it go unchecked and calls for immediate action. He instructs the assembled church to hand the sinner over to Satan for the destruction of his flesh so that his spirit may be saved in the day of the Lord (1 Cor 5:5). The action he prescribes is not punitive but restorative. He anticipates the result will be the man's repentance and ultimate salvation.[8] But in the meantime, the health of the church must be protected, and its reputation must be rehabilitated among outsiders.

To address other moral failures, Paul adopts a risky rhetorical strategy. He acknowledges what is perhaps a Pauline slogan, "all things are lawful for me," and then qualifies it. Freedom in Christ does not mean "anything goes." The proper standard is this: Is the action helpful to the cause of Christ? Is it consistent with the demands of the Lord Jesus on one's life? Essentially, the body (individual) is "for the Lord" and not for immorality (1 Cor 6:13). Despite the claims of the spiritual elite that what they do with their bodies carries no eternal weight, Paul counters that the resurrection of Jesus means that our bodies matter on this side of the parousia. The Greek philosophers were wrong to say the body was merely the shell or prison of the soul. Bodily existence calls for holiness now, because the physical bodies of believers are "members of Christ" (1 Cor 6:15).

For Paul, it is inconceivable that someone would cavalierly join one of Christ's members with the physical body of a prostitute. To do so is tantamount to Christ himself engaging the services of a harlot. The unity of the believer with the Lord ought to preclude this kind of behavior. Furthermore, sexual immorality injures the body (individual and corporate) in ways other sins do not (1 Cor 6:18). Paul concludes (1 Cor 6:19): "do you not know that your body [the individual's physical body] is a temple of the Holy Spirit within you, which you have from God and that

---

[8]In Paul's dyadic world, being shunned by one's community was socially, emotionally and often financially devastating. In much of the modern Western world, a Christian might merely change churches, thereby, rendering church discipline impotent.

you are not your own?" As a temple of the Holy Spirit, the bodies of Christ-believers are God's house and not their own to do with as they please. Having been bought with a price (the sacrifice of Jesus), the only proper response is to bring glory to God with their bodies. But how do sexual beings bring glory to God with their bodies?

SO WHAT?
"Who Cares What Another Christian Does?"

"What they do in the privacy of their own homes is their own business." Paul didn't see it that way. To him, sins "against the body" included the body of Christ. Both the individual Christian and the church are a temple of the Holy Spirit. Therefore unholy behavior "against the body" is a sacrilegious act, violating the temple of God. This is what makes Christians accountable to each other. Together we reveal the presence of God. So the individualistic saying "all things are lawful to me" does not give Christians liberty to do whatever they want regardless of the church. What we do affects other people, whether we realize it or not. But notice what this did not mean. Paul did not command the church to "discipline" the fornicators by kicking them out. Instead, he reminded them all of their allegiance to their master. The motivation for glorifying God in our body is grounded in our belonging to Christ.

Should husbands and wives abstain from sexual relations altogether as some Corinthians were saying: "It is well for a man not to touch a woman" (1 Cor 7:1)?

Paul's response to this first question posed by the Corinthians covers the gamut of marriage, celibacy and divorce. Marriage, he argues, turns out to be a good antidote to sexual immorality. Couples may choose to abstain from sexual relations for short periods to devote themselves to prayer, but generally they have a mutual responsibility to satisfy one another's sexual needs. Although the apostle promotes marriage, he himself favors singleness and urges more people to seek the gift of celibacy (1 Cor 7:7). He cites two reasons: (1) the nearness of the end and (2) the troubles associated with marriage. The imminence of the parousia calls for an urgency that is unsettling to long-term commitments. Singles can devote themselves completely to the Lord and his church, while the married will always have divided loyalties. His basic rule, however, is this: remain as you were when God called you (7:17-24).

SO WHAT?
Should We Take Paul Seriously About Marrying or Staying Single?

Well, this is one of the most important decisions people make in their lives. For modern, Western Christians "normal" means growing up, marrying and having children. Wanting to be normal, most marry as soon as "the right person comes along." Unfortunately, the right person often ends up not being so right after all. In America half of first marriages end in divorce. Fewer and fewer children grow up with their biological mothers and fathers. Christian marriages end in divorce at about the same rate as non-Christian marriages. Still, celibacy is not considered a serious lifestyle option unless you are going to be a priest. So most Christians don't think Paul was addressing them. They think he was talking to somebody else, or at least they hope so. Clearly Paul believed singleness had a lot of advantages. That's why he advised it. Perhaps we need to listen.

Regarding divorce, Paul apparently appeals to the teaching of Jesus (perhaps Mk 10:1-12): believers are not to initiate divorce (1 Cor 7:10-11). If they do, they are to seek reconciliation or remain single. Believers are not to divorce a spouse simply because he or she is not a believer. The reason is that the marriage bond has a sanctifying effect upon the unbelieving partner and the children (1 Cor 7:14). Whether Paul means the faith of the one provides a positive influence toward God or something more substantial is not clear. What is clear, however, is that believing partners are instruments of peace and salvation even in partly Christian families (1 Cor 7:14-16).

To eat or not to eat. Some in Corinth (perhaps Jewish Christians) believed Christ-believers should abstain from meat offered to idols. To them eating this meat amounted to idolatry. They were deeply hurt when other believers went ahead with these meals without a care. The question was complicated by a number of factors including where the meal was taking place (in a pagan temple or in a private home) and who was present at the table (those offended or not offended by the practice).

Some had made this divisive issue a matter of knowledge; Paul makes it a matter of love (cf. 1 Cor 13:1). Knowledge can lead to an arrogant disregard for others. Love always builds up. Initially, Paul sides with those who ate the meat sacrificed to idols by appealing to their common knowledge of God's oneness (Deut 6:4). If there is only one God, then idols are really nothing at all. Yet, despite their common confession, Paul understands that some are more sensitive to the constant and insidious nature of idolatry in Corinth. Such take offense, convinced they are defiled when other Corinthian Christians make the decision to eat because uncleanness is contagious. (See "Contagious Matters" on p. 156). Recognizing the gravity of the situation, Paul calls on those who feel free to eat meat to consider that their liberty has become a "stumbling block to the weak" (1 Cor 8:9). This is particularly true when the meal at which they eat this meat takes place in a pagan temple. Paul urges believers to set aside cavalier acts of autonomy and consider the effect their freedom has on others. Though it is not a sin to eat food sacrificed to idols, it nevertheless becomes sin when the motivation is showing off one's knowledge and the result is an offended brother or sister. Paul's principle can be stated simply: for Christ-believers personal freedom must always yield to the needs of the other (cf. Phil 2:1-11).

Paul finds Israel's story instructive for the new narrative being written about the people of God in Achaia. In the problems at hand Paul relies on the wilderness experience of Israel as a guide and an example (*typoi*, 1 Cor 10:6; perhaps warning).[9] For him, the story of Israel is the story of the Corinthian church now writ large in his scriptural imagination. If the Corinthian believers do not alter their current course, they are in danger of falling. He writes: "These things happened to them [Israel] to serve as an example, and they were written down to instruct us, on whom the ends of the ages have come" (1 Cor 10:11). The times have indeed changed. The end of the ages has already begun. The decisive event of history—the death and resurrection of Jesus—has occurred, which makes the current moment critical. The next big event in the world is the second coming of Jesus, which looms large on the horizon. The divisions, immorality and arrogant elitism of those "with knowledge" in Corinth are serious problems that have eternal consequences, and eternity is just around the corner. So Paul urges them to take the way of escape God is providing—listen to Paul!—and not let temptation bring their ruin.

Divided by worship. The Corinthian church was so divided that even their gatherings for worship caused more injury than good. First, there were gender issues separating men from women, specifically, how women prayed and prophesied and how they related to the men (and angels). Second, there were social issues sep-

---

[9]The discourse is full of scriptural echoes of Israel's desert experience. Paul appears to have expected his audience to recognize these accounts. The Jewish population of the church was likely large and their scriptural literacy was considerable.

WHAT'S MORE . . .
Culture Wars and 1 Corinthians 11:2-34

For Paul the gospel was more than a collection of theological ideas; it was a
lifestyle, a set of traditions to live by (1 Cor 11:2, 23-26). But, what happened when Paul's way of life clashed with local customs? Consider the
Corinthians, who exchanged their apostle's traditions for their own when it
came to worshiping God (1 Cor 11:3-16) and sharing table (1 Cor 11:17-
34). Paul tried to set them straight, and he used every kind of argument to
make the point. For example, in his instructions regarding the behavior of
husbands and wives during worship, Paul relied upon theological arguments
based on biblical texts, that is, that man is made in the image of God,
woman was made from man, wives should cover their heads because of the
angels (from Gen 1:26; 2:21-23; 6:1-2). But he also appealed to common
social practices (women should not shave their heads, 1 Cor 11:5-6) and
natural behavior ("Does not nature itself teach you that if a man wears long
hair, it is degrading to him, but if a woman has long hair, it is her glory?"
1 Cor 11:14-15). Here Paul is being culturally relevant: Corinthians (like
other Roman citizens) thought men with long hair were effeminate, shameful. But, to Jewish men long hair was a sign of honor, distinguishing those
who were keeping a Nazirite vow. In fact, Paul had long hair when he wrote
1 Corinthians, for he had made such a vow at least two years previously
(Acts 18:18). Obviously, for Paul some customs were universally applicable
and others were merely provincial practices. Therefore, when local customs
compromised his gospel, a culture war ensued. With all the talk about heads
and hair, husbands and wives, honor and shame, it is quite apparent Paul
was trying to strike a balance with indigenous traditions when making the
gospel culturally relevant for his time. If a provincial practice helped his
cause, he used it. If a local custom violated the essence of his gospel and the
traditions he taught, he acted to change it.

arating the haves from the have-nots; particularly, the poor were not getting their
fair share of the food at regularly scheduled fellowship meals. Third, there were
spiritual and relational issues separating those who possessed or did not possess
certain highly prized spiritual gifts. The irony of the situation, for Paul, was troubling: what was supposed to exalt God was now dividing his people.

The issue before the apostle is whether men and women ought to wear veils (or cover their heads) when prophesying or praying in public. The question is not, can men and women speak for God or pray in their gatherings? Paul clearly expects both to pray and prophesy in public (1 Cor 11:4-5). Although we don't know the exact situation, it seems that some adult—and thus married—women were praying and prophesying unveiled, violating local customs of sexual distinctiveness and decency.[10] Sexual identity, modesty and dress are culturally determined. Every culture decides what is appropriate. But even cultural issues are not without theological nuance and, for Paul, a proper understanding of creation provides the basis necessary for maintaining order in the community. Viewed from below, (1) woman was created for man; yet (2) man is born from woman; and (3) all things are from God (1 Cor 11:8-12). Paul is able to affirm any cultural or social practice that does not violate these basic principles. Since the veiling of women (wives) in worship maintains the husbands' honor (in that culture), it is a practice worth keeping. But when men wear head coverings[11] in worship, it leads to disorder. Even nature, he thinks, teaches the same lessons (1 Cor 11:14-15).

The Lord's Supper. Paul's account of Jesus' last meal with his disciples is the earliest on record[12] and becomes the basis for the later church practice known as "the Lord's Supper." For Paul the Lord's Supper does four things: (1) it commemorates the past sacrifice of Jesus; (2) it proclaims the present reality of salvation purchased by Christ's broken body and spilled blood; (3) it unifies the many members who come together into one body; and (4) it anticipates the future consummation. So Paul expects the church to gather at the Lord's Table "until he comes" (1 Cor 11:26). Yet despite such lofty musings, the Corinthians were eating the Lord's Supper in an unworthy manner and their guilt had brought dire consequences. Instead of building solidarity, their way of handling the Supper brought shame to the poor. Paul writes: "For all who eat and drink without discerning the body, eat and drink judgment against themselves" (1 Cor 11:29). By "body" Paul does not

---

[10]Paul's statement that a woman should wear a veil "because of the angels" presents an interpretive question. The answer appears related again to creation. Genesis 6:1-4 was being interpreted in Paul's day (*1 Enoch* 6—9; *Jubilees* 5) as a story of lustful angels (sons of God) who came down and engaged in sexual relations with women and fathered a race of beings that brought great tragedy to mankind. This may explain Paul's concern. On the other hand, Winter thinks that Paul is concerned about female modesty when male messengers *(angeloi)* (as spies) visited house churches; see Winter, *After Paul Left Corinth*, pp. 136-37.

[11]Winter argues that men covered their heads with the edge of their toga when performing priestly duties. Claiming a special status (priest) subverted the "natural order" that Paul saw in the universal gifting of the Spirit; see Winter, *After Paul Left Corinth*, pp. 121-23.

[12]Paul's account of the Lord's Supper bears narrative resemblance to the Lukan report (Lk 22:19-20; cf. Mk 14:22-24; Mt 26:26-28).

mean the bread; he is referring to the collective members of the body of Christ. Judgment comes, according to Paul, upon the body because some devour the sacred elements, with little consideration for the other members of the body.[13] So Paul urges them to examine themselves and judge themselves so they will not experience God's judgment (1 Cor 11:28, 31-32).

WHAT'S MORE . . .
Contagious Matters

Ancient people often learned by observation. They had figured out that when a person associated closely with someone with a fever (what we might call the flu), often he too got a fever. They also noticed that when a person associated closely with someone immoral, often he too began to act immorally. We say one is the result of viruses; the other results from influence. Either way, something has seeped into the other person. Christians acting improperly at the Lord's Supper were causing this "disease" to spread to others. "One bad apple spoils the whole bunch," both biologically and ethically.

Spiritual gifts in the body of Christ. Paul answers the Corinthians' question about spiritual gifts by acknowledging the unity and diversity of the gifts. He writes: "Now there are varieties of gifts, but the same Spirit; and there are varieties of services, but the same Lord; and there are varieties of activities, but it is the same God who activates all of them in everyone" (1 Cor 12:4-6). For Paul, the spiritual gifts have a divine origin, a christological focus and an ecclesiastical nature. Regarding their divine origin, Paul credits the Spirit, the Lord (Jesus) and God (the Father)[14] as the source of these gifts (cf. 2 Cor 13:13). Regarding their christological focus, all the gifts point to the lordship of Jesus (2 Cor 12:1-3) and enable the church to extend the mission of Christ. By ecclesiastical nature we mean two things. First, Paul teaches that the Holy Spirit gives to every believer at

---

[13]Stanley Hauerwas rightly reminded us Paul does *not* say that those who are "sick or have died" are necessarily the ones who ate unworthily. The church had allowed a contagion (sin/the world) to invade the body. Christ and Christians healed the body by casting out demons. Paul commands the Corinthians to cast out the one who contaminates the body; "The Sanctified Body: Why Perfection Does Not Require a Self," in *Embodied Holiness*, ed. S. M. Powell and M. E. Lodahl (Downers Grove, Ill.: InterVarsity Press, 1999), pp. 24-28.

[14]Passages like this, which are implicitly trinitarian, provided the raw materials for later doctrinal development along a trinitarian trajectory.

least one gift (1 Cor 12:7), distributed according to his sovereign will (1 Cor 12:11). Second, Paul explains that the manifestations of the Spirit are for the common good (1 Cor 12:7). They are not for the benefit of one or a few but for the entire church.[15]

The human body provides Paul an appropriate analogy for the church's unity in diversity. In 1 Corinthians 12 the apostle develops his notion of the church as "the body of Christ." As the human body is one and has many "members" with various functions, so the body of Christ, the church, is one and has many members (1 Cor 12:12-26). The unity of Christ's body, for Paul, begins in Spirit baptism. All believers are baptized into one body by the one Spirit. The diversity that characterizes people outside the body (e.g., racial, cultural, religious and social) is overcome in baptism. Baptism constitutes the previously diverse population into a new unity in diversity, a diversity of function in the one body. In the new diversity of Christ's body, equality and hierarchy coexist peacefully. Similarly, the diversity of the bodily members acknowledges their interdependence. Every part is necessary. He writes: "If one member suffers, all suffer together with it; if one member is honored, all rejoice together with it" (1 Cor 12:26).

The unity and mutuality of the body is not upset by the variety of gifts, since they have a common, divine source. God has appointed apostles first, prophets second, teachers third, and then miracle workers, healers, helpers, leaders and various kinds of tongues. As founders of churches and those commissioned by the risen Jesus, apostles occupy the highest "office" in the church and, if Paul is an example, appear to exercise many if not most of the gifts.[16] Prophets are those who proclaim the "word of the Lord" during worship and are recognized as men and women uniquely inspired by the Spirit.[17] Teachers seem to have exercised a pastoral role (Eph 4:11) in addition to passing on the church's tradition. The reason that Paul places speaking in tongues last is likely because some in Corinth flaunted this gift and disrupted worship (1 Cor 14:6-40). While no gift is possessed by all—despite the claims of

---

[15]E. Earle Ellis, *Pauline Theology: Ministry and Society* (Grand Rapids: Eerdmans, 1989), pp. 26-37.

[16]This is clearly the earliest meaning of *apostle*. If being commissioned by Jesus during his earthly ministry is an essential element, then there are no longer apostles today; yet then Paul would not have qualified. If being commissioned by Christ to found churches in new areas is the essential element, then apostles are still found today (largely in "mission" areas). Could this explain the large number of miracles often reported there?

[17]It is challenging to understand how Paul could affirm women prophets/pray-ers in 1 Corinthians 11 and then restrict their participation in worship in 1 Corinthians 14:34-36. To address this seeming contradiction, some exegetes have argued that 14:34-36 was a later scribal addition (Gordon Fee), a Corinthian slogan (D. W. Odell-Scott), the contribution of Sosthenes (Richards), pertained only to chattering (Moffatt), or that Paul restricted a wife's judging of her husband's prophetic speech (Witherington, Thiselton, thus, "Let them interrogate their husbands at home").

some—he urges them to seek the greater gifts along the path of love. For Paul, love is not so much a spiritual gift as it is "the way" (1 Cor 12:31), the manner in which all the gifts are practiced. Gifts of inspired speech without love are simply noise. Great generosity or sacrifice incites nothing outside of love's motivation. So Paul celebrates the path of love as he instructs the church on the proper uses of the gifts.

According to Paul, the spiritual gifts are destined to pass away when "the perfect comes" (1 Cor 13:10). The "perfect" refers to the consummation of the age at the second coming of Jesus. All gifts, including prophecy, speaking in tongues and gifts of knowledge, will come to an end at the parousia. Though the spiritual gifts celebrated by the church come from God, the knowledge and abilities they impart are imperfect and partial. The church awaits that day when imperfection gives way to perfection and partial knowledge is eclipsed by seeing God face-to-face. When that day comes, faith, hope and love, the triad of Christian virtue, will accompany the saints into the age to come. They are needed by the church now in the imperfect world; they will be needed in the future when the new creation has fully come (1 Cor 13:13).

The resurrection of the dead. Paul concludes this magisterial letter with his most thorough explanation of the resurrection of Christ and the general resurrection at the end of the age. For him the death, burial, resurrection and the appearances of the risen Messiah make up the center of his gospel (1 Cor 15:3-8). Although some in Corinth argued there is no resurrection of the dead, Paul takes on the naysayers with a rather simple argument: Christ's resurrection guarantees that resurrection from the dead is a current reality and future hope for those who belong to Jesus. If Jesus has not been raised, then (1) Paul's preaching and the Corinthians' faith is empty, (2) sins are not forgiven, and (3) those that have fallen asleep will have perished forever. But the resurrection of Jesus, an event for which there are ample witnesses, disproves their improbable claim. His awakening demonstrates that the end of the age has already commenced. Christ is "the first fruits" of those who have fallen asleep (1 Cor 15:20). At the second coming, all who belong to Jesus will also be resurrected.

As Paul ponders the significance of these events, he envisages Jesus as a type of Adam (cf. Rom 5). By virtue of his resurrection, Christ, the "new Adam," stands at the head of the new creation, and he remedies the problem of death set in motion by the first Adam. As Adam brought death into the world, so the new Adam brings resurrection from the dead. As all die in Adam, so all will be made alive in Christ (1 Cor 15:21-22).[18] Christ, the new Adam, reverses the curse of death.

---

[18]Ellis argues for the translation "All in Adam die; all in Christ will be made alive" (Ellis, *Pauline Theology*, pp. 10-17).

Those who die prior to the parousia will experience the resurrection when he comes. After the parousia death itself is swallowed up and dies along with all the other powers that stand contrary to God. Finally, when all creation is related properly to God's Son, the Son will hand over "all things" to God so that God might be "all in all" (1 Cor 15:24-28).

After his brief sketch of last things, Paul turns to the nature of the resurrection body (1 Cor 15:29-41). Death and burial, he writes, are like planting a seed in the earth. In due time, the seed springs to life with a "body" different from the original, a body of God's choosing. Again, the diversity of flesh and the splendor of the heavenly bodies are a clue to the resurrection body and its glory.[19] These analogies provide some help in understanding the continuity and discontinuity between the body that dies and the body that is resurrected. Regarding continuity, the resurrection does not obliterate individual identity; the "self" remains intact. Regarding discontinuity, the resurrection is a radical transformation from one kind of life to another. The present body is perishable. The resurrection body will be imperishable. The present body is mortal, subject to sin and death. The resurrection body will be immortal, liberated from the powers of sin and death. The present body bears the image of Adam, the man of the earth. The resurrection body will bear the image of the second Adam, the man from heaven.[20]

As a herald of Christ, Paul concludes by disclosing to the Corinthians a "mystery": "We shall not all sleep [the sleep of death], but all of us will be changed, in a flash, in the blink of an eye, at the last trumpet; for the trumpet will blast and the dead will be raised as immortals and we shall be changed" (1 Cor 15:51-52, author's translation). This scheme is similar to what he writes to the Thessalonians (1 Thess 4:13-18). When the heavenly trumpet sounds, the dead are raised and the living are transformed. This massive, world-shattering metamorphosis takes less than a second. Immediately, mortal nature is clothed with immortality and "death is swallowed up in victory" (1 Cor 15:54, quoting Is 25:8, NASB.). For Paul,

---

[19]Paul's analogy of the stars and resurrection owes its substance to Daniel 12:1-3, the clearest affirmation of bodily resurrection in the Old Testament. According to Daniel, those who sleep in the earth will awake, some to life and others to utter disgrace and contempt. Those who are wise and teachers of righteousness will shine like the stars forever. For Paul those who belong to Christ are the wise, righteous teachers who will be transformed in the resurrection and share in the luminous, glorious nature of the stars.

[20]Some interpret Paul's statement that the resurrection will bring a "spiritual body" to mean that he does not believe in bodily resurrection but only spiritual transformation (1 Cor 15:44). This is unlikely given his Pharisaic and apocalyptic background, his gospel and other affirmations of bodily resurrection elsewhere. As Alan Segal argues, the "spiritual body" is "the ordinary body subsumed and transformed by the spirit" (Alan Segal, *Life After Death: The History of the Afterlife in Western Religion* [New York: Doubleday, 2004], p. 430).

this scenario is not wishful, utopian thinking; it is guaranteed by the victory the Lord Jesus Christ won decisively over sin and death.

SECOND CORINTHIANS

Although little time had passed, much had happened between the writing of 1 and 2 Corinthians. Paul had made the painful visit to Corinth, trying to bring a rebel under control (2 Cor 2:1-11). Evidently, the face-to-face encounter didn't work since some of the members refused to back Paul. So, after returning to Ephesus,[21] Paul sent Titus to Corinth, carrying a "sorrowful letter" that was supposed to cause the Corinthians to repent and kick out the obstinate member. While eagerly awaiting word from Titus upon his return, Paul fell into difficulty in Ephesus, narrowly escaping death (Acts 19?). Consequently, Paul was forced to leave town and change his travel plans, deciding he would try to meet up with Titus somewhere in Macedonia (2 Cor 1:8—2:12; 7:5-7). Titus reports that the sorrowful letter had the desired effect: the church shunned the rebellious member and remained loyal to Paul. Paul responds with 2 Corinthians, partly because the Corinthians had gone too far; they wouldn't let the repentant member back into their fellowship. In 2 Corinthians, Paul falls all over himself praising his converts for their loyalty, encouraging them to forgive the disobedient member, reminding them of his ministry of reconciliation (2 Cor 2:5—5:10). After all, Paul was once a rebel before he was reconciled to God. Now, as God's ambassador, Paul challenged the Corinthians: "be reconciled to God" (2 Cor 5:20).

According to Paul, his converts had failed to recognize what the ministry of reconciliation required. It meant "carrying in the body the death of Jesus" (2 Cor 4:10), and "walk[ing] by faith, not by sight" (2 Cor 5:7), "regard[ing] no one from a human point of view" (2 Cor 5:16) and living as "having nothing, and yet possessing everything" (2 Cor 6:10). In other words, it meant living like Jesus ("though he was rich, yet for your sakes he became poor, so that by his poverty you might become rich," 2 Cor 8:9), and emulating Paul ("as servants of God we have commended ourselves in every way: through great endurance, in afflictions, hardships, calamities, beatings, imprisonments," 2 Cor 6:4-5). The Corinthians

---

[21]Why not stay until the matter was resolved? We have no way to know Paul's reasoning, but the answer will lie in their culture and not ours. For example, sometimes an intermediary (the Greek Titus) was the culturally appropriate way to resolve such a conflict; see Margaret Mitchell, "New Testament Envoys in the Context of Greco-Roman Diplomatic and Epistolary Conventions," *Journal of Biblical Literature* 111 (1992): 643; or perhaps Paul had found a ship willing to risk a late fall trip across the Aegean and thus made the trip to Corinth. The ship's schedule may have required Paul to leave sooner than he wished.

needed to learn what it meant to become living sacrifices for the welfare of others. This is why the paradox of Christian existence is the leading motif of 2 Corinthians: "for whenever I am weak, then I am strong" (2 Cor 12:10). The strength-in-weakness theme pervades the entire letter in a variety of apparent contradictions, including joy in suffering, generosity in poverty and life in death. For Paul the theological basis for this paradox is the life, death and resurrection of Jesus. In weakness and suffering Jesus descended into death; in power and joy God raised him from the dead. Therefore, weakness is strength, death is life, and humiliation is glory.

The new covenant and its delegates. The prophets Jeremiah (Jer 31:31-34) and Ezekiel (Ezek 36:24-27) foresaw a day when God would establish a new contract with his people, writing the law on their hearts, cleansing them of their sins and putting a new heart and spirit within them. The old covenant came with glory, indeed so much glory that the Israelites could not look upon Moses' face because of its brightness (2 Cor 3:7). But, in agreement with Ezekiel and Jeremiah, Paul knows that the new covenant has a surpassing glory. According to Paul, it accomplishes what the old covenant does not.

The new covenant, written on the heart by the Spirit, brings (eternal) life. It

---

WHAT'S MORE . . .
Comparing Old with New

Old Covenant	New Covenant
Written on tablets of stone (2 Cor 3:3, 6-7)	Written on the heart by the Spirit (2 Cor 3:3)
Ministry of death (2 Cor 3:6-7)	Ministry of the Spirit (2 Cor 3:6)
Came with glory (2 Cor 3:7)	Comes with greater glory (2 Cor 3:3, 10-11)
Ministry of condemnation (2 Cor 3:9)	Ministry of righteousness (2 Cor 3:9)
Fading away (2 Cor 3:11)	Abiding (2 Cor 3:11)
Veiled and hidden (2 Cor 3:13)	Proclaimed with boldness (2 Cor 3:12)

does more than condemn sin; it establishes righteousness. Furthermore, it will not fade away; it is an everlasting covenant between God and humanity.

Paul believes that whenever the books of Moses are read in the synagogue, a veil lies (metaphorically) over the minds of unbelievers. But when a person turns to the Lord, that veil is removed (2 Cor 3:16; alluding to Ex 34:34). Until this age runs its course and Christ returns, the "god of this age" will continue to veil the truth from those who are perishing. Paul nevertheless proclaims "Jesus Christ as Lord" because the God who created light in the beginning (Gen 1:3) illuminates their hearts with the knowledge of the glory of God in the face of Christ (2 Cor 4:6). Ultimately, for Paul, to see the face of Christ is to encounter the glory of God. And, as the many generations of mystics before and after him also believed, to behold this glory is to be transformed into the image and likeness of God. Yet, when Paul describes seeing the face of Jesus, he has more in mind than mystical experiences. As one who has seen the risen Jesus himself (1 Cor 9:1), he knows firsthand the power of such experiences, but he does not imply that such visions are normative. So, besides in visions and revelations, in what way can one see Jesus? Paul's answer is found again in the nature of apostolic ministry.

The apostles bear this transcendent vision of glorious transformation in their own bodies and ministry. Compared to the spectacular treasure of divine glory, they are only "earthen vessels" (2 Cor 4:7; clay pots). Still they carry in their bodies always the death of Jesus so the life of Jesus may be revealed in their bodies (2 Cor 4:10-12). To say it another way, Paul's ministry is an exhibition of the cross and resurrection of Jesus (cf. Gal 3:1). To see and to hear Paul—and the other apostles with similar ministries—is to see Jesus. To see Jesus, whether in a vision or in the lives of the apostles, is to become more like him. Ultimately, to become more like Jesus is to experience the cross and the resurrection and to be ushered into God's glory-presence. So, the afflictions that the Corinthians experience in this age are only slight and momentary compared with the eternal weight of glory awaiting them in the age to come (2 Cor 4:16-18). In fact, Paul understands that in some way these hardships (cross) are producing the weight of glory (resurrection) to be received on the other side of Christ's return.

Taking down the tent. In 2 Corinthians 5 Paul attempts to describe these invisible, eternal realities by reflecting on what lies beyond death for Christ-believers. The current life is temporary and destined for destruction; our bodies are "earthly tents" that will one day be taken down.[22] But in the future we will receive "a build-

---

[22]This passage is one of the most difficult to interpret. It is also possible Paul is talking corporately and not individually; thus, this present age is an earthly tent to be torn down.

ing from God, a house not made with hands, eternal in the heavens" (2 Cor 5:1). Paul does not say precisely when the dead will receive their permanent dwelling. There are two ways in which his teaching has been taken. The first is often called "soul sleep" (e.g., 1 Cor 15; 1 Thess 4:13-18). It presumes the human being is a body-soul that cannot be separated. At death a person "sleeps" until the parousia, at which time he or she wakes up and receives a new, transformed body.[23] Those sleeping, of course, are not aware of the passage of time. They close their eyes in death, and the next moment of their consciousness they awaken at the resurrection. The second way Paul's teaching is interpreted may be called immediate presence (cf. Phil 1:20-26; 2 Cor 5:1-9). It presumes the human being has a body-soul that can be separated and exist independently. At death, the body is laid in the earth; the soul is present immediately with God in heaven. At the parousia, God will unite the souls of those who have died with new, transformed bodies.

The main point for Paul is to confront those intellectual heirs of Plato who used terms like "tent" for the body and "naked" for the disembodied soul. They considered the body the prison of the soul and likened salvation to release from the constraints of the body-prison. Paul, based on his Jewish heritage, affirms the goodness of the body. Salvation is not about escaping the body; salvation is receiving from God a new, transformed body. For Paul, the basic human disposition toward embodiment is positive not negative. We do not long to be "naked souls" (souls apart from bodies); we long for immortal life to swallow whole our mortality (2 Cor 5:4).

God is the one who made us this way and has given to the church the witness of the Holy Spirit as a down payment on the acquisition of eternal bodies at the parousia—the same Spirit that raised Christ will raise us on the last day. But until then, though we are at home in this earthly body, we are away from the Lord (2 Cor 5:6), even if we would rather it be the other way around (2 Cor 5:8). This should not be interpreted to mean that Paul preferred a disembodied state. It is rather a straightforward expression of his desire to be with Jesus.

The ministry of reconciliation. Paul's message is based fundamentally on this truth: God was in Christ reconciling the world to himself (2 Cor 5:19). For Paul, reconciliation is a central, soteriological metaphor drawn from relational or diplomatic circles. Reconciliation is the act by which a situation of estrangement is overcome and peaceful relations are restored between enemies (cf. Rom 5:8-11).[24]

---

[23]Many tombstones read "Rest in Peace," reflecting this kind of understanding of what lies beyond death prior to the parousia.

[24]Stanley Porter, "Peace, Reconciliation," in *DPL*, pp. 695-96.

SO WHAT?
Does It Matter If We Will Be Disembodied Souls or Not?

The modern image of a winged soul sitting on a cloud and playing a harp is not a biblical picture. (Thank goodness!) Heaven is not our final reward. The goal of eternal life is not to escape from the earth—God's purpose is to reclaim it. The New Testament envisions humans again indwelling a garden on a new, "resurrected" earth (Rev 22). Working and learning will be as much a part of the new garden as the old. Popular theology imagines that after death we will know all things. The Bible does not say this. Paul wrote, "I will know fully, even as I have been fully known" (1 Cor 13:12). In the end, we will know God as we are "fully known" by him—face to face, as it were. But how will we know each other? How will we recognize each other? Will we know everyone "automatically" or will we get to know each other? How will I speak to my Korean brothers? Maybe I'll have to learn to speak Korean. (I'll have time.) Or, perhaps we'll all have to learn a new, heavenly language. There is so much we don't know about life in the age to come. All the more reason we must avoid the temptation of relying upon the ancient Greeks or our modern culture to tell us what eternal life will be like. Maybe the resurrection of Jesus is all we need to know for now.

For Paul, God took the initiative in this work of reconciliation by sending Christ (2 Cor 5:14-15). The appropriate human response to Christ's reconciling work is to accept him and to devote one's energy and vitality to him. The people who undertake this commitment find themselves "in Christ" and part of the "new creation" (2 Cor 5:17). The old, unreconciled creation is doomed to pass; indeed the turning point has already arrived. Therefore, no longer is it appropriate to deal with others "according to the flesh" (2 Cor 5:16), that is, in purely human terms without regard to God's plan and power. The new, reconciled and reconciling reality has come in ways that many never fully anticipated. Those whom God reconciles are given the ministry of reconciliation (2 Cor 5:18-19), that is, they are to announce God's actions and forgiveness in the world and invite all to enter the new creation.

For the apostle, the reconciliation of sinners involved an interchange: "For our sake he [God] made him [Christ] to be sin who knew no sin, so that in him

[Christ] we might become the righteousness of God" (2 Cor 5:21). Put another way, the sinless became sin so the unrighteous could become righteous. Although Paul does not say how Christ became sin—he could be referring to the incarnation ("sending his own Son in the likeness of sinful flesh," Rom 8:3)—most interpreters believe Paul was referring to Christ's death. On the cross Christ became sin, Paul believes, because sinners were on the cross with him. When he died, all died. When he rose, all rose. As a result, all who were with him on the cross have their sins forgiven and become what he essentially is, the righteousness of God. This interchange of sin for righteousness is what makes reconciliation possible. Paul sees himself, and perhaps all reconciled believers, as "ambassadors for Christ" (2 Cor 5:20), diplomats for the heavenly corps. Their main task is to take the message of reconciliation to the world and thereby to establish peace. This is why Paul endures tribulations (2 Cor 6:3-5) and commits himself to virtue (2 Cor 6:6-8). The result is a ministry where God's strength becomes evident through every human weakness.

The collection for the saints in Jerusalem. At this strategic point in the letter, Paul turned his attention to the relief offering—another sacrifice for the welfare of others (2 Cor 8:1—9:15). Since the Corinthians preferred boasting, they might have been pleased to know Paul had been boasting about them to the Macedonians. Even though the Macedonian believers had given a lot of money—beyond their means or what Paul expected—Paul had bragged to them that the Corinthians were prepared to exceed that amount. But what if they weren't ready? What if they hadn't been collecting the money as Paul instructed? Or "if some Macedonians come with me and find that you are not ready, we would be humiliated—to say nothing of you—in this undertaking" (2 Cor 9:4). So Paul reminded the Corinthians of the many reasons why collecting the relief offering was a must: (1) sowing the gospel seed bountifully will mean a bountiful harvest, (2) God blesses abundantly those who give cheerfully, (3) the relief offering will cause the Jerusalem church to thank God for the Gentile mission, and (4) it will confirm the obedience of the Corinthians (2 Cor 9:6-15). Paul was so confident the Corinthians would come through with a sizeable gift that he offered praise to God in advance of his arrival: "Thanks be to God for his indescribable gift!" (2 Cor 9:15). The pressure was on. The Corinthians had to reveal their thankfulness for God's grace by finishing the task.

The word "grace" *(charis)* occurs throughout 2 Corinthians 8—9. For Paul its most basic meaning is God's unmerited favor (undeserved kindness) directed toward humanity in the life, crucifixion and resurrection of Jesus. In 2 Corinthians 8—9 Paul weds the collection for the impoverished saints in Jerusalem with a theology of grace; he expands the meaning of *grace* to refer to the act or opportunity of participating in the collection (e.g., 2 Cor 8:4, 6, see the NRSV footnotes). In this sense the gracious response of the Macedonians (2 Cor 8:1) to help the poor Judeans exhibits the grace they have received from God. To put it another way, to whom much is given (God's grace) much is required (the Corinthian participation in the collection). So the Macedonians were the perfect example for the Corinthians to emulate. Despite severe affliction, their abundant joy and deep poverty had overflowed into an extraordinary act of generosity (2 Cor 8:2). They gave beyond their means. The odd juxtaposition of poverty and joyful generosity offered Paul another example of how Christ makes strength in weakness "normal." In Christ's grace, generous poverty is not an oxymoron; it is business as usual. This kind of giving begins, in Paul's mind, with giving oneself to the Lord and then to his agents (2 Cor 8:5). Once that is done, it is easy to open the purse to alleviate poverty and suffering among brothers and sisters.

As we see throughout his letters, Paul's theology is grounded in the life and work of Jesus. He turns from the generosity of the Macedonians to that of Jesus in order to revive the Corinthians' stalled interest in the relief offering for Jerusalem. He writes: "For you know the generous act [lit., grace] of our Lord Jesus Christ, that though he was rich, yet for your sakes he became poor, so that by his poverty you might become rich" (2 Cor 8:9). This verse restates an earlier theme of the interchange that took place in Christ's life and death:

The sinless one became sin so the unrighteous could become righteous. (2 Cor 5:21)

The rich one became poor so the poor could become rich. (2 Cor 8:9)

Strength in weakness. Paul ended 2 Corinthians with a final warning about Corinthian misperceptions: what is strength and what is weakness, what is honorable and what is shameful, what is worth boasting about and what is irrelevant. As a matter of fact, Paul's tone changes dramatically in this section (2 Cor 10:1—13:13). One minute he is lavishing praise upon the Corinthians for their obedience, the next he is lashing out at them for their impertinence. What happened? Some think that this section of the letter may be an imbedded version of the "sorrowful letter" and that 2 Corinthians is actually a collection of fragments. Others account for the abrupt shift in Paul's attitude to a report he received while composing the letter (which often took weeks): intruders have corrupted Paul's gospel work in Corinth (see 2 Cor 11:4-6, 20-23).[25] It could simply be, however, that Paul first wanted to encourage the congregation he nearly lost to the rebel member, praising them for their loyalty and reminding them of their commitment to the relief offering. Then, afterwards, he turned to the problem reported by Titus. In other words, Titus had brought good news and bad news. At first Paul celebrated the good news (a rarity when it came to the Corinthians), then he took up the bad news, ending his letter with a stinging rebuke.[26] Here Paul exposes the same kind of personal feelings and vulnerabilities as he did throughout the letter, that is, how Paul doesn't measure up to the Corinthians' standards (2 Cor 10:1-11), especially when compared to other teachers/apostles (2 Cor 10:12—12:13), and how he anticipates his next meeting with the Corinthians will not go well (2 Cor 12:14—13:4). It all has to do, once again, with the way Paul sees things and the way the Corinthians see things. To Paul, weakness is strength, shame is honor, foolishness is wisdom, and humility is the power of God. This is why the Corinthians did not appreciate Paul, did not understand the gospel and therefore did not realize what was required of them (2 Cor 13:5-10).

In the midst of cataloguing his weaknesses and difficulties, Paul narrates the accounts of two mystical ascents into heaven in the third person ("a man in Christ," 2 Cor 12:1-10). The reason for such a rhetorical tangent is to focus attention away from the fact he is boasting momentarily in something other than weakness. He is a man in Christ who has had visions and revelations of the Lord. He has been caught up to the third (the highest) heaven. He has seen the heavenly paradise. He has heard things no mortal could or should speak of. This kind of report may sound puzzling to us, but it was common enough in Paul's day (cf. Rev 4). In the apocalyptic tradition mystics often sought visions and practiced techniques in order to receive revelations.[27] We are not privy to exactly how the man in Christ experienced these ascents. Even he is not sure how he makes the journeys (whether

---

[25]We have examples of other letters where late news caused the letter writer to shift his tone abruptly (see Cicero *Letters to Friends* 2.13.3). Letter-writing practices offer another possibility as well. Since 2 Corinthians was from Paul and Timothy (2 Cor 1:1), perhaps the tempering influence of Timothy is gone for the letter's conclusion. The "we:I" ratio reverses between chapters 1—9 and 10—13. Such autographed postscripts were not uncommon; Paul seems to emphasize his role in 2 Corinthians 10:1; and it matches a possible severity in other postscripts (e.g., Philem); see Richards, *First-Century Letter Writing*, pp. 174-75.

[26]See Ben Witherington III, *Conflict and Community in Corinth: A Socio-Rhetorical Commentary on 1 and 2 Corinthians* (Grand Rapids: Eerdmans, 1995), pp. 429-32; Paul had been answering incendiary charges brought against him throughout the letter (2 Cor 1:17; 2:17; 3:1; 4:2; 6:3; 7:2), but turned directly to address those making the accusations in this section.

[27]Alan Segal, *Paul the Convert: The Apostolate and Apostasy of Saul the Pharisee* (New Haven, Conn.: Yale University Press, 1990), pp. 35-37.

in the body or out of the body). But these glorious events ultimately remind him of weakness because God has given him "a thorn in the flesh" to keep him from being carried away by such ecstasies. Precisely what his thorn in the flesh is, we do not know. Some speculate it is a physical or emotional illness—he does mention eye problems on one occasion (Gal 4:15). Others opine it is his opponents—he does call the thorn a "messenger" rather than a "message." Whatever the case, he believes God sent this "messenger of Satan" to harass him and keep him from unseemly celebration (2 Cor 12:7). Three times Paul prays to the Lord Jesus that this thorn will leave him.[28] He ceases when the Lord speaks: "My grace is sufficient for you, for power is made perfect in weakness" (2 Cor 12:9). From that day Paul begins to boast in his weaknesses so the power of Christ can rest fully on him. For Christ's sake he is content with weakness, hardship and persecution: "for whenever I am weak, then I am strong" (2 Cor 12:10). Therefore his converts should need no more "proof that Christ is speaking in me" (2 Cor 13:3).

CONCLUSION

Reading through 1 and 2 Corinthians, we are privileged to only half of a conversation that at times became very tense. As Paul and his letters traveled back and forth across the Aegean, we see a man vacillating between anxiety and elation over the progress of his spiritual children. Though he desired to be with them as they worked through divisions, moral and legal questions, and other spiritual ills, he could be present often only through letters and couriers that represented him. But these letters had a profound impact upon the church as they sifted through every word to discover the import of Paul's glorious gospel.

The Corinthian experiment worked. If Paul's law-free gospel produced a church of obedient believers in Corinth, then it would work anywhere. Paul probably didn't think in such pragmatic terms. Nevertheless, the fact Paul was able to rein in the wild behavior of the Corinthian converts provided more proof that the only things Gentiles needed to lead holy lives were the power of the Holy Spirit and the gospel according to Paul. That Paul wrote his letter to the Roman church while he was in Corinth, envisioning new territories for his gospel ministry, reveals the confidence of an apostle who knows whereof he speaks. His gospel changed lives, even immoral pagans in Corinth. He knew God called him to be the apostle to the Gentiles. Therefore, he was convinced he would be the one to take the message of Christ to all the nations, as far as land would take him, to the end of the

---

[28]The "three times" prayer may recall that Jesus prays three times in the garden for the cup of suffering to be removed. Ultimately, Jesus surrenders to the will of the Father (Mk 14:32-42 and par.).

world. And he would need Rome to do it. Opportunity and need had come together.[29] It was time to write another letter.

READ MORE ABOUT IT

DPL Articles:

"Corinthians, Letters to the," pp. 164-79, by S. J. Hafemann.

"Discipline," pp. 214-18; esp. "2. Evidence of Paul's Disciplinary Practice," pp. 215-18, by T. E. Schmidt.

"Gifts of the Spirit," pp. 339-47, by G. D. Fee.

"Man and Woman," pp. 583-92, by C. S. Keener.

"Marriage and Divorce, Adultery and Incest," pp. 594-601, by G. F. Hawthorne.

"Strong and Weak," pp. 916-18, by M. B. Thompson.

"Wisdom Christology," pp. 969-71, by E. J. Schnabel.

---

[29]Paul had the time and living situation necessary to write a letter; it would take the Corinthians time to gather the offering—Luke tells us three months (Acts 20:3). The availability of Tertius (Rom 16:22) may also have encouraged Paul to write. There are some indicators that Tertius had skills beyond that of the ordinary agora secretary; see Richards, *Letter Writing*, pp. 130 n. 29, 151-52.

7

The Itinerant Paul

Romans

BY THIS TIME IN HIS MINISTRY, Paul had earned a reputation that had reached the ears of Rome. Since Paul had not preached the gospel in Rome, the Christians there must have heard about Paul and his law-free gospel from friends (Rom 16:3, 7, 11, 13) and foes (Rom 3:8). Obviously, the apostle to the Gentiles did not start the church in Rome (Rom 1:10-13); we do not know who did. But, since all roads led to Rome, it is not surprising the gospel had reached the city before Paul had a chance to visit. In fact, there is evidence a church had formed in Rome before A.D. 49. Suetonius recorded that the Emperor Claudius expelled Jews from Rome because of problems related to conflicts over "Chrestus."[1] Also, when Paul first came to Corinth, he met Prisca and Aquila, two Christian tent makers who were victims of Claudius's edict (Acts 18:2). Indeed, Prisca and Aquila may have been the connection whereby Paul learned of the church in Rome and the Romans heard about Paul. In any event, by the time Paul wrote his letter, the church had been in existence in Rome for at least a decade. Christians in Rome had been meeting for quite some time without the apostle's help or advice. Yet, for some reason, Paul decided to send the believers in Rome a letter—the longest of them all. Why? What business did Paul have with the Roman Christians? Why did he believe it was his prerogative to offer pastoral advice to a group of people who were not his converts? And, why did Paul write such a lengthy letter, when all he wanted was to ask Ro-

---

[1]Did Suetonius confuse *Christus* (a Latinized form of "Christ") with *Chrestus,* a common slave name? If so, the dispute was likely between Jews and Jewish Christians.

man Christians for help in his westward mission to Spain?

Romans was the only Pauline letter sent to establish contact with a congregation. Paul stated such a purpose in the beginning and toward the end of his letter. First, Paul wrote to the Romans in order to tell them of his plans to visit them—that he wanted to establish a friendship by exchanging spiritual gifts, and that he hoped to add converts to their number "as I have among the rest of the Gentiles" (Rom 1:11-13). Then, toward the end of the letter, Paul comes back to the purpose of his writing. His letter was meant to help them with matters of faith (Rom 15:14-15), to explain the purpose of his ministry (Rom 15:16-21), to ask for their support of his mission to Spain (Rom 15:22-29), and to ask for their prayers in light of the dangers awaiting him in Jerusalem (Rom 15:30-32). His purpose is rather straightforward. Paul was trying to make friends in Rome. He needed their help. It's what comes between these stated purposes that leaves scholars puzzling over the occasion of Romans.

THE OCCASION OF ROMANS

From Romans 1:16—15:13, Paul offered the fullest theological explanation of his gospel found anywhere in all of his letters. Unlike in 1 Corinthians, where Paul was taking on issue after issue, in Romans the apostle was seemingly fixed on one topic: the righteousness of God in Christ. Indeed, the letter reads like one extended argument ("therefore/then" occurs forty-eight times in Romans!).[2] This has led some interpreters to believe that what we have in Romans is a complete version of the gospel according to Paul—a systematic theology of sorts. There is no doubt that Romans contains some of Paul's best work. His logic is tight; his arguments proceed with clarity and force, each building upon the other, leading the reader (listener) to conclude that one God has revealed one gospel for all people, for all time, regardless of ethnicity. And Paul seems to cover every theological base in his argument: theology and anthropology, Christology and soteriology, ecclesiology and eschatology. Several doctrines, however, are missing from this important letter; for example, where is the teaching regarding the return of Christ, or the importance of the Lord's Table? So Romans is no compendium of Pauline theology; Paul wasn't trying to get down on paper everything he believed. Nevertheless, the question still remains: why did Paul make such an elaborate argument for the singularity of his gospel to a church he never visited? Was his emphasis on the universality of his mission (good news for Jews and Gentiles) intended as

---

[2]The Greek word is *oun*.

groundwork for soliciting support for his plan to go to Spain—a "this is what I preach so you can help me" appeal? Or, like his other letters, was Paul writing to address issues in the church in Rome? Does Paul's "neither Jew nor Greek" argument provide a social commentary on ethnic problems in Rome? In other words, was the occasion of this letter prompted by Paul's need or Roman issues?

A closer reading of the letter, however, reveals that Paul had more in mind than establishing a friendship and seeking their help. That was his stated purpose. But the length of the letter and the presence of so many ethnic references (Rom 1:16—4:25; 9:1-11:32; 15:7-33) suggest that Paul had other reasons as well. Perhaps Paul

---

SO WHAT?
Roman Problems or Paul's Needs: Does It Matter?

Well, if Paul was summarizing his gospel in Romans in order to introduce himself, then we can use the letter to suggest these are the themes that are nearest and dearest to Paul's heart, perhaps the center of his gospel. In this case, "justification by faith," a major theme in Romans, is a central theme and worthy of leading a Reformation. On the other hand, if the problems addressed in the letter arose from the Roman church, then perhaps "justification by faith" is no more the essence of Paul's theology than is "the unity of the body of Christ"—the emphasis of 1 Corinthians.

---

kept emphasizing that Jews and Greeks needed the gospel, that God is the God of Jews and Gentiles, that God was still going to make good on promises he made to the Jewish people, and that Gentiles shared in the covenant promises God made to Abraham because Christians in Rome were divided along ethnic lines.[3] Some have suggested Claudius's edict was to blame. Once Jews were allowed to return to Rome after Nero lifted the ban in A.D. 54, Jewish Christians faced a dilemma. They were not welcome among their countrymen in the synagogues but did not belong in the Gentile house churches either. Gentiles had grown accustomed to meeting with Gentiles. Notice, Paul did not address his letter to the *ekklēsia* in Rome, choosing instead the more curious expression "all God's beloved" (Rom 1:7). And Romans 16:3-16 gives evidence there were at least five cell groups of Christians meeting in different locations in Rome (the "house church" of Prisca

---

[3]See Philip Esler, *Conflict and Identity in Romans: The Social Setting of Paul's Letter* (Minneapolis: Fortress, 2003).

and Aquila, Rom 16:5, those of Aristobulus, Rom 16:10, those of Narcissus, Rom 16:11, the "brothers and sisters who are with" Asyncritus et al., Rom 16:14, and "all the saints who are with" Philologus et al., Rom 16:15). Some Roman Christians had distinctive Jewish names (Mary, Andronicus, Junia), while others had Greek names (Narcissus, Hermes, Philologus, Olympas) or slave names (Ampliatus, Urbanus, Stachys). Since Jewish names are clustered together in Paul's list of greetings, it may confirm that house churches fostered ethnic divisions. Indeed, some scholars even see Paul's instruction to "greet one another with a holy kiss" as an innocuous way of forcing these subgroups to acknowledge each other in the faith (Rom 16:16). If it is true that ethnic tensions led to divisions in the church at Rome, then it makes Paul's theological argument less "theoretical" and more critical to the success of his mission.

But, did Paul's argument for Gentile inclusion in Romans lead to Jewish exclusion? In other words, did the gospel according to Paul require the dissolution of Jewish identity? At times he certainly seems to suggest the idea, for example when he places all humanity under the same indictment of sin (Rom 1:18—3:20). Since Jews and Greeks both need the gospel, then Paul was essentially saying to the divided congregation that "there is neither Jew nor Greek in the body of Christ"— these things don't matter. But if that were the case, why would Paul hold up the claim there was unfinished business between God and his elect in Romans 9—11? God made a covenant that was ethnocentric. Jewish identity was still important to God. Abraham's covenant was still in effect. So, the question for Paul (as well as all Jews), then, wasn't whether God still had a covenant with Israel or that Gentiles should be included in Abraham's covenant, but how? Of course, Paul believed faith in Jesus Christ made Gentiles members of the covenant. But, did that mean Jews had to believe in Christ to receive the promises God made to Abraham? And, if so, did they have to give up Jewish identity—circumcision, dietary laws, sabbath days—to maintain covenant obedience?

This is where the great scholarly divide appears in the Romans debate.[4] Ironically, where Paul has been the most forthcoming with his theological ideas—Romans!—scholars have developed the most diverse opinions regarding the implications of the apostle's theologizing. First, some scholars take ethnicity out of the context of Romans, diffusing the explosive issue of covenant relations. In other words, Paul wasn't addressing a particular problem in Rome when he wrote this letter. Paul was simply making generic statements about the implications of his

---

[4]See Karl Donfried, ed., *The Romans Debate* (Peabody, Mass.: Hendrickson, 1991).

gospel, for Jews and for Greeks. Ethnic references were systemic to the universality of the gospel he preached. Therefore, dietary issues concerning the "weak" and "strong" in Romans 14:1—15:6 should not be taken as analogous to Jews and Gentiles. In fact, it is argued that problems Paul had recently faced in Corinth influenced the apostle's vocabulary as he extended these regional issues to a universal audience—like the church in Rome. Thus, Paul was not addressing any particular groups in Rome. Paul had no pastoral influence or purpose in his letter to the Romans. Paul was working out the theological significance of his gospel in general—it just so happens the Christians in Rome were the beneficiaries of his ruminations.[5] But, would Paul write such a lengthy letter, at quite an expense, without a target audience? Paul appears very intentional in his letters to other churches. Besides, even if the first two-thirds of the letter could be seen as a generic argument for the verity of his gospel, how does one explain the rather specific instructions Paul gives in Romans 12:1—16:20? The letter reads like a word on target.

Second, a few scholars have argued that Paul was not trying to make Jewish people accountable to his gospel. Instead, Paul was arguing for Gentile inclusion without Jewish exclusion. That is to say, in Romans Paul was setting forth the idea of two covenants: one for Jews and another for Gentiles. This explains why Paul holds the idea that circumcision is valuable in light of covenant obedience (Rom 2:25). Paul did not maintain that covenant promises belonged only to those who believed in Christ Jesus. He was simply claiming Gentiles could be grafted into the olive tree of Israel without keeping the law, that is, via his gospel. Jews were saved by grace through the law; Gentiles by grace through faith in Jesus. So Paul argued passionately for Gentile inclusion in order to gain the support of the Jewish contingency in the Roman church for his mission to Gentiles. His contention with Israel was they failed to be the light to the Gentiles. What Israel did not do, God has done through the gospel according to Paul.[6] The problem with this line of thinking, however, is the curse Paul wished upon himself, to be "cut off from Christ for the sake of my own people" (Rom 9:3). If the Jewish people were safe without Christ, why would Paul have such "great sorrow and unceasing anguish" over their unbelief (Rom 9:2)? As far as Paul was concerned, Jews who rejected his gospel rejected God's righteousness for themselves (Rom 10:3). The only thing he could hope for would be that his kinsmen according to the flesh

---

[5]In this view, the dialogical nature of the letter was due to a particular style of rhetoric, the diatribe, and not to an actual dialogue with the Roman church.

[6]See Lloyd Gaston, *Paul and the Torah* (Vancouver: University of British Columbia Press, 1987), pp. 135-50.

would not "persist in their unbelief" but would be grafted back into the olive tree of God's salvation before the last day (Rom 11:23-27).

Third, some scholars try to reconcile the implications of Paul's gospel and Jewish identity by centering on the apostle's view of the law. Since keeping the law was the exclusive means of maintaining covenant for Jews, then how Paul dealt with the law (in his argument for the righteousness of God) could help us clarify questions of ethnicity and covenant relations. Indeed, a literal interpretation of the Hebrew Scriptures leads to Judaism. If Gentiles obeyed the whole law, they would become Jews.[7] That would make Paul's gospel (not to mention Christ's death) unnecessary, since a right relationship with God could be maintained by keeping covenant—obedience to the Law—a Jewish privilege. Therefore, Paul objected to the law on ethnic grounds—it excluded Gentiles by definition.[8]

But didn't Paul object to the law because it promoted boasting in human merit?[9] Paul argued for the righteousness of God based on faith and not works. Therefore, the law and Paul's gospel would be mutually exclusive, because the law required works and the gospel according to Paul required only faith in Christ. After all, Paul did not discover the righteousness of God in Christ because of his obedience to the law. Instead, his Damascus Road experience came by grace through faith.[10] So, according to this reversion to the "Lutheran" view of Paul, the apostle objected to the law on theological grounds—no man will be able to stand before God on the last day and claim righteousness because of his meritorious works, that is, obedience to the law.

Finally, some scholars think we have misunderstood the occasion of Romans by ignoring the political intent of Paul's theologizing. Paul's arguments for the "righteousness of God apart from works of law" should not be read as a polemic against Judaism per se. Instead, Paul had bigger designs for his mission; he was attacking the social injustices of Roman imperialism—the so-called Roman peace that came by strength, law and the worship of Caesar (this letter was written to Romans). This is why Paul started the letter by listing the failures of iconic worship and the social problems that resulted from such "ungodliness." The rhetorical strategy of Paul's argument is plain: Roman "righteousness/justice" is a far cry

---

[7]According to Stephen Westerholm, Paul objected to the law because Gentiles could not keep it (it was given only to Jews), see *Perspectives Old and New on Paul: The Lutheran "Paul" and His Critics* (Grand Rapids: Eerdmans, 2004), pp. 418-19.

[8]So Sanders and the "New Perspective."

[9]See Simon J. Gathercole, *Where Is Boasting? Early Jewish Soteriology and Paul's Response in Romans 1-5* (Grand Rapids: Eerdmans, 2002), pp. 197-215.

[10]See Seyoon Kim, *Paul and the New Perspective: Second Thoughts on the Origins of Paul's Gospel* (Grand Rapids: Eerdmans, 2002), pp. 51-53.

from the righteousness of God that is revealed by the gospel according to Paul. Indeed, what most Romans would consider shameful—a message about a crucified Lord who restores the whole world—Paul sees as the very power of God for salvation. "In the place of the salvation of the Pax Romana, based on force, there is the salvation of small groups, cooperatively interacting with one another to extend their new forms of communality to the end of the world."[11] This is why Paul sent Phoebe (a patroness) to Rome with this letter: to solicit support among the tenement (poor) and house (wealthy) churches for his missional effort to extend the network of churches even to the "barbarians" in Spain.[12] So, Paul was speaking generally of social justice, not particularly of individual righteousness, when he argued for a justification by faith that comes without works of law.[13]

Yet in Romans (more so than any other letter) Paul quotes Jewish law in his arguments against the righteousness of God via works of law. Why? Although there are many "key passages" to Paul's argument in Romans, the issue could be resolved if we knew what Paul meant by these two statements: "For it is not the hearers of the law who are righteous in God's sight, but the doers of the law who will be justified" (Rom 2:13), and "For Christ is the end of the law so that there may be righteousness for everyone who believes" (Rom 10:4).

Was Paul speaking about "the doers of the law" "Christianly" or "Jewishly"? Was Paul arguing for the finality of the law or the necessity of its fulfillment? When he wrote "end," did he mean "over and done with" or "goal"? Was he saying faith in Christ replaces the law as the means of maintaining covenant—exchanging one kind of righteousness for another? Or, was he suggesting righteousness in Christ completes the law, so that Christ-believers keep the law better than anyone? That is, through the indwelling Spirit, Christ-believers are empowered to keep the law.

At times, Paul sounds like he believes the old age of law is over—it's a power that doesn't work anymore: "But now, apart from law, the righteousness of God has been disclosed . . . . But now we are discharged from the law, dead to that which held us captive" (Rom 3:21; 7:6). Therefore, that which divides Jews from Gentiles (the law!) is no longer operative. Ethnic distinctions are erased. On the other hand, elsewhere Paul suggests the law is still in effect: it convicts sinners (Rom 3:19-20) and is fulfilled by Christ-believers (Rom 8:4). In other words, Paul argued that righteousness via faith in Christ is the climax of a covenant still in

---

[11]Robert Jewett, *Romans*, Hermeneia (Minneapolis: Fortress, 2007), p. 143.
[12]Ibid., pp. 88-80.
[13]Ibid., p. 273.

force.[14] The gospel is the fulfillment of a story that began with Abraham. So Abraham is the model believer before the gospel of Jesus Christ—for the circumcised and uncircumcised (Rom 4:3-12). Abraham is the father of Christ-believing Gentiles because he was God's first Gentile convert. Abraham is the father of Christ-believing Jews because he had "resurrection" faith that God would bring his dead loins and Sarah's dead womb to life (Rom 4:19-24). Therefore, according to Paul, Jewish identity markers remain—established by the law—in the working out of God's covenant promises (even God still recognizes the difference between natural and grafted branches, Rom 11:17-21).

Paul seemed to hold two sets of competing ideas:

1. Those who obey the law keep covenant with God, and yet righteousness can only be found by faith in Christ; and

2. The gospel replaced the old covenant, establishing a new age of righteousness, and yet the righteousness of God in Christ fulfilled/continued the prior covenant of Abraham.

A few scholars have said this is fairly typical of Paul; he is inconsistent and therefore incoherent (in the technical sense of not having a view that "coheres"). Paul did not have a unified field theory when it came to the cosmology of salvation.[15] Paul himself had not yet figured out the connection between law, covenant and faith in Christ.

Most interpreters, however, find Paul to be theologically astute and coherent, especially in Romans. Jews have an advantage in the righteousness of God because they have the law, but all people are equally under the power of sin and in need of salvation through Christ. God shows no favorites—he is the God of Jews and Gentiles—yet Israel is his chosen people. The law is holy and good, serving its divine purpose, and yet God has revealed righteousness apart from the law. Circumcision is still valuable for those who keep the law, and yet only those who live by the power of Christ's Spirit fulfill the law. Nothing shall separate those in Christ Jesus from the love of God, but branches can still be broken off the olive tree. Israel failed to obtain salvation, but God's choice is irrevocable. Abraham is not only the father of Jews according to the flesh, but also of Gentiles according to the spirit. Paul could speak of ethnic distinctions as fixed realities in the economy of God's salvation and still maintain that the mercy of God is a mystery that changes every-

---

[14]See N. T. Wright, *The Climax of the Covenant: Christ and the Law in Pauline Theology* (Minneapolis: Fortress, 1992), pp. 231-57.

[15]See E. P. Sanders, *Paul, the Law, and the Jewish People* (Minneapolis: Fortress, 1993), pp. 75-81; and Heikki Räisänen, *Paul and the Law* (Minneapolis: Fortress, 1986), pp. 128-54.

thing: "O the depth of the riches and wisdom and knowledge of God! How unsearchable are his judgments and how inscrutable his ways!" (Rom 11:33). Indeed, Romans reveals not only Paul's attempt at uncovering these mysterious ways of God, but also how such theologically diverse ideas hold together.[16]

The argument in Romans divides easily into two unequal halves: chapters 1-11 deal with the righteousness of God in Christ, and chapters 12-16 describe what that life is supposed to look like—individually and corporately. The first half of the letter is comprised of three arguments: (1) why everyone needs the righteousness of God in Christ (Rom 1—4), (2) what this righteousness does for the Christbeliever (Rom 5—8), and (3) how this righteousness fits into God's covenant with Israel (Rom 9—11). Then, in the second half of the letter (Rom 12—16) Paul offered several bits of advice for the Roman congregation on how to live faithfully like Christ: as a living sacrifice (Rom 12:1-21), by submitting to God (Rom 13:1-14), by deferring to others (Rom 14:1—15:13), by supporting the apostle's ministry (Rom 15:14-33), and by welcoming Phoebe and each other (Rom 16:1-27).

THE GOSPEL (GOOD NEWS) HE PREACHED

Paul begins Romans with a clear statement of his apostolic call and the gospel. He is a servant of Christ Jesus, called to be an apostle and set apart for the gospel of God (Rom 1:1). His apostleship is a work of divine grace for the express purpose of leading Gentiles to the "obedience of faith" for Jesus' name (Rom 1:5). Paul uses the same phrase in Romans 16:26, so that the entire letter is framed by the notion of faithful obedience to the gospel.[17] For Paul, faith is a comprehensive term that expresses the heart of the gospel. This "good news" (1) begins in the covenant faithfulness of God, (2) is manifested in Jesus' faithfulness to his cross-centered mission and (3) demands a response of faith and obedience on the part of humanity. Paul's divinely inspired message stands in continuity with the preaching of Israel's prophets (Rom 1:2). Utilizing a preformed Christian tradition, Paul describes the content of the gospel in terms of Jesus' sonship. First, Jesus is the Son of God from the line of King David according to the flesh (Rom 1:3). He fulfills the messianic prophecies that speak of David's son as the son of God (2 Sam 7:12-

---

[16]See Francis Watson, *Paul and the Hermeneutics of Faith* (London: T & T Clark, 2004) who believes that Paul's contradictory positions on the law's effectiveness regarding righteousness is due to dissonant voices within the law, what Watson calls the "optimism" and "pessimism" of the law. Sometimes, the law implies that righteousness can be found by obeying its decrees. At other times, the law is completely resigned to the fact that "no one" obeys God; see especially pp. 66-77.

[17]In cases like this, when a writer uses similar or identical phrases or ideas at the beginning and end of a portion of text in order to bracket, or frame, material, scholars refer to it as an *inclusio*.

16; cf. 4QFlor). Second, in the resurrection God installs him as the "Son-of-God-in-power." This new stage of Jesus' sonship begins at the resurrection, the supreme act and promise of power energized by the Holy Spirit.

The theme of the Roman letter is stated succinctly in Romans 1:16-17:

> For I am not ashamed of the gospel; it is the power of God for salvation to everyone who has faith, to the Jew first and also to the Greek. For in it the righteousness of God is revealed through faith for faith; as it is written, "The one who is righteous will live by faith."

Despite the scandal of the cross, Paul is not ashamed of the gospel. This is because God's power is revealed in the gospel and makes salvation a reality for everyone who believes, Jews first, then Greeks. In Paul's vernacular, *salvation* is a comprehensive term that incorporates all of the benefits of the gospel. It includes (1) the forgiveness of sins, (2) reconciliation and living at peace with God, (3) adoption into God's eternal family, (4) redemption from slavery to sin, death and other spiritual forces, (5) resurrection from the dead at the parousia, (6) acquittal at the final judgment and (7) glorification with him for eternity. So salvation is not merely going to heaven after death; it is a wide-ranging program of transformation for humanity and creation. Specifically, Paul unpacked the salvation found in the gospel as the revelation of "the righteousness of God" (Rom 1:17), a theologically loaded phrase. First, righteousness describes the character of God. God is righteous and just, faithful to his covenant obligations. Second, since character reveals itself in action, "the righteousness of God" refers to the saving activity of God that extends righteousness to all creation. For Paul, it was not enough for God to be righteous; he must act consistently with his righteousness to establish justice in the world.[18] He did this by sending his Son. Paul believed that what God had accomplished in Christ demonstrated his covenant faithfulness and established salvation for Jews and Gentiles.

The revelation of God's righteousness is qualified as being "through faith for faith" (Rom 1:17). "Through faith" emphasizes the divine source of righteousness. "For faith" describes the requisite human response to God's gift. In other words, the basis for God's saving activity now revealed in the world through Christ is found in God's faithfulness to his promises made to Abraham, Moses, David and his other covenant partners. In sending his Son, God fulfills the commitments he made previously. But God's covenant faithfulness also prompts human faith in the

---

[18]The English terms "righteousness" and "justice" are both acceptable translations for Paul's term here: *dikaiosynē*.

gospel. Ultimately, in order to be saved, people must believe and obey the gospel message. So the goal of God's saving acts is to create a righteous people identified by faith (what Paul called "predestination"). Paul had come to this understanding by re-reading Habakkuk 2:4 in light of his experience with Christ. Paul's gospel confirms what is written: "The one who is righteous will live by faith" (Rom 1:17). Paul took from the prophet two truths: (1) righteous(ness) is necessary for life and salvation and (2) faith is the means of righteousness.

THE BAD NEWS: THE REVELATION OF GOD'S WRATH

Before Paul elaborates on the good news, he reflects on the bad news, the reality of God's wrath that is already in the world because of the ungodliness and wickedness of all people (Rom 1:18). Three times he uses the phrase "God gave them up" to indicate that God's wrath is evident in something of a hands-off policy toward the world. The wrath he describes consists primarily of God's stepping aside and leaving us to our own devices. Paul does not mean that God is taking a passive, wait-and-see disposition toward the world; it is best understood as an active absence, a divine decision to allow the unredeemed human will to reach its determined and just end (cf. Is 5; 1 Cor 5:5). If God's presence is salvation and blessing, then God's "absence" is destruction. But the "already" nature of God's wrath, for Paul, does not preclude the not-yet, eschatological wrath to come. A day of wrath is coming for all who persist in their sinful ways. Yet the apostle's point here is to emphasize the shape of divine wrath already in the world in contrast with the "but now" revelation of God's righteousness (Rom 3:21).

God's wrath is already seen in that "God gave them up" to impurity that dishonors their bodies and is fueled by their lusts (Rom 1:24-25). For Paul, the pervasiveness and foolishness of idolatry proved the sinfulness of humanity and was one crucial reason for God's displeasure with the world. Second, "God gave them up" to dishonorable passions as men and women exchanged natural for unnatural sexual acts (Rom 1:26-28). Paul's thoughts on sexuality are rooted in Genesis 1 and the conviction that the creation order is "good." Any deviation is, by definition, not good and a violation of creation. By natural intercourse, Paul means heterosexual unions, unions consistent with nature and capable of leading to procreation ("be fruitful, multiply, fill the earth"). For Paul, the presence and pervasiveness of homosexual practice constituted the cause and effect of God's wrath in the world. Finally, "God gave them up" to a debased mind and improper conduct (Rom 1:28-31).

If idolatry or homoerotic practice did not apply to his audience, then the next list of sins would likely encompass everyone left. He named wickedness, covetousness, envy, gossiping, deceit, slander, arrogance, boasting, disobedience to parents and foolishness, among other things. These sins are not merely Gentile problems. God's judgment, unlike human justice, is impartial (Rom 2:11) and truthful (Rom 2:2). The problem of sin will extend to Paul's own people, the Jews. The point is straightforward: all have sinned and are subject to God's wrath (cf. Rom 3:23).

God's wrath is not spent in this age only. A day of judgment is coming when God will render to everyone according to his works (Rom 2:6; cf. Prov 24:12; Ps 62:12). Tribulation and distress await all who work evil, both Jews and Gentiles. Glory, honor and peace await those who work "the good," both Jews and Gentiles.

SO WHAT?
Does It Matter If Paul Was Denouncing Homosexual Practices of His Day?

Wasn't he just reflecting local cultural attitudes, as he did when he seems to endorse slavery? "Times have changed"; "society is more accepting of homosexuality than it used to be." Actually, the opposite is true. Greek society in Paul's day was affirming of bisexual practice among men. Paul's position flew in the face of much popular opinion among Gentiles. Paul knew what he was saying was going to be unwelcome by many.

When the righteous judgment of God is revealed, some will enter into eternal life and others will meet divine wrath. Their eternal destiny will not be based upon who was a Jew or a Gentile (Rom 2:11); God's judgment will be based upon the quality of their works, each one's deeds. Gentiles sin and die without God's law. Jews sin and die under God's law (Rom 2:12). But it is not enough to possess the law; God expects obedience. Sometimes Gentiles do what the law requires despite not having it (Rom 2:13-14). According to Paul, this shows that God's law is written on the heart. Ultimately, this inner law becomes the standard by which Gentiles will be judged. In the final analysis, what matters is performance and not possession of the law (whether a heart-law or Torah).

No boasting allowed. Paul turns next to the Jewish reliance on the law and boasting in their covenant with God (Rom 2:17-24). Properly understood, law and covenant are grounds for boasting.[19] However, because many Jews failed to keep their part of the covenant, they brought dishonor to God, as their prophets pointed out: "The name of God is blasphemed among the Gentiles because of you" (Rom 2:24, quoting Is 52:5). Paul's critique of his Jewish contemporaries takes its cue from the canonical prophets, who condemned the hypocrisy of those who claimed to be in covenant but continually broke it. Circumcision is a good example. Circumcision matters, according to Paul, if you observe God's law. But if you break it, circumcision becomes irrelevant. It should have generated "shame" as a sign that they were covenant breakers. On the other hand, Gentiles who keep the law's precepts might as well be circumcised because they are keeping the law in their hearts (Rom 2:24-27). The true Jew, therefore, is not just Jewish on the outside; he's Jewish on the inside, where it counts. True circumcision involves the heart, as the law taught (Deut 10:16) and the prophets confirmed (Jer 4:4).

Jews have quite an advantage in matters of righteousness, but in the end they are no better off because of sin (Rom 3:1-10). The advantage comes because Jews have been entrusted with the oracles of God (Rom 3:2). Nevertheless, God has not ignored Jewish infidelity to the covenant. He has judged it, demonstrating that he is righteous even though his people are not.

The problem of sin for Jew and Gentile. Despite their many advantages, the power of sin eclipses any benefits for Jews (Rom 3:9). They are "without excuse" on the last day because the law defines sin (Rom 3:19-20). To underscore this, Paul pulls together a chain (or *catena*) of scripture texts—drawn chiefly from the Psalms—that charge that sin and its consequences bring ruin, violence and misery to every man (Rom 3:10-18). Paul uses the word "sin" *(hamartia)* in two ways. First, he uses it to refer to a willful act of disobedience against God—the usual meaning today. Second, Paul uses *sin* to describe a power at work in human lives causing people to behave in ways they wish they did not. In this case, sin is not deliberate because sin's power trumps human choice. Regardless, both the power of sin and deliberate sins constitute a major problem for Jews and Gentiles. Any solution to the problem has to address sin's dual nature.

"BUT NOW" (MORE ON THE GOOD NEWS): THE REVELATION OF GOD'S RIGHTEOUSNESS

Paul returns to the "the righteousness of God" as the solution to humanity's plight.

---

[19]Boasting was not always a negative characteristic as it is in modern society. In Paul's context boasting was a way to affirm honorable status, in this case, Jewish honor as members of the covenant *and* God's honor as giver of the covenant.

God's righteousness has been revealed to deal completely with sin, entering the world apart from the law. In the past God's righteousness was revealed through the law; "but now" it has been made available outside the law. God's saving righteousness has been achieved by the faithfulness of Jesus, whom God put forward as an atoning sacrifice. His life and especially his death demonstrate his fidelity to God and his generous love for humanity. Now that Christ has come, God's righteousness is extended to all who have faith, without distinction, both Jews and Greeks. For Paul, faith is the comprehensive response of trust and absolute dependence on God; it is a commitment to the covenant established by Jesus' blood. Those who put faith in Jesus discover that God's righteousness has been communicated to them. As a result they are justified by faith. This means that (1) God has forgiven their sins and (2) they now enter into a blessed relationship with God, a relationship characterized by peace (Rom 5:1). Paul understands this right standing to be a gift of divine grace in Christ. For the apostle, the death of Jesus deals completely with the sin-problem of humanity. First, for sins—deliberate acts of disobedience—the cross offers forgiveness. Second, for sin—the power that causes misery and frustration—the cross provides redemption, namely, the liberation from sin's power.

Although Paul seldom uses sacrificial terminology to describe Jesus' death, he does so in Romans 3:25. His point is that God, not man, supplied the sacrificial victim. The Messiah's blood atoned for humanity's sin. In the past God had passed over our sins showing his patience. "But now," in the present age, God shows his righteousness through what Jesus has done (Rom 3:26). This means that no one is put into a right relationship with God by works of law (circumcision, dietary rules and sabbath observance, cf. Gal 2:16). Boasting is therefore excluded. There is one way for all to be justified, the way of faith. But the way of faith does not set aside the law; according to Paul, it upholds it, as the story of Abraham illustrates.

Our father Abraham. Abraham's story proves valuable to Paul as he considers how a person is made right with God. According to Paul, Genesis 15:6 establishes that righteousness has always been a matter of faith and not works. God declared Abraham righteous apart from works because the patriarch entrusted his future to God's promise. The righteousness "reckoned" to Abraham by faith (Gen 15:6) is connected with and explained as the blessed state of a man against whom the Lord does not "reckon" sins (Ps 32:1-2).[20] In fact, Paul points out that Abraham was

---

[20]Paul connects a Davidic psalm (Ps 32:1-2) to Abraham's faith-reckoned righteousness by applying a rabbinic hermeneutical principle *(Gezera Shawa)* that allows for texts to be linked and interpreted based on a common word, in this case the word *reckoned*.

reckoned righteous before he was circumcised (Rom 4:9-11). According to Paul's reading, Abraham's circumcision was a sign of faith-reckoned righteousness. Therefore, the patriarch became the father of all nations—circumcised and uncircumcised—because God reckons righteousness by faith apart from circumcision (Gen 17:5). Abraham believed the promise despite the childless state of his marriage to Sarah and their advanced ages (Rom 4:13-21). He waited in hope for the promise that he and his descendants would inherit the world and that he would be the father of many nations.

Because of his mindset, Paul reads the Hebrew Scriptures as prefiguring the story of Jesus and his followers. He believes his converts (Jews and Gentiles) are the spiritual heirs of Abraham and his faith. All who put faith in Jesus' atoning death and resurrection, according to Paul's gospel, will be declared righteous or justified. From Abraham's story, Paul learns that righteousness, without which there is no salvation, has always been by faith, not by circumcision and other works of the law.

For Paul righteousness by faith has past, present and future implications. Justification takes place in the past whenever Jews and Gentiles believe in Christ's atoning work. As a result, they live in a state of blessedness Paul describes as "peace with God" and access to God's grace (Rom 5:1-2). Still, justification places Christ-believers on a journey (sanctification) that will end in their glorification when they will share in the glory of God (Rom 5:2). Thoughts of partaking in the divine glory lead Paul to acknowledge the present existence with Christ as one of suffering. Even in suffering the believer can rejoice knowing what blessings await when tribulations arise:

suffering→endurance→character→hope.

Paul is not talking about all suffering here. He has in mind suffering that comes as a result of being on the spiritual journey toward glorification, not sufferings that result from sin or transgression.

For Paul the death of Jesus on the cross provided the means to justification by faith. The situation for humanity was dire. We were weak, ungodly, unrighteous, sinners destined for wrath. But Christ's death on the cross demonstrated God's immense love and reconciled us to God. Now that we have been justified by his blood, we will certainly be saved from God's wrath both now and in the future judgment (Rom 5:8-9). Furthermore, though we were his enemies, God took the initiative to reconcile us to him through the death of Jesus. If we are now reconciled by his death, in the future we will be saved by his resurrection life. So if there is any boasting to do, it is not because we have attained this on our own. It is because God through the Lord Jesus Christ has provided us the gift of reconciliation (Rom 5:11).

SO WHAT?
Why Does It Matter What Paul Means by "Saved"?

Paul describes salvation as more of a process than it is often thought to be today. In one sense, I (Richards) was saved on June 25, 1970, but in another sense, I am still being saved. My problems with sin and suffering didn't disappear then. Many of the promises of salvation (no more tears, no more death) are not yet realized in my life. The death rate for humanity is still 100 percent. My salvation began in 1970 and continues to gradually blossom within me—as my character becomes more like Christ's. Then on the Day of the Lord, I will be raised and what began in 1970 will be completed.

Adam and Christ. As Paul reflected on the plight of humanity, his thoughts turned to the (still) universal problems of sin and death. From the story of Adam, Paul learned that death had come into the world as a result of sin (Gen 1—3). Sin and death were, for Paul, two sides of the same coin; they needed a single, comprehensive solution. Accordingly, the apostle envisages Jesus as a new, or second, Adam who came to reverse the curse of death brought on by sin. In Jesus' death God dealt with sin once-and-for-all. In Jesus' resurrection he set in motion the general resurrection at the end of the age whereby death's grip over humanity is loosed and ultimately death itself dies. As Paul understood it, Adam was a "type" of the one to come. Just as Adam stood at the head of the first creation, Jesus now represents and embodies the new creation.

The universality of death proves that sin is universal, but how does Adam's sin and death relate to the sin and death of Adam's children? Paul writes: "Therefore, just as sin came into the world through one man, and death came through sin, and so death spread to all *because all have sinned*" (Rom 5:12, italics added). The italicized words are the sticking point. Some interpret the phrase as "in whom [Adam] all have sinned." This means the children of Adam were collectively "in Adam" when he sinned. Therefore, we die because Adam sinned. Others interpret it as "because all have sinned." This means that the children of Adam sin like their ancestor. Therefore, we die because we sin and not because Adam sinned. Paul acknowledges that death reigned from Adam to Moses, even over those whose sin was not like Adam's transgression. This clearly suggests that their sin, even if it was different than Adam's, was death's cause.

Paul develops this Adam-Christ typology to portray Jesus as the head of the

WHAT'S MORE . . .
Baptism: Buried and Raised with Christ

Although Romans 6:3-5 is not a comprehensive statement on Paul's theology of baptism, it is his most complete description of the rite of Christian initiation. Baptism is the "but now!" moment for the believer; it is the turning point.[a] Everyone who is "baptized into Christ" (christologically and ecclesiologically) has been "baptized into his death." As the waters of baptism wash over Christ-believers, they are mystically buried with Christ into his death. As they come up out of the waters, they are united with Christ in his life to walk "in newness of life" (Rom 6:2-4). For Paul, baptism unites the faithful with Christ in his death and burial. In a real sense, they died in Christ's death and lived again in Christ's resurrection. The baptized now walk in newness of life, anticipating the parousia, when all things become new and there is no vestige of sin, death and the weakness of mortal flesh. So for the baptized, the old self has been crucified, potentially putting an end to sin's dominance.s

[a]Gorman, *Apostle of the Crucified Lord,* p. 368.

new creation. The old order established in Adam has been dominated by sin and death. The new order created in Christ abounds in grace and life. Through Adam's transgression and disobedience all men are condemned as sinners. Through the righteous act and obedience of Jesus, the second Adam, all—both Jew and Gentile—can experience life and stand before God as righteous (Rom 5:18-19).[21]

Paul sensed his Jewish readers would wonder about the role of the law in this. Adam had introduced sin and death into the world. The law had been given to curb sins (i.e., willful acts), but it was helpless in dealing with the power of sin. While it did name "sins," the power of sin reigned in our mortal bodies. Had the law been sufficient to put an end to sin, death too would have died. But the reign of death meant that the law was powerless to deal effectively with sin. In fact, sin,

[21]Some have used passages like this to argue for universalism. Universalism is the belief that all people will ultimately be saved regardless of what they believe or do. We think this pushes the Adam-Christ typology too far and ignores Paul's clear teaching elsewhere that some will experience God's wrath. Three things are certain for Paul. First, he believes all could be saved; salvation is not limited to a select few. Second, he understands not all will be saved. Some will face an eternity separated from God. Third, he holds all who are saved will be saved by what Christ has accomplished; there is no other way of salvation.

insidious as it is, used the law to increase sins. A greater power was needed. Now that Christ has come and the new age has arrived, the unchecked influence of sin (and death) has met its match. As sin increases, grace increases all the more.

Paul's interlocutor chimes in: "If what you say is true, shouldn't we remain in sin, so grace can abound?" The apostle forcefully responded, "No, not at all" (Rom 6:1-2). The reason is simple: believers are dead to sin as their baptism dramatizes.[22] Sin cannot reign over those who are identified through baptism with the crucified, buried and risen Lord. Likewise, as sin's twin, death no longer has dominion in the presence of the resurrected one. In light of this, Paul admonishes his followers to consider themselves dead to sin and alive to God through Christ Jesus (Rom 6:11). Furthermore, he continues:

> Do not let sin exercise dominion in your mortal bodies, to make you obey their passions. No longer present your members to sin as instruments of wickedness, but present yourselves to God as those who have been brought from death to life, and present your members to God as instruments of righteousness. (Rom 6:12-13)

By saying "do not" Paul is showing that death to sin is not automatic. Baptism's meaning must be appropriated into daily life. It was possible to "backslide" and become a slave to sin once again, but that would not happen as long as Christ-believers intentionally lived as God's obedient servant. For Paul, everyone serves a master; there are no free agents.

There was a time when the Romans were slaves to sin and owed no debt to righteousness. "But now" they have been set free from sin to serve God. Those who serve sin have only death to look forward to, but for those who serve God "the free gift of God is eternal life in Christ Jesus our Lord" (Rom 6:23).

PAUL AND THE LAW

As we have already seen, one of the thorniest problems involved in studying Paul is coming to grips with his understanding of the law. Romans 7 is one of the other "hot spots" in interpreting Paul. Working from the analogy of marriage, Paul argues that just as death frees the surviving spouse to marry another, so death to the law frees a person to belong to another. Believers, he thinks, have died to the law so they can belong to another (Jesus). For those who don't know Christ, sinful passions exploit the law and bear the fruit of death. "But now" those who have died to the law are discharged from serving sin that held them captive (Rom 7:5-6).

---

[22] Some Christians will say, "Baptism is just a symbol." But few realities are more powerful than a symbol, and the word *just* implies a diminution that must be rejected. Baptism has a mystical element, and while baptism may not be soteriological, it is ecclesiological and christological.

Paul is quick to insist the law is not sin; it does, however, make sins known. In fact, the power of sin takes advantage of the commandments and incites all kinds of sins, leading to death. The real culprit for Paul is not the law; it is sin. The law is good, just and holy, offering covenantal means to find forgiveness for sins. It could not, though, overcome the power of sin (and thus death). The law promised life but sin exploits the commandments, deceives and brings death (Rom 7:7-11). Sin is such a wretched scourge that it takes the goodness of God's law, distorts it and produces death.

In Romans 6:11 Paul declares Christ-believers are dead to sin and then admonishes them not to allow sins to reign unchecked. In Romans 7:14-25 he tries to address this ambiguity, but his answer is difficult to understand. The main interpretive issue involves the identity of the "I" who is struggling with sin. Does it refer to Paul alone or to humanity in general? Paul's statements seem more than autobiographical. He is not just talking about himself; he is describing the struggle of every person for whom sin and flesh have caused frustration and despair. By "I" Paul certainly means himself, but he is discussing a universal problem, the problem of every son of Adam and daughter of Eve. Sin working in our flesh produces a fractured, fragmented world for whom Christ, and not the law, is the only answer.

But another question about the "I" still remains: Is Paul talking about preconversion or postconversion Christian experience? Does this frustrated state refer to someone who has not (yet) been saved or also to a believer? We can't be sure. The passage suggests to us Paul is describing believers. The present tense verbs throughout the section suggest Paul is describing a current condition. Furthermore, the "I" section is sandwiched between two passages that urge believers not to let sin reign in their bodies (Rom 6:12) and to walk in the Spirit not in the flesh (Rom 8:1-11). What we have then in Romans 7:14-25 is a passage that describes the experience of believers who are not living as if they were dead to sin and are therefore walking in the flesh. It is not the ideal Christian life, but it is nevertheless a real part of the spiritual journey.

LIFE IN THE SPIRIT

Chapters and verses are artificial divisions inserted in the Bible hundreds of years after its books were written. Here is a place where the chapter division interrupts the train of thought. Paul has shared the painful frustration of all believers who are at war with sin and the flesh. The only hope for this state of wretchedness is the gift and grace of the Lord Jesus (Rom 7:14-25). Romans 8 completes the answer to the problem of sin and its exploitation of the law. There is no transition in Paul's thinking here. The Romans 8 life in the Spirit provides the alternative to the Romans 7 life under sin and death. Despite the struggle, there is ultimately no condemnation for those in Christ Jesus (Rom 8:1). That is because the law of the Spirit of life in Christ liberates them from the law of sin and death. Frail flesh and the power of sin are no match for the Son whom God sent in the likeness of sinful flesh. He condemned sin so that those who walk in the Spirit can fulfill the law's righteous demands (Rom 8:4). Paul then compares life in the flesh with life in the Spirit.

Life in the Spirit provides the gracious alternative to a life lived in the flesh under sin. But the Spirit's control is not autocratic. Believers must choose to walk in the Spirit. To be "in the Spirit" means to have the Spirit of God dwell in you (Rom 8:9). In Pauline thought, the Christian life consists primarily of living coopera-

---

WHAT'S MORE . . .
Walking in the Flesh vs. Walking in the Spirit

Mind set on the flesh (Rom 8:5)	Mind set on the Spirit (Rom 8:5)
Death (Rom 8:6)	Life (Rom 8:6)
Hostile to God (Rom 8:7)	Peace (Rom 8:6)
Does not submit to God's law (Rom 8:7)	Fulfills the righteousness of the law (Rom 8:4)
	Spirit of God dwells in you (Rom 8:9)
	Belong to Christ who is in you (Rom 8:10)
	Spirit's alive because of righteousness (Rom 8:10)
	Life to your mortal bodies (Rom 8:11)
You will die (Rom 8:13)	You will live (Rom 8:13)
Spirit of slavery (Rom 8:15)	Spirit of sonship (Rom 8:15)
Fear (insecurity) (Rom 8:15)	"Abba" (security) (Rom 8:15)

---

tively with the Spirit of Christ who dwells within.[23] When Christ is present in a
life, the human spirit is alive to righteousness. But more than that, the present experience of the indwelling Spirit offers hope that mortal bodies will live forever.

As in Galatians 4:4-5, Paul uses the metaphor of adoption to depict one aspect
of the reality of salvation in Christ. Although rare among the Jews, adoption was
a common part of family life in the Mediterranean world. The Greek word *huiothesia* means literally "to make [someone] a son." Broadly speaking, it refers to
"the creation of kinship relationships between two or more people through legal
and/or ritual means."[24] Paul employs the term here (cf. Gal 4:4-5; Eph 1:5) to describe a change of status from an existence characterized by slavery to freedom in
the Spirit. Through adoption Christ-believers enter into an intimate relationship
with God through Jesus. The intimacy is reflected in the "Abba! Father!" address
in prayer and the inner witness of the Spirit (Rom 8:15-16). Still the apostle understood this sonship in two stages: (1) it is "already" present through the work of
the Spirit, but (2) it is "not yet" fully realized until the resurrection. God's children
have the first fruits of the Spirit; yet the current reality entails suffering and groan-
ing as we await our complete "adoption as sons, the redemption of our bodies"
(Rom 8:23).[25] So the adoption metaphor provided Paul with yet another way to
portray the already/not-yet aspect of Christian hope.[26]

Since inheritance rights were an important part of adoption in the Roman Empire, it made sense for Paul to recognize that God's adopted children will also be
"heirs of God and joint heirs with Christ" (Rom 8:17). By this he likely refers to
the glory, power and honor God's children will enjoy in the kingdom of God. This
stands in contrast to the current suffering God's children must endure. (In the ancient world one's status often had to do with how much suffering one endured.)
Our present suffering is not a true indicator of our coming status. Those who
would be fellow heirs must be fellow sufferers if they wish to be glorified together
with him. Only those who suffer now with Christ can rest in the blessed assurance

---

[23]For Paul the Spirit of God and the Spirit of Christ refer to the same indwelling reality. This suggests
the most intimate connection possible between God and his Messiah.

[24]David B. Capes, "Adoption in the First Century," *Biblical Illustrator* 32, no. 1 (2005): 39. It is important to note the apostle never uses the word *adoption* to describe the sonship of Jesus. While Jesus is
"the Son of God," "his Son" or "the Son" (e.g., 1 Thess 1:10; 1 Cor 15:28; Rom 1:3-4; Gal 2:20), Paul
knows Jesus' sonship is of a different order than that of his followers. Still, those who are adopted as
sons into God's forever family are adopted on the basis of the accomplished work of Jesus.

[25]James C. Walters notes that adoption included the cancellation of all debts as well as the promise of
an inheritance; see "Paul, Adoption and Inheritance," in *Paul in the Greco-Roman World,* ed. J. P. Sampley (Harrisburg, Penn.: Trinity Press International, 2003), pp. 50-51, 54.

[26]James Scott, "Adoption, Sonship," in *DPL,* p. 17.

of sharing his future glory. Still, the suffering of the present is nothing compared to the glory that will be revealed in his coming (Rom 8:18). Even creation longs for the revelation (apocalypse) of God's children.

Since the fall, creation has been in the throes of the curse brought about by human sin. This cosmic emptiness and decay continues until the day when it will share in the glorious liberty awaiting God's children. Paul describes the creation's tribulation as "labor pains," a typical apocalyptic image for the struggle prior to the birth of the new age. Like a cosmic mother, creation groans in travail waiting for a new creation. At the parousia, the children of God will experience the glorious redemption of their bodies and creation will be liberated from its slavery to decay

SO WHAT?
What's the Significance of Calling Jesus "Son of God"?

"Son of God" is one of the titles that Jesus bears, as is "son of David." It is based on a Jewish idiom, where "son of" indicates sharing a common nature. Thus, we are "sons of light" (1 Thess 5:5). Others are "sons of the evil one/devil" (Mt 13:38; Jn 8:44). But the phrase "Son of God" can be misunderstood. Arabic, for example, does not use this idiom. "Son of" indicates biological paternity only. "Son of God" would thus mean that God and Mary, . . . well, produced Jesus. Muslims find the phrase offensive. In that sense, we would find it extremely offensive also. We agree with their expression: "God does not beget and he is not begotten." This misunderstanding over "Son of God"—not to downplay its seriousness—arises from cultural and translational problems. Likewise, when Paul uses a Mediterranean metaphor (adoption), he is careful. Christians are "sons of God" (Rom 8:14-23) in the Mediterranean sense of adoption, but only partly in the Jewish sense of "shared nature" and not at all in any anachronistic sense of biological descent.

(Rom 8:21-23). Until that day believers enjoy the firstfruits of the Spirit, who helps in weakness, guides in prayer and intercedes for saints (Rom 8:26-27).

To those who love God and live out their call faithfully, all things are working together for good (Rom 8:28). Put another way, Paul believes human weakness cannot threaten the ultimate plan of God. He paints that plan in broad strokes: (1) foreknowledge, (2) predestination, (3) calling, (4) justification and (5) glorification (Rom 8:29-30). These five acts constitute God's plan and work to save the world. For Paul, God is the ultimate actor in this drama of redemption; humans are the beneficiaries of this gracious work. The goal of the plan is to create a worldwide family of people conformed to the image of God's Son with Jesus as the elder brother. This Christoformity takes place first in the mind and will of God and then is worked out in subsequent stages of salvation history.

Romans 8 ends with one of the most memorable bits of prose in all Paul's letters. It is a joyous celebration of assurance that nothing can separate God's chosen from his love expressed in Christ Jesus (Rom 8:31-39). God demonstrates how much he is "for us" by not sparing his Son and by justifying his elect through faith (Rom 8:31-33). Christ Jesus died, was raised and is seated at the right hand of God, where he lives to intercede "for us" (Rom 8:34). According to Paul, these lavish expressions of divine love can't be frustrated by any tribulation, persecution or hardship. "The elect" are "super-victors" because of God's love for them. While others in Paul's day trembled in the face of death and unknown malevolent forces, he rejoices that absolutely no heavenly or earthly power can separate believers from God's love.

JEWS AND GENTILES IN GOD'S PLAN

In Romans 9—11 Paul moves on to discuss the relationship between the new and the old covenant. If nothing can separate believers of the new covenant from the love of God, then what happened to those who belonged to the old covenant? Since Christ-believers are eternally secure in their relationship with God because of his promises, then does the same security apply to the promises God made to Israel? At this point in the argument, exalted prose gives way to mournful longing when Paul realizes the majority of Jews had not embraced his gospel and were therefore at risk of incurring the wrath of God. Despite their obvious privileges— their election, the glory, the covenants, the law, the temple worship, the promises, the patriarchs and the messianic hope (which should have prepared them to welcome God's Messiah)—Paul's kinsmen according to the flesh had persisted in unbelief. But their unbelief did not compromise God's faithfulness. The promises of God will come true in the end: all Israel will be saved. Yet, in the meantime, Paul is willing to be cut off from Christ if only his fellow Jews would be saved.[27] As he

---

[27] As Paul moves toward Christlikeness, he exhibits more of the love of Jesus, a love that made him willing to lay down his life for others.

deals with his questions and grief, Paul turns to Scripture and mines the story of Israel.

As it is written . . . Paul acknowledges first that not all of Israel is true Israel. From the story of Abraham, he learns that not all of Abraham's physical descendants are children of the promise. Abraham had other sons, but the spiritual heirs of Abraham would come through Isaac (Rom 9:7, quoting Gen 21:12). Likewise Rebecca and Isaac had two sons, but God chose Jacob rather than Esau as the bearer of the covenant (Rom 9:12, quoting Gen 25:23). This in no way constitutes injustice on God's part. He has been true to his promises to extend blessings to Abraham's descendants even if those descendants did not include all his children.

Paul learns from the story of Moses and Pharaoh that God is sovereign. The Lord offers mercy and compassion to whomever he wishes (Rom 9:15, quoting Ex 33:19). Ultimately, election depends on God's mercy, not human will or effort. As the Pharaoh of Egypt discovered, God hardens the hearts of whomever he wills (Rom 9:17-18, quoting Ex 9:16; cf Ex 10:1, 20, 27). His decisions are not open for discussion. He is the potter; we are the clay. The potter can make of the clay what he wishes. If God has chosen (corporate election or corporately) for the Gentiles to be recipients of his glory and mercy, that is his business. In a sense the prophet Hosea recognizes this when he writes

> Those who were not my people I will call "my people,"
>   and her who was not beloved I will call "beloved."
> And in the very place where it was said to them, "You are not my people,"
>   there they shall be called children of the living God.
> (Rom 9:25-26, quoting Hos 2:23; 1:10)

According to the prophet Hosea, Israel had lost her standing as God's chosen and had become like the Gentiles. Paul interprets this oracle according to his own day and applies it to believing Gentiles who are now included among "my people."

Isaiah's prophecies too were instructive in this regard. He championed the idea of the "remnant," namely, that only a part of Israel had remained faithful to God and would be saved. The majority was going to face God's judgment. The prophet declared that unless God had left a remnant, Israel would have been wiped out like Sodom and Gomorrah (Rom 9:27-29; quoting Is 10:22 and 1:9). Paul finds the same reality present in his mission. A "remnant" of Israel is remaining true to God and responding in faith to his gospel. So Paul finds in Scripture a way of coping with the grief he faced. The current failure of many Jews to respond to his gospel does not mean God is unfaithful to his promises; likewise it does not mean he rejects his people. Rather Paul sees in his day what Scripture foresaw: the faithful-

WHAT'S MORE . . .
Paul's Favorite Prophet

Paul's favorite prophet was probably Isaiah. The apostle quoted him more than any of the Old Testament prophets. For him, Isaiah was the quintessential seer, the faithful witness, the one who—perhaps more than any—saw Israel's and the world's future with the coming of the Messiah. Specifically, Paul discovered in Isaiah that many Gentiles would find salvation in the beautiful message of the gospel he preached (Rom 10:20, quoting Is 65:1). But he also read that not all who heard the powerful story would believe the good news (Rom 10:16, quoting Is 53:1). Finally, it was Isaiah who convinced Paul that Israel's unbelief and disobedience are not new; they have characterized the contrary members of God's covenant people all along (Rom 10:21, quoting Is 65:2).

ness of the remnant, the inclusion of the Gentiles, the sovereign election of God and fulfillment of his promises.

Righteousness by faith in Jesus. The problem for many unbelieving Jews, according to Paul, is how they understand righteousness. They think correctly that righteousness is essential to salvation. The question is, how is saving-righteousness achieved? The Gentiles are stumbling into true righteousness, namely, a righteousness based on faith (Rom 9:30). At the same time, many Jews are stumbling over the work of God because they are seeking a law-based righteousness (Rom 9:31-32). Again, the prophet Isaiah predicted this (Is 8:14; 28:16). God's saving work, symbolized here as the construction of a new temple,[28] will cause some to stumble and others to be saved (Rom 9:33). Those who fall have a zeal for God and righteousness, but it is pursued in ignorance—they don't know that the righteousness that comes from God is not law-based righteousness; it is faith-based righteousness. Paul writes: "For Christ is the end of the law so that there may be righteousness for everyone who believes" (Rom 10:4). By "the end of the law," then, Paul means its goal not its finish (demise). In other words, all along the law has been pointing Israel to the Messiah. With Christ the law reaches its goal. Before the Christophany, Paul's life had been focused on the law. "But now" that

---

[28]The same passages, Isaiah 8:14 and Isaiah 28:16, are quoted in 1 Peter 2:6-8 in reference to the spiritual temple established with Jesus Christ as the cornerstone. Paul's use of Isaiah's stone passages here may suggest that he reads them as constituting a new temple.

Christ has come, his center of gravity shifted from Torah to Christ. This did not mean, however, that he abandoned the law altogether. It means that he finds that Christ's life of faithful obedience, death and resurrection had been the endgame all along. As Paul was incorporated into Christ through faith and baptism, the gift of righteousness became his. He exchanged a righteousness of his own[29] (living under the law) for the righteousness that comes through faith in Christ (Rom 10:5).

Paul reads the story of Jesus, as well as his own life story as a herald of the gospel, against the backdrop of God's gift of the law. The life and prosperity offered to Israel by keeping the law (Deut 30:15-20) finds its true fulfillment, for Paul, in the gospel of universal salvation through faith in Jesus. As God's apostle, he announces salvation to all Jews and Greeks who confess "Jesus is Lord" and believe that God raised him from the dead (Rom 10:9). With the prophecies of Joel echoing in his mind, Paul writes: "For, 'Everyone who calls on the name of the Lord shall be saved'" (Rom 10:13, quoting Joel 2:32).[30]

A remnant does remain. So Paul refuses the charge that Israel's unbelief means that God is rejecting his people. He, for one, is proof that a remnant remains. But the issue for Paul is not about individuals; it is about the nation of Israel as God's covenant people. He recalls the time when Elijah complained against God that he alone remained faithful, only to be reminded that a sizeable company (seven thousand) had not bowed the knee to the idol (Rom 11:2-4, alluding to 1 Kings 19:9-18). At the present moment, Paul says, "there is a remnant, chosen by grace" (Rom

---

[29]This is where the influence of E. P. Sanders weighs heavily upon our shoulders. Paul's language is understood two ways: as referring to ethnicity or to personal merit. (1) Did Paul believe his righteousness under the law was due to his "efforts," or due to his election by virtue of the covenant with Abraham? By "a righteousness of my own" was Paul talking about *a Jewish* kind of righteousness? If so, the emphasis is ethnic. (2) The more traditional "Lutheran" emphasis on meritorious works argues (such as Gathercole) that Paul had a problem with Jews who believed that they earned their righteousness via meritorious works. "You that boast *in the law*" (Rom 2:23). But, were the Jews boasting in the privilege of the law or their human effort? This is a complex and debated issue. While many scholars still contend Paul was combating Jews who thought they were earning their salvation through the law, others suggest Paul knew there was a righteousness according to the law (he even claimed it for himself, Phil 3:6). The problem was a "better" righteousness has come along via his gospel because it includes Gentiles without Jewish law, thus fulfilling the promises of God to Abraham. Therefore, Paul objected to the law because it excluded Gentiles.

[30]"Calling upon the name of the Lord" referred to the ritual invocation of God's name (YHWH) in the temple. Paul refers this YHWH text to Christ whom believers confess as "Lord." This is a remarkable appropriation of God's name. It means that, for Paul, the risen Jesus bears God's name and is identified with him. It also implies that the ritual invocation and worship of Jesus characterized the early Christian churches with which Paul associated. For a full treatment of this and other YHWH texts see David B. Capes, *Old Testament Yahweh Texts in Paul's Christology*, Wissenschaftliche Untersuchungen zum Neuen Testament 2, no. 47 (Tübingen: J. C. B. Mohr, 1992).

11:5). Believing Jews, like Paul and many of his coworkers, prove that God has not left Israel behind. Many Jews have stumbled over God's revelation of righteousness in Christ, but they will not ultimately fall. Their unbelief is temporary, intended to allow salvation to come to the Gentiles (Rom 11:11). Furthermore, the salvation of the Gentiles will provoke Israel to jealousy when it sees God's promises and blessings resting upon the other nations.

Nevertheless, Paul turns to the Gentile believers with a warning against pride. Working from an agricultural image of pruning and grafting an olive tree, he remarks that some in Israel have been pruned because of unbelief. But Gentile believers, whom he calls "a wild olive shoot," have been grafted into the trunk to share in the tree's richness (Rom 11:17). Before they become boastful of their self-awarded superior status,[31] Paul reminds them the root supports the branch, the branch doesn't support the root. If natural branches can be pruned because of unbelief and lack of productivity, how much more can grafted branches be pruned for the same (Rom 11:21-24)? Indeed Paul expects the natural branches to be grafted back onto the tree when unbelief gives way to faith.

All Israel will be saved. Paul wanted his Roman audience to understand a mystery. God had let his apostle in on a secret. God was hardening the hearts of some in Israel until the full number of Gentiles enter into Christ. Afterward all Israel will be saved (Rom 11:25). This conclusion is consistent with the Scripture that declares that all ungodliness will be removed from Jacob (i.e., Israel) and all sins will be taken away in the (new) covenant (Is 59:20; Jer 31:3; Is 27:9). Though Paul did not see the greater part of the Jews coming to faith, God's salvation had been offered first to the Jews, then to the Greeks. In the end Israel will be saved because the gifts and call of God are irrevocable (Rom 11:29).

Paul does not explicitly say how and when all Israel will be saved. Three observations seem warranted. First, given the importance Paul placed on Jesus' coming, death and resurrection, it is unlikely he envisioned Israel's salvation apart from the person and work of the Messiah. Second, the word he used, "saved," is a soteriological image with a future orientation. This probably means that he expected "all Israel" to be "saved" at the parousia, or in the Day of Judgment. Third, he has already established that "Israel" does not refer to every physical descendant of Abraham but to those upon whom God's mercy is extended. Taking these points to-

---

[31]Paul has not abandoned the problems of the Roman church to engage in theological discussion. Behind his description here is Paul's injunction to the Gentile believers in the church in Rome not to become boastful of what God had accomplished through them during the five years their Jewish Christian brothers were absent.

gether, it seems Paul believed that after the full number of Gentiles heard and received the gospel, a great turning of the Jews to faith in the Messiah would take place prior to his coming. Together with all the Gentiles, believing Jews would bow their heads and bend their knees in worshipful recognition of his Lordship (Phil 2:9-11). That scenario provided the Jewish apostle the hope he needed to curb his grief and to sustain his efforts. If Gentile conversions provoked jealousy and precipitated the day all Israel would be saved, Paul was willing to do all in his power to bring that about.

THE ETHICS OF RIGHTEOUSNESS

Space does not allow us to unpack the significance of the specific instructions Paul gave to the Roman church in Romans 12—16. Instead, we will summarize a few of his admonitions.

1. In light of all God's mercies (Romans 1—11), Christ-believers are to devote themselves completely to God. They are to avoid conformity to the world's ways as they move toward Christoformity (Rom 12:1-2; cf. 8:29).

2. As members of Christ's body, believers are to exercise their spiritual gifts according to the faith and grace God provides (Rom 12:3-8).

3. Love toward the church expresses itself in brotherly affection, generosity and hospitality. Love toward God elicits prayer, patience, joy and service (Rom 12:9-13).

4. Following the teachings of the Lord Jesus, believers are to bless their enemies, live at peace with all men, not seek revenge and overcome evil by doing good (12:14-21).

5. Since God establishes every human authority, Christ-believers are to respect the governing authorities and submit to their rule. This includes obeying the laws, paying taxes and giving appropriate honor to officials (Rom 13:1-7).[32] This is not to say that Paul called for "blind allegiance" to the emperor and his representatives. In fact the Christian claims about Christ ("Jesus is Lord"; Caesar is not) and the loyalty of Christ-believers to a higher authority were to prove subversive to the absolute claims of Rome.

---

[32]Again, the chapter division here falls at a poor place, and likewise, we can see this from an *inclusio*. In Romans 12:19, Paul warns against taking individual revenge for wrongs, "Leave room for the wrath of God" and then in Romans 13:4, he concludes his argument by citing the emperor as an agent of "wrath" for dealing with such wrongs. "Therefore," Paul concludes, "one must be subject [to the authorities]" (Rom 13:5).

6. All believers should avoid debt, with one exception—they are to regard themselves as debtors in love to their neighbors. Love fulfills the entire law—another dominant theme of the teachings of Jesus and Paul (Rom 13:8-10).

7. Because salvation draws closer every day, the faithful are to set aside revelry, drunkenness, sexual misconduct and divisiveness. Instead they are to "put on the Lord Jesus Christ" (Rom 13:14)—live like Christ—and not seek to gratify the flesh.

8. Following the example of Christ, weak brothers (Jewish believers?) are to welcome strong brothers (Gentile believers?). Likewise Gentile believers are to receive kindly their Jewish counterparts. Ultimately the One God desires for his people to be one. This includes especially the common table around which much of their life together revolves (Rom 14:1—15:13).

9. Since all belong to God and all will stand before the judgment seat of God, believers must avoid passing judgment on one another (Rom 14:5-12).

THE CALL FOR UNITY

Paul ends his injunctions to the Roman church with a call for unity, confronting for a last time the ethnic division wracking the church (Rom 15:1-6). With strong language (as he often ended his letters) Paul states, "Welcome one another, then, just as Christ has welcomed you" (Rom 15:7). Paul uses "unity" as a segue into his plans to visit Rome on his way to Spain. He mentions how these other regions have shown their unity by supporting his ministry (Rom 15:19-29). Just as there should be no division between Jew and Gentile in the Roman church, so there should be no hesitation in supporting Paul's efforts to take the gospel to the end of the earth.

As the church is expected to welcome Paul when he finally arrives, they are expected in the interim to welcome Phoebe, a church leader from Cenchrea (Rom 16:1-2). Adopting the format of a typical recommendation letter, Paul commends her and asks the church to facilitate her visit there.[33] Paul ends with a long list of greetings (not at all typical for Paul), probably to bridge among the various factions, and a closing benediction instead of a typical health-wish. In the benediction, he writes of his plan to "bring about the obedience of faith" (Rom 16:26) of his Gentile converts—a goal that would take him once again to Jerusalem and

---

[33]Since recommendation letters were usually carried by the person being recommended, Phoebe may well have been the letter carrier for this very "weighty" letter.

WHAT'S MORE . . .
Jesus and Paul

Some of Paul's pastoral counsel echoes Jesus' teaching. Since Paul was not one of the original disciples, it is debated how much of Jesus' teachings Paul knew or even wanted to know.[a] For Paul, what Christ did (on the cross) overshadowed anything he said. Moreover, Paul composed all his letters before any of the Gospels were written. But does this mean he did not have access to some of Jesus' sayings, parables and scriptural expositions? The fact that Paul seldom quotes the known sayings of Jesus leads some scholars to conclude—wrongly in our judgment—that the apostle is not interested in the earthly Jesus. Echoes of "the Jesus tradition" may be heard in many of Paul's letters, but they are concentrated in Romans, 1 Corinthians and 1 and 2 Thessalonians. Romans 12 provides several examples:

- Bless those who persecute you; bless and do not curse them (Rom 12:14; Mt 5:44; par. Lk 6:28a)

- Do not pay back to anyone evil for evil (Rom 12:17; Mt 5:39b-41; Lk 6:29)

- Live peaceably with all men (Rom 12:18; Mk 9:50; Mt 5:9)

- Do not seek revenge . . . overcome evil with good (Rom 12:19-21; Lk 6:27, 35)

---

[a]For a review of the issues see Seyoon Kim, "Jesus, Sayings of," in *DPL*, pp. 474-92; also John M. G. Barclay, "Jesus and Paul," in *DPL*, pp. 492-503; David Wenham, *Paul and Jesus: The True Story* (Grand Rapids: Eerdmans, 2002).

---

bring him back to Rome. But, it wouldn't be under conditions either he or the church would have expected. Paul would come to Rome, not as a missionary to Spain, but as a prisoner of the empire.

READ MORE ABOUT IT

DPL Articles:

"Abraham," pp. 1-9; esp. "3. Abraham in Romans," pp. 6-8, by N. L. Calvert.
"Adoption, Sonship," pp. 15-18, by J. M. Scott.
"Israel," pp. 441-46, by W. S. Campbell.

"Righteousness, Righteousness of God," pp. 827-37, by K. L. Onesti and
   M. T. Brauch.
"Romans, Letter to the," pp. 838-50, by J. D. G. Dunn.
"Rome and Roman Christianity," pp. 850-55, by M. Reasoner.
"Wrath, Destruction," pp. 991-93, by G. L. Borchert.

8

The Imprisoned Paul

Letters to Churches

THE GOOD NEWS OFTEN LED PAUL INTO BAD SITUATIONS. Nearly everywhere he went, preaching the gospel of Jesus Christ got him into trouble. Acts tells the story of repeated incidents in which Paul's gospel ministry brought him face to face with Jewish authorities and Roman magistrates. In his letters, Paul often wrote of persecutions he endured at the hands of both his "own people" and "the Gentiles": beatings, prison, riots and stoning (2 Cor 6:5; 11:26; 1 Thess 2:14-16). And it is easy to see why Paul offended Jewish leaders. Many of the statements we read in his letters about Jewish law, holy days and dietary regulations are inflammatory (even today, some scholars accuse Paul of being "anti-Jewish"). Opposition to Paul came primarily from Jewish leadership, which is why most of his letters are filled with vitriolic language against many things Jewish, sharply distinguishing faith in Christ (a Jewish figure) from works of Jewish law. The gospel according to Paul was not religion-as-usual for Jews or Gentiles. Jewish opponents, of course, certainly recognized Paul's message as a dangerous threat to their way of life. So, until recently, scholars have been satisfied with attributing the source of Paul's struggles to his ongoing battle against "Jewish imperialism." Whenever Paul set aside the covenant requirements of circumcision, obedience to the whole law and ethnic identity, he encountered resistance. From his opponents' point of view, holiness required compliance; rebels had to be punished (Deut 13:1-5); such situations called for "zeal." Like Jesus, Paul ran into trouble from "the Jews." We've heard this story before.

And there's the rub. Paul may have "received from the Jews the forty lashes minus one" five times for violating Jewish law, but he was hauled off to prison several times (how many? we don't know) because he was accused of breaking Roman law (2 Cor 11:23-24). Jewish squabbling over Torah cannot explain Paul's Roman troubles. Why did the gospel of Jesus preached by Paul get him in trouble with governmental authorities? Scholars are turning their attention to exploring how the politics of Paul became the primary source of his problems.[1] Perhaps Paul was imprisoned for the same reason Jesus was crucified. Caesar is Lord. Defy the sovereignty of Rome, whether you were an imperial subject (Jesus) or Roman citizen (Paul), and the charge would be the same: treason. When Paul went about the Roman Empire proclaiming a Lord other than Caesar, he was bound to get in trouble. Acts of treason against Rome were punishable by death. That which was considered subversive ranged from the egregious to the inane. People who uttered murderous threats (even using sorcery) against Caesar and his household met with the same punishment as a man who dared to receive hometown honors on Caesar's birthday (Tiberius had the man put to death).[2] Caesar guarded jealously his imperial claims of power and allegiance.

Conflict is inevitable when an irresistible force meets an unmovable object. Was Paul surprised by his troubles with Roman authorities? When he was imprisoned several years for preaching the gospel, did he shake his head in disbelief that such unfortunate circumstances befell him? Was Paul the typical jailbird, always chirping about the injustices of Roman law with protests of innocence: "You've got it all wrong, fellas. I'm innocent, I tell you. This is all one big misunderstanding!" Or did Paul know exactly what he was doing? Did he realize from the beginning that preaching the gospel of Jesus Christ would not only offend Jews but would also provoke Romans, that his message was politically charged, that hailing the lordship of Jesus would land him in prison? Paul knew. In fact, more scholars are beginning to see that Paul was not only trying to change the religious devotion of Jews (Jesus is Lord and Messiah) but was also subverting the Roman Empire by converting its citizens, whose "minds are set on earthly things. But our citizenship is in heaven" (Phil 3:19-20). Paul knew his gospel was in opposition to the designs of the Roman Empire.[3] He knew swearing allegiance to Christ would lead to denying Caesar's deity. Citizens

---

[1] See Richard A. Horsley, ed., *Paul and Politics: Ekklesia, Israel, Imperium, Interpretation* (Harrisburg, Penn.: Trinity Press International, 2000).

[2] Suetonius *Tiberius* 58.

[3] See N. T. Wright, "Paul's Gospel and Caesar's Empire," in *Paul and Politics*, ed. Richard A. Horsley (Harrisburg, Penn.: Trinity Press International, 2000), pp. 160-83.

would be forced to choose: do I continue to burn the ashes at Caesar's shrine, support the imperial cult and sacrifice to idols? Maybe Paul targeted Roman colonies for this very reason. Perhaps it was not simply a matter of geographic expediency that led Paul to urban populations. Paul may have had demographic designs in his gospel intentions. Among the outposts of Roman rule, Paul was establishing competing colonies for the kingdom of Christ. Advancing the gospel and planting churches, then, could be seen as acts of subterfuge, reaching all the way to Rome's outer limits, from Jerusalem to Spain.

When the story of Acts ends, Paul had not yet made it to Spain. When Paul took the relief offering to Jerusalem, he was arrested and imprisoned. Once again, Jewish problems led to Roman intervention. In this case, an angry Jewish mob accused Paul of violating temple rules, forcing a magistrate to take Paul into custody, eventually transferring him to Caesarea Maritima. After spending two years awaiting trial in Caesarea, Paul appealed to Caesar in order to be tried in Rome.[4] This is where the narrative in Acts ends—with Paul under house arrest at Rome (Acts 28:16-31). While Paul was in prison waiting for his day in court, he wrote several letters; we have five of them: Philippians, Colossians, Ephesians, Philemon and 2 Timothy. In these letters Paul makes reference to prison conditions—being in "chains" (Phil 1:7; Col 4:18; Philem 10)—talks about his trial (2 Tim 4:16) and its possible outcome (Phil 2:23; 2 Tim 4:6), or refers to himself as a "prisoner of the Lord" or "of Christ Jesus" (Eph 4:1; Philem 1). Traditionally it has been understood that Paul wrote these letters while he was imprisoned in Rome: the four so-called captivity letters during his house arrest (Acts 28:16) and 2 Timothy during a later, harsher, second imprisonment. In Philippians Paul refers to the imperial guard and the household of Caesar (Phil 1:13; 4:22), establishing a Roman provenance. Recently, however, some scholars have questioned whether Paul wrote these letters (especially Philippians) while he was imprisoned in Rome. First, Paul seems to emphasize the discomfort of his prison experience by constantly referring to the pressure of his "chains." This hardly sounds like the mild conditions described in Acts, where Paul looks like he's in detention rather than in a Roman prison. Second, and more substantively, some scholars have doubted whether there was enough time during a Roman imprisonment for all the correspondence to have transpired between Paul and the Philippians.

Did Paul play up the desperate situation in Philippians in order to win sympa-

---

[4]Or in order to avoid being released from Roman custody (and thus protection) in Judea.

thy? He acts like he's going to die (Phil 1:21; 2:17). Or does the uncertainty of the result of Roman justice (who would trust Nero?) coupled with the customary procedure of soldiers keeping watch over their charge with chains explain Paul's precarious situation highlighted in Philippians and minimized in Acts? Indeed, the situations described in Acts and Philippians are not that far apart. That Paul was able to receive visitors (and money!) and write letters implies he was under house arrest, chained to a guard.

The larger question is whether there was enough time during a Roman imprisonment for Paul to write Philippians. The problem is distance. The number of trips implied in the letter would have taken more than two years (Acts 28:30). First, someone carried news to the Philippians that Paul was in prison in Rome. Then the Philippians sent a gift via Epaphroditus. Along the way Epaphroditus became deathly ill. Word was sent to the Philippians about the illness. The Philippians sent word to Paul of their concern. Paul then sent the letter via Epaphroditus explaining why it took so long to respond to the gift and assure them of Epaphroditus's well-being. That's five trips (more land than sea) totaling more than four thousand miles. This time crunch has led some scholars to suppose Paul wrote Philippians during an Ephesian imprisonment, shortening the distance required to around fifteen hundred miles (mostly by sea).

The solution, however, rests on several assumptions. First is the assumption that Paul's comments on being mistreated in Ephesus mean that he was imprisoned there (1 Cor 15:32; 2 Cor 1:8-11). But most take the reference to Paul fighting the "wild animals at Ephesus" as figurative, and neither Acts nor 2 Corinthians speak of a lengthy imprisonment, only that Paul's colaborers were brought before the magistrate and released (Acts 19:28-41). Furthermore, Paul never mentioned he had been imprisoned in Ephesus, only that he had received a "sentence of death" (2 Cor 1:9), which could mean any number of things. Second, it is assumed that references in the Philippian letter to the imperial guard and Caesar's household apply to posts outside of Rome. Yet one wonders whether, if distance were not an issue, anyone would presume to suggest these were not references to Paul's Roman imprisonment. Finally, is distance really a problem? It is assumed that word had to travel between two fixed points, Rome and Philippi. But do the facts require this? Once Paul appealed to Caesar from Caesarea, news could have traveled to Philippi from Caesarea via one of Paul's companions while Paul himself was brought to Rome.[5] Also, once Epaphroditus

---

[5]Paul was sent by ship too late in the sailing season, so his friends would likely have traveled by land, making a stop in Philippi highly probable.

WHAT'S MORE . . .
Paul's Imprisonment

According to Acts, Paul was held in prison at least three times: in Philippi, in Caesarea and in Rome. More than likely there were several other occurrences, since he claims to have endured "far more imprisonments" in a letter written before he was arrested in Jerusalem and imprisoned in Caesarea/ Rome (2 Cor 11:23). The conditions of his imprisonment seem to match the three kinds of incarceration used by Roman magistrates. The *carcer* entailed the harshest conditions for the worst criminals. Prisoners feared this form of custody since many died from malnutrition, exposure or disease. There were no food rations or state-issued clothing for criminals or laws governing due process. These prisons operated at the discretion of the magistrate; many prisoners were left to rot in jail. Luke's description of Paul and Silas's imprisonment in Philippi sounds as though they were in a *carcer*. Under these conditions, no one was supposed to aid prisoners in their distress. It was just the opposite case for prisoners under house arrest. High-status defendants, or even those charged with lesser crimes, could rent their own quarters while awaiting trial or sentencing. Sometimes the prisoner would be chained to a guard. Most often the accused would merely be confined to quarters with a guard posted at the entrance. In either situation, these "free prisons" allowed visitors to take care of the needs of the prisoner, providing food, clothing and other personal effects and comforts. Luke describes Paul's Roman imprisonment using these terms (Acts 28:16-31). Finally, military custody was similar to free prisons in that the incarceration could occur anywhere; the only difference was that soldiers were given charge of the prisoners (Phil 1:13), determining where the criminal would be held. Therefore, in all three cases, it was the guard (whether military or civilian) who controlled prison conditions, not only allocating food and clothing, but determining whether the prisoner was to be chained, fettered or even isolated from outsiders.

---

fell ill during his trip to Rome, it is assumed these travelers would have met no one heading the opposite direction—someone who could have carried word to the Philippians of Epaphroditus's illness. Actually, only two trips between Rome and Philippi must be inferred from Paul's letter to the Philippians: Epaphroditus's coming and going. More than likely, Paul wrote Philippians, as well as Colossians, Ephesians, Philemon and 2 Timothy, from a Roman detention.[6]

While he was in prison, Paul wrote a lot about power. Philippians, Colossians and Ephesians are filled with power talk, and most of it centers on Christ. In Philippians Paul pictures every knee bowing at the name of Jesus, longing for the power of his resurrection, a power that enables Christ "to make all things subject to himself" (Phil 2:10; 3:10, 21). In Colossians Christ rescues his faithful from the powers of darkness, disarming the rulers and the powers at the cross, causing the peace of Christ to "rule in your hearts" (Col 1:13; 2:15; 3:15). And in Ephesians Paul speaks of the immeasurable greatness of the power of Christ, who is seated in heaven above all other powers and provides the power that is at work within the church, protecting Christ-believers from the "cosmic powers of this present darkness" (Eph 1:19-21; 3:20; 6:12). It is probably no coincidence that while Paul was detained in prison, chained to a Roman soldier, the victim of Roman sovereignty, he wrote of the wonder-working power of Christ. A supreme power, a cosmic kingdom, a Christ ruling over all powers, in heaven and on earth—this is the good news sent by a man in chains. To unbelievers Paul's letters would confirm a delusional state. Imprisonment was getting the best of him. If Christ is king, what is his ambassador doing in chains? To his converts, on the other hand, these messages from prison reaffirmed what they already knew: their allegiances belonged to the Christ who rules over all. According to Paul, Christ had already won the battle for the ages (Col 2:15). His coronation brought the highest honor (a name above all names, Phil 2:9) and the most powerful throne (seated above the heavens, Eph 1:20). All that was left for his heavenly colonists was to march against all foes, vanquishing all opposing powers (Eph 6:12). Indeed, it took a prisoner of Rome to teach citizens and subjects of the Roman Empire how to wear the armor of God (Eph 6:13-17) and to fight a good fight to the end (2 Tim 4:7). All they had to do was imitate him and become a prisoner of the Lord (Phil 3:17).

PHILIPPIANS: REJOICING IN CHAINS

It probably did not surprise Paul's converts in Philippi when they found out their apostle was in a Roman prison. Several years before, during Paul's first mission visit to Philippi, some of its citizenry had accused Paul of "disturbing our city" and "advocating customs that are not lawful for us as Romans to adopt or observe"

---

[6]The only other possibility would be during Paul's two-year imprisonment in Caesarea, where the distance for letter traffic between Paul and his churches would have been even greater.

(Acts 16:20-21). As far as these colonists were concerned, Paul's gospel ministry violated the Roman way of life—their social identity, their reason for having special status. Loyalty to the emperor compelled them to take extreme measures in silencing the troublemaker. That time, in the thoroughly Roman city of Philippi, Paul's offense led to a public beating and literal incarceration (remember, the *carcer* was the harshest form of imprisonment). So, it is quite understandable if Paul's converts in Philippi were sympathetic to Paul's circumstances when they heard he was "in chains" in Rome (especially the Philippian jailer who was led by his prisoner to "believe on the Lord Jesus," Acts 16:31). Knowing Paul would need help with provisions during his imprisonment, the Philippians sent a gift. This seems to be the occasion for Paul's letter to the Philippians. At the beginning and toward the end of his letter, Paul thanked his converts for their support (Phil 1:5-7; 4:10-19). But, as was his habit, Paul used the occasion to deal with other issues as well: conflict, unity, false teaching, true citizenship. Sorting out Paul's intentions and Philippian problems, scholars try to figure out how this letter did its job. Some look for clues in the letter in order to reconstruct the historical circumstances that prompted Paul to write what he did. Others maintain this is not a helpful strategy, arguing Paul wrote what he wrote because of the rhetorical conventions of writing a certain type of letter and not because he was addressing actual problems or opponents within the church.

Paul identifies several opponents throughout the letter: (1) those who "proclaim Christ out of selfish ambition," trying to add pressure to Paul's chains (Phil 1:17), (2) those identified by Paul as "your opponents," who were trying to "intimidate" the Philippians (Phil 1:28), (3) the "dogs" who "mutilate the flesh" (Phil 3:2), and (4) the "enemies of the cross of Christ" (Phil 3:18). The question, however, is whether Paul was identifying several different opponents of his gospel or offering several descriptions of the same Philippian troublemakers. That is to say, were the Philippian opponents identified in the beginning of the letter actually the same nefarious persons whom Paul called "dogs" and "enemies of the cross" at the end of the letter? Those who answer "yes" argue Paul was battling the same opposition he confronted in Galatia and Rome: the Judaizers. They fit the description. They are the "dogs of circumcision" who put confidence in the flesh (ethnic identity), whose "glory is in their shame" (a euphemism for genitals, thus referring to circumcision), whose "god is their belly" (referring to dietary laws) and who persecuted the Philippians and tried to ruin Paul's reputation.

This seems a reasonable solution. Yet nowhere in the letter does Paul take on Judaizer issues as he did in Galatians or Romans. If the Judaizers had infiltrated the church, shouldn't Paul have written somewhere in Philippians a warning like "don't get circumcised" (as in Galatians) or "stop fussing over food" (as in Romans)? Rather, Paul talks about unity and strife (Phil 2:1-4, 14-15; 4:2-3). The problem was a divided church. But, the opponents Paul attacks don't seem to be insiders (like in Corinth). Perhaps the better solution is sorting out whether Paul's instructions concerning the proper behavior of the Philippians have something to do with the explicit warnings he gives regarding their opponents. In other words, is it possible that when Paul was encouraging his converts to "be of the same mind" and "join in imitating me," he was countering the false teaching of the "dogs" and/or the "enemies of the cross"?

Trying to make the connection, scholars have put forward several proposals: (1) the opponents were Jewish Christian perfectionists (the law makes one holy), or (2) anti-Paulinists ashamed of his imprisonment, or (3) local church leaders trying to usurp Paul's authority, or (4) Philippian pagans requiring support of the imperial cult. A good case can be made for each of these, leading some to suggest the variety of possibilities may reveal Paul was confronting several opponentsy, not just one. He wrote one letter to deal with multiple opponents. Other scholars maintain we cannot identify a single opponent because Philippians is a literary composite of several letters.[7] Paul wrote multiple letters to deal with multiple opponents. This would explain why Paul sounds like he's ending the letter several times ("finally" appears twice, in Phil 3:1 and 4:8), why transitions between completely different subjects are so rough (between Phil 3:1 and 3:2 and between Phil 4:9 and 4:10), and why it is difficult to find a unifying theme in the letter. There is no manuscript evidence, though, for such a reconstruction.

These problems—difficulty in establishing the identity or identities of Paul's opponent(s) or the uneven nature of the Philippian letter—do not require such complex solutions. Perhaps the reason the opponents are so enigmatic and the issues addressed are so eclectic is because Paul was writing what has been called a friendship letter. Rather than assume Paul was attacking actual opponents in Philippi, some scholars argue the concerns Paul expressed were generic warnings (against potential enemies) common among friends. And when friends wrote each other, they customarily tightened the bonds of their alliance by reminding each other of their common enemies. Thus Paul's letter to the Philippians men-

---

[7]Over a long period of time, Paul had written several letters to the Philippians, addressing several issues (dealing with different opponents, addressing problems within the church, expressing thanks for the gift), and these fragments were eventually compiled as one letter; see Pheme Perkins, "Philippians: Theology for the Heavenly Politeuma," in *Pauline Theology*, ed. Jouette M. Bassler (Minneapolis: Fortress, 1991), 1:89-104.

tions opponents because it is a friendship letter.

In Paul's day to have friends was the same as declaring mutual enemies. Friendships were as much an alliance against common foes ("us" versus "them") as a relationship due to shared interests.[8] Threats, real or perceived, against a group of friends produced enmity. Stoking the fires of enmity helped steel the solidarity of friendships. This is why Paul kept talking about opponents when he was thanking the Philippians for their gift and addressing mutual concerns. What looks like a fragmented letter—moving to and fro between unrelated topics—is in reality a lit-

---

WHAT'S MORE . . .
An Example of a Friendship Letter

Even though I have been separated from you for a long time, I suffer this in body only. For I can never forget you or the impeccable way we were raised together from childhood up. Knowing that I myself am genuinely concerned about your affairs, and that I have worked unstintingly for what is most advantageous for you, I have assumed that you, too, have the same opinion of me and will refuse me in nothing. You will do well, therefore, to give close attention to the members of my household lest they need anything, to assist them in whatever they might need, and to write to us about whatever you should choose. (Pseudo-Demetrius, "Epistolary Types," c. 200 B.C.—A.D. 200)[a]

---

[a]"Ancient Epistolary Theorists," trans. A. J. Malherbe, *Ohio Journal of Religious Studies* 5 (1977): 33.

---

erary device in which sharing of resources and talking about outsiders were common among friends. Indeed, these letters were intended to overcome distance and to make up for the absence of friends. Recurrent themes of "I can't wait to see you" and "we really need each other" run throughout friendship letters. Additionally, insider talk about enmity and mutual affections, contrasting the behavior of terrible enemies and good friends, was part and parcel of friendship. Consequently, neither the dogs of circumcision nor the enemies of the cross should be identified

---

[8]The popular television series *Survivor* demonstrated this well. Picking some members as friends automatically made other enemies. Likewise, such "friendships" often had little to do with feelings and much to do with social survival.

as actual people causing problems within the Philippian church.[9] Instead, what Paul was doing was reminding his converts of their common enemies. Essentially he was saying: "Since we're friends, watch out for these types of people: they put confidence in the flesh and they live for earthly things." That is not to say, however, that Paul wasn't dealing with actual problems in the church. It is quite evident, for example, that certain members within the circle of friendship were not getting along (Phil 2:1-4; 4:2-3). Therefore, Paul wrote the Philippian letter using the selfless behavior of Christ, of Timothy, of Epaphroditus and even of himself in order to correct problems within and identify threats without.

I'm in prison. Rejoice! The letter to the Philippians is often referred to as "the epistle of joy," because "joy" and its sister traits (hope and peace) abound in the letter. Despite the circumstances attending the letter—Paul's imprisonment, the threat of false teachers and apparent rifts in the congregation—Paul prays with joy (Phil 1:4), endures incarceration with joy (Phil 1:18), instructs the Philippians in joy (Phil 2:1-11), ponders the possibility of death with joy (Phil 2:17-18) and admonishes them to live joyfully (Phil 3:1; 4:4). For the apostle, joy *(chara)* is not a mood that can be attained apart from faith; it is the byproduct of the work of divine grace *(charis)*. Those who have received God's favor *(charis)* through Christ Jesus are able to experience joy *(chara)* even in the midst of suffering. Therefore joy is not dependent on favorable circumstances. A believer is able to rejoice in suffering with the full assurance that these hardships are producing in them patience, character and hope (cf. Rom 5:3-4).

It is ironic that this letter was dispatched by a prisoner in Rome, the capital of the empire, to an imperial outpost, Philippi, to encourage colonists to stand firm in their heavenly citizenship by having the same mind as Christ who died on a Roman cross. Over the course of the letter, Paul gives several reasons why the Philippians should join him in rejoicing over his circumstances and their partnership in his ministry. His imprisonment: (1) helped spread the good news (Phil 1:12-18), (2) gave him an opportunity to honor Christ by choosing to die for him (Phil 1:19-26)[10] and (3) encouraged the Philippians to follow his example, suffering for

---

[9]See Stanley Stowers, "Friends and Enemies in the Politics of Heaven," in *Pauline Theology*, ed. Jouette M. Bassler (Minneapolis: Fortress, 1991), 1:105-21.

[10]But what choice did Paul have? Some think Paul was speaking hypothetically—if he could choose, he would die for Christ—that no choice was available to him. Some think Paul was contemplating suicide. Reeves argues the Philippians sent their gift to help Paul bribe his way out of prison. By refusing to use the gift in that way, Paul was choosing to die for Christ; see Rodney R. Reeves, "'To Be or Not to Be?' That Is Not the Question: Paul's Choice in Philippians 1:22," *Perspectives in Religious Studies* 19 (1992): 273-89.

Christ, standing firm against their opponents (Phil 1:27-30). But Paul's joy was not full; the Philippians were not acting like Paul or Christ when it came to how they treated each other (Phil 2:1-4). To make his point, Paul quoted the lyrics of an early Christian hymn the Philippians had probably sung many times (Phil 2:6-11).

The hymn to Christ. Paul earnestly desires for the "mind" of Christ to shape the lives and community in Philippi. So he sets up Jesus as the lordly example of humility and selfless service. The hymn he cites is constructed around two movements: (1) the descent from equality with God to the humiliation of the cross and (2) the ascent from death to exaltation by God and universal acclamation by all creatures.

One of the important interpretive questions in the hymn has to do with the meaning of the phrases "existing in the form of God" and "did not consider equality with God as something to be grasped" (Phil 2:6, our translation). Most scholars take these as references to the preexistence of Christ. Prior to his entrance into the world, he existed in the form of God. Nevertheless, he decided not to hold on to his equality with God. Instead he emptied himself and became a human being. According to this view, the hymn espouses the preexistence and incarnation of a divine person. But not all agree that the doctrine of the preexistence of Christ was

---

WHAT'S MORE . . .
Philippians 2:6-11

THE DESCENT (2:6-8)	THE ASCENT (2:9-11)
Though he was in the form of God	the Father
He did not consider equality	To the glory of God
with God as something	"Jesus Christ is Lord"
to be grasped	Every tongue confess that
He emptied himself	subterranean beings)
Taking the form of a servant	(of heavenly, earthly and
Becoming in the likeness	Every knee shall bow
of men	So at the name that belongs to Jesus
Being found in form as a man	above every name
He humbled himself	And bestowed on him the name
Becoming obedient to	Therefore God highly exalted him
death	Even death on a cross

---

grasped early enough by the church to have been included in the Philippian letter.[11] We think it likely that the hymn assumes some form of preexistence.[12] If he
had to "become man," he was not previously "man."

As a result of his faithful obedience, God super-exalted *(hyperypsōsen)* the
crucified Jesus and gave him the name above every name (Phil 2:9). Given the language in the hymn and the reverence accorded the name of God in Hebrew Scriptures, the name must be LORD *(kyrios)*, God's holy, unspeakable name (in the Hebrew, YHWH). This conclusion is confirmed by the universal acclamation of all
heavenly, earthly and subterranean creatures. When the name that belongs to
Jesus is expressed, "every knee [will] bow, . . . every tongue [will] confess that Jesus
Christ is Lord" (Phil 2:10-11, alluding to Is 45:23). This language belongs to one
of the most significant monotheistic passages in the Old Testament and refers
originally to the worship of YHWH.[13] The hymn writer has deliberately taken
scriptural language regarding the worship of Israel's one God and applied it to the
risen Jesus. This is a remarkable appropriation of God's name and worship. Since
the Father has bestowed his name upon the crucified Jesus, the worship of Jesus
by all creatures brings glory to God (Phil 2:11).

Men with the mind of Christ. Even though Paul talked much about what the
Philippians should think, for him the gospel was more than a set of beliefs. It was
a way of life—a koinonia (fellowship) of purpose worth sharing (Phil 1:7), an attitude worth adopting (Phil 2:5) and an example worth imitating (Phil 3:17).
What happened to Christ will happen to those who believe in him. The gospel
story is replicated in every believer. This was the ultimate reason to rejoice, to be
"poured out as a libation" offering, a sacrifice of faith (Phil 2:17). Indeed, a life of

---

[11]Interpretive schemes abound for unraveling the meaning of this hymn. James Dunn (*Theology of Paul
the Apostle* [Grand Rapids: Eerdmans, 1998], p. 286) notes the scriptural allusions to Adam and concludes that the Christ hymn in Philippians 2 is "the fullest expression of Adam Christology in the
NT" (cf. Heb 2:5-9). In particular he notes that Adam is made in the image of God (cf. Gen 1:27)
and is tempted to grasp at equality with God (cf. Gen 3:5). The first man fails, of course, and becomes
an obedient slave to corruption and death. For Dunn and other interpreters, Jesus provides the con-
verse of Adam. The second Adam did not try to grasp for equality with God (something he did not
possess). Rather he emptied himself and humbled himself by being willing to die a criminal's death
on the cross. Since Adam-Christ typologies are common in Paul's letters, a subtle allusion to Jesus as
a new Adam, who reverses the curse of Adam's sin, may underwrite the hymn. Michael Gorman
(*Cruciformity: Paul's Narrative Spirituality of the Cross* [Grand Rapids: Eerdmans, 2001], pp. 88-94)
suggests that the humiliation-exaltation structure in the hymn is based on a similar pattern found in
the fourth servant song (Is 52:13—53:12; augmented by Is 45:23).

[12]Cf. Douglas McCready, *He Came Down from Heaven: The Preexistence of Christ and the Christian Faith*
(Downers Grove, Ill.: InterVarsity Press, 1995), pp. 73-80.

[13]David B. Capes, *Old Testament Yahweh Texts in Paul's Christology,* Wissenschaftliche Untersuchungen
zum Neuen Testament 2/47 (Tübingen: J. C. B. Mohr, 1992), pp. 157-67.

gospel sacrifice, looking out for the interests of others, had already been modeled by Timothy (Phil 2:19-24), Epaphroditus (Phil 2:25-30) and especially Paul (Phil 3:2-16).

Paul, like Christ, did not regard his honorable status as something to be preserved at all costs. Prior to his Christophany, Paul had quite a résumé and enjoyed a number of bragging rights (Phil 3:4-6). The pre-Christian Paul benefited from a status nearly all would have envied. But as the hymn suggests, Paul took on the attitude of the preincarnate Christ; he emptied himself of those gains and wrote them off as losses for the sake of Christ (Phil 3:7). Indeed, he suffered the loss of all things and considered them "dung" compared to the excellence of what it means to "know Christ" and be found in him (Phil 3:8-10).[14] As Paul identified with the humiliation and death of Jesus, he expected also to share in his resurrection/exaltation (Phil 3:10). In that sense, Paul's own story will be absorbed one day into the wider story of Christ. So Paul invites the Philippians to join him in imitating Christ and to pay attention to those, like Timothy and Epaphroditus, who present a model for how to live.[15]

True citizenship. While the Philippians took pride in their Roman citizenship, Paul urged them to understand their true citizenship is in heaven. As "resident aliens" they will not be at home in the world, for they belong to another city. Paul earnestly desired for the Philippian church to be an alternative community in the world. For that to be true they must not look to Rome for guidance; they must look to heaven. They must refuse to worship Caesar as Lord; they must worship the Lord Jesus. They must expect only small benefits from any so-called earthly saviors; they must wait for a Savior from heaven who will transform the world with power. Those who pattern their lives on the story of the Christ's humiliation and exaltation can expect their humbled bodies to be transformed into a body like his (Phil 2:9; 3:21). In the end, the Christ hymn provides Paul with more than a pattern for humble service to others; it also offers the (implicit) promise that believers who enter into his humiliation will also enter into his glorious exaltation (Phil 3:20-21).

---

[14]To "know Christ" implies intimacy and a knowledge based on experience. It is knowledge of a person, not knowledge about a thing. The upshot of Paul's own Christ-patterned humility is that he exchanged a law-based righteousness for the faith-based righteousness of God made possible through the faithfulness of Christ's obedient sacrifice on the cross (Phil 3:9).

[15]The imperative in Phil 3:17 is difficult to translate. It means either "join together in imitating me" or "join me in imitating Christ." Both are possible since Paul clearly urged believers to imitate Christ elsewhere and he also encouraged others to imitate him as one who imitates Christ (see Eph 5:1; 1 Thess 1:7; 1 Cor 11:1; cf. Phil 4:9).

Power in contentment. Paul waited until the end of the letter to thank the Philippians for their gift. It gave him an opportunity to write about the contentment he had learned through his many ups and downs. Unfortunately many translations obscure the point. Note particularly the NASB translation: "I can do all things through Him who strengthens me" (Phil 4:13). The context is contentment, not "doing." The passage is better rendered: "I have strength to be content in every sit-

---

SO WHAT?
Is It Significant That Paul Thanks the Philippians for the Gift?

In our culture, Paul's manner of giving thanks has led some to accuse Paul of offering a "thankless thanks." At the very least, to say "I didn't really need it" seems an odd way to say "thanks." As we mentioned in chapter one, Paul lived in a world where all gifts came with strings attached. In fact, a serious challenge for Paul throughout his ministry was accepting assistance from wealthy benefactors without becoming entangled in a patron-client relationship. Normally, accepting a gift such as the Philippians sent would make Paul a client. Paul needed to express gratitude without becoming a paid client. It's possible the "Philippian" gift was actually from an individual such as Lydia or the jailer. Paul then thanked the church, rather than the individual, thereby demonstrating how Christian gift giving is different. The giver is a steward of God's resources so the beneficiary becomes a client of God, rather than of the steward.

---

uation through the one who empowers me." Paul knew the power in contentment. He understood that lack of contentment is the root of all sorts of personal and social failures (e.g., coveting, stealing, adultery, murder). Contentment, on the other hand, leads to peace and joyful satisfaction. But Paul had to "learn" contentment in the rugged situations of life. It is unnatural. Discontent is the normal state of man, as Henry David Thoreau understood: "The mass of men live lives of quiet desperation." But Paul found the secret of contentment for every situation through Christ's power resident in him.

Paul knew his converts would "keep on doing the things that you have learned and received and heard and seen in me" (Phil 4:9), because, as he wrote at the beginning of the letter, "the one who began a good work among you will bring it to completion by the day of Jesus Christ" (Phil 1:6). This was Paul's confident hope, confirmed by the Philippians' gift, which was another reason for rejoicing. The gift proved they were looking out for the interest of others. Even though Paul didn't need it (Phil 4:10-14), the Philippians did the right thing by sending it (Phil 4:15-19)—"a fragrant offering, a sacrifice acceptable and pleasing to God" (Phil 4:18). By assigning the gift to God, Paul remained a slave of Christ and avoided the appearance of becoming a client of the Philippians. Indeed, as a colony of heaven, the Philippians were to live as citizens worthy of the gospel (Phil 1:27) by sacrificing to God (not Caesar!), confessing Jesus as Lord (not Caesar!), and sharing in the good news of Paul (not Caesar!). Suggestively, this fellowship of purpose would extend the reach of their friendship even to the household of Caesar. So Paul cleverly ends the letter with greetings coveted by any colonist: "The friends who are with me greet you. All the saints greet you, especially those of the emperor's household" (Phil 4:21-22). Rejoice!

COLOSSIANS: FULLNESS OF LIFE IN CHRIST

As readers of Paul's letters, we come to a different world when we read the Epistle to the Colossians. First, it is quite apparent Paul did not start the church in Colossae (Col 2:1); the gospel came to the Colossians due to the preaching of one of their own, Epaphras, Paul's missionary partner (Col 1:7; 4:12). That Paul wrote a letter to a church he had not founded was not new (recall Romans). The difference, however, is that Paul had a hand in the beginnings of the gospel ministry at Colossae, since Epaphras was his coworker. In other words, Paul was the Colossians' "grandfather" in the faith. This makes for an intriguing relationship. Why was Paul the one who wrote the letter to the Colossians?[16] He did not know them; they had probably never met him (Col 2:1). Since the letter addressed specific problems within the church, shouldn't the letter have come from Epaphras? Epaphras was the Colossians' father in the faith and knew the situation firsthand, but he could not go because he was imprisoned along with Paul at the time (Philem 23). Nevertheless, it was Paul and not Epaphras who wrote letters to Colossae as well as Laodicea (Col 4:13-16), another church founded by Epaphras in the same region. Even though Paul had no firsthand knowledge of the persons involved (as with Romans), he still wrote the letter as if he were directly involved in the affairs

---

[16]One precipitating factor may have been the Philemon/Onesimus problem. It is clear why Paul would write to Philemon, but writing to Philemon (a church leader in Colossae) without addressing the church may have been seen as rude. Also, Paul wants to bring corporate pressure on Philemon to deal well with Onesimus, so he mentions publicly that Onesimus is a faithful and dear brother (Col 4:9), preventing Philemon from burying the problem out of sight; see also Philemon 21 and Colossians 4:1. Nonetheless, this alone cannot explain the letter.

of the church. Unlike Romans, where he was trying to gain a hearing, Paul acted as if the Colossians were his converts.

Second, Colossians does not read like a letter from Paul. Those who read Greek can see the difference better than those who rely on translations. The vocabulary is different. The style is different. Even the major themes are different when contrasted with the letters we have studied so far. We maintain the differences in vocabulary, style and themes in Colossians (as well as in other so-called deutero-Pauline letters) are attributable in some measure to conventions of letter writing in the first century.[17] Corporate authorship, the influence of secretaries, the dynamics of letter composition and the insertion of preformed material (like hymns and confessions) during different stages of writing contribute to the variable qualities of Paul's letters. Even though Paul's name appears at the head of the letter, these writings did not come from Paul alone. He had help—a lot of help. Therefore, one cannot dismiss a letter as non-Pauline simply on the basis of stylistic, linguistic or theological peculiarities. In fact, one cannot speak of a Pauline style since the production of all of his letters involved the input of many people. Paul did not author these letters by himself; he never claimed he did.

But even so, why is Colossians different? We must consider whether Timothy had a greater role in its composition, or Paul used his secretary differently, or the problems Paul corrected were unique and required different vocabulary. It may be that it is a combination of all three factors that sets Colossians apart from other Pauline letters. Besides, the theological ideas highlighted in Colossians are not altogether absent from Paul's earlier letters; for instance, 1 Corinthians 8:6; 15:25-27 and Romans 8:18-31 speak of Christ reigning over creation and conquering his enemies.

Why then did Paul send this rather unusual letter to the Colossians, with its grandiloquent description of Christ at the beginning and mundane instructions on domestic matters at the end? To most scholars, the occasion for the letter depends upon how one identifies the so-called Colossian heresy that surfaces in the middle of the letter. Paul wanted to make one thing plain: this teaching did not come from him and it had nothing to do with Christ. Where did this false teaching come from? Once again, we are reading someone else's mail. We are faced with the difficult task of trying to identify Paul's opponents based on his comments. In other words, where Paul is pushing hard, there must be resistance. And since we know

---

[17]See E. Randolph Richards, *Paul and First-Century Letter Writing: Secretaries, Composition and Collection* (Downers Grove, Ill.: InterVarsity Press, 2004).

very little about the Colossians,[18] scholars are forced to argue from a broader context, either Hellenistic, Jewish or Roman. Because Paul characterized the false teaching as a "human tradition" and a "philosophy" based on the "elemental spirits of the universe," with ascetic practices apparently derived from a cosmic dualism (in which flesh = evil, spirit = good), most commentators have been satisfied with assigning the false teaching to the influence of regional mystery religions. It is argued that certain Christ-believers had combined their new beliefs with their old ones (local mythologies), a syncretism resulting in the bizarre beliefs and practices of the "Colossian heresy." Recently, scholars have taken references to Jewish practices (circumcision, sabbaths, dietary code) as an indication that Paul was countering a mystical form of Judaism found in Phrygia—a region known for its fascination with magic. Perhaps Paul was, once again, trying to distinguish Jewish ways from gospel living for a church that may have received its start in the synagogue.[19] Finally, some interpreters have found subversive language in Colossians, claiming Paul was fighting for the allegiances of his converts in the face of the ever-present imperial cult. At the very least, Paul was taking on the Roman way of life when he affirmed the all-ruling, all-powerful Christ and told the Colossians how to run their households.[20]

The Colossian hymn. Whatever the source of the "philosophy," Paul believed this false teaching challenged the all-sufficient, comprehensive work of Christ. This is why Paul started the letter with a picture of an exalted Christ, the "[visible] image of the invisible God" who created all things and rules over all things. Paul drives home the sufficiency of Christ by quoting what appears to be a preformed tradition that commemorates the person and finished work of Christ.[21] The hymn is based broadly on the Jewish wisdom tradition in which divine wis-

---

[18]The site where Colossae was located (on the south bank of the Lycus River, ten miles east of Laodicea, in the Phrygian region of the senatorial province of Asia Minor) has not yet been excavated. As of our writing, the last two years have seen significant archaeological work in the Lycus valley, but no published reports have yet appeared. What we know about Colossae is gleaned from historians: a hundred years before Paul, Colossae was a prosperous city with a significant population, known for its textile industry (the Lycus valley provided ideal pasture for sheep). But by the first century A.D. the city had lost its preeminence to the neighboring cities of Hierapolis (ten miles west/northwest of Colossae) and Laodicea. We also know that a devastating earthquake destroyed Laodicea around A.D. 60, a tremor that probably affected Colossae as well.

[19]See James D. G. Dunn, *The Epistles to the Colossians and to Philemon* (Grand Rapids: Eerdmans, 1996), pp. 29-35.

[20]See Brian J. Walsh and Sylvia C. Keesmaat, *Colossians Remixed: Subverting the Empire* (Downers Grove, Ill.: InterVarsity Press, 2004).

[21]Based on its content, it seems likely someone within the Pauline circle is the author of this piece, whether Paul or an associate.

dom reflects the divine glory and serves as the agent of creation and the agent of redemption (Wisdom of Solomon 7:22-28; cf. Prov 8). Early theologians like Paul found wisdom language helpful in providing Christ-believers with a wealth of symbols and images to describe their newly found faith in a variety of ways and contexts. The hymn can be divided into two parts: (1) the Son as Creator of all things (Col 1:15-17) and (2) the Son as Head of the church and Reconciler of all things (Col 1:18-20).

The first stanza of the hymn declares the Son to be "the image of the invisible God, the firstborn of all creation" (Col 1:15). The phrase "image of God" recalls the Genesis narrative where a similar phrase refers to the creation of "the Adam" in God's image and likeness (Gen 1:27; cf. 1 Cor 11:7). But the Son is not Adam's twin; he is the agent of creation, the one through whom, in whom and for whom all things are made (Col 1:16). For "all things" the hymn explicitly cites heavenly and earthly entities, visible and invisible realities, along with the entire assortment of angels, principalities and powers. These are the spiritual powers feared and placated in the folk religions around Colossae. Whether or not these powers acknowledge it, they exist because of the Son who holds all things together (Col 1:17).

The second stanza celebrates the headship of the Son over the church and the (eventual) reconciliation of all things by the cross. Paul writes: "He is the head of

---

SO WHAT?
Does It Matter That Jesus Is the "Firstborn"?

Some interpreters take the phrase "the firstborn of all creation" to mean the Son is a created being. Yet in the next line he is heralded as the creative agent behind "all things in heaven and on earth" (Col 1:16; cf. wisdom in Prov 8). "Firstborn" in biblical times did not refer to sequence but to status, as Colossians 1:17 makes clear ("he himself is before all things"). The Western mind has a hard time grasping this. For us *firstborn* refers to birth order. Therefore it cannot be changed. But *firstborn* in the ancient world referred primarily to status and inheritance. Thus Jacob, the second-born, buys the title from Esau, and becomes the "firstborn." Again, we see that Jesus has many titles, "Son of God," "Son of David," "the Christ" and now "firstborn," each of which conveys a special meaning.

the body, the church" (Col 1:18). The line combines two potent Pauline emphases: (1) the church as the body of Christ (1 Cor 12:12-29 and Rom 12:3-8) and (2) the headship of Christ (1 Cor 11:3; cf. Eph 4:15). Here the focus is on Christology not ecclesiology, as the apostle emphasizes the headship and preeminence of Christ over against his people. As "the firstborn from the dead" (Col 1:18), the Son leads the way from death to life. He is the beginning of the new creation: in him the resurrection from the dead has begun.

The hymn continues, "For in him all the fullness of God was pleased to dwell" (Col 1:19). This is an especially evocative statement of what theologians refer to as the incarnation, namely, the man Jesus is the fleshy place of God's complete indwelling. This makes him uniquely qualified to serve as the agent of reconciliation (Col 1:20). Reconciliation assumes that humanity and the rest of creation has fallen out of God's favor. As Paul figures it, nothing below is able to establish peace. So God's Son comes into the world and establishes peace through his blood on the cross. For Paul, Christ on the cross is the locus of reconciliation. And this reconciliation is not partial; it bestows benefits in heaven and on earth (Col 1:20).

Christ in you. Paul sees his imprisonment as part of the drama of redemption. His suffering is not pointless; it is for the sake of the Colossian believers. As he endures the harshness of imprisonment, he continues his ministry through suffering. He writes: "I am now rejoicing in my sufferings for your sake, and in my flesh I am completing what is lacking in Christ's afflictions for the sake of his body, that is, the church" (Col 1:24). He does not mean, of course, that in some way the death of Jesus is not sufficient for his church. After all, he has recited a hymn that declares the ultimate sufficiency of Christ for the reconciliation of all things. The phrase "what is lacking" may be best interpreted "what is remaining"; so we render it, "I am completing in my flesh what remains of Christ's afflictions." For Paul, Christ's sufferings are the main act in the drama of redemption. Still, Christ-believers like Paul continue those sufferings until the end of the age because they are his body. Then again Christ identifies with his persecuted and afflicted people so thoroughly that it can be said that he suffers with them.

God's plan is to include the Colossians with the covenant people so that they become equal partners, thoroughly vested with God's glory. Paul sums it up: "Christ in you, the hope of glory" (Col 1:27). Stated another way, the one in whom God's fullness dwells (Christ) now dwells in and among the Colossians. Typically Paul locates believers "in Christ." In Colossians he turns it on its head to say that Christ is located in them. This notion of mutual indwelling becomes a hallmark of Pauline theology. Residing within and among them is the fullness of God's power and wisdom. If that is true, then there is no need to look anywhere else for help in overcoming the problems they face. They can press on to maturity. They have the All-Sufficient One in them. So, Christ is the answer to Paul's initial prayer for the Colossians (Col 1:3-8).

The Colossian heresy. Although the Colossians have received the true gospel, Paul turns now from discussing the sufficiency of Christ to addressing more directly certain beliefs that make up the Colossian heresy. We cannot tell from the letter whether these beliefs and practices represent a single heretical movement or two or more diverse movements. If they do reflect a single movement, attempts to identify it will remain elusive because they do not correspond precisely to any known religious group. Most likely, we have here a blending of Jewish and pagan religious beliefs combined with practices unique to the Colossae region. This alternative gospel threatens to derail these believers completely if they do not decide to return to faith in Christ alone and allow him to take root in their lives (Col 2:6-7).

Paul perceived that the Colossians' faith was imperiled by shifting allegiances to human tradition, "philosophy" and real or imagined spiritual forces. In Colossians 2:8-23 Paul warned his converts about a "philosophy" that would take them captive like prisoners of war. It was a deceptive, empty, human tradition, "according to the elemental spirits of the universe, and not according to Christ" (Col 2:8). Evidently some of the Colossians were succumbing to its teachings, living by prohibitions such as: "Do not handle, do not taste, do not touch" (Col 2:21). Those who refused to submit were condemned as impious, since they did not control their fleshly desires in "matters of food and drink or of observing festivals, new moons, or sabbaths" (Col 2:16). The philosophers also claimed to have special visions of heaven, "insisting on self-abasement and worship of angels" (Col 2:18). Perhaps they practiced some kind of corporal mortification, punishing their bodies in order to enter the presence of God and to join the angels in worship. Or maybe their ascetic ways had something to do with acknowledging human weakness, observing taboos as they worshiped angelic powers. Whatever the reason, Paul questioned these practices as vacuous ("shadow of what is to come," Col 2:17) and temporal ("these regulations refer to things that perish with use," Col 2:22). These "human commands" had "the appearance of wisdom" but were worthless in fighting self-indulgence (Col 2:22-23), serving only to inflate the egos of those who kept them (Col 2:18).

The household code. The letter to the Colossians contains one of the oldest surviving household codes from the early Christian movement (cf. Eph 5:21—6:9; 1 Pet 2:18—3:7). These household codes typically provide guidance to family

WHAT'S MORE . . .
Key Elements of the Colossian Heresy

1. Philosophy and human traditions (Col 2:8). Some in Colossae were pursuing wisdom "according to human tradition" with little regard to the revelation of Christ, the wisdom of God. According to Paul, the fullness of the deity is embodied in Christ (Col 1:19; 2:9) so those who are in him have already entered into the fullness of life (Col 2:10). Compared to God's revelation in Christ, the benefits of human philosophy pale.

2. Spiritual powers (Col 2:8, 15, 22). The Colossians were living in fear of spiritual beings and following local customs on how to appease them. According to Paul, believers no longer need to worry, for on the cross Christ defeated "the principalities and powers" and led them in "triumph" (Col 2:15, 20 NKJV). The "triumph" was a spectacular parade that took place after a great military victory. The triumphant general would lead a procession of conquered, humiliated prisoners on their way to execution or slavery. According to the apostle, Christ triumphed over the spiritual powers on the cross, so believers should welcome their champion, Christ, and enjoy the benefits of his victory.

3. Jewish practices (Col 2:11, 16, 20-21). Some Gentiles in Colossae had begun adopting Jewish practices such as circumcision, dietary codes and holiday observances. Paul counters by insisting that even the uncircumcised belong to the true circumcision in Christ. For Paul, baptism is the "mark" of the new covenant. Better than any other symbol, it expresses the unique, cross-centered story of the Christian life. Through the cross Christ erases sin and cancels the legal demands that condemn humans; so Gentiles do not benefit by observing Jewish law (Col 2:14).

4. Ascetic practices (Col 2:18, 23). To achieve some advantage over fleshly desires, some Colossian Christians were fasting and engaging in severe forms of bodily discipline. Paul argues against extreme ascetic acts because they have limited value and place the emphasis on things below rather than things above (Col 3:1-2). Spiritual transformation, he believes, comes through a threefold strategy: (1) meditation on eternal realities, (2) setting aside sin and (3) taking on Christ-centered virtues (Col 3:1-17). It is not enough merely to deprive the flesh; one must fill the void with a proper mindset and upright behaviors modeled on the love of Christ.

5. Worship of angels (Col 2:18).[a] The Colossian heresy included some element of the veneration of angels. Paul deals preemptively with this sacrilege by pointing to Christ who is the fullness of deity in bodily form. Reverence is to be accorded to God and his Messiah, not to the angels.

---

[a]The phrase "worship of angels" is obscure. It can mean either joining the angels in the worship of God (subjective genitive) or bowing before the angels in worship (objective genitive). Given the pagan context and rarity of monotheism, the latter seems most likely.

members on how to relate to one another in a manner consistent with the gospel. If "Jesus is Lord," then Christian households will look and act differently than their pagan neighbors. Often the phrase "in the Lord" punctuates passages like this. It signifies the ethical imperative of the gospel, the demands made upon believers in light of God's saving activity in Christ.[22] So, for example, wives are to be subject to their husbands "in the Lord" (Col 3:18), children are to obey their parents, for this is pleasing "in the Lord" (Col 3:20), and slaves are to obey their masters out of the fear of the Lord (Col 3:22). Consequently, Christian family life is to be lived "in the Lord," that is, under his complete authority.

Modern families, particularly in the West, are in certain respects notably different from their ancient counterparts. The ancient family was primarily an ex-

---

WHAT'S MORE . . .
Paul's Household Code in Colossians 3

Wives, be subject to your husbands (Col 3:18)	*Husbands*, love your wives (Col 3:19)
Children, obey your parents (Col 3:20)	*Fathers*, do not provoke children to anger (Col 3:21)
Slaves, obey your masters (Col 3:22-25)	*Masters*, deal with your slaves justly and fairly (Col 4:1)

---

tended unit, often slave owning, thoroughly patriarchal. Thus, a typical household code emphasized how each group (wife, children, slave) related to the master. The modern, Western family, on the other hand, is a smaller, nuclear unit, not slave holding, and occasionally patriarchal. The theological context for the Colossian household code is the appropriation of the new nature—the character of Christ, the peace of Christ, the word of Christ—and the encouragement to do everything in the name of Christ (Col 3:10-25), modifying how relationships should be addressed. Thus, Paul seems to begin with the basic code but then adds the reciprocal responsibility of the "master of the house."

Any attempt to interpret Paul's counsel must take into consideration both the

---

[22]See J. Christiaan Beker, *Paul the Apostle: The Triumph of God in Life and Thought* (Philadephia: Fortress, 1980), pp. 272-74.

WHAT'S MORE . . .
A Matter of Interpretation

Some earlier generations of Christians took Paul's counsel regarding slavery as tacit permission to own slaves themselves. They concluded that slavery was a God-ordained, honorable institution. They held slaves and fought anyone who tried to intervene on behalf of their "property." Fortunately, other Christians read Paul and the full counsel of Scripture differently and started a movement to abolish slavery. These abolitionists interpreted Paul's comments against the background of life in the Roman Empire where (1) between 20 to 30 percent of people were slaves (some estimate that up to 90 percent of the people in Rome were) and (2) where slavery was not a matter of race. After a good deal of study and prayer, they determined that Paul's admonitions did not provide a universal warrant for slavery, especially the kind of racialized slavery that developed in the West.

Like our ancestors in the faith, we must be alert and careful in determining how to interpret and apply Paul's teachings. In order to read Paul well, we must come to know his culture and our own. Only then will we be able to divide rightly the word of truth.

cultural and theological contexts. It is always best to try to understand Paul on his own terms rather than on ours. So, when Paul instructs wives to submit to their husbands, he does so in conformity with pagan culture around him. Wifely submission is the typical advice of every moralist during Paul's time. But Paul's instruction is different. First, Paul addresses the wife, not her husband. He considers the wife a free, moral agent, a sister in Christ, perfectly capable of understanding and following his teachings. Other household codes at the time are addressed to the male head of household about how to keep the family in line. By addressing the wife, Paul immediately elevates her status in the community.

Second, Paul's counsel has a qualitative distinction epitomized by the phrase "in the Lord." Wives' submission to their husbands may well be the cultural norm, as is slavery, but it has been illuminated by the light of the Christian story. It is qualified by mutual love, forgiveness and kindness. It is attenuated by a husband's love and gentleness. Finally, Paul does not consider every situation. He is laying the foundation for a general approach to the family based upon the new creation. He does not deal with circumstances in which husbands abuse their wives or are

perpetually unfaithful. In making modern application, we should avoid pressing
Paul's instruction into service for which it was not intended.

Given the pervasiveness of slavery in Paul's world, it is no surprise that Paul's
churches were populated with slaves and often led by slave owners. He turns first
to the slaves and instructs them: "Slaves, obey your earthly masters *[kyriois]* in
everything, not only while being watched and in order to please them, but whole-
heartedly, fearing the Lord *[kyrion]*" (Col 3:22). For Paul the bottom line is this:
whatever service slaves provide is for the Lord, not for their masters. As a result,
they should work hard, recognizing that the Lord will reward or punish them (Col
3:23-25). The advice to the masters is brief but weighty: "Masters *[kyrioi]*, treat
your slaves justly and fairly, for you know that you also have a Master *[kyrion]* in
heaven" (Col 4:1). The play on words is intentional. The apostle hopes to shape
the behavior of the slave owners by appealing to the lordship of Jesus. They might
be called "lords" or "masters" on some human level, but he reminds them that they
were ultimately servants of a heavenly Lord who expected justice and fairness.

Indeed, the peace of Christ's rule would be seen in the way families behaved
toward each other (Col 3:18—4:1), the way Christ-believers treated unbelievers
(Col 4:2-6), and the way different churches encouraged each other through their
faithful service (Col 4:3-17). The household code would have been especially important to Christ-believers since they met for worship in each other's homes. So
Paul introduced his teachings with the challenge: "Let the peace of Christ rule in

SO WHAT?
Does the Kind of Peace Make a Difference?

Peace is peace, right? The Romans kept peace with a sword. It was the ces-
sation of hostility rather than the peace that comes from love—loving each
other, loving our enemies. That kind of peacemaking only happens when
the "peace of Christ rules in [our] hearts" and we "clothe [our]selves with
love" (Col 3:15, 14). Sadly, many American Christians are quicker to cheer
for a militarily produced peace rather than to pursue the things that truly
make for peace. Some have said the pax Romana has been replaced by a pax
Americana. Christ enjoined us to be peacemakers. True, but how we bring
peace should be determined by the way Christ has brought peace to us (Col
2:14-15).

your hearts" (Col 3:15). Paul had proven that Christ was sufficient for all things, cosmic and domestic—a pax Christi that eclipsed the pax Romana. Amazingly, this letter of peace, extolling the universal power of Christ, came from a man who asked nothing for himself except: "Remember my chains" (Col 4:18). For Paul the prisoner, Christ was sufficient.

EPHESIANS: POWER AND UNITY IN CHRIST

Paul's letter to the Ephesians reads like a shotgun sermon: it covers a wide array of topics and is aimed in only a general direction. As a matter of fact, if it weren't for two words appearing at the beginning of the letter, "in Ephesus" (Eph 1:1), Ephesians could be categorized as a "General Epistle" or "catholic letter," much like 1 Peter or 1 John. The generic quality of these letters is evident in several ways: (1) there seems to be no specific occasion for them, (2) no particular opponents are identified, (3) general instructions for the church and the home are given, (4) the usual personal greetings at the end of the letter are practically missing, and (5) the significance of the person and work of Christ is put forward in broad, sweeping terms applicable to all believers. What makes this comparison even more suggestive for Ephesians is that the earliest copies of this letter actually omit the words "in Ephesus." In other words, if our Bibles reflected the text of Ephesians found among the earliest Greek manuscripts, we might call this letter "1 Paul," and interpret its meaning without establishing a specific historical context. We would simply recognize it for what it most likely is: a generic letter, copied and circulated in a particular region, meant to be read by several churches who called Paul their apostle.

Yet the question remains: why do we call this letter Ephesians? Why do critical editions of the Greek New Testament retain the words "in Ephesus" even though the earliest (and most would argue, best) manuscripts omit them? The simple answer is: because church tradition says so. Canonical lists, patristic quotations and all manuscripts (even the earliest copies that omit "in Ephesus" in the first verse) affix "to the Ephesians" as the title of this letter. Yet accepting Ephesus as the destination for this letter proves to be troublesome. Paul sounds like he doesn't know the people he's addressing; and they, in turn, have only heard about him from others (Eph 1:15; 3:2-3). That doesn't square with what Acts tells us. In fact, according to Acts, Paul spent more time in Ephesus (over two years) than anywhere else during his mission trips (Acts 19:10). Also, the impersonal tone of Ephesians doesn't fit well with the intimate knowledge Paul would have had of the house churches in Ephesus. And since no specific problems were addressed in the letter, one is left with the impression that either the believers in Ephesus had no significant problems (really?) or this letter was not intended only for them, that is, generic issues were raised and addressed because it was written for a general readership. That could explain why the earliest Greek manuscripts have no addressee: Ephesians was either a circular letter sent out to the churches of Asia Minor, coming to rest in Ephesus, or Paul sent the Ephesians a letter he intended for them to publish among the churches of the region. Thus there was no specific occasion for this letter. We can hypothesize that while he was a prisoner in Rome, Paul, the apostle of the Gentiles, wanted to send one last letter to the churches he worked so hard to establish, reminding them to walk worthy of their calling in Christ Jesus.

But Paul had recently sent a letter to Colossae, a city only one hundred miles east of Ephesus, and had asked them to exchange letters with another church in Asia Minor. Why would he send another letter, very similar in content, to the same region and at about the same time? Indeed, Colossians and Ephesians are epistolary paternal twins, sharing several literary features: they seem to follow the same general outline, deal with the same topics, and even end the same way (the commendation of Tychicus is exactly the same, word for word). This literary symmetry has led many scholars to suspect that Ephesians didn't come from Paul at all. They argue that Paul wouldn't have written a generic letter like Ephesians: (1) he wouldn't copy himself, (2) Paul always sent letters to address specific problems, (3) the style of Ephesians is too lofty and grandiose, (4) the theology is inconsistent with other Pauline statements (e.g., Paul would never have said that the law was "abolished," Eph 2:15; cf. Rom 2:25), and (5) the narrative of Paul's ministry in Ephesians 3:1-13 sounds more like a eulogy for a dead man than a self-description of an active apostle. So it is argued that Ephesians is a pseudonymous letter written by an admirer of Paul long after the apostle died in order to preserve the allegiances of the apostle's churches in Asia Minor. This "someone" knew Paul's theology and vocabulary so well that he was able to write a letter that sounded much like Paul.[23]

We maintain, on the other hand, that Ephesians sounds like Paul because it came from Paul. Why must Paul's death be a precondition for a letter like Ephesians to appear and gain acceptance among the churches? Couldn't Paul have endorsed (or even produced) a letter like Ephesians, despite its differences? It is true that those who accept the Pauline authorship of Ephesians need to account for the differences between Ephesians and the rest of the Pauline corpus, more particularly

---

[23]See Andrew Lincoln, *Ephesians*, Word Biblical Commentary (Word: Dallas, 1990), 42:60-73.

the generally recognized "authentic" letters of Paul. Once again, we believe that the peculiarities of Ephesians can be attributed to Paul's use of a secretary, the factor of corporate authorship (in this case, the influence of Colossians), the incorporation of preformed material and the occasion of the letter. What we have here is what scholars have suspected all along: Paul took previously existing notes, quotations, arguments (and in this case, Colossians), reworked it to fit particular occasions, incorporated other voices, used preformed material and issued letters that were meant to be read by several house churches. What makes Ephesians unique is that it had such a broad readership (Asia Minor), and yet it was still written as a "word on target." In other words, Paul had his reasons for writing Ephesians.

According to Clinton Arnold, Paul wrote Ephesians to address the problems his converts faced when they gave up their magical arts for the gospel of Jesus Christ.[24] Ephesus was the home of the temple of Artemis (Diana), one of the seven ancient wonders of the world. The Cayster River connected Ephesus to the Aegean Sea, and thus the capital of Asia Minor was a seaport town, where thousands of merchants would bring their wares to the great agora at the harbor. The massive temple situated on the harbor hill in Ephesus was easily seen from the marketplace. In fact, magic (or what we might more commonly call sorcery) was a marketable trade; its popularity was not restricted to Ephesus. The inhabitants of Asia Minor (especially Phrygia) were known for their devotion to magic. Devotees would ascend the temple in Ephesus, pay their respects to Artemis and purchase magical amulets to protect them from malevolent powers. It was customary to hire priests to inscribe magical incantations (curses and blessings) taken from the legendary mysterious writing found on a rock that fell from the sky (Acts 19:25, 35). Paul's converts had disposed of their magical charms, leaving themselves unprotected and vulnerable to their enemies (both celestial and terrestrial). According to this reconstruction of the situation, Paul wrote Ephesians in order to encourage the house churches, not only in Ephesus but also in the surrounding region, to remain strong in their faith. This is why the letter is filled with power language. From the beginning, Paul purposefully presents Christ as exalted above all powers through his resurrection, picturing the church as the body of Christ, thereby placing "all rule and authority and power and dominion" under the feet of Paul's converts (Eph 1:18-23). Consequently, at the end of the letter, Paul encourages the Ephesians to put on the "whole armor of God," and to fight against "the cosmic powers of this present darkness" (Eph 6:10-17). They need no magical

---

[24]See Clinton Arnold, *Ephesians: Power and Magic* (New York: Cambridge University Press, 1989), pp. 51-69.

amulets, for Christ is their protection against "the wiles of the devil" (Eph 6:11).

The problems magic caused for Paul's converts may provide a context for the basis of his argument at the beginning of the letter and his advice near the end. But what about the heart of the letter, where Paul spends much time writing about diversity, unity, the purpose of his ministry and the requirements for holy living? It could be Paul was heading off a potential isolationist movement within the predominantly Gentile church in Ephesus. Markus Barth maintains that Paul's letter was intended for Gentile converts who came into the church after Paul left Ephesus and were dismissive of the church's spiritual heritage and Jewish roots.[25] This explains: (1) why the letter seems to be addressed exclusively to Gentiles (Eph 2:11-13), (2) why Paul emphasized the diversity (Jew and Gentile) and unity of the church ("one Lord, one faith, one baptism" [Eph 4:5]) using Jewish metaphors ("commonwealth of Israel," "household of God," "holy temple"[Eph 2:12, 19, 21]) and thereby affirming a Jewish heritage, (3) why Paul relied so heavily upon preformed material drawn from early Christian worship services (baptismal confessions [Eph 5:14], hymns [Eph 1:4-10], early catechisms [Eph 4:8])—implying that idiosyncrasies must give way to long-held traditions—and (4) why Paul seems practically to be introducing himself to his readers in Ephesians 3. The apostle was setting these newcomers straight about faith in Christ. Nowhere was it more evident that Christ had broken down the wall of separation between Jews and Gentiles than when they worshiped the God of Israel together. This is why, at the heart of the letter, there are declarations of and invitations to praise God for the redemption he planned before the foundation of the world. Paul knows worship unleashes the power of transformation. So with worship never more than a few thoughts away, he hopes to forge a new identity for Christ-believers so they can properly relate to the new creation already begun in the cross and resurrection of Jesus.[26]

Spiritual blessings in heavenly places. Ephesians immediately erupts in praise to God with a style of Jewish thanksgiving called *berakah* ("blessed be" or "praise be"; Eph 1:3).[27] The opening section (Eph 1:3-14) is composed of one long sentence

---

[25]Markus Barth, *Ephesians: Introduction, Translation and Commentary on Chapters 1-3*, Anchor Bible (New York: Doubleday, 1974), pp. 10-12.

[26]Andrew Lincoln and A. J. M. Wedderburn, *The Theology of the Later Pauline Letters* (Cambridge: Cambridge University Press, 1993), p. 91.

[27]The *berakah*-formula consists of three parts: (1) a form of the word "blessed"; (2) a name(s) or title(s) of God; and (3) benefit(s) from God that elicit the praise. The formula occurs in the Old Testament (e.g., Gen 24:27; Ps 103 [LXX 102]; 104 [LXX 103]; 144 [LXX 143]), the Apocrypha (e.g., 1 Maccabees 4:30-33), and the Dead Sea Scrolls (1QS11). It is found in other New Testament books (e.g., 1 Pet 1:3-12). Paul employs the expression here and in 2 Corinthians 1:3-7 with adjustments made for his unique Christian theology.

in Greek, punctuated three times by the phrase "to the praise of his glory" (Eph 1:6, 12, 14). The blessings bestowed on believers are qualified by two phrases: "in the heavenly places" and "in Christ." "In the heavenly places" is a unique phrase found only in Ephesians (Eph 1:3, 20; 2:6; 3:10; 6:12). Given Paul's use of the expression elsewhere, "heavenly places" appears to mean the spiritual location occupied by Christ-believers in this age.[28] In this "place" believers are spiritually raised—the first rumblings of the general resurrection at the parousia—to fellowship with Christ, enjoying many "blessings" even as they wait for the full flowering of salvation. Still, "heavenly places" is not the final destination for the faithful because of the spiritual conflicts that are constantly being waged there.

Second, the spiritual blessings which Paul enumerates are granted by God "in Christ." The phrase "in Christ" is common in Paul but concentrated here in Ephesians. Two primary notions underwrite it: (1) Christ is the one through whom God has acted to redeem the world. This is the instrumental sense, because Christ is the means of salvation. (2) Christ is the place where believers are located. This is the local or incorporative sense, because Christ-believers are united with the crucified and risen Jesus. The byproducts of this vital connection with Christ (or being "in him") constitute "every spiritual blessing."

Paul then proceeds to unpack some of the spiritual blessings available in Christ in the heavenly places:

1. predestination (Eph 1:4)—chosen in Christ before the foundation of the world
2. adoption (Eph 1:5)—adopted as sons through Jesus Christ
3. redemption (Eph 1:7)—redeemed through his blood
4. forgiveness (Eph 1:7)—forgiven for our trespasses
5. revelation (Eph 1:9)—made known to us the mystery of his will
6. sealed (Eph 1:13)—sealed with the Holy Spirit of promise
7. inheritance (Eph 1:14)—the Holy Spirit is "the pledge of our inheritance"

These blessings describe some aspect (past, present and future) of the salvation Paul finds available in Jesus Christ.

Predestination and election are theological ideas widely misunderstood. A close look at what Paul has to say can help clear up some of the confusion. Paul employs the concept of election in a uniquely Christian way. He states that God "chose us

---

[28]This often confuses modern readers because we use "heaven" to describe realm(s) above us. In Jewish thought, the various realms are layers of heavens, with the third heaven being the highest.

in Christ before the foundation of the world to be holy and blameless before him"
(Eph 1:4). The apostle understands election as having a christological and communal focus. By christological we mean that God predestined and chose Christ to
be the redeemer before the world was created. He is "the Chosen One." By communal we mean that God elects a people, a community of faith located in Christ.
Nowhere in Paul's letters does he suggest that God chooses individuals; the language is always corporate. In effect, Paul's teaching on election and predestination
can be understood this way: God chose Christ from the beginning and chooses
those who choose Christ. According to Paul, God's plan is to create a community
that is holy and blameless (Eph 1:4). These are not conditions of acceptance; they
are the consequences of God's saving work.

The berakah concludes with the role played by the Spirit in the spiritual blessings (Eph 1:13-14). The Holy Spirit seals those who hear the gospel and believe.
To "seal" is to confirm or authenticate (e.g., letters and books are sealed with a
mark establishing authenticity). Packages (and tombs! Mt 27:66) were sealed to
insure nothing was stolen from them. Biblical prophets borrowed the image to depict how God marks his elect to preserve them from judgment (e.g., Ezek 9:3-6;
Rev 7:1-17). Paul adopts this prophetic image to portray the Spirit's role in confirming, authenticating and ultimately safeguarding Christ-believers until the Day
of Judgment. The Holy Spirit, he says, serves as "the pledge of our inheritance"
(Eph 1:14). By "pledge" he means "down payment," the spiritual power available
to all Christ-believers on this side of the parousia.

Seated at the right hand. The theological basis for the spiritual blessings realized
by Christ-believers is found in the resurrection and Lordship of Jesus. According
to Paul, God "raised him from the dead and seated him at his right hand in the
heavenly places . . . [and God] has put all things under his [Jesus'] feet" (Eph
1:20-22). The image of Jesus sitting at God's right hand means that their crucified
Lord occupies the place of sovereign power over the universe. Psalm 8 praises
God's majestic name for the (first) creation, particularly granting humans dominion and putting all things under their feet (Ps 8:6). For Paul, the resurrection and
exaltation mark the beginning of a new creation and a return to God's original design that sin corrupted and Christ corrected. The dominion of Christ, the new
Adam, extends beyond the fish, birds and animals to include "all rule and authority
and power and dominion, and above every name that is named, not only in this
age but also in the age to come" (Eph 1:21). By this Paul underscores that the risen
and exalted Christ currently reigns over those spiritual powers most feared by citizens of Asia Minor. Paul believes that all these powers (fate, demons, spirits,

curses, gods and assorted magical practices) have been subjected to Christ by the actions of God.[29] As Christ's body, the church stands as the blessed beneficiary of Christ's headship over all things (Eph 1:23). The ultimate redemption of the cosmos has begun and the church is the first wave of God's glorious plan. At the parousia the rest of the creation will follow the church's lead in bowing and confess-

---

SO WHAT?
Why Does It Matter if "They" Have "Their" Church and "We" Have "Ours"?

Paul was accused of violating the "dividing wall" in the Jerusalem temple (Acts 21:28). That incident began the process that led to his imprisonment in Rome, where he was writing. This issue was personal for Paul. The Jew-Gentile divide is just one example of the barriers that we erect. Racial, sexual, religious, social, economic and educational barriers threaten Christ's church in our time. As Paul proclaims the radical unity of Jew and Gentile in one body for his day, he announces a revolutionary vision in which Christ's new creation dismantles the old nature with its prejudices, enmities and strife that divide contemporary churches. Through the cross Christ "put to death the hostility" that comes with bigotry (Eph 2:16). Martin Luther King Jr. once mourned the fact that the most segregated hour during the week was Sunday at eleven a.m. According to Paul, anyone who maintains and promotes such divisions denies the ultimacy of the cross and the lordship of Jesus through whom all barriers have been overthrown. Bigots are enemies of the cross.

---

ing "Jesus Christ is Lord."

From death to life. The Ephesians were once dead in trespasses and sins. They were ruled by passions of the flesh and were on the path destined for destruction and everlasting wrath (Eph 2:3). "But now" all of that has changed. Death has given way to life. Despite their former state, God made them alive together with

---

[29]For recent attempts to come to grips with Paul's language of "the powers" see C. E. Arnold, *Powers of Darkness: Principalities and Powers in Paul's Letters* (Downers Grove, Ill.: InterVarsity Press, 1992). Walter Wink, *Naming the Powers: The Language of Power in the New Testament* (Philadelphia: Fortress, 1984) attempts to demythologize the powers, claiming they were not spiritual beings but "inner and outer aspects of any given manifestation of power" (p. 5). These would include social structures, institutions, states and religious movements (pp. 104-5).

Christ. He raised them and seated them together with him in heavenly places (Eph 2:5-6) so that his destiny becomes theirs. In that sense salvation is an event of the past, accomplished in Christ Jesus. But the abiding result of that salvation accompanies those who accept God's gift of grace into a new way of life (Eph 2:8-9). Grace is God's disposition toward humanity that brings salvation to a society of rebels. Faith is the means by which salvation is experienced and appropriated. The entire plan—its origin, execution and result—is the gift of God. While others are walking after the flesh, its passions and false gods (cf. Eph 2:1-3), Christ-believers are called to walk in the good works prepared by God.

Through Christ God has reached out to those far from grace to bring them near (Eph 2:13), both Jews and Gentiles to himself, making the two groups into one (Eph 2:14). Ultimately, the one God is creating one new people in the Messiah, a new race uniting all the sons of Adam and daughters of Eve into a single, reconciling community. The Messiah accomplishes this by tearing down "the dividing wall, that is, the hostility between us" (Eph 2:14). By "dividing wall" Paul has in mind (1) the literal wall in the temple separating the Gentiles from the Jews (see Josephus *A History of the Jewish War* 5.194; cf. Acts 21:27-36) and (2) the figurative wall made up of enmity on both sides. This wall has been dismantled "in his flesh," that is, by the cross.

A life worthy of the call. In Ephesians 4—6 the imprisoned Paul pleads with his audience to "lead a life worthy of the calling to which you have been called" (Eph 4:1; cf. 1 Thess 2:12). The worthy life, he says, is characterized by humility, gentleness, patience, forbearance and love. These are the ways of Christ. Armed with these attributes, Christ-believers are to strive to maintain the unity of the Spirit in the bond of peace (Eph 4:3). No effort is to be spared in the attempt to hold on to the precious unity that God wills, fragile though it be. But believers are not required to create that unity. The Spirit has already done that. Their job is more modest but no less important; they are to guard the unity. This unity is grounded in the oneness of God and its corollaries: one body, one Spirit, one hope, one Lord, one faith, one baptism and one God and Father of all (Eph 4:4-6).

The one body (of Christ) is composed of many members, each graciously gifted (Eph 4:7; cf. 1 Cor 12:7, 11). But rather than list the gifts given to each member of Christ's body (cf. Rom 12 and 1 Cor 12), Paul lays out job descriptions for the gifted leadership: (1) to equip the saints to do the work of ministry; (2) to build up the body of Christ; and (3) to move the church toward unity and maturity (Eph 4:12-14). Because all are gifted, every member of Christ's body is to serve, trained by the leadership. But without competent leadership the church is not encouraged, unity is not maintained, and false doctrines continue to assail the weaker members.

Put off ... put on: Living the good life (empowered by the Spirit). According to Paul, Christ-believers are to put aside (off) their old nature since it belongs to the former age and has been corrupted by deceitful lusts (Eph 4:22). In its place they are to put on the new nature, which is part of the new creation, fashioned after righteousness, holiness and truth (Eph 4:23-24). He admonishes the "children of light" not to engage in the sexually impure and covetous lifestyles of the disobedient (Eph 5:7), quoting an early baptismal liturgy: "Sleeper, awake! Rise from the dead, and Christ will shine on you" (Eph 5:14). Christ-believers, Paul reminds them, have already experienced a type of spiritual resurrection that unites them with the risen Jesus. Though they will one day arise bodily, they walk even now in Christ's light that shines on and through them. As a result, they are able to reflect the light of Christ and expose the spiritual and moral darkness around them. Paul exhorts them to be filled with the Spirit (Eph 5:18) by singing (Eph 5:19), by making melody (Eph 5:19), by giving thanks (Eph 5:20) and by submitting to one another (Eph 5:21). This last idea, of submitting to one another, segues Paul into a household code.

The household code. The Ephesian household code[30] originates in the directive regarding mutual submission.[31] Mutual caring and yielding to others are constant themes in Paul's letters (cf. Phil 2:1-11; 1 Cor 8). And yet in the Ephesian code Paul is occupied primarily with the responsibility of the husband. Mutual submission is to manifest itself in a husband's love for his wife (Eph 5:25-29), with Christ's sacrifice providing the basis and standard. Husbands are to love their wives as they love and care for their own bodies. For Paul, husbandly love is a healthy form of self-love, because in marriage the two become one (Eph 5:31, quoting Gen 2:24). Sacrificial love protects the ideal of marriage established from the beginning.[32] In the end the husband's love for his wife actualizes the second great commandment: "love your neighbor as yourself" (Lev 19:18; cf. Eph 5:33).

---

[30]See the background comments on the household code in Colossians 3:18—4:1.

[31]Ephesians 5:22 does not contain a verb. It takes its verbal idea, "be subject to," from 5:21. This fact alone demonstrates how tightly connected are mutual and wifely submission. As Michael Gorman (*Apostle of the Crucified Lord: A Theological Introduction to Paul and His Letters* [Grand Rapids: Eerdmans, 2004], p. 524) rightly notes, the household code in Ephesians is not an attempt to impose pagan, patriarchal values on the church but to impose spiritually empowered, mutual submission on a pagan, patriarchal structure.

[32]For Paul the ideal of marriage is laid out clearly in Genesis. It consists of four elements: (1) one man, (2) one woman, (3) one-flesh relationship and (4) commitment for life. If someone seeks to change or leave out any element, one misses the ideal. Polygamy, divorce, homosexual unions, adultery, one-night stands and so on all violate the ideal established by God from the beginning.

The armor of God. Paul's final admonitions create a memorable image. Believers, Paul writes, are to put on the full armor of God to do battle with spiritual powers that threaten them (Eph 6:12). They are to appropriate the Lord's strength and protect themselves with the "whole armor of God" so that no matter what the devil throws their way, they will be able to stand (Eph 6:10-11). The battle, Paul believes, is not against human enemies but against principalities, powers, agents of darkness and evil spirit-beings. Inspired by the prophets, he links each piece of protective armor to some aspect of God's power and work. For example, Paul urges that their feet be protected with the "gospel of peace" (Is 52:7: "How beautiful upon the mountains are the feet of the messenger who announces peace, who brings good news"). The breastplate of righteousness and the helmet of salvation echo Isaiah's oracle (Is 59:16-17; cf. Wisdom of Solomon 5:17-20). The other armor includes loins girded with truth, the shield of faith and the sword of the Spirit, which is the word of God (Eph 6:14-17). The armor provides believers with the defensive and offensive power they need. Each piece of armor reminds the faithful that they are fully protected by God's great might—and so safe from the magical powers that threaten them. The letter draws to a close with an admonition for believers to pray through every situation by the Spirit (Eph 6:18) and to intercede for all the saints, and especially for Paul, the ambassador in chains.

We may never know for certain the situation that prompted Paul's letter to the Ephesians. What is apparent, however, is that this letter captures the heart and soul of his gospel ministry, the essence of his Christology and ecclesiology. From the beatific blessing of Ephesians 1:3-14 to the battle armor of God in 6:10-17, Paul's pastoral concern for his converts shines through every line as he celebrates the present tense of God's salvation. These one-time pagans are presently raised with Christ Jesus, seated in the heavenly places—the temple of the living God. Jew and Gentile (Eph 3:7-19) are the one body of Christ (Eph 4:1-16), walking in truth (Eph 4:17-32), imitators of God and children of light (Eph 5:1-20). Their homes belong to Christ (Eph 5:21—6:9), and they wage a war against enemies who are not "blood and flesh" (Eph 6:10-17), because they are strong in the Lord. Wearing the armor of God, Paul summoned these soldiers to fight alongside their apostle, a prisoner in chains. Their mission? To bring the peace of God "to the whole community" because of their "undying love" for Christ (Eph 6:23-24). It's no wonder some scholars believe this letter fits well the church of the second century. Ephesians is a letter for the church universal, a message for the ages.

READ MORE ABOUT IT

DPL Articles:

"Citizenship," pp. 139-41, by M. Reasoner.

"Colossians, Letter to the," pp. 147-53, by P. T. O'Brien.

"Ephesians, Letter to the," pp. 238-49, by C. E. Arnold.

"Households and Household Codes," pp. 417-19, by P. H. Towner.

"Hymns, Hymn Fragments, Songs, Spiritual Songs," pp. 419-23, by R. P. Martin.

"Lord," pp. 560-69, by L. W. Hurtado.

"Philippians, Letter to the," pp. 707-13, by G. F. Hawthorne.

"Prison, Prisoner," pp. 752-54, by D. G. Reid.

9

The Imprisoned Paul

Letters to Individuals

PAUL GAVE ADVICE TO THE VERY END. He considered personal problems within the church as his business. Up to this point, Paul had written letters for a corporate setting, requiring the different house churches in a particular city to gather together to hear their apostle identify and correct particular problems within the fellowship, occasionally calling out individuals by name (Phil 4:2; Col 4:17). But with his letters to Philemon, Timothy and Titus, Paul took a different approach. With regard to Philemon, Paul wrote a personal letter from prison and addressed it not only to Philemon but also to the house church that met in his home (Philem 1, 2), not to all of the Colossian Christ-believers (evidently the group that met in Nympha's house didn't need to hear the letter, Col 4:15). In the case of 2 Timothy, the imprisoned Paul chose not to send another letter to the Ephesians. Rather, he wrote this letter directly to Timothy in hope that his young apprentice would take matters into his own hands, confronting false teachers and correcting corrupt teaching in the house churches of Ephesus. In other words, rather than having 1 and 2 Colossians and 1, 2 and 3 Ephesians in our canon, we have both corporate and personal letters: Colossians and Philemon, Ephesians and letters to Timothy. Why did Paul do it this way? Does this indicate that Paul changed his epistolary strategy toward the end of his life? Or, in these cases, did unusual circumstances within the house churches require a different tactic?

PHILEMON: CONFIDENT OF OBEDIENCE

Paul wrote a letter to the Colossians telling them, among other things, that slaves should obey their masters and that masters should be fair to their slaves (Col 3:22-4:1).[1] But there was a problem of certain complexity in one of the house churches—the one that met in Philemon's home—that required more attention than what a generic, pastoral word of advice would cover. What can be inferred from the letter to Philemon is that Onesimus (whose name means "useful"), a slave of Philemon, had become a convert of Paul while the apostle was in prison (Philem 10). Tychicus was carrying the letter to the Colossians, along with (or escorting) Onesimus, who was returning to Philemon with this letter in hand (Col 4:7-9). In this personal letter, Paul made three requests: (1) Philemon should welcome the slave as a "beloved brother," as if Onesimus were Paul (Philem 16-17), (2) Paul should be allowed to repay any debt Onesimus owed Philemon (Philem 18-19), and (3) Philemon should prepare a guest room for Paul when he came to Colossae (Philem 22). Paul also stated that he would have preferred to keep Onesimus as a personal assistant, making a pun on the meaning of the slave's name: "Formerly, he was useless *(achrestan)* to you, but now he is indeed useful *(euchrestan)* to you and to me" (Philem 11). He even toyed with the idea of using his apostolic authority to order Philemon to release his slave to Paul (Philem 8-9). But he decided, rather, to appeal to Philemon's conscience, reminding him of his debt to Paul ("your owing me even your own self"), hoping that Philemon would consent to sending Onesimus back to the apostle (Philem 12-19).

Even though Paul implies many things in the letter, there is much we don't know: (1) where Paul was imprisoned when he wrote the letter, (2) whether the letter to Philemon was sent around the same time as Colossians, (3) the identities of Apphia and Archippus, (4) the kind of relationship that existed between Paul and Philemon, whom the apostle calls a "dear friend and co-worker" and "partner," (5) the debt Onesimus owed Philemon and the debt Philemon owed Paul, (6) the circumstances under which Paul and Onesimus met, (7) how Onesimus had become "useless" to Philemon, (8) what "benefit" Paul was expecting from Philemon, (9) what Paul was implying when he expected Philemon to do "even more than I say," and (10) why Paul asked Philemon to prepare a guest room for him even though he was in prison. Because of these teasing innuendoes and suggestive implications, inquiring minds try to draw out inferences, filling in the information gaps in hopes of making sense of the "whole story." If we could figure

---

[1]We cannot be certain the letters were written at the same time, but if not, then Onesimus made two trips from Rome to Colossae, which seems unnecessary.

out the events leading up to this letter, then we might be in a better position to answer the question of why Paul felt it necessary to write a separate letter to Philemon.

Paul and Onesimus. Much of the mystery would be solved if we knew for certain the circumstances under which Paul and Onesimus met. There are three possibilities. (1) If Onesimus had been sent by Philemon to minister to the imprisoned apostle, then Paul was asking Philemon to release Onesimus, sending him back to help Paul while he was in prison. Given this scenario, no problems existed between Philemon and Onesimus. Basically, Paul wrote the letter to call in a debt: "I did something for you, now do something for me." This reconstruction is plausible, but it is difficult to explain Paul's comment that Onesimus was "useless" to Philemon (Philem 11), hardly the sort of slave likely to be sent on such an important task. (2) If Onesimus was a runaway slave who was converted by the imprisoned Paul, then it seems quite obvious what Paul was up to. He was trying to get Philemon to take back a rebellious slave without punishing him since Onesimus had changed his ways and had become Philemon's "brother" in the faith. And Paul was hoping that Philemon would voluntarily release Onesimus to the service of

---

WHAT'S MORE . . .
Legally Running Away

Slaves were required by law to protect their master's property, including themselves. If a slave did something that so angered his master that the master might well kill or injure the slave, then Roman law stated the slave could remove himself or herself from the master's reach until he cooled off. The slave's best option was to flee to an *amicus domini*, a "friend of the master," who would hopefully intercede for the slave, calm the master and avoid a "loss of property" for the master. For this to work, the "friend" really needed to be of equal or greater status than the master and (obviously) inclined to help. It also helped if the "friend" was nearby, because the slave was a runaway until he was in the "friend's" custody. If this were the case, why would Onesimus run all the way to Rome to find a friend of his master? It is difficult to explain. It is possible that whatever he had done was so grievous, he wasn't going to find a supporter nearby. Yet he had heard his master speak of Paul and this new faith (and its emphasis on forgiveness), and Onesimus decided this Paul and his gospel were his only hope.

Paul. This would require Onesimus to "obey his master," and carry the letter to Philemon, regardless of the consequences. While this is a popular reconstruction, it is difficult to explain how a runaway slave could have met a Roman (Paul) who was under house arrest. (3) If Onesimus was seeking out Paul to adjudicate a grievance against his master, which was allowed by Roman law, then Paul was taking sides with Onesimus. This would require Philemon to treat his slave "justly and fairly." Paul is appealing (virtually commanding) Philemon on the basis of their friendship to accept Onesimus back—despite whatever he had done—and even hinting at freeing him.

Any one of the three scenarios would explain why Paul needed to send a personal letter to Philemon. But the fact that the letter was not only intended for Philemon but was supposed to be read to the entire group of Christ-believers who met in his home may indicate Paul was trying to add social pressure to get Philemon to comply with his "request." The balance of judgment may fall, therefore, on the side of the second and third scenarios, where additional pressure would make better sense (if Paul simply wanted Onesimus, he would only have needed to ask for him, since Philemon had already shared his slave with the apostle). There must have been a problem between master and slave. In the legal world, Philemon was the master, Onesimus his slave and Paul his friend. But in the church world, Paul was father and apostle to both Philemon and Onesimus, where slave and master had become equals—brothers. Since we must first sort out the loaded terms Paul used in this tangled web of social and spiritual relations, it is difficult to figure out the problem Paul was trying to solve. No doubt the onus was on Philemon. Paul was the broker trying to work a deal, and Onesimus was the bone of contention—either "useless" or "useful." Yet, regardless of the circumstances, according to Paul, Onesimus's conversion had changed everything. The gospel was supposed to enable a master and a slave to act like brothers. And Paul would travel to Colossae to make sure of it. Indeed, his request to "prepare the room" may have been more of a threat than a promise. But, then again, Philemon's "love for all the saints" and "faith toward the Lord Jesus" were well known, having reached the ears of a man under arrest (Philem 4-7). Since Philemon, a man of such great faith, was praying for Paul's release, it would only be a matter of time before the apostle would be free and would need a guest room in Colossae (Philem 22). Most likely, then, Paul wrote this letter toward the end of his first Roman imprisonment.

The question of slavery. For the imprisoned apostle, the gospel was a powerful social engineer, capable of making brothers of a freeman and a slave, eradicating class distinction, closing the social distance (cf. Gal 3:26-28). A key reference to Paul's attitude is found in Philemon 15-16: "Perhaps this is the reason he was separated from you for a while, so that you might have him back forever, no longer as a slave but more than a slave, a beloved brother—especially to me but how much

---

SO WHAT?
A World Without Slaves?

Christians today often struggle to understand why Paul (and other Christians) couldn't see the inherent injustice in slavery. Scholars often say, "They could not imagine a world without slaves." We wonder, "Why couldn't they?" Well, slaves did most of the cooking, building, farming, shop keeping and industry. In the ancient world, slaves filled the role that wage-earning employees fill today. Our society today couldn't function without employees—at least we can't imagine how it could. In fact, the similarities are more striking. Most ancient slaves "got off work" about five p.m. They could, if they chose, work a night job and earn personal money. They could even own slaves of their own. Many slaves were "freed" at about age thirty. We are not suggesting ancient slavery was somehow "not so bad"; it was a terrible injustice. However, the virtual slavery of the minimum-wage employee in America (or even worse in developing countries) is not so different, and many modern Christians remain silent. Can we imagine a society without them? What will future Christians say of us?

---

more to you, both in the flesh and in the Lord." But we should avoid drawing too many conclusions from this statement regarding Paul's attitude toward slavery. As a man of his day, when one in every three or four people was a slave, he likely accepted slavery as part of the fabric of society. Nevertheless, his admonitions to Philemon played an important role in helping later generations of Christ-believers see that slavery is ultimately incompatible with the Christian faith. Paul postulates that the interruption in Onesimus's service has a greater good in view. They are separated briefly (by God perhaps) as master and slave to be united forever as brothers in Christ (Philem 15-16).

Conspicuously absent from Philemon is any reference to the death, resurrection or parousia of Christ. This is due to the occasion of the letter, not that Paul had changed his theological commitments. In fact, the person and work of Christ form the substructure of the letter. As in all his other letters, the Lord Jesus and God the Father are the sources of grace and peace (Philem 3, 25). Jesus is the object of Philemon's love and the focus of every good work (Philem 4-6). He is the reason for Paul's imprisonment (Philem 9) and for his boldness in approaching Philemon. He is the content of the gospel for which Paul is in chains (Philem 13). His is the kingdom where slaves can be named brothers (Philem 16). So while Christology may not be center stage in Philemon, it is the foundation that drives Paul's appeal.

LETTERS WITHOUT HISTORICAL CONTEXT: FIRST TIMOTHY AND TITUS

Evidently, Philemon's prayers worked. Paul was released from prison. Acts, on the other hand, gives no impression that Paul ever got out of jail. Luke ends his story with Paul preaching the gospel to the ends of the earth from a Roman prison. Yet in 1 Timothy and Titus, Paul is a free man, giving instructions to his coworkers whom he left behind in Ephesus (Timothy) and Crete (Titus). According to 1 Timothy, Paul was somewhere in Macedonia when he sent this letter to Timothy (1 Tim 1:3), probably in or going to Nicopolis (Achaia) when he wrote to Titus (Tit 3:12). Although a few scholars have tried to fit these details into Paul's itinerary as recorded in Acts (maybe Paul wrote these letters during his third mission trip), most believe that 1 Timothy and Titus were written sometime after Paul's first Roman imprisonment. As a matter of fact, the greater number of Pauline scholars today believe these "Pastoral Epistles" to Timothy and Titus were written long after Paul died; they are pseudonymous literature. Where the majority of scholars accept the Pauline authorship of seven of thirteen letters attributed to the apostle (Galatians, 1 Thessalonians, 1 and 2 Corinthians, Romans, Philippians, Philemon), and split somewhat evenly over the authenticity of three (2 Thessalonians, Colossians and Ephesians), the scales of scholarly opinion tip decidedly against the Pastoral Epistles (1 and 2 Timothy and Titus) as being genuine Pauline letters. The arguments against Pauline authorship hinge, once again, upon the vocabulary, style and content of these letters when compared to the uncontested "authentic" letters of Paul.

For example, the Pastorals have a higher percentage (over 35 percent higher) of unique words (*hapax legomena*, a Greek expression meaning "written once") compared to other Pauline letters. Is it feasible that, toward the end of his life, Paul demonstrated a sudden burst of vocabulary, a verbal flourish unprecedented in his writing? Furthermore, the style of these letters is very different from others; the author uses many "faithful sayings" or proverbs or confessions, often quoting other people. Would Paul, a man who boasted he did not receive his gospel from men (Gal 1:12) and who had no problem relying upon his own authority to solve problems (1 Cor 7:25), find it necessary to quote others to beef up his pastoral advice, particularly advice for a close colleague like Timothy or Titus? In fact, some scholars argue that much of what was written in the Pastoral Epistles would have been very familiar to Paul's faithful coworkers—common instructions Timothy helped dispense to other churches as Paul's co-author (the household advice is very similar to what was written to the Colossians). Why would Paul write what his associates already knew? Regarding the parts of the letter that would have appeared as novel to Timothy or Titus, scholars argue that these instructions were too advanced for first-century churches. For example, issuing requirements for church offices like bishops and deacons sounds more like the organization of the second-century church as seen in the letters of Ignatius.

In fact, some scholars think all this talk about "church order" and "tradition" and the proper behavior of women in response to church problems is the opposite of what Paul promoted in his ministry. The life "in the Spirit" advocated by the

WHAT'S MORE . . .
Letter from Ignatius to the Magnesians

> I exhort you: Be zealous to do all things in harmony with God, with the bishop presiding in the place of God and the presbyters in the place of the Council of the Apostles, and the deacons, who are most dear to me, entrusted with the service of Jesus Christ, who was from eternity with the Father and was made manifest at the end of time. Be then all in conformity with God, and respect one another; and let no man regard his neighbour according to the flesh, but in everything love one another in Jesus Christ. Let there be nothing in you which can divide you, but be united with the bishop and with those who preside over you as an example and lesson of immortality. As then the Lord was united to the Father and did nothing without him, neither by himself nor through the Apostles, so do you do nothing without the bishop and the presbyters.[a]

[a]Ignatius *To the Magnesians* 6.1-7.1.

"real Paul" was creative and open-ended, and did not discriminate according to gender, ethnicity or social status. Additionally, when Paul took on heresy, he attacked the teaching itself, not the character of its proponents, which is what happens throughout the Pastoral Epistles.

Taken together, these are fairly weighty arguments against Pauline authorship. Those who defend the Pastoral Epistles as Pauline maintain, on the other hand, that each argument does not bear the weight of the scrutiny it delivers.[2] Quite frankly, many of the arguments are overstated. For example, it has been demonstrated that other uncontested Pauline letters would fail the same *hapax legomena* test. Paul's vocabulary in 1 Thessalonians and 2 Corinthians is very different from other "authentic" letters.[3] Which letter or letters should we use to establish the standard of Pauline vocabulary, since the standard determines the variation? Also, that Paul relied upon preformed tradition is not new (1 Corinthians has several examples) and in turn, this factor changes the standard of deviation (the more Paul quotes another the less he sounds like Paul!).

Regarding church order, no instructions regarding the duties of the bishop or deacon are given in the pastoral letters—they are assumed. And, the importance of their authority, such as one finds in Ignatius, is completely ignored in Paul's letters. Paul was more concerned about the character of the church leaders. The onus was on the leaders to behave and not the membership to obey: an "overseer" (bishop) and a "servant" (deacon) must be of good reputation, among outsiders and insiders. Besides, these were not offices to be claimed or titles to be held. They were functions to be performed. To translate these words *episkopos* and *diakonos* as "bishop" and "deacon" is anachronistic, since such terms carry the freight of later church usage. Further, it's not as if church order didn't exist prior to the second century (cf. Phil 1:1). Paul set up rules for church conduct, divided along gender lines, when life "in the Spirit" went too far even for him (1 Cor 14:1-40). Finally, Paul was known to attack the character of his opponents, often questioning their sincerity and credibility (see Gal 4:17; 6:12-13; 2 Cor 11:12-15).

This is a complicated issue. There are other arguments for and against Pauline

---

[2]See Luke Timothy Johnson, *First and Second Letters to Timothy*, Anchor Bible (New York: Doubleday, 2001), 35a:55-90. See also the recent "tongue-in-cheek" example by Harold Hoehner, where he applies to Galatians (one of the few letters "unquestionably" Pauline) the same arguments used to reject Ephesians, reaching the same results: "Did Paul Write Galatians?" in *History and Exegesis: New Testament Essays in Honor of Dr. E. Earle Ellis for His Eightieth Birthday*, ed. Sang-Won (Aaron) Son (New York/London: T & T Clark, 2006), pp. 150-69.

[3]See William D. Mounce, *Pastoral Epistles*, Word Biblical Commentary (Nashville: Thomas Nelson, 2000), 46:88-118.

authorship that deserve our attention, and the debate is far more technical than we have been able to discuss here. Instead, we have tried to give examples of how the questions of authorship are like swords that cut two ways. Oftentimes the point for authenticity becomes the counterpoint against Pauline authorship and vice versa. It depends upon how you work the argument. Some see the letters as generic, impersonal instructions that could have come from any admirer of Paul; others argue that Paul offers his most personal and direct advice in these letters. Obviously, the question of authorship determines the occasion of these letters. If they didn't come from Paul, then an imposter was trying to wield the authority of Paul to combat the second-century heresy, Gnosticism: "Timothy, guard what has been entrusted to you. Avoid the profane chatter and contradictions of what is falsely called knowledge" (1 Tim 6:20). Those who subscribe to Pauline authorship see an apostle trying to get his young delegates to correct false teaching, to live a godly life and to help indigenous church leaders do their jobs. Timothy and Titus weren't "pastors" of these churches in Ephesus and on the island of Crete. It is quite apparent that local church leaders were already filling that role. Yet Paul believed that his gospel, his traditions and his ways were still under attack. Working under the premise, then, of the Pauline authorship of these misnamed Pastoral Epistles, the question remains: why were false doctrine and church disorder such problems in these particular churches? Paul had already left his two most trusted coworkers to iron out the difficulties. Why did he have to send letters as well?

The very fact that we have so many letters from Paul (versus only two from Peter!) may reveal that Paul very much wanted his churches to rely upon him for leadership. In other words, establishing local indigenous leadership within his churches may have been a matter of necessity rather than the result of a well-conceived missionary strategy. Early on, we see Paul guarding his converts like a mother hen, warning them about interlopers who preach "another gospel." Essentially, Paul maintained, "If it doesn't come from me, you shouldn't believe it." We see evidence of his protective ways when he was careful to send and identify delegates that came from him. Paul had an inner circle of trusted companions, of whom Timothy and Titus were major players, upon whom he could rely to teach his converts "his ways" and nobody else's (see 1 Cor 4:17). Eventually the lack of local leadership created a power vacuum within the churches that led to a variety of problems: divided loyalties, fractious house churches, amorphous traditions, vulnerabilities to false doctrine, identity crises. No amount of traffic in letters or personal emissaries from their apostle could straighten out all of the problems within Paul's churches. The more Paul traveled and the broader the reach of his influence became, the more difficulty he had in keeping his converts true to his gospel. What we have in 1 Timothy and Titus, then, is Paul's attempt to affirm local leadership (he didn't write these letters directly to the churches) yet still keep his protective hand over the welfare of his churches. In other words, these epistles represent the later methods of the final stages of Paul's apostolic ministry. This is why Paul used more preformed tradition, why he addressed issues of church order, why he identified his opponents by name, and why he encouraged Timothy and Titus to pay attention to sound doctrine. These were, indeed, Paul's "last days." Now an old man, he only had so much time to get his house in order.

False teaching in the church. Paul asked Timothy to remain in Ephesus in order to safeguard the church from the persistent threat of false teaching (1 Tim 1:3-11). He left Titus behind on Crete to put the church in order and to appoint elders (Tit 1:5). He hoped his loyal coworkers would be able to hold the churches together despite many defections. The exact nature of the false teachings is difficult to figure out.[4] He describes the opponents as those who want to be teachers of the law but lack any understanding of it (1 Tim 1:7-11). They are unruly deceivers "of the circumcision" who are fascinated with Jewish myths (Tit 1:10-14). These rebels like to pass on strange doctrines and are morbidly interested in controversies, myths and endless genealogies (1 Tim 1:3-4; 6:3-4). They forbid marriage and advocate abstention from certain foods (1 Tim 4:3; cf. Tit 1:15-16). The error of some is so severe that Paul's only recourse is to turn them over to Satan in hope that their blasphemy will cease (1 Tim 1:20; cf. 1 Cor 5:3-5). Some scholars argue that the heresy in Ephesus is an early form of Gnosticism. Whether these descriptions represent a single strain of heretical virus or multiple mutations is unclear.[5] As we read these letters, we get the picture that Timothy and Titus superintend churches that are not altogether well. Paul hopes his representatives in Asia and Crete will remember his example, fight for the true faith and bring health to God's household.

The true faith. The remedy for the doctrinal illness threatening the churches is found in passing on the true faith. For Paul the word "faith" means both (1) trust in God and Christ and (2) the entire way of life—belief and practices—that char-

---

[4]Are the opponents in Ephesus similar to the ones in Crete? Should we even assume the opponents of 1 and 2 Timothy are the same?

[5]Some of the descriptions suggest a probable Judaizing component. Carl Smith (building on the theories of his mentor, Edwin M. Yamauchi) argues that a group in the time of Trajan pulled together various existing ideas, creating a system that is later termed Gnosticism; see Carl B. Smith, *No Longer Jews: The Search for Gnostic Origins* (Peabody, Mass.: Hendrickson, 2004).

acterize the Christian community (cf. Gal 1:23; 2 Cor 13:5).[6] Despite Saul's blasphemous rampage against the church, God entrusted him with this faith (Tit 1:3). Now, as an apostle, Paul entrusts Timothy and Titus to carry on that work. He trusts that passing the gospel along through "faithful sayings," hymns, confessions and Scripture will ensure its faithful transmission to the next generation. The "faithful sayings"[7] introduce or conclude various soteriological passages: for example, "Christ Jesus came into the world to save sinners" (1 Tim 1:15); "For to this end we toil and struggle, because we have our hope set on the living God, who is the Savior of all people, especially of those who believe" (1 Tim 4:10). The "faithful sayings" provide a vehicle to recollect, pass on and celebrate God's goodness, mercy and salvation revealed through the appearance of Christ. When the message is apprehended by faith, believers are saved, not because of their righteousness, but through the rebirth and renewal of the Holy Spirit (Tit 3:4-7).

Confessions and hymns also liturgize[8] the essence of the true faith. Paul writes:

> For there is one God;
>> there is also one mediator between God and humankind,
> Christ Jesus, himself human,
>> who gave himself a ransom for all. (1 Tim 2:5-6a)

Often these hymns focus on the finished work of Christ:

> Without any doubt, the mystery of our religion is great:
>
> He was revealed in flesh,
>> vindicated in spirit,
>>> seen by angels,
> proclaimed among Gentiles,
>> believed in throughout the world,
>>> taken up in glory. (1 Tim 3:16)

The "faithful sayings," hymns and confessions may reflect preformed traditions that Paul adopts or compositions from within the Pauline circle. Regardless, these letters depend heavily upon preformed materials that Paul hopes Timothy and Titus will help him pass along. Earle Ellis reckons that nearly half of 1 Timothy and

---

[6]Leon Morris, "Faith," in *DPL*, pp. 285-91.

[7]The formula is translated as "faithful is the word." It occurs in 1 Timothy 1:15; 3:1; 4:9; 2 Timothy 2:11; Titus 3:8. The bishop is supposed to have a good grasp of the faithful word (Tit 1:9). Timothy is supposed to remind his congregants of these faithful sayings (2 Tim 2:11-14).

[8]*Liturgize* is a neologism that refers to the process of turning the Christological and soteriological narratives into confessions, hymns and prayers that are used by the church in worship to pass on its tradition.

SO WHAT?
Orthodoxy or Orthopraxy: *Does It Matter Which Comes First?*

Isn't this a "chicken and the egg" question? If our goal is "right living," then it may not matter how we get there. Behavior modification, social pressure, self-help books and legislating morality might all be effective ways to lead (or push) someone into "right living." But, is mere orthopraxy the final goal? "What difference does it make if I believe the right thing? As long as I do the right thing, that's all that matters." Some people try to separate orthodoxy from orthopraxy, as if one can exist apart from the other. At least one of the authors grew up in a small town in the southern United States. In those days most people conformed to perceived Christian standards of behavior. But did "right living" produce orthodoxy (right teachings) or genuine faith? Even then racism, sexism and classism were not "perceived" as heretical practices. The same problem exists today. Many TV preachers proclaim a gospel that's thin on content but heavy on positive thinking and self-help. Being "successful" has become more important than being faithful, and so we hear sermons that legitimize opulent lifestyles and the pursuit of happiness regardless of what Paul taught about becoming "living sacrifices." Paul maintained believing and doing are inseparable: what we believe impacts how we live, and what we do reveals what we believe. This is why Paul kept warning his colaborers about "false doctrine." Right thinking (orthodoxy) should lead to right living (orthopraxy). If Paul is right, then sermons today need more substance (doctrine) and fewer "Principles for Successful Living."

Titus draw upon preformed materials.[9] Receiving and transmitting the church's tradition will keep in check wild-eyed heretics who swerve wide of the truth and endanger the well-being of the church. The byproduct of sharing this sound teaching will be "love that comes from a pure heart, a good conscience, and sincere faith" (1 Tim 1:5-6). Furthermore, since correct practice (orthopraxy) follows from correct doctrine (orthodoxy), Paul anticipates that the true faith will bring an end to lawlessness, rebellion and sin in the church (1 Tim 1:8-11; Tit 3:8-11).

Our Savior. Although the title *Savior* occurs occasionally in Paul's other letters (see, e.g., Phil 3:20; Eph 5:23), it is prominent in 1 Timothy and Titus, where it

---

[9]E. Earle Ellis, *The Making of the New Testament Documents* (Leiden: Brill, 2002), pp. 116-17. For the traditioning process and the criteria to determine the presence of preformed traditions see pp. 52-60.

is applied to God and to Christ. The title means simply "the one who saves, delivers or protects." In Paul's day it was used to refer to pagan gods, legendary heroes and powerful rulers who were said to preserve lives and improve the lot of citizens. Paul's increased use of the title may reflect the Christian "answer" to the growing influence of the imperial cult. Caesar was very fond of the title *Savior*. Ultimately, however, the content of the title derives from its Old Testament use to refer to Israel's God as "Savior."[10] Though Paul describes the Father as "the Savior of all people" (1 Tim 4:10), his salvation is mediated through the accomplished work of Jesus Christ, who gave himself a ransom for all (1 Tim 2:3-6; cf. Tit 3:6). Because of this, Paul is able to use *Savior* in reference to Jesus as well. In his first coming he abolishes death and brings "life and immortality to light through the gospel" (2 Tim 1:10). In his second coming, he ushers in salvation "with eternal glory" (2 Tim 2:10) as the bodies of our humiliation are transformed by his great power (cf. Phil 3:21). In the present, believers wait for "the blessed hope and the manifestation of the glory of our great God and Savior, Jesus Christ" (Tit 2:13). For Paul, God the Father and the Lord Jesus are distinct persons even if their roles in salvation do overlap.

Qualifications for leaders. Without positive leadership Paul knows the church will not fare well against the claims of the false teachers. He congratulates those who aspire to become a bishop (*episkopos*, 1 Tim 3:1)[11] and lists a number of qualities Timothy, Titus and the rest of the church should look for when selecting leaders. The bishop must be above reproach, faithful in marriage, prudent, respectable, hospitable, able to teach, not addicted to wine, not contentious, gentle and free from the love of money. He should be able to manage his own family well and not be a new covert. He ought to enjoy a good reputation with those outside the church (1 Tim 3:2-7; cf. Tit 1:5-9).[12] Deacons must possess many if not all of the same qualities (1 Tim 3:8-13). Paul expects women to serve as deacons (1 Tim 3:11) though probably not as bishops.

Paul does not lay out a job description for these congregational leaders (cf. Eph 4:11-16). The term translated "bishop" may be better rendered "overseer" or "superintendent." Apparently Paul expects them to have responsibility for the general well-being of the community. This means passing on the church's traditions through teaching and preaching (1 Tim 3:2) as well as refuting those who

---

[10]The title *Savior* is concentrated in Psalms and Isaiah, two of the early Christians' favorite "books" of Scripture.

[11]The two "offices" mentioned in Ephesians 3 are bishop ("overseer" or "superintendent") and deacon ("minister" or "servant"). The same roles appear in Philippians 1:1.

[12]The term *elder* may be synonymous with or overlap the term *bishop* (cf. Tit 1:5-9 and 1 Tim 3:1-7).

contradict sound doctrine and practice (Tit 1:9-11; see also 2 Tim 2:24-25). It means further that they serve as examples to the church and the broader society (Tit 1:6; 1 Tim 3:7). Ultimately Paul thinks the entire church should be subject to the ruling authorities and ready to do every good work (Tit 3:1), but the bishops, deacons and elders are to lead the way in hospitality, reputation and charity. The term *deacon* implies service to the congregation. Those who serve well obtain

---

WHAT'S MORE . . .
The Husband of One Wife

Scholars disagree as to what Paul was intending to teach when he wrote that the bishop and deacon must be "the husband of one wife" (1 Tim 3:2 NASB) or "married only once" (1 Tim 3:2 NRSV). There are four ways in which this difficult phrase is interpreted: the bishop/deacon (1) must be married; (2) must not be a polygamist; (3) must not be divorced; or (4) must be faithful in marriage. For Christians in Paul's day, the greater danger was not adding or exchanging a wife—such actions had legal, social and economic ramifications—but widespread prostitution (from temples to banquets) and female slaves in the house. Moreover, the first three interpretative options regard a candidate's marital status; the last regards one's personal character. Since the other qualifications have to do with character, it seems appropriate that this statement does as well. After all, if Paul had wished to say "married," "not divorced" or "not a polygamist," there are perfectly good ways of doing that in Greek. We take the phrase to mean essentially that the bishop/deacon is to be "a-one-woman-kind-of-man," that is, an individual capable of marital fidelity.

---

a high standing and great confidence in the faith (1 Tim 3:13). Given the context of the letter, it is clear Paul believes that gifted, qualified leaders are necessary to protect the church from the ravages of false teaching and immorality attendant with it. Without these leaders, those who make up the household of God do not know how to act (1 Tim 3:15). With them the church is able to maintain its doctrinal and moral purity.

Ordering their common life. Another important component of these letters is the directions Paul offers on how believers are to order their life together. Included here are instructions on worship, modesty, the treatment of widows and the relationships between young and old. In these kinds of issues, culture plays a central role.

When the church gathers to worship, Paul urges that prayer and intercession be made for all people, but especially kings and those who have authority (1 Tim 2:1-2). The salvation God provides manifests itself even during this age in societies characterized by peace, godliness and dignity. Paul expects men to take the lead in prayer and lift up holy hands. Women are to join in the prayers, dressing modestly[13] and wrapping themselves in good works out of reverence for God. Paul's instruction on the silence of women in worship is highly controversial. Some take it as universally applicable, others culturally determined. Whatever he means in 1 Timothy 2:11-15, the silence is not absolute, because elsewhere he describes women praying and prophesying in the church (e.g., 1 Cor 11:5). The appeal to Eve's deception of Adam and its consequences (1 Tim 2:13-14; Gen 3) suggests that the passage may reflect a local problem in which wives of congregational leaders had become advocates for false doctrine. Such women must not be allowed to take authority over their husbands or other men in the congregation. Another possibility is that incompetent, unlearned women (probably wealthy patronesses, perhaps even the hostess for the church) were exercising their newfound freedom in Christ and trying to become teachers. If this is the case, the issue is not that they are women but that they are not competent to teach. Paul concludes that women "will be saved through childbearing, provided they continue in faith and love and holiness, with modesty" (1 Tim 2:15). The statement can be interpreted two ways: (1) despite Eve's transgression, women can be saved (eternally) by fulfilling the command "be fruitful and multiply, and fill the earth" (Gen 1:28) in faith, love and holiness; (2) women of faith will be brought safely through childbirth. In that day childbirth presented many dangers for women, and it was often the topic of prayer.[14]

Widows are worthy of honor and in some cases financial assistance by the church (1 Tim 5:3-16). "Real widows" are those who have no other means of support, live above reproach and are devoted to a ministry of prayer. Although Paul instructs younger widows to marry and have families, he expects some older widows to choose this special work in the church. When they do so and have no children for financial support, they may rightfully be enrolled in the benevolence min-

---

[13]Western Christians typically assume Paul means "sexually modest." Perhaps Paul meant "economically modest."

[14]Craig Keener, *Paul, Women and Wives: Marriage and Women's Ministry in the Letters of Paul* (Peabody, Mass.: Hendrickson, 1992), pp. 101-21.

istry of the church. Another interpretive option is that "widows" may have been the common term for a female elder, since virtually all women married. Once she was mature and released from family duties (= a widow), this godly elder was qualified to serve and to be paid by the church.

In Titus 2 Paul instructs his younger colleague on the proper conduct expected of the various generations in the church. Older men are to serve as examples of temperance, faith and love. Older women are to instruct the young mothers on how to love their husbands, care for their children and manage the domestic affairs in the Christian household. Younger men are to exhibit self-control, model good works and teach with integrity and sound speech. Like everything else in these letters, this generational code promotes "sound doctrine" and is grounded ultimately in the grace of God that brings salvation to all (Tit 2:11-15).

SECOND TIMOTHY: REMAINING FAITHFUL

We can tell from 2 Timothy that Paul was imprisoned when he wrote this letter. The circumstances surrounding the letter seem different from the other captivity letters. Timothy was with Paul when he wrote Philippians and Colossians; he was the co-author. Apparently Timothy was somewhere in Asia Minor when he received 2 Timothy (2 Tim 1:18; 4:13, 19). At the end of the so-called captivity letters, Paul acts like he knows he is going to be released from prison (Phil 1:19; 2:24; Philem 22). In 2 Timothy, however, Paul is resigned to death since his "first defense" before the courts did not result in his release (2 Tim 4:16): "the time of my departure has come. I have fought the good fight, I have finished the race, I have kept the faith. From now on there is reserved for me the crown of righteousness" (2 Tim 4:6-8). Paul wanted Timothy to make the long trip to Rome as soon as possible—before winter would prevent him from traveling—stopping by Troas along the way to retrieve some of his belongings (2 Tim 1:17; 4:9-13). To mesh these comments with the more optimistic tones of Colossians, Philemon, Philippians and Ephesians, it is often suggested that Paul was freed from prison in Rome, traveled to Crete and Ephesus, and headed toward Nicopolis, writing 1 Timothy and Titus during this time. Since Nicopolis was a good port for sailing west, Paul may have sensed the growing opposition specifically targeting him and decided it was a good time to pursue his plans to minister in Spain. The new territory would keep him out of reach of his opponents. Before those plans could be made, however, Paul was arrested and sent back to prison in Rome for the second and final time (1 Tim 1:3; Tit 1:5; 3:12). Therefore, as far as we know, 2 Timothy was Paul's last letter.

Why did Paul write 2 Timothy? It is hard to tell. There seems to be a contradiction of purpose in Paul's last letter. The letter is filled with pastoral advice for Timothy: how to behave, how to deal with problems within the churches, how to serve faithfully as a minister at all times. Then, after Paul spent most of the letter telling Timothy how to take care of matters in Asia Minor, he makes the urgent request: come to me as quickly as you can. If Paul expected his young associate to travel to Rome as soon as he received this letter, then most of what he had written—such personal advice—could have been given to Timothy face to face. Why go to all the expense and trouble of sending such a lengthy letter when a simple note, "come to Rome," would suffice? Maybe Paul was afraid Timothy wouldn't make it to him before he died. Or, it could be Paul wrote the letter for the benefit of other readers. He expected Timothy to share the contents of the letter with the churches of Asia Minor, especially Ephesus. The last line reveals the intended audience: "Grace be with you" (2 Tim 4:22). The pronoun is plural. To be sure, throughout the letter Paul speaks directly to Timothy. Singular pronouns dominate as Paul gives personal instructions for his apprentice, singling out false teaching, naming troublemakers. But at the very end Paul addresses a larger audience. His last words consist of a blessing for his converts as well: "Grace be with you." Like his letter to Philemon, Paul wrote a personal letter intended for a corporate setting. Why did he do it?

Several clues within 2 Timothy may explain the occasion for the letter. First, it is apparent Timothy needed Paul's clout in straightening out crooked people. At the beginning of the letter, Paul devoted quite a bit of space to building up Timothy, encouraging him to do what needed to be done: faithfulness to the truth of Paul's gospel would lead to suffering like Paul (2 Tim 1:6—2:13). Timothy may have been reticent to say what needed to be said and to follow in his mentor's steps; conflict inevitably led to difficulties. In his absence, however, Paul needed Timothy to confront the false teachers (2 Tim 2:14-19), to ignore foolish arguments (2 Tim 2:20—3:9) and to guard the treasure of Paul's teaching by keeping to sound doctrine (2 Tim 3:10—4:5). This letter gave Timothy the ammunition (and the encouragement) to do what Paul was requiring. By sending it to Timothy but having it read in the presence of all—even the false teachers—Paul's authority would be publicly lent to Timothy's voice. Second, Paul may have doubted whether his letter would have been read directly to the churches of Asia Minor (in particular, Ephesus) because they were no longer loyal to him (2 Tim 1:15).[15] So Paul had to

---

[15] Some scholars believe that the state of affairs as revealed in the circular letter to the seven churches in John's Revelation may indicate how little influence Paul had in Asia Minor toward the end of his life. For example, two churches are chastised by the risen Christ for eating meat offered to idols—a deadly sin equal to fornication (Rev 2:14, 20). Of course, Paul allowed the practice of eating idol meat under certain conditions (1 Cor 8:1—11:1).

write the letter to Timothy in hope that his understudy would be able to do what he could not: preserve his legacy (2 Tim 2:2), correct the misinterpretations of his teaching ("the resurrection has already taken place," 2 Tim 2:18) and keep his converts in the fold of his apostolic work (he had sent Crescens, Titus, Tychicus, Erastus and Trophimus to churches in other regions for the same reason, 2 Tim 4:10-12, 20). Finally, it is possible Paul wrote this personal/public letter because he was trying to set up Timothy as his successor. Seeing the end of his life approaching, Paul needed to pass the torch of his gospel light to his "child in the faith" so that the churches of Asia Minor would remain loyal to the gospel according to Paul.

Imitating Paul. "All who want to live a godly life in Christ Jesus will be persecuted" (2 Tim 3:12). Paul wrote Timothy to remind him of this rock-bottom reality of the gospel. The gospel had already taken root in Timothy's life (2 Tim 1:3-7). Timothy had seen how the gospel brought suffering in Paul's life due to his unrelenting faithfulness to it. Paul was imprisoned because of the gospel; nearly all of his friends (except for Onesiphorus) had forsaken him (2 Tim 1:8-18). Perhaps Onesiphorus had even died for the faith; helping a prisoner in Rome under Nero's reign of terror was a risky venture.[16] Now it was Timothy's turn to join in the suffering, to be faithful to Paul and his gospel, which was confirmed by the Spirit and abandoned by the ungodly (2 Tim 2:1-13). The proof of Timothy's faithfulness to the gospel would be seen when he confronted the false teachers in Ephesus (2 Tim 2:14—3:9). One cannot help but wonder if Timothy's timidity (2 Tim 1:7) had something to do with his reticence to speak against Paul's opponents in Ephesus—their false teaching (2 Tim 2:16-18), their useless arguments (2 Tim 2:23-25) and their immoral behavior (2 Tim 3:2-9). Did such confrontation bring persecution? Or was Paul addressing two unrelated issues in Timothy's life: his avoidance of persecution and his reluctance to correct false teachers? We don't know. But one thing is certain: Paul recounted in his own life how persecution and correcting false doctrine went hand in hand (2 Tim 3:10-13). "Distressing times will come"; this was the troubling reality of the last days (2 Tim 3:1).

The present distress, however, gives way to the pressing reality that one day Timothy will stand before God, "who is to judge the living and the dead" (2 Tim 4:1). How should Timothy prepare for that day? He should be true to the Scriptures, for they are the resource for teaching the wise and correcting the foolish (2 Tim 3:14-17). He should proclaim the message he learned from the beginning, whether he felt like it or not, whether listeners liked it or not (2 Tim 3:14; 4:2-4).

---

[16]See the arguments pro and con for Onesiphorus's martyrdom, I. Howard Marshall, *The Pastoral Epistles*, International Critical Commentary (Edinburgh: T & T Clark, 1999), pp. 718-19.

He must endure suffering, carry out his ministry and live a God-fearing life (2 Tim 4:5)—just like Paul. Then one day Timothy will receive the same reward as Paul—a "crown of righteousness"—because he longs for the appearing of Christ (2 Tim 4:8). The crown Paul envisions is not the jewel-encrusted, fur-lined headpiece we have seen on European monarchs. It was the laurel given to the runner who won the race. The athletic metaphor has served Paul well before in reference to discipline and endurance (1 Cor 9:25; Phil 4:1). The Greek construction *crown of righteousness* can mean either "crown for righteousness" or "crown, that is, righteousness." Thus Paul is either referring to the reward for righteousness (resurrection) or the reward that is righteousness (final vindication). Both ideas are prevalent in Paul's writings. Indeed, it would be not only their own but Paul's crowning achievement for his converts to receive just recompense for a faithful life on the last day (see 1 Thess 2:19). Speaking of the last day, Paul's last days were presently dawning on him. His time on earth was nearly over. Timothy would have to take up the charge of fighting the good fight like a good soldier, finishing the race like a good athlete and keeping the faith like a good farmer (cf. 2 Tim 2:4-6; 4:7).

Paul's departure. When Paul comes to the end of this letter, he knows he is not long for this world. The confident face he has shown in earlier prison letters seems all but gone. The difference between "house arrest," with a hopeful outcome, and *carcer*, with a likely death sentence, would affect any, even the apostle to the Gentiles. There is an air of sorrow and resignation about this letter. The elder statesman of the church writes the famous lines:

> As for me, I am already being poured out as a libation, and the time of my departure has come. I have fought the good fight, I have finished the race, I have kept the faith. From now on there is reserved for me the crown of righteousness, which the Lord, the righteous judge, will give me on that day, and not only to me but also to all who have longed for his appearing. (2 Tim 4:6-8)

Paul takes comfort in the fact that he has run the race of faith well and that God is just. His life has been a sacrificial offering to God. Although none stood with him at his first defense, the Lord supported him and gave him strength. Ultimately, Paul believes, the Lord will rescue him from these evil attacks and bring him safely into the heavenly kingdom (2 Tim 4:16-18). Throughout his letters we have seen the importance Paul places on righteousness. It is the first and last requirement for salvation. It is the "gift of God" when one first believes (Rom 6:23) and the gift of God at the end of the race (2 Tim 4:8).

Even though Paul was resigned to the fact he was going to die, we do not know when that happened. All we have is church tradition—a tradition that says Paul was beheaded during Nero's reign of terror (around A.D. 68). Today a shrine marks the traditional spot where Paul was executed; his body is supposedly buried on the Via Ostiense outside the walls of Rome. We do not know if he ever made it to Spain, if his letters worked, if the relief offering had its desired effect, or if every church he started remained true to the gospel of Jesus Christ. But we do know this: Paul wrote letters, and his letters were among the first documents accepted by the early church as Holy Scripture. Paul was the major contributor to the New Testament, a body of literature he never dreamed would exist. Ironically, although he didn't write letters to preserve his legacy, that is exactly what happened. For all his efforts to pass along his gospel by establishing churches and training future leaders, Paul's gospel endured the test of time because he put pen to papyrus. What were his dying words? We don't know. His last words for the church, on the other hand, have been immortalized: "Grace be with you."

CONCLUSION

Paul wrote these letters toward the end of a nearly thirty-year career as Christ's apostle. The younger Paul seems confident he will be alive until the parousia, but now in his last days Paul realizes that his churches will go on without him. His imprisonments, shipwrecks and near-death experiences focus his attention on the necessity and inevitability of Christian suffering for the sake of Christ. For him that will mean martyrdom on behalf of the faith communities he founded and loved until the end. The Paul we find in the later letters is not a lone pioneer on the edge of the empire. He is a vital link in the chain of the church's tradition. Therefore he transmits to the next generation the hymns, confessions and faithful sayings in use in all the churches. He sets in motion the selection and development of leadership to carry the churches into their post-Pauline phase. He places before the less mature believers examples for them to imitate. He continues his assault— a lifelong enterprise—on false teaching and improper piety. He encourages the Christ-believers to walk worthy of the gospel they have received in faith by the enabling of the Holy Spirit. He orders their life together through the wisdom found in the household and generational codes, knowing to some extent that the future of the church depends on how they pass the faith along. Finally, as Paul moves toward his certain end, he comes to grips with the universal and cosmic implications of his gospel. The message of salvation for the Jew first and then for the Greek does not end until "all things" are summed up under the headship of Christ. One day every knee will bow and every tongue will confess that "Jesus Christ is Lord."

READ MORE ABOUT IT

DPL Articles:

"Pastoral Letters," pp. 658-66, by E. E. Ellis.

"Suffering," pp. 919-21, by S. J. Hafemann.

"Philemon, Letter to," pp. 703-7, by A. G. Patzia.

"Slave, Slavery," pp. 881-83, by A. A. Rupprecht.

10

Paul's Theology

PAUL ENTERED AND LEFT THIS WORLD A JEW, at least by the standards of his day. His Jewish identity was one of the most significant factors in how he lived (religion), what he believed (theology), and how he saw the world (worldview). When he came to faith in Christ, he did not think he was leaving the faith of his fathers; rather he thought he was entering the fulfillment of the covenant promises God made to Abraham, Moses, David and the rest of his kin. At the deepest level of Paul's religion, theology and worldview lay convictions he inherited directly from his Jewish ancestors.[1]

BUILT ON A JEWISH FOUNDATION

Paul identifies himself as a Pharisaic Jew (Phil 3:5-6; Gal 1:14; 2 Cor 11:22). Most Pharisees of that day shared a set of core convictions. We will consider five of the most significant: (1) one God; (2) one people of God; (3) one future with God; (4) one book from God; (5) one place to worship God. As a Diaspora Jew, Paul pledges to live according to these convictions; but even after the Damascus road, he retains these allegiances in modified form.

One God. Paul inherits the belief in the oneness of God (monotheism). He confesses the central tenet of his faith regularly among his people (the Shema, Deut 6:4-6). For him God is the sole power in the universe, the Creator, Provider and ultimate Judge. When Paul became a Christ-believer, he did not abandon monotheism. He continued to confess the oneness of God, but his understanding

---

[1]James D. G. Dunn, *The Theology of Paul the Apostle* (Grand Rapids: Eerdmans, 1998), pp. 713-16.

of God was revolutionized by Christ. After the Christophany on the Damascus Road, he came to see Jesus as Lord, the image of God, the one who uniquely bears God's name. So Christ reveals a new aspect of the identity of the God of Abraham and Israel. Because God acts in Christ, Paul confesses a new Shema of the one God the Father and one Lord Jesus Christ (1 Cor 8:6). This was not ditheism (the belief in two gods); it was monotheism recast to include Jesus within the divine identity. There is only one God, Paul believes, and Jesus reveals a new dimension, a new reality of that one God. For Paul, God's oneness is retained but reimagined to include a second, distinct person.

Monotheism involves more than what a person believes; it comes to life particularly in how one worships. As a Pharisee, Paul worshiped only one God. He prayed to him, confessed him and sang psalms to and about him. When he attended the temple, he took vows and offered sacrifices to him. Now as a Christ-believer, Paul worships Jesus along with God. He prays to the Lord Jesus, confesses him, sings hymns about him, eats meals in his honor and baptizes in his name. He devotes himself totally to the lordship of Jesus. From the outside, one might get the idea that Paul has two gods. But from the inside, Paul knows that devotion to Christ legitimately expresses devotion to God the Father. To bow down to Jesus and confess him as Lord is to do the will of God (Phil 2:9-11).

Despite the close association of Jesus with God the Father, we should recognize that for Paul they remain distinct persons. Although the titles and functions they share sometimes blur the lines between them, Paul did not confuse Christ with God the Father. Christ is the Son. God is the Father. On the last day the Son will submit everything to the Father (1 Cor 15:20-28). The Son has been, is and always will be subordinate to the Father.

One people of God. According to Jewish tradition, the one God had a "chosen people." The family of Abraham was destined to be his representatives in the world. God elected his descendants to become a great nation, to occupy a strategic plot of land and ultimately to extend God's blessing to all the people of the world. Israel was God's servant in the world, an elect nation whose identity was determined by birth, circumcision, faith and obedience. The covenant between God and Israel was an act of divine grace, but to inherit the gifts and remain in the covenant, Israel had to obey God's law.

When Paul encountered Jesus on the Damascus road, his thinking about election changed. He continued to believe the one God was working to create one people, but his understanding of how to get in and stay in the one people of God was revolutionized. Before Christ, people became members of God's elect community by virtue of birth (i.e., having a Jewish mother) or conversion (including circumcision and baptism/purification), and they stayed in because they observed Torah (in short, by living like Jews). "But now" Paul believes membership in the new covenant is open to Jews and Greeks by virtue of Christ's finished work on the cross. Baptism in Christ, not circumcision, marks the new covenant community. As Paul rereads the Scriptures in light of his Christ-revelation, he sees that God's plan all along has been to include Gentiles in the one people of God. But Gentiles do not have to live like Jews to receive God's favor; they enter the covenant people by faith in God's crucified and resurrected Messiah.

One future with God. As we survey the letters, we find that Paul was a Pharisaic Jew with apocalyptic expectations. Pharisees believed in the resurrection of the body at the end of the age. While some Jews were agnostic on the question of life after death, Pharisees answered with Scripture and tradition affirming that the righteous dead will be given a new body and live in a utopian "world to come" with God. For an apocalyptic Pharisee like Paul, the resurrection of Jesus and the new creation he inaugurated bring history as we know it to an end. But the end of the age is not the end of the world. There is a glorious future to which all creation is headed.

Apocalyptic is easier to describe than it is to define. It is a worldview that finds expression in a variety of religions in Paul's day. Among Jews, the Pharisees, the Essenes and the followers of Jesus operated with an apocalyptic outlook. The term *apocalyptic* comes from a Greek word meaning "unveiling" or "revelation." It affirms the presence of an invisible, eternal world (heaven) running alongside the visible, temporal world (earth) we know through our senses. Although most people are unaware of it, some people ("seers") are attuned to this alternate reality and can see earth's future (in the present) through visions and heavenly journeys. Apocalypticism enters Jewish religion through the prophetic voices that announce the ultimate victory of God and his people over evil (e.g., Dan 8:1-14; Zech 5:1—6:8; *1 Enoch* 90:1-42; 91:11-17; 93:1-10; *4 Ezra* 3:1—5:13). It arises out of a social context of at least deprivation and possibly persecution.

At the heart of the apocalyptic worldview is a linear view of history. History is headed somewhere; it is not an endless series of cycles. Paul's apocalyptic history consists of two ages: the present evil age and the world to come (or the kingdom of God). The present age is ruled by powerful spiritual forces contrary to God. Sin, death and evil dominate everything. In contrast, the age to come will turn the old world upside down. Righteousness, life and eternal peace replace the darkness of the first age. The turning point, in the apocalyptic view, is not from below; it in-

SO WHAT?
Does Apocalypticism Matter?

Why does it matter if Paul had an apocalyptic worldview? What's in a label? While one of your authors was overseas, the movie phenomenon of *Friday the 13th* happened. When he returned, he saw a movie advertised as *Friday the 13th, 3*. Knowing nothing about it, he asked his students if he should go see it. "It's a slasher film," one student responded. After some investigation, he learned about this genre. Even if you know nothing about a movie except that it's a slasher film, you already know to expect: (1) poor lighting, (2) large pieces of cutlery, (3) women who cannot run more than ten feet without falling down, and (4) hands that suddenly thrust through doors. Often there will be shower curtains, open windows and dark basements with rickety stairs. Likewise, even if you know nothing about a Judeo-Christian writing except that it's apocalyptic, you already know to expect: (1) a pessimistic view of this world, (2) the seeming dominance of evil, (3) God's intervention just in the nick of time and (4) when God acts finally and decisively, the wicked are punished and the innocent are set free to enjoy eternal bliss. That is also how Paul saw the world: (1) cosmic powers exercise their cruel dominion in this present darkness (Eph 6:12), (2) the days are evil (Gal 1:4; Eph 5:16), (3) God sent his Son in the "fullness of time" (Gal 4:4), and (4) the "day of the Lord will come like a thief in the night"—sudden destruction for the wicked, immediate reward for Christ-believers (1 Thess 5:2-3; 1 Cor 15:52). This is why Paul thought the end of the world was near: the gospel was an apocalyptic reality breaking into history—where old things have passed away and everything is becoming new.

---

volves God's intervention from above. Properly speaking, the turning point is not the end of the world but the end of the world as we know it. But often the change is viewed as so complete and abrupt that the apocalyptic message arrives in end-of-the-world language.

From everything we read in his letters, Paul inherits and operates with an apocalyptic worldview. The Christian Paul, however, differs from the apocalyptic Saul, because he is now convinced the turn of the ages has already arrived in the death, burial and resurrection of Jesus. His resurrection was the first. Soon, he believes, the remaining righteous will follow Jesus and receive their resurrection bodies. As a result he looks at the present age as winding down, soon to pass away forever. The spiritual forces that rule this age have lost the war, but "mopping up" exercises continue after the decisive victory. Christ-believers therefore continue to battle, now outfitted with the full armor of God.

For Paul, believers live between two crucial moments: the resurrection and the parousia of Jesus. As a result salvation has both an "already" and a "not yet" component. Because of the resurrection, Christ-believers are already united with Jesus, sealed with the Spirit, forgiven of their sins and more than conquerors. On the other hand, salvation is not yet complete because sin and death are still active, though wounded, adversaries. Until the parousia they remain constant threats. But when Christ returns, the dead are raised, the living are transformed and sin along with death is destroyed. Although believers are already "saved" by virtue of Christ's faithfulness, they await the full flowering of their redemption in the second coming of Jesus. According to Paul, this is the one future with God toward which everything moves.

WHAT'S MORE . . .
People of the Book

By "book" we do not mean the "codex"-styled Bible we know today, a collection of books between two covers. What we call "the Book," Paul knew as a loose collection of holy writings he calls "Scripture" *(graphē)*, copied by hand on scrolls. Furthermore, unlike today, few Jews if any ever saw a complete set—even the concept is anachronistic—for the Hebrew canon and text were not fixed.[a] Quite possibly, there were sacred writings that Paul had never heard or read, and this would be even more true for a common man from Nazareth. Why does Jesus quote from Deuteronomy, Isaiah and the Psalter? Those were likely the writings his hometown synagogue owned; they were the texts that were commonly used during weekly and annual festivals. Interestingly, these were also the biblical books found in multiple copies among the Dead Sea Scrolls. This suggests these books were favorites among the covenanters of Qumran. Only scribes were familiar with "all the Scriptures" since they were the professional transcribers. Today ordinary Christians (in the West) have access to the entire collection of Scripture.

---

[a]Peter Flint, ed., *The Bible at Qumran: Text, Shape, Interpretation* (Grand Rapids: Eerdmans, 2001), pp. 27-29.

One book from God. Jews are people of "the Book." They believe God has revealed himself to patriarchs, prophets and poets who in turn wrote down these revelations for future generations. These revelations are contained in a book. Like other Jews in his day, Paul encountered Scripture primarily in the synagogue where he studied and worshiped.

Pharisees especially had a deep love for Scripture. They read it, memorized it, debated it and attempted to put it into practice daily. The spiritual heirs of the Pharisees were Jews who survived the nation's destruction in A.D. 70 and moved to Galilee to start rabbinical schools, keeping the faith alive through the study of the one book from God. As a Pharisaic Jew, Paul inherited this book of divine revelation, the very words and will of God in ink on parchment. Moreover he received from his teachers a way of reading Scripture, interpreting it and applying it to life. For the Pharisees, these "oral traditions" were equal to the Scriptures in importance and authority. Initially, the way Paul/Saul read Scripture and kept to the oral tradition put him at odds with the followers of Jesus. But then he met the risen Savior.

Afterward Paul's Christian theology developed in large part through Spirit-inspired interpretations of Israel's sacred texts. For the apostle, the gospel of Christ fulfills God's promises to Israel (e.g., Rom 1:2-3). The death, burial and resurrection of Jesus are "according to Scripture" (1 Cor 15:3-8). By that Paul means that he finds the story of Jesus a compelling climax to God's covenant with his people.

For all practical purposes Paul is a man immersed in Scripture. He speaks its language. He thinks, hopes and imagines in its symbols. He writes his letters with it resonating in his ears. Like a tuning fork, it provides for him pitch, even as he produces the timbre. He situates his arguments and apostolic advice within the symbolic world created by Israel's sacred texts. But already these Scriptures were awash in what scholars call "intertextuality," fragments of earlier stories echoing in the later chambers of sacred words and promises. Later Jewish texts and stories, like Isaiah's sermons on return from exile, are told with allusions to earlier stories, like the exodus. Paul continues the interpretive practices of his ancestors in faith, extending Scripture beyond their day to his own, finding its fullness in the Lord Jesus Christ.[2]

One place to worship God. In the first Christian century Jews were scattered all over the world, but according to tradition, God had set aside one place for sacrifice and worship. That was the temple in Jerusalem. Hundreds of years before Paul, King Josiah had mandated that Israel's one God receive exclusive worship in the Jerusalem shrine. So Jerusalem became the center of the world for Jews, even those

---

[2]Richard Hays, *Echoes of Scripture in the Letters of Paul* (New Haven, Conn.: Yale University Press, 1989), pp. 14-15.

WHAT'S MORE . . .
Paul's Use of the Old Testament

When writing to his churches, Paul uses the Old Testament in three ways: (1) quotations, (2) allusions and (3) appropriations of biblical themes. Some of these are intentional; others appear to be unintentional. But this is what you would expect from someone steeped in the stories and language of Scripture. Although it is not possible to distinguish completely between a quotation and an allusion, most scholars conclude that Paul cites the Old Testament ninety to one hundred times in his letters.[a] He quotes from sixteen books altogether, but mostly from the Pentateuch, Psalms and Isaiah. The majority of his quotations are found in Romans, 1 and 2 Corinthians and Galatians. As you might expect, allusions to Scripture are more numerous. Sometimes just a few words can conjure up a suitable biblical image for Paul to make a point. There are some letters without explicit citations, but echoes of scriptural themes and biblical imagery show up in nearly all the apostle's correspondence.

[a]Moises Silva, "The Old Testament in Paul," in *DPL*, p. 630. When we look carefully at Paul's use of the Old Testament, it seems most of his quotations are from the Greek versions. Although he refers to himself as a "Hebrew of Hebrews" (Phil 3:5 NIV), the fact that he writes his letters in Greek may account for some of his dependence on the Greek versions. An earlier generation of scholars addressed the issue of whether Paul's Old Testament citations were closer to the Hebrew Masoretic text or to the Greek Septuagint. They assumed that Paul drew from standardized Greek and Hebrew texts. They interpreted the variations from those standardized texts as memory lapses or interpretive comments. Recent work has set aside these working assumptions and shown that the Hebrew and Greek biblical texts were not as fixed as we had thought. In particular, the biblical scrolls from Qumran exhibit a lot of variation within a single Jewish library. See, for example, E. C. Ulrich, "The Qumran Biblical Scrolls: The Scriptures of Late Second Temple Judaism," in *The Dead Sea Scrolls in Their Historical Context*, ed. T. H. Lim (Edinburgh: T & T Clark, 2000), pp. 67-87.

living away from the land of promise. During Paul's lifetime the covenant people considered Herod's temple—so called because of the extensive renovations he sponsored—the holiest place in the world, the locus of God's presence. Paul inherited from his ancestors a sense of sacred space.

Paul retained the idea of sacred space but not its location. His experiences of the risen Christ taught him that the community of faith makes up the true temple in the new age. This was a theological move already made by the desert-dwelling Essenes who wrote many of the Dead Sea Scrolls. Disgusted over the

WHAT'S MORE . . .
The Temple in Jerusalem

Most Jews considered the temple to be God's earthly home:

> In my distress I called upon the LORD;
>> to my God I cried for help.
> From his temple he heard my voice,
>> and my cry to him reached his ears. (Ps 18:6)

Likely what infuriated the audience of Stephen, resulting in his stoning, was that he retold the story of Israel by noting all the activities of God apart from Jerusalem and the temple, culminating with the indictment that God does not live in man-made houses. Saul no doubt shared the audience's anger (Acts 8:1).

---

corrupt temple leadership, they decided to abandon Jerusalem altogether, retreat to the desert and create a new temple—a people founded on prayer, piety and the study of Scripture. Early Christians had their own accounts of temple cleansings and predictions of the temple's destruction. It is no wonder Paul replaces the sacred place of the temple with the sacred space of Christ-believers gathered in his name.

Other influences in Paul's theology. As we have already made evident, the Christophany[3] on the Damascus Road marked the turning point of Paul's life, the moment when everything changed. It provided the energy and the orientation for much, if not most, of his subsequent theological reflection. At the heart of the Christophany was (1) the recognition of Jesus' true identity as Messiah and Lord, (2) the revelation that Gentiles are welcome in God's one people apart from law, and (3) Paul's role in bringing about their obedience. Paul spent the rest of his life unpacking the meaning of what he saw that day on the road to Damascus, but he never completely exhausted its power or fully exploited its significance.

Another source for Paul's theology was the traditions he received from those who were Christ-believers before him.[4] Paul often handed on these traditions to

---

[3]In chapter three we laid out in detail these crucial events. We will not retrace those steps here.

[4]Paul distances his gospel and apostleship from human authority (especially Jerusalem) in Galatians. This has more to do with the purpose of the letter than his general practice. His other letters show his reliance on the Christ-believers before him.

SO WHAT?
Is One Space Exclusively Sacred?

Why does it matter if Paul redefined "temple"? Paul retained the language and symbols of the temple while transforming their meaning. For example, the body (physical body) is the temple of the Holy Spirit (1 Cor 6:19). Christ's death is the mercy seat or atoning sacrifice (Rom 3:25) in the temple. In his death Christ destroyed "the dividing wall of hostility" that separates the Jewish court from the Gentile section of the temple (Eph 2:14-15). "I don't need to go to church," insists Danny, "I can worship him just as well on the golf course." We are still called to worship God in sacred space, but Paul argues that all of us together form a new dwelling for God, "in him the whole structure is joined together and grows into a holy temple in the Lord" (Eph 2:21). The local community is God's temple where the Spirit dwells (1 Cor 3:16-17; cf. 2 Cor 6:16-18). In the end, Paul takes from his Jewish ancestors a sense of sacred space, but the revelation of Christ causes him to reevaluate the real estate in Jerusalem for the real state of holiness in Christ's church.

---

his converts. The content of these sayings has to do primarily with the person and work of Christ, the gospel he preached, and worship. The following list provides an overview to some of the preformed traditions Paul used in his letters:

1. Hymns about Christ—Philippians 2:6-11; Colossians 1:15-20; 1 Timothy 3:16

2. Confessions, such as "Jesus is Lord"—Romans 10:9

3. The "Abba" address to God—Galatians 4:6; Romans 8:15

4. The Maranatha prayer "Our Lord [Jesus], come"—1 Corinthians 16:22

5. The "Amen"—Galatians 6:18; 1 Timothy 1:17

6. The Lord's Supper—1 Corinthians 11:23-25

7. The Kerygma (Gospel)—1 Thessalonians 1:9-10; Romans 1:3-4; 1 Corinthians 15:3-7

8. "Faithful is the Word" sayings—Titus 3:8; 1 Timothy 3:1; 2 Timothy 2:11

Since Paul often quotes preformed hymns, prayers and summaries of the gospel, we see the extent to which he relies on the preaching and practices of the early church. He is no "Lone Ranger" out on the edge of the empire. He is in frequent conversation with believers who enrich his understanding of this new covenant. He passes on to his churches the traditions they hold dear.[5]

Paul spent roughly thirty years as the apostle to the Gentiles. During that time he traveled widely, established churches, suffered imprisonment and other persecution, debated opponents, enjoyed the camaraderie of coworkers and had several near-death experiences. Although it is impossible to say exactly how these experiences affected his theology, it is likely that they influenced how he preached the gospel and related to his churches. It is commonly argued, for example, that Paul's preaching of justification by faith and his understanding of the law owes its substance to the Judaizing forces that seemed to pursue him throughout most of his career. Such strident opposition to a circumcision-free gospel caused him to reread Scripture and to formulate a response for how Gentiles can be included in God's people apart from works of law. In some of the later letters, we notice a growing awareness of the universal scope of Christ and his salvation and the need to appoint leaders and protect the deposit of faith. While we can only speculate regarding the causes, we may question whether Paul's imprisonments, advanced age and/or near-death experiences may have persuaded him that he would not always be around for his churches. The early Paul seems convinced that he will accompany them until the parousia. The later Paul is not so sure. Eschatology may well be the preoccupation of youth. But for the aging Paul, the survival of the church and the quality of the next generation takes center stage.

THE CENTER OF PAUL'S GOSPEL

Paul's theology was the result of many forces and factors, none of which occurred in isolation. As we have indicated, however, the primary sources for his theology were his Jewish background, his Christophany, the traditions he inherited and his missionary experiences over a thirty-year career. All these worked together (through the Spirit) to form a unique perspective on the gospel by one of the church's greatest founders. As scholars have discussed Paul's theological contributions to Christianity, they have arrived at this question: Is there a center to Paul's theology?

The majority have answered "yes," but disagree what the center is and by what criteria it should be determined.[6] But there is a prior question: what do we mean

---

[5]In some passages (e.g., 1 Cor 11:2; 15:3-7) Paul uses the technical language for receiving and passing on traditions. This demonstrates his dependence on the formulas and preaching of the church in his own mission.

[6]Some scholars question the project of determining a center. Their concern is based mainly upon the available evidence. Paul's letters are occasional documents. They are not systematic treatises on his theology. True. While this fact makes the task more difficult, it does not automatically invalidate it.

by the theological center? First, the center of Paul's theology is the starting point, the conceptual "place" from which his theologizing emerges. Second, the center of Paul's theology is that which explains, supports and holds together everything else. To that extent, the center pervades the whole as a theme in a symphony or as leaven in bread. Take it away and the whole collapses into an ill-defined lump. The

---

SO WHAT?
Why Quest for a Center?

Why does it matter whether or not we can find the "center" of Paul's theology? The reason scholars want to discover the center of his theology is because Paul holds to so many diverse theological ideas. Not all of them are easily understood, as Peter complained (2 Pet 3:16). If we could find the center, the essence, of what Paul believed, then we might be in a better position to explain some of his more ancillary theological ideas. If we could discover the generative source of his theology, then we might be able to map out his convictions: that idea developed into this, which further led to that. Knowing the source of an idea can sometimes provide enough missing pieces to flesh out a thought that was too sketchy to understand previously.

---

problem, of course, is how you go about determining the center of Paul's thought from the occasional documents known as his letters.

J. Christiaan Beker states the problem clearly. In his monumental work *Paul the Apostle: The Triumph of God in Life and Thought* Beker argues that there is a "coherence" to Paul's thought that can be discovered amid the "contingent" circumstances of the letters. Paul's theology consists of a constant interaction between the coherent center of the gospel and its contingent application. For Beker, coherence resides at the deep level (the "secret center behind his theological thinking");[7] it is the primordial experience of Paul's Christophany. Contingency, on the other hand, sits on the surface; it is the result of Paul's application of his gospel to the current problems of his churches. According to Beker, before we can describe how Paul's theology coheres, we need to consider the contingent expressions of his gospel—Paul's occasional letters. Indeed, as we have already seen throughout his letters, Paul was

---

[7]J. Christiaan Beker, *Paul the Apostle: The Triumph of God in Life and Thought* (Philadelphia: Fortress, 1980), p. 7.

able to make the gospel a "word on target" to address the problems his churches faced without compromising or diluting the essence of his theology.[8] Many common themes emerge in Paul's letters, but what is the center of his theology?

Determining the center. How can the center of Paul's theology be determined? Put another way, what criteria will lead us to the center? We think the center will be that aspect of Paul's theology that best satisfies the following criteria:

The center must be

1. integral: it finds expression in all parts of all his letters.

2. generative: it participates in—and to some degree generates—all his theologizing. It can help to explain everything else.[9]

3. experiential: it results from encounters he has with the risen Jesus.

4. traditional: it is consistent with the traditions he inherits and uses.

5. scriptural: it serves as the interpretive key to new readings of Scripture.

6. theological: given Paul's commitment to monotheism, the theological center is ultimately a word about God, explaining and revealing him.

7. presuppositional: at times it sits beneath the surface of Paul's letters, supporting and limiting the argument.

The aspect or aspects of Paul's theology that fit these criteria are likely candidates for the center of Paul's theology.

Some possible centers. Scholars offer various opinions on Paul's theological center. Protestant German scholarship of the twentieth century continues to be influential. For many years the Lutheran emphasis on justification by faith (in Christ) dominated the approach to this question. With some modifications, that view was argued skillfully by Ernst Käsemann.[10] Albert Schweitzer, however, argued that justification by faith was part of the apostle's doctrine of redemption. Since it is derived from something else, it cannot be the center. He also noted that justification by faith is prominent only in Galatians and Romans. Based on the criteria above, justification could not be the center since (1) it is not integral to all of Paul's letters and (2) it is not generative; it is derived from some deeper cause.

Schweitzer posited that the true center is the mystical doctrine of being-in-Christ. He famously wrote: "The doctrine of righteousness by faith is therefore a

---

[8]Ibid., pp. 11-12.

[9]E. P. Sanders, *Paul and Palestinian Judaism: A Comparison of Patterns of Religion* (Philadephia: Fortress, 1977), p. 441, states it negatively: "a theme cannot be central which does not explain anything else."

[10]Ernst Käsemann, "'The Righteousness of God' in Paul," in *New Testament Questions of Today*, trans. W. J. Montague (Philadephia: Fortress, 1969), pp. 168-93.

subsidiary crater, which has formed within the rim of the main crater—the mystical doctrine of redemption through the being-in-Christ."[11] This "Christ-mysticism" can be summarized as follows: Christ-believers are "in Christ," that is, they are mystically united with him in his death, burial and resurrection. Although they live in this world dominated by sin and hostile powers, they are raised above it by their incorporation in him. Jesus' resurrection guarantees the future resurrection of every one found in him. Schweitzer's proposal remains influential. Sanders modifies it and recasts it as "participation in Christ."[12]

Although being-in-Christ or participation in Christ are important categories for Paul and likely lay near the center, we do not think they represent the center, because they are derived ultimately from something else, the comprehensive saving acts of God through Jesus the Messiah. Being and participating in Christ, for Paul, depend upon the cross and resurrection of Jesus. This is understood and expressed by scholars in a variety of ways. Beker, for example, suggests that the coherent center of his gospel derives its symbolic structure from a Christian apocalyptic worldview. At the heart of the matter is the triumph of God realized in and through the Christ-event. God's victory over the powers and evil that once ruled the age is inaugurated in Christ and will result in the redemption of the entire created order. Paul's letters are constantly rendering this coherence using various metaphors and symbols appropriate to the changing circumstances of the churches.[13]

Ralph Martin finds earlier attempts at describing Paul's center to fall short of success. He posits that reconciliation is the center. According to Martin, the entire gospel and its effects can be summarized and explained in this: God was in Christ reconciling the world to himself. Reconciliation was not a Pauline innovation; the apostle inherited it from the churches (cf. Col 1:15-20; 2 Cor 5:18-21). And he interpreted the concept in both vertical and horizontal dimensions. Vertically, reconciliation deals with the enmity between God and humanity. Horizontally, it addresses the hostility between Jews and Gentiles through the cross (e.g., Eph 2:11-22).[14]

Toward the center: A narrative approach. A promising proposal has emerged recently from scholars who maintain that the coherent core to Paul's theology

---

[11]Albert Schweitzer, *The Mysticism of Paul the Apostle*, trans. William Montgomery (New York: Seabury, 1968), p. 225.

[12]Sanders, *Paul and Palestinian Judaism*, pp. 502-8, 518-23.

[13]Beker, *Paul the Apostle*, pp. ix, 15-17.

[14]Ralph Martin, *Reconciliation: A Study of Paul's Theology*, New Foundations Theological Library (Atlanta: John Knox, 1981), pp. 1-6. See also Marvin Pate, ed., *The Story of Israel: A Biblical Theology* (Downers Grove, Ill.: InterVarsity Press, 2004).

is not found in theological ideas or constructs. Instead, they think the center is a narrative substructure, the story beneath the letters.[15] According to this approach, the letters are not isolated principles and pastoral advice from one who shoots from the hip when addressing various church problems. Properly understood, the discourses, exhortations and arguments in Paul's letters are birthed in stories about God's saving actions in the world. This approach finds an agreeable analogy in the faith of Israel. Israel's religion was constituted primarily in the stories of the exodus and covenant in the Pentateuch. Weekly and annually their festivals liturgized those stories, creating a narrative world available to all.

Richard Hays argues it is possible to observe the narrative foundation no matter how well it may be obscured by the discursive building above. Two moves are necessary. First, we must identify allusions to the underlying story (or stories) and attempt to construct its characters and plot. Second, we must track how the story (or stories) shapes the logic of Paul's arguments.[16] We may not always be able to hear the story, but we can see its effects through his pastoral advice.

According to N. T. Wright, stories form the heart of our intellectual history. They give shape to individual thought, fashion communal identity and articulate a culture's worldview. By their nature stories express worldviews in ways propositions and ideas cannot. Worldviews lie at a foundational level, supporting the whole "cognitive map" of any culture. Indeed, in the culture of the New Testament, theology has a decidedly narrative shape that emerges from a particular worldview.[17] According to Wright, Paul's theology is composed of retelling the essentially Jewish story around Jesus. It is "the whole story of God, Israel and the world as now compressed into the story of Jesus."[18] The apostle reads the stories from Scripture and finds that the climax of God's covenant with Israel arrives in Jesus. Narrative theologians differ as to the number of stories operative in Paul's correspondences. Some argue that it should be heard as one grand story (macrostory). Others say it should be read as several narratives that intersect, collide, overlap but ultimately merge together.[19]

---

[15]The shift from modernity (ideas) to postmodernity (narrative) is no doubt formative here.

[16]Richard Hays, *The Faith of Jesus Christ: An Investigation of the Narrative Substructure of Galatians 3:1—4:11*, Society of Biblical Literature Dissertation Series 56 (Chico, Calif.: Scholars, 1983), p. 29.

[17]N. T. Wright, *The New Testament and the People of God* (Minneapolis: Fortress, 1992), pp. 122-23.

[18]Ibid., p. 79.

[19]At least four stories seem to be present in Paul's letters: (1) God and creation (especially Adam), (2) Israel, (3) Jesus and (4) Paul. In a monotheistic setting all plots and subplots surface and eventually resolve into the grand story of God and his creation.

Conclusion: The essence of what Paul believed. All of the suggestions regarding a theological center for Paul have one thing in common. They relate their doctrinal or narrative center to the person and work of Christ (e.g., justification by faith in Christ, participation or being-in-Christ, reconciliation through the work of Christ, and the story of Jesus fulfilling God's covenant story with Israel). Given the criteria above, we believe the person and work of Christ as told in the essentially Jewish story of Jesus constitutes the true center of Paul's theology.[20] Christ is integral to all parts of all Paul's letters, as we hope our previous chapters have shown. His story of Christ as the climax of God's covenant explains most other aspects of his theology. His personal story of the risen Christ on the Damascus road shapes and transforms his life. Yet this experience is complemented and informed by the traditions about Christ that Paul inherits from the Jerusalem and Antiochean churches. He finds in Scripture the story of Jesus prefigured and discovers him to be the key to unlocking the mysteries of God. At the same time the word about Jesus is also a word about God, for Jesus reveals the true identity of the Eternal One. In a sense, the One God is logically and reverentially[21] prior to the One Lord (1 Cor 8:6). To say that Christ and his story form the center of Paul's theology is to recognize that fundamentally Christology is a word about God. Richard Bauckham has coined the phrase "christological monotheism" to get at this perspective.[22] In the final analysis, Paul's Christology expresses his commitment to the identity and uniqueness of Israel's one God. This is not theology in some abstract, impersonal sense or what one thinks about God. Rather it is theology in the concrete, personal sense of the new covenant.

Christological monotheism resides on the surface and in the depths of Paul's letters. It is explicitly expressed and implicitly presuppositional. As with most presuppositions, it leaves its marks in ways that point toward the center. For example, the oneness of God demands the oneness of God's people (Eph 2:11-22). So God acts through the cross of Jesus to make that oneness a reality. Again, the oneness of God demands unity among his people. Therefore the apostle urges the members of the body of Christ to strive to maintain unity (Eph 4:1-6) and to see themselves as members of one another (1 Cor 12:12-31). And again, the oneness of God means that the creation redeemed through the victory of Christ in the resur-

---

[20]Joseph Fitzmyer, *Pauline Theology: A Brief Sketch* (Englewood Cliffs: N.J.: Prentice-Hall, 1967), p. 16; Dunn, *Theology of Paul*, pp. 729-30.

[21]By that we mean that the reverence previously given to God by people of the first covenant accords with the reverence offered Jesus by the people of the new covenant.

[22]Richard Bauckham, *God Crucified: Monotheism and Christology in the New Testament* (Grand Rapids: Eerdmans, 1998), p. 7.

rection and parousia is ultimately subjected to the Father "so that God may be all in all" (1 Cor 15:23-28).

So the center of Paul's theology is christological monotheism narratively constructed in the presuppositions, traditions, arguments and paranesis of the letters. It is not a principle; it is a person. It is not a big idea; it is a relationship with God through Christ. It does not reside in the realm of myth and legend; it is the turning point of history. Viewed conceptually, christological monotheism is the key concept that organizes and makes sense of all Paul's theology. Viewed narratively, christological monotheism tells the story of Jesus whose preexistence, life, death, resurrection and second coming form the climax of God's covenant with the world.

READ MORE ABOUT IT

DPL Articles:

"Apocalypticism," pp. 25-35, by D. E. Aune.

"Center of Paul's Theology," pp. 92-95, by R. P. Martin.

"Eschatology," pp. 253-69, by L. J. Kreitzer.

"Old Testament in Paul," pp. 630-42, by M. Silva.

"Temple," pp. 923-25, by P. W. Comfort.

"Tradition," pp. 944-45, by M. B. Thompson.

11

Paul's Legacy

WHAT IS THE CONNECTION BETWEEN the Paul who argued theology with his colleagues in a third-story apartment and the Paul we argue about in our Bible studies? How did we get from there to here, from first-century Antioch (Syria) to First Church, Antioch (Texas)? Acts ends with Paul under arrest (Acts 28:30). In our last word from Paul himself, he tells us "everyone deserted me" (2 Tim 4:16 NIV). The greetings that follow indicate not every one had actually washed their hands of Paul. Nonetheless, Paul's life ends with a few faithful friends and a few struggling churches in western Turkey and Greece (four "regions": Galatia, Ephesus, Macedonia and Achaia). Most, if not all, of the churches Paul had started disappeared within a generation or two. Paul appears to drop off the radar screen quickly. Compared to other apostles, there are few references to Paul for the first hundred years after his death.[1] Yet this does not match our modern image of Paul. For us, Paul looms large, overshadowing all other figures in Christian history. By the time of Augustine, the bishop of North Africa in the fourth Christian century, Paul is the undisputed heavyweight among the early disciples.

It was not Paul's churches that brought him this prestige. It was his letters. More surprisingly, his letters do not appear to have been esteemed initially. At first glance, we see no evidence early Christian leaders viewed Paul's letters as particularly important. In fact, our initial evidence suggests the opposite. In his story of

---

[1]Wilhelm Schneemelcher ("Paulus in der griechischen Kirche des zweiten Jahrhunderts," in *Zeitschrift für Kirchengeschichte* 75 [1964]: 4-13) argues there are no unambiguous citations of Paul before Irenaeus. The earlier references, according to Schneemelcher, are traditions quoted by both Paul and the early fathers. Schneemelcher is overly pessimistic; see *1 Clement* 47:1-3.

Paul in Acts, Luke doesn't even mention that Paul wrote letters. Did Luke think it wasn't worth mentioning? Second Peter seems to give Paul's letters a mixed review:

> So also our beloved brother Paul wrote to you according to the wisdom given him, speaking of this as he does in all his letters. There are some things in them hard to understand, which the ignorant and unstable twist to their own destruction, as they do the other scriptures. (2 Pet 3:15-16)[2]

This is not to say Paul fell into disrepute.[3] Rather, the value of his letters, which Paul himself probably considered secondary to his actual ministry, had not yet been fully recognized.

THE COLLECTION OF PAUL'S LETTERS

If Paul's letters were not immediately valued, preserved and locked away, how do we manage to have copies today? How did his letters go from seemingly private letters of specific congregations to published editions handed down through the centuries to us? In actuality, we need to back up and ask a more basic question, How did the individual letters to churches scattered around the countryside become a collected set?

Many readers of the New Testament have not stopped to wonder how someone got a copy of a letter of Paul to the Romans and a copy of the one to the Galatians, even though the regions were over a thousand miles apart. What ancient evidence do we have for how these individual letters became a published set? We might expect to find that our oldest copies came to us as individual letters and then, at some point in history, published sets begin to appear. Unfortunately, this is not the case. Like the rest of the Bible, we do not have any autographs[4] of Paul's letters. We do not have any direct copies of an autograph. We have copies of copies. In fact our

---

[2]This passage is often debated. Many consider 2 Peter to be pseudonymous. The writer seems to equate Paul's letters with Scripture. Furthermore, 2 Peter seems to imply an existing collection of Paul's letters. For the connection of 2 Peter 3:15 with the question of the Pauline canon, see E. Randolph Richards, *Paul and First-Century Letter Writing: Secretaries, Composition and Collection* (Downers Grove, Ill.: InterVarsity Press, 2004), pp. 221-22.

[3]E. J. Goodspeed argued that Paul's reputation turned from positive to negative in the decades after his death, resulting in the neglect of his letters. Donald Guthrie, *New Testament Introduction* (Downers Grove, Ill.: InterVarsity Press, 1974), pp. 654-55, demonstrates there is no evidence that Paul was disdained.

[4]This term *autograph* means the document written in the author's own hand. By this, scholars mean "the original." We suggest this term is a poor fit. Even the original was not in the author's handwriting, but in a secretary's. Also, there may have been at least two "originals," the one dispatched and the retained copy. Nonetheless, the term *autograph* remains a common designation for the "original manuscript."

WHAT'S MORE . . .
Papyrus 46

This manuscript was made of a single quire[a] and originally had 104 leaves. Seven leaves were lost on the outside (meaning 14 pages from the front of the book and 14 pages from the end).

This is the earliest known copy of Paul's letters. It also has an unusual order: Romans (beginning at 5:17), Hebrews, 1-2 Corinthians, Ephesians, Galatians, Philippians, Colossians and 1 Thessalonians.

It is assumed the remaining seven pages contained 2 Thessalonians. Bruce Metzger argues the missing pages "would have been insufficient for the Pastoral Epistles,"[b] raising questions about whether the scribe even knew of these letters, suspected them as non-Pauline, or just didn't intend to copy them. What about Philemon? However, the writing in the codex becomes increasingly smaller as the book progresses, suggesting to some that the scribe was becoming concerned he would not have sufficient room to finish his text. If the scribe only intended 2 Thessalonians and even Philemon, then there was more than adequate space. Because the manuscript is damaged, we should be cautious of using $\mathfrak{P}^{46}$ to argue the Pastorals were not part of the Pauline corpus in A.D. 200.[c]

---

[a]A book (codex) was made from large sheets (leaves) folded over. Thus one sheet folded in half made four pages (when written front and back). Often about four sheets would be stacked, folded over together and sewn along the folded edge. This sewn bundle was called a quire. Books (codices) were usually made of multiple quires stacked together (as books often are today). Too many sheets in one quire (as in $\mathfrak{P}^{46}$) caused the inside sheets to be too small, since the edges were trimmed to be even.

[b]Bruce Metzger, *Manuscripts of the Greek Bible* (Oxford: Oxford University Press, 1981), p. 64.

[c]So also David Trobisch, *Paul's Letter Collection: Tracing the Origins* (Minneapolis: Fortress, 1994), p. 22.

---

earliest copy of any of Paul's letters originated about 150 years after the original was written. To further complicate the matter, the earliest manuscript, called $\mathfrak{P}^{46}$ (dated about A.D. 200), is not a copy of a single letter of Paul but is already a collection.

Other manuscripts vary from the list of the "Pauline" letters in $\mathfrak{P}^{46}$. The manuscript evidence, therefore, does not present a clear picture.

In addition to the actual manuscript copies of Paul's letters, we have three other early significant sources of data: the early church fathers, Marcion and the Muratorian Canon. We will consider these later in the chapter. For now, suffice it to say the apostolic fathers, whose writings date to about A.D. 90-150, refer to at least some but not all of Paul's letters. Marcion, a church leader eventually rejected by the church for his heretical teachings, gave Paul's letters primacy, apparently publishing his own set of Paul's letters around A.D. 140. Marcion's list differs slightly from what we traditionally consider the letters of Paul. The Muratorian Canon (traditionally dated c. A.D. 200) contains a list of Paul's letters that differ from the testimony of the early fathers and Marcion.[5]

To complicate the matter further, the history of the investigation into the Pauline canon (the collected set of Paul's letters) has traditionally been fueled by the prevailing scholarly opinions about the authenticity of select letters of Paul. When scholarly opinion (in the late 1800s and early 1900s) primarily concluded against the authenticity of the Pastorals as Pauline, the question naturally arose as to how they found a home in the Pauline canon. As additional letters became suspect, such as Ephesians or 2 Thessalonians, the question became more pressing, since our earliest extant copies do include those letters. This impetus gave rise to several theories about how Paul's letters were collected and published. Proponents fell into two general categories, those who argued the process was gradual (like a snowball rolling down a hill and increasing in size) and those who argued an individual provided momentum resulting in a quick move (a "big bang") to collect and publish the letters.

Snowball theories. The various snowball theories[6] may be divided into two groups: those who think the gradual process was finished within 50 to 100 years (by about the time of Marcion [A.D. 140]) and those who argued it took longer, 100 to 150 years (finishing about A.D. 200, the early date for the Muratorian Canon). Theodor Zahn suggested that interest in Paul's letters was immediate.[7] He argued that churches read Paul's letters publicly in worship, a custom Paul may have initiated (Col 4:16). Thus a desire arose in various churches to collect other

---

[5]Recent scholarship has argued the list is probably from Syria of the fourth century and is consistent with other lists from that place and time. If correct, this eases the tension somewhat.

[6]Harry Gamble, *New Testament Canon: Its Making and Meaning* (Philadelphia: Fortress, 1985), p. 36, popularized this image. Stanley E. Porter ("When and How Was the Pauline Canon Compiled? An Assessment of Theories" in *The Pauline Canon*, ed. Stanley E. Porter [Leiden: Brill, 2004], p. 99 n. 10) indicates that C. F. D. Moule may have been the first to coin the term.

[7]Zahn, a scholar who was underappreciated in his native Germany of his time, has still not received the full attention he deserved. We three authors were required as doctoral students to read his *Grundriss der Geschichte des Neutestamentlichen Kanons* [Outline of the History of the New Testament Canon] (Leipzig: Deichert, 1904).

letters of Paul. Finally, around A.D. 80-85, a church (Rome, Antioch or Corinth) finalized the collection with a set of ten letters (excluding the Pastorals). Adolf Harnack also argued for a gradual collection of Paul's letters. He thought the drive to publish a Pauline collection arose not from church use but rather as a response to heretical teachers (notably Marcion) who were publishing their own lists of "approved scriptures." Thus, according to Harnack, a complete Pauline canon (including the Pastorals) existed by A.D. 140.

Other snowball theorists suggested that the process may have begun immediately after Paul, but it took longer. Kirsopp Lake pointed out that references made by early church fathers to some of Paul's letters don't necessarily mean the writer knew all of Paul's letters. Furthermore, the variations in the arrangement of Paul's letters in the later extant copies indicate, in Lake's assessment, that there were multiple partial collections. The process of standardizing the collections took longer and culminated by the time of the Muratorian Canon (about A.D. 200).

Although there is much to commend the snowball theory—a position still held by many—scholars have noted several significant weaknesses. First, even though a Christian writer failed to mention a particular letter of Paul, it does not mean it was unknown. This is an argument from silence.[8] Second, the evidence does not support a gradual growth. From Marcion to the Muratorian, the list of Paul's letters increases; however, Tertullian and Origen have shorter lists. Therefore, the length of a list indicates canonical development and not the gradual formation of the collection. Lastly, snowball theories lean heavily upon three historical "pillars": (1) Acts doesn't mention the letters of Paul; (2) P^{46} had only ten letters plus Hebrews; and (3) the Muratorian Canon represents a thirteen-letter collection by A.D. 200. Recently, all three of these "facts" have been called into serious question,[9] leaving no clear basis for suggesting a growing snowball of letters. Indeed, "one cannot help but think that the gradual collection theory of the Pauline corpus—as popular as it has been—is one of expedience . . . without a firm foundation."[10]

"Big bang" theories. In opposition to snowball theories with their gradual coalescing of the Pauline canon, "big bang" theories suggest an individual (or a com-

---

[8]See Guthrie, *New Testament Introduction*, p. 646.

[9]Obviously, we cannot discuss these here. See for (1) William Walker, "Acts and the Pauline Corpus Reconsidered," in *The Pauline Writings*, ed. S. Porter and C. Evans, *Biblical Seminar Series* 34 (Sheffield: Academic, 1995), pp. 63-70; for (2) J. Duff, "P46 and the Pastorals: A Misleading Consensus?" *New Testament Studies* 44 (1998): 578-90; and for (3) G. M. Hahnemann, *The Muratorian Fragment* (Oxford: Clarendon, 1992).

[10]Porter, "When and How," p. 103.

munity) took it upon himself to collect and publish the letters of Paul. There was
no groundswell movement, no culmination of a trend. The sudden impetus of an
individual caused the rapid appearance of a published collection of Paul's letters.
But what caused the big bang? It could have been a response to (1) a sudden interest in Paul's letters after a period of lapsed interest, (2) the rise of a heresy or (3)
a motivated follower's desire to preserve Paul's legacy through his letters.

According to Edgar J. Goodspeed, an unnamed disciple in Ephesus was
spurred on by the publication of Acts and initiated the collection. Goodspeed argued that Paul was not initially esteemed after his death. Then, because of the
publication of Acts around A.D. 90,[11] Paul was recast dramatically and powerfully
as the apostle to the Gentiles,[12] which prompted someone to seek to collect the
letters of Paul.[13] Since in A.D. 90 Ephesus (1) had become, thanks to the ministry
of John, the second largest Christian center, (2) had received a prominent position
in the book of Acts, and (3) was noted for letter writing activity at that time (Revelation and the letters of Ignatius), then Ephesus was the church most likely to
publish Paul's letters. Ephesians was written by a disciple of Paul to stand at the
head of a collection of nine letters (excluding the Pastorals). Ephesians fit Goodspeed's theory, for the letter seemed—at least to some—to be a summary of Paul's
theology, and it may well have been a circular letter, intended for multiple destinations.[14] John Knox expanded significantly upon his teacher's theory. In addition
to strengthening the arguments, Knox added three items. The collection was intended to be a sevenfold Pauline corpus, capitalizing upon the ancient love of
"seven."[15] Knox suggested it was Onesimus who collected the letters. Although the
letter to Philemon is closely connected to Colossians, how does one explain
including a personal letter in such a select collection? Knox suggested it was

---

[11]Why is Acts dated so late? At that time, it was quite popular in scholarship to view Acts as a late
document reflecting second-generation Christianity. Following Hegel's view of history, "thesis" (early
Palestinian [Petrine] Christianity) had been opposed by "antithesis" (later Gentile [Pauline] Christianity), which later resolved into early Catholic Christianity, as represented by Acts. This reconstruction required that Acts be dated later.

[12]E. J. Goodspeed, *The Meaning of Ephesians* (Chicago: University of Chicagao, 1933), pp. 82-165.

[13]Stanley Porter rightly complains that Goodspeed's thesis is more complex than is usually presented
in summaries such as this. For a more detailed and even-handed description, see Porter, "When and
How," pp. 103-7.

[14]In our discussion of Ephesians, we suggested it is quite possible Ephesians was written with the intention of being sent to multiple destinations. This "circular letter" theory is independent of Goodspeed's theory.

[15]Sevenfold is reached by grouping the letters in this manner: (1) Ephesians, (2) Romans, (3) Galatians, (4) Philippians, (5) the Corinthian letters, (6) the Thessalonian letters and (7) Colossians/
Philemon.

Onesimus's influence.[16] Knox further suggested Marcion worked from this original collection. Marcion moved Galatians to the front (displacing Ephesians as the head letter), in keeping with Marcion's anti-Jewish theme. In the years that followed, various modifications were offered to the Goodspeed-Knox theory. The genius of Goodspeed and Knox is clear; however, there is no evidence of any kind that Ephesians was ever the head of any collection of Paul's letters.[17]

Walter Schmithals suggested the rise of Gnosticism in the early second century fueled an orthodox movement to oppose it. This movement quested about for "authoritative" material, such as the Gospel of John, to publish in opposition to Gnostic teaching. The book of Acts had placed Paul in a position of authority. Schmithals suggested an unknown editor gathered fragments of authentic Pauline letters. These fragments were edited, elaborated and organized into "seven" letters and then published as letters of Paul.[18] Schmithals has not persuaded scholars, primarily because there is no solid evidence there was ever a collection of only seven letters.

Recently, a general consensus has begun to emerge that some key figure, such as Luke, Timothy or Onesimus, may have played an initial role. Then other nameless disciples of Paul continued the process, including editing letters and even writing other letters (such as the Pastorals) in Paul's name, seeking to apply Paul's thought to new situations. These new letters, pseudonymously written under Paul's name, were noble efforts, some argue, to apply Paul's theology to contemporary church problems.

But the "deutero-Pauline" approach to pseudonymity assumes the early church would have accepted the idea of an "honorable" forgery.[19] If these deutero-Pauline authors were not trying to deceive but rather to honor, would they write in Paul's name? Pseudonymous writings were common at that time but fell into two categories: writings in the name of a contemporary author with the intention to deceive, or writings in the name of an author from centuries before, where one may assume the contemporary readers were not deceived. Scholars have seriously chal-

---

[16]In a letter by Ignatius to the church in Ephesus, he identifies a bishop by the name of Onesimus.

[17]Our earliest collections concur. P[46] has Romans first; Marcion lists Galatians, and if the Muratorian canon is early, it has 1 Corinthians. So Günther Zuntz, *The Text of the Epistles: A Disquisition upon the Corpus Paulinorum* (London: British Academy, 1953), p. 276. See Porter, "When and How," pp. 105-7, for a thorough critique.

[18]Walter Schmithals, "On the Composition and Earliest Collection of the Major Epistles of Paul," in *Paul and the Gnostics*, trans. J. E. Steely (Nashville: Abingdon, 1972), pp. 239-74.

[19]Terry Wilder (*Pseudonymity, the New Testament, and Deception* [Lanham: University Press of America, 2004]) recently argued "no." On the other hand, Mark Harding, "Disputed and Undisputed Letters of Paul," in *The Pauline Corpus*, ed. Stanley E. Porter (Leiden: Brill, 2004), p. 149, argues "the concept of the noble lie is crucial" to classical thought and used by Christian writers, citing Clement of Alexandria *Stromateis* 7.53 and Origen *Contra Celsum* 4.19.

lenged the existence of innocent apostolic pseudepigrapha (writings under a false name, claiming apostolic authority).[20]

Paul as the first publisher. Theories that a close associate of Paul, such as Luke or Timothy, took an early interest in Paul's letters allow the possibility that it was not an associate but Paul himself who first initiated the process of a collection. After all, Paul was the first to encourage churches to make copies and exchange letters (Col 4:16). David Trobisch argues the Pauline corpus stood originally with four Pauline letters, like F. C. Baur's Hauptebriefe,[21] and was then augmented after his death with Ephesians as the head of this expansion, as in Knox's theory, with the process overseen by a key individual, such as Luke or Timothy. Perhaps most intriguing is Trobisch's contention that the initial publication was instigated by none other than the apostle Paul himself. Trobisch noted the various collections we have of Paul's letters (the manuscripts like $\mathfrak{P}^{46}$, the references in the early fathers, and the lists of Marcion and the Muratorian list) reveal a system to the arrangement of the letters. Trobisch began with what is commonly recognized. Paul's letters to churches were grouped first, beginning with the longest to the shortest. Paul's letters to individuals were grouped next, starting with 1 Timothy and ending with Philemon. Within this scheme, letters to the same congregation or individual were kept together.[22]

Galatians and Ephesians are out of sequence. Ephesians is slightly longer. This break in order suggests to some scholars that we should see a seam here in the Pauline corpus. Trobisch argues the Pauline corpus began originally with four letters: Romans, 1-2 Corinthians and Galatians, explaining why Galatians is before Ephesians. This order is well preserved in our manuscript tradition. He credits Paul with initially publishing the four letters. Romans was reworked slightly, with Romans 16 intended as a "cover letter." Galatians was reworked into the format of a legal defense to justify Paul's collection for the saints in Jerusalem and his stance on the Mosaic law. 1 and 2 Corinthians are actually the compilation of seven letters of Paul: a letter about quarrels (1 Cor 1:10-4:21), a letter about the immoral

---

[20]See D. A. Carson, "Pseudonymity and Pseudepigraphy," *Dictionary of New Testament Background*, ed. Craig Evans and Stanley Porter (Downers Grove, Ill.: InterVarsity Press, 2004), pp. 857-64.

[21]The four letters, Romans, 1-2 Corinthians and Galatians, have long been designated the *Hauptebriefe*, German for "chief letters." There is a rich theological history behind this designation; however, it is often used regardless of one's evaluation of the theories of F. C. Baur.

[22]Of course, Hebrews is an exception to this. It is shorter than 1 Corinthians and longer than 2 Corinthians. In the case of $\mathfrak{P}^{46}$, Trobisch thinks the scribe did not want to stick Hebrews between the two letters and so listed it before 1 Corinthians. However, among the manuscripts, Hebrews varies in where it appears. Many, including Trobisch, think this variation is another sign it was added later to an already established Pauline corpus.

WHAT'S MORE . . .
Multiple Editions of Romans

Extant manuscripts of Romans reveal an interesting phenomenon. We have one manuscript copy of Romans with only chapters 1—15 (ms 1506). Marcion had a version of Romans with only fourteen chapters. It was long assumed that Marcion had edited down his copy, although it is hard to see why chapters 15 and 16 should have offended him. Through a careful study, Harry Gamble has demonstrated the fourteen-chapter edition existed in the eastern part of the empire and was used rather than created by Marcion.[a]

How can we explain multiple editions? We suggest the editions originate from Paul. He composed the sixteen-chapter version from Corinth, dictating it to Tertius (the secretary, Rom 16:12), who perhaps took it down rapidly in shorthand. How did Paul know so many people to greet in Rome, when he had never been there? Again, we think Tertius is the connection. A case can be made for Tertius being from Rome. Why else would he feel free to insert his own greetings into Paul's letter? This is rare in antiquity and was done only by secretaries who were personally known to the recipient.[b] Paul, who preferred merely generic greetings, probably asked Tertius to greet the important members of the church there by name.[c]

Once in prison, Paul decided other churches should read what he wrote to the church in Rome. (Notice that while in a Roman prison, he encouraged the same practice to the Colossians.) When he made another copy of his letter to Rome, there was no need to include the recommendation letter for Phoebe or the greetings (Rom 16). The travel plans in Romans 15 didn't work out as he had hoped and also didn't need to be copied, certainly from verse 14 onward. Rather than claiming a later disciple of Paul took it upon himself to edit Romans, we should consider the possibility that Paul himself did. Ancients loved to share copies of letters with others. For example, Cicero notes "Take care that you get from Lucceius the letter I sent him" and "I have sent you a copy of the letter I wrote to Pompey.[d] We should not be surprised that a shortened copy of Romans appears in the East among the churches Paul loved.

---

[a]Harry Gamble, *Textual History of the Letter to the Romans: A Study in Textual and Literary Criticism*. Studies and Documents Series 42 (Grand Rapids: Eerdmans, 1977).

[b]See E. Randolph Richards, *The Secretary in the Letters of Paul*, Wissenschaftliche Untersuchungen zum Neuen Testament 2/42 (Tübingen: Mohr/Siebeck, 1991), pp. 76, 170-71.

[c]When Paul personally picks up the pen to end his letters, his greetings are brief and usually generic. See 1 Corinthians 16:24; 2 Corinthians 13:12-13; Galatians 6:16; Ephesians 6:23; Philippians 4:21-22; Colossians 4:18; 1 Thessalonians 5:26; 2 Thessalonians 3:18; Titus 3:15. Only Philemon and 2 Timothy have a few named greetings from Paul's hand.

[d]Cicero *Letters to Atticus* 4.6 and 3.9.

brother (1 Cor 5:1—6:11), a letter answering questions from Corinth (1 Cor 6:12—16:24) and so on. Trobisch argues these were originally separate letters that Paul himself edited into the present format for publication.

Paul as a private collector. Older collection theories share a commonality. They connect the issue of collection with the process of publication. In other words, it is assumed the person (or persons) publishing the letters was the one who collected them.[23] It is also assumed the letters were collected from the dispatched copies. That is to say, someone traveled around and made copies of the received letters; for example, the published copy of Paul's letter to the Philippians came from making a copy of the letter retained by the Philippian church. Practically, such a scenario is possible. Ancients traveled frequently. Because of the early Christian emphasis on hospitality, when a Christian was visiting another city, it is not unreasonable to assume he stayed in the home of another Christian. During the meal, he perhaps heard a letter of Paul read, as reading aloud was a common form of after-dinner entertainment (and certainly more appropriate for Christians than other forms of after-dinner revelry). The guest might request a copy to take home to his church.[24]

This scenario has two weaknesses. First, even though it can easily explain the exchange of letters, as Paul himself encouraged (Col 4:16), it doesn't account for how a complete set of letters was collected from such a wide geographical area. Second, there is no evidence from the first century that the letters of Paul were particularly valued. By the second century, when evidence begins to appear that churches esteemed the letters, we already have complete collections. Tying collection to publication pushes publication back into the first century, where it seems unlikely, or pushes collection into the second century, which seems equally unlikely. We suggest it is more plausible historically to separate the convoluted publication process from the question of how an original set of Paul's letters came into being.

Retaining personal copies. When an ancient publisher wished to produce a set of collected letters, he had two sources. He could collect copies from the various recipients by making copies of the dispatched letters, or he could make copies of the letter-copies retained by the author himself. Classical scholars have long known ancient letter writers routinely retained personal copies of their letters.[25] It is now

---

[23]Of course, most theories allowed for partial, local collections.

[24]Cicero *Letters to Atticus* 8.9. In similar fashion, it is also possible the publisher sent a letter to Philippi asking them to make a copy and send it back, presumably providing the necessary funds.

[25]R. Y. Tyrell and L. C. Purser, *The Correspondance of M. Tullius Cicero* (Dublin: Hodges and Figgis, 1915) 1:59, "There seems considerable evidence that the senders of letters . . . were accustomed to keep copies of letters, even, perhaps, letters which might seem to us to be of no great significance."

being recognized in New Testament circles.[26]

Ancient letter writers recognized the value of retaining a copy. The most immediate reason was that letters were sometimes lost during delivery.[27] Yet letter writers had at least two other common purposes for retaining a copy. First, they often shared the letter with another person on another occasion. Dolabella asked for a copy of a letter he had heard that Cicero had sent to another. Cicero dismissed it as a "little nothing he had written." Nonetheless, he had a copy of it at his Pompeii home, and he sent a copy (Cicero *Letters to Friends* 9.12.1) to Dolabella. Second, the writer would sometimes reuse a portion of one letter in a letter to another. We have multiple examples of this, and there appears to have been no stigma attached to the practice.[28] More than thirty years ago, Bruce Metzger suggested this may explain the similarities between Paul's letters to the Ephesians and the Colossians.[29]

We have no direct evidence that Paul retained copies of his letters.[30] He makes no explicit comments about doing so. On the other hand, Paul makes little or no comment on other epistolary practices either. We see no evidence why Paul would not have retained a copy. He seems to hold his letters in high regard and encourages others to make copies (Col 4:16). With the time and expense involved in preparing one of his letters, it would be foolhardy not to retain a copy.[31]

Paul's personal collection. We argue that Paul's letters were not collected by someone circulating among the churches and gathering up copies of the dispatched letters. Rather, the first collection of Paul's letters was his own personal dossier. But contrary to Trobisch, we suggest Paul did not retain copies in a push to have his letters published. His concerns were more immediate. After his death, his personal effects, including his notebooks, fell into the hands of his disciples. Among the books

---

[26]For a more detailed discussion, see Richards, *Letter Writing,* pp. 156-61. Harry Gamble notes, "Ancient writers often kept copies of their private letters even when no particular literary merit of topical importance was attached to them; and copies of instructional, administrative letters were all the more likely to be kept." See Gamble, *Books and Readers in the Early Church: A History of Early Christian Texts* (New Haven, Conn.: Yale University Press, 1995), p. 101.

[27]See, e.g., Cicero *Letters to Friends* 7.25.1 or *Letters to Quintus* 2.12.4.

[28]See Richards, *First-Century Letter Writing,* pp. 160-61.

[29]Bruce Metzger, in his classic introduction in *The New Testament: Its Background, Growth, and Content,* 3rd ed. (Nashville: Abingdon, 2003), p. 216.

[30]There are some subtle indicators; see E. Randolph Richards, "The Codex and the Early Collection of Paul's Letters," *Bulletin for Biblical Research* 8 (1998): 159-60.

[31]See, e.g., Gamble, *Books and Readers,* pp. 100-101: "It seems unlikely that Paul would have written the kinds of letters he wrote without retaining copies"; and Ben Witherington III, *The Paul Quest: The Renewed Search for the Jew of Tarsus* (Downers Grove, Ill.: InterVarsity Press, 1998), p. 102; and Porter, "When and How," p. 125; see also Jerome Murphy-O'Connor, *Paul the Letter Writer: His World, His Options, His Skills,* Good News Studies (Collegeville, Minn.: Liturgical, 1995), 41:118.

of personal notes, Scripture excerpts, early traditions, and so on, were notebooks of material he was currently working on and also copies of his letters. Thus, we have one set of the collected letters of Paul before others recognized their value. The drive to publish the letters arose independently and subsequently to this collection.

This theory reconstructs how a single set of Paul's letters became a collection. It explains how certain letters were preserved. Other letters were "lost," not because a church discarded them or a collector disdained them but rather because Paul did not make a personal copy. Why would Paul not make a copy before dispatching it? We have no way of knowing. However, we should allow for more mundane reasons, such as not having enough time to make a copy before the original needed to be sent. We should also note, as Trobisch does, that not even Cicero made personal copies of every letter, even those he later wished to publish. Sometimes Cicero felt pressure from the letter carrier to hastily finish a letter so he could leave (e.g., Cicero *Letters to Friends* 15.17.1-2); sometimes he had no secretarial help with him (e.g. Cicero *Letters to Atticus* 5.12). It is mere speculation why Paul did not make a personal copy of a particular letter. It is sufficient to note only that such things happened.

The weakness in this approach is that it explains only the first collection. It does not address how Paul's letters were arranged and published. For those questions, we still need to explain why and how the burgeoning church came to make extensive use of Paul's letters.

FINDING PAUL'S ENDURING LEGACY

We began the chapter by saying that Paul's letters did not seem particularly esteemed at first. This however would apply only to the first few decades, perhaps A.D. 60-90.[32] Later, believers did begin to find them useful. How do we know this? A closer look at Christian writings shows many used Paul's letters. This observation was summed up by E. J. Goodspeed:

> Every Christian document shows acquaintance with Paul's letters—the Revelation, Hebrews, I Clement, I Peter, the letters of Ignatius and Polycarp, the Gospel of John. This is, in fact, the key to the later literature of the New Testament; *it is all written in the presence of the collected Pauline letters.*[33]

---

[32]We take 2 Peter as Petrine and thus as evidence of a Pauline collection in the early 60s. However, we think Peter had seen the *original* collection and thus 2 Peter is not evidence of an early veneration of Paul's letters. See the discussion in Richards, "Codex," pp. 165-66.

[33]E. J. Goodspeed, *An Introduction to the New Testament* (Chicago: University of Chicago Press, 1937), p. 211; emphasis ours.

While comments about Paul's letters are scarce, the evidence is plentiful that others were reading them. Since folks were reading collections of Paul's letters, how were these collections made available? In other words, how were the letters of Paul published as authoritative writings?

The canonization of Paul's letters. History clearly pronounces that the legacy of Paul was the Pauline canon. Our English word "canon" derives from the Greek *kanōn*. This Greek word originally referred to a tool for measuring straightness. It denoted function. From this root idea, *kanōn* came to mean "a rule," and later "a list," a meaning more connected to form. This double connotation of form and function carried over into our English usage. "Canon" in Pauline studies clearly refers to a fixed form, a very specific list of particular letters; yet it also has a functional meaning. To be "canonical" (in the Pauline canon) means a letter is on the list, but more than that, the letter is normative (straight and true) for the Christian faith by virtue of being on the list, and it is regarded as authoritative in the life of the community. We shall limit our discussion here to the contents of the Pauline canon. Also, for our purposes here, the term "Pauline corpus" (or *corpus Paulinum*) will be used interchangeably with "Pauline canon."

The publication of Paul's letters. When our students hear about Paul's letters being published, they often think of large publishing houses, printing presses, marketing departments and so on. They wonder, "How many copies were made for the first print run of the book?" Ancients operated by an entirely different system. Books were hand-copied, usually one at a time. When we speak of publishing Paul's letters, we are referring to when copies of Paul's letters began to circulate more widely. With that definition in mind, we can examine the earliest published collections we have of Paul's letters.

Trobisch correctly draws several inferences from this data. The various locations of Hebrews are likely explained by its being added to an existing collection of Paul's letters and that it took some time to decide where to place it. $\mathfrak{P}^{46}$ listed Hebrews according to its relative length. The remaining orderings (if they included Hebrews) placed it at the end of the letters to churches (after 2 Thess) or at the end of the entire collection. Hebrews initially did not belong with the letters of Paul.

The study of the manuscripts led Trobisch to conclude we have no manuscript evidence to indicate there were ever partial editions of Paul's letters: the various collections scattered around "not only ordered the letters the same way but also had access to exactly the same number of letters—thirteen."[34] The manuscript ev-

---

[34]Trobisch, *Paul's Letter Collection*, p. 22. He rightly notes that when manuscripts are missing their endings (like $\mathfrak{P}^{46}$ or 03), we are unwise to make conjectures about what letters they contained originally.

WHAT'S MORE . . .
The Arrangement of Paul's Letters in Select Manuscripts

Marcion	𝔓46	01, A, B, C	Muratorian Canon[a]	D (onward)
2nd century	2nd century	4th century	4th century	5th century+
Gal	Rom	Rom	Corinthians	Rom
1 Cor	Heb	1 Cor	Eph	1 Cor
2 Cor	1 Cor	2 Cor	Phil	2 Cor
Rom	2 Cor	Gal	Col	Gal
1 Thess	Eph	Eph	Gal	Eph
2 Thess	Gal	Phil	Thessalonians	Col
Laodiceans	Phil	Col	Rom	Phil
Col	Col	1 Thess	"Again to Corinthians"	1 Thess
Phil	1 Thess	2 Thess	"Again to Thessalonians"	2 Thess
Philem		Heb	Titus	1 Tim
		1 Tim	"Two to Timothy"	2 Tim
		2 Tim		Tit
		Tit		Philem
		Philem		Heb

[a]We are following the sequence indicated in lines 50-61 of the Muratorian fragment. It is questionable how much this was intended to indicate a sequence, for it offers a different sequence for Hauptebriefe in lines 42-44.

idence thus leads us to conclude that the early church knew a collection of thirteen letters arranged in a fixed order.[35] Original publishers were working from a fixed collection. We suggest the collection originated from Paul's set of letters.

Evidence for a Pauline canon. The rise of the New Testament canon is not the study of how twenty-seven books came into a single collection. Rather, it is the study of how three collections took place. In the centuries that followed, these

---

[35]The slight variations (such as switching Galatians and Ephesians) are explained as theological (as in Marcion) or just accidental. Murphy-O'Connor's careful study of ancient systems of determining length (counting lines) shows Ephesians and Galatians are very similar in length. See Murphy-O'Connor, *Paul the Letter-Writer*, pp. 123-24; and Trobisch, *Paul's Letter Collection*, p. 17.

collections came to be viewed as a single set, a "collection of collections."[36] The three collections were: (1) the four Gospels, (2) the letters of Paul and (3) the General Epistles. Only two documents stood somewhat independently of these: Acts and the Revelation. (Hebrews was usually listed with Paul's letters.) Acts was the second volume of Luke's Gospel. The Revelation was quickly tied to the letters of John. The story of how each of these collections came into being is fascinating, but we shall limit our discussion to the Pauline collection, specifically how the unpublished set of Paul's letters—which we think arose from Paul's personal set—became an accepted list of authoritative letters. Evidence comes in two forms. Church leaders quote sections from Paul's letters, demonstrating they owned and accepted a letter as Pauline and authoritative. Second, church leaders list letters to be accepted as authentically Pauline. Let's look briefly at each type of evidence.

Barnett's Evidence of Paul's Letters in the Early Church Fathers[a]

This early church father:	appears to know these Pauline letters:
Clement of Rome (*c.* 95)	Rom, 1-2 Cor, Gal, Eph, Phil, Col, Pastorals[a]
Ignatius (*c.* 115)	Rom, 1-2 Cor, Gal, Eph, Phil, Col, 1 Thess, Pastorals[a]
Polycarp (*c.* 110-120)	Rom, 1-2 Cor, Gal, Eph, Phil, Col, 1-2 Thess, Pastorals
Justin Martyr (*c.* 152)	Rom, 1 Cor, Gal, Eph, Col, 2 Thess
Theophilus (*c.* 170-180)	Pastorals
Athenagoras (*c.* 170-180)	Pastorals

[a]The primary data for this chart is condensed from the excellent summary in Mark Harding, "Disputed and Undisputed Letters of Paul," in *The Pauline Canon,* ed. S. Porter (Leiden: Brill, 2004), pp. 130-31, n. 4. The dates given are for the writing that contains the proposed citation. Barnett does not see allusions to the Pastorals in the letters marked with an [a]; other scholars do. Barnett does, however, see evidence of the Pastorals in Polycarp's letter to the Philippians but argues the Pastorals used Polycarp (he dates the Pastorals late); see Albert E. Barnett, *Paul Becomes a Literary Influence* (Chicago: University of Chicago Press, 1941), pp. 182-83.

Citations. First, as church leaders across the empire gained access to material, they cited it in their own writings. The earliest writings are by church leaders commonly called the apostolic fathers (Clement of Rome, Ignatius, Polycarp and Justin Martyr). There seems to be early and widespread evidence that various letters

---

[36]To use Harry Gamble's terminology in "Canon," *Anchor Bible Dictionary,* ed. David Noel Freedman (New York: Doubleday, 1992), 1:853.

of Paul were read and used by early church leaders.

Early evidence is wonderful to have. Nonetheless, it is a tricky matter. If an early father cited the letter, then he knew of the letter and presumably considered it Paul's. If he made no mention of a particular letter, say Philemon, it may be because he did not know of the letter, or because he rejected the letter as pseudonymous, or because he did not happen to feel the need to quote anything from it. Furthermore, the evidence of the earliest fathers is more tenuous. Clement of Rome explicitly ascribes a citation to Paul, noting it was from Paul's first letter to the Corinthians (*1 Clement* 47.1-3). Clement seems to imply he is aware of more than one letter.[37] Ignatius notes Paul remembered the Ephesians "in every letter" (*Letter to the Ephesians* 12.2). Is he implying Paul wrote more than one letter to the Ephesians? Ignatius's comment is too vague to be clear. Polycarp, in his letter to the Philippians, reminds them that Paul wrote "letters" to them (*Letter to the Philippians* 3.2). Was Polycarp misunderstanding Philippians 3:1, or did he know of other letters we don't have? Furthermore, the actual citations from the fathers are very brief, often little more than snippets. Some scholars have suggested they are not citing Paul's letters at all but merely quoting formulas and echoing traditions that Paul himself also cited.[38] Nonetheless, most scholars agree the evidence is sufficient to show at least some of Paul's letters were known to many of the early fathers.[39]

Lists. A second type of evidence overcomes some of the weaknesses we just noted. When a church father listed a book as "approved" or "rejected," we are not left wondering if he was aware of the book. He has stated his opinion. If he fails to mention a New Testament writing, we are more confident in saying that he was unaware of it; otherwise, he would have placed it in a category. This type of early evidence provides wonderful testimony as to how the letters of Paul were perceived by one individual or by a community represented by that individual. But that is also its weakness. We are left to decide if that individual is a reliable gauge of how Christians of his day perceived Paul's letters. In other words, was he representative of all or most Christians, or was he aberrant, perhaps a leader of a "heretical" sect?

The earliest surviving list of Paul's letters comes from Marcion (c. A.D. 140). We know of Marcion's list, however, only through Tertullian (c. A.D. 200) and Epiphanius (c. A.D. 375). These two men were writing against the heretical teach-

---

[37]This also implies he was *un*aware of the so-called previous letter, suggesting Clement was working from a collected set like ours and *not* from his personal experience in Corinth; see Richards, "Codex," p. 166.

[38]So argues Schneemelcher, "Paulus in der griechischen Kirche des zweiten Jahrhunderts," 4-13.

[39]See, e.g., Mark Harding, "Disputed and Undisputed Letters of Paul," in *The Pauline Corpus*, ed. S. Porter (Leiden: Brill, 2004), pp. 129-31.

ings of Marcion. In book five of his *Adversus Marcionem,* Tertullian mentions Marcion's *Apostolikon,* his set of Paul's letters. According to Tertullian, Marcion's *Apostolikon* contained Galatians, 1-2 Corinthians, Romans, 1-2 Thessalonians, *Laodiceans,* Colossians, Philemon and Philippians.[40] Since Tertullian lists the letters in an order different from the canonical order (which Tertullian followed), scholars assume Tertullian is preserving the arrangement of Marcion. Why is Galatians first? Tertullian does not say. Most assume that Marcion was privileging Galatians, for it fit best with his theology. Tertullian says the letter to the Laodiceans was a "mutilated" version of Ephesians. Tertullian also notes Marcion rejected the Pastorals.

Although the testimony of Marcion is very early, using his evidence is more difficult. Since Marcion was known not only for his heretical teachings but also for his willingness to expunge unwanted texts from Scripture—for example, he did not recognize the entire Old Testament—we cannot read anything into his rejection of the Pastorals.[41] Thus, for our general purposes, we may conclude that Marcion's canon gives evidence that at least ten letters of Paul were known in Asia Minor by early in the second century.

The sporadic evidence of the early fathers changes dramatically with the writings of Irenaeus (who was active c. 175-195), who frequently quotes from Paul's letters, clearly ascribing them to Paul. Irenaeus cites twelve letters of Paul (all except Philemon).[42] From the time of Irenaeus onward, Paul figures more and more prominently in the writings of church leaders. From the time after Irenaeus, we also begin to have manuscripts of Paul's letters, demonstrating which letters of Paul were accepted. In the third century, the letter to the Hebrews begins to find widespread acceptance as a fourteenth letter of Paul, yet often with reservations.

Noncanonical Letters. The letter of Hebrews may be safely removed from our discussion of the Pauline canon since the letter itself does not claim to be Paul's and the early church was at best ambivalent about assertions of Pauline authorship. We have not, however, finished discussing the establishment of an authoritative Pauline canon. We must also consider eight other letters that claim to be Paul's: *3 Corinthians, Laodiceans* and six letters to Seneca. Since most readers of the New

---

[40]For a fuller description, see Harding, "Disputed and Undisputed," pp. 132-33.

[41]F. C. Baur (1875) argued the unusual arrangement in Marcion's canon was because he listed authentic letters first (Gal, 1-2 Cor, Rom [Baur's *Hauptbriefe*]), then the forged letters (1-2 Thess, Col, *Laodiceans* [Eph], Philem, Phil). The Pastorals had not even been written yet, according to Baur. This reconstruction has not been persuasive.

[42]Irenaeus speaks generally of letters to the Thessalonians and Corinthians and the Pastorals, not distinguishing these individual letters.

WHAT'S MORE . . .
Hebrews in the Pauline Canon

Clement of Alexandria (c. A.D. 155-220) considered Hebrews a letter of Paul. As a Greek speaker himself, he recognized the letter was not Pauline in style. He explained this (according to Eusebius, *Historia Ecclesiastica* 6.14.2) by saying Paul wrote the original letter in Hebrew. Luke then translated it into Greek. Origen (c. A.D. 185-254) likewise considered it Pauline but was similarly troubled by the difference in style. He claimed (according to Eusebius, *Historica Ecclesiastica* 6.25.11-14) that Paul generated the contents but a later follower composed the actual letter. This uncertain opinion led Eusebius to support a thirteen-letter canon of Paul and then to argue for Hebrews as a fourteenth letter, aware that "some doubted," particularly in the western half of the Roman Empire (Eusebius, *Historica Ecclesiastica* 3.38.2-3).

The eastern half of the empire seems to have quickly accepted Hebrews as authoritative. Most prominently, Athanasius (*Thirty-Ninth Festal Letter*, A.D. 367) argued for a fourteen-letter Pauline corpus. When doubts were raised over Hebrews, its early defenders "gave it an excellent pedigree in ascribing it (quite falsely) to the apostle."[a] It is particularly noteworthy that early Greek-speaking church fathers, such as Clement and Origen, recognized the difficulty of claiming Pauline authorship for Hebrews when the letter was so clearly non-Pauline in style. Ancients used broad stylistic measures (like argumentation and tone) as indicative of authorship. Cicero recognized a letter as genuine because he recognized the person's style: "I have never seen anything more Sestian in its style" (Cicero *Letters to Atticus* 15.3).

Nonetheless, Hebrews remained within the Pauline canon until the Reformation, when Erasmus, Calvin and Luther questioned its status as a letter of Paul. No modern scholar accepts it as Pauline. The letter is anonymous. Paul never projected himself as the sort to write anonymously (see 2 Thess 3:17; 2 Cor 10:8-9).

---

[a]Harding, "Disputed and Undisputed," pp. 135. We are heavily indebted to his excellent discussion, pp. 134-36.

Testament are not familiar with these, we'll offer a very brief description.

Early versions of the Armenian New Testament contain *3 Corinthians*. The earliest extant copy dates to the third century. Purportedly it is Paul's response to yet another letter from Corinth concerning the disruptive teachings of Simon and Cleobius. The teachings of these "false teachers" were actually the problems facing second-century Christianity, which were largely Gnostic issues. "Paul's" response

---

WHAT'S MORE . . .
Excerpts from 3 Corinthians

(1) I, Paul, the prisoner of Jesus Christ, to the brethren in Corinth—greeting! . . . (4) For I delivered to you in the beginning what I received from the apostles who were before me. . . . (5) that our Lord Jesus Christ was born of Mary of the seed of David, when the Holy Spirit was sent from heaven by the Father into her. . . . (34) But if you receive anything else, do not cause me trouble; for I have these fetters on my hands that I may gain Christ, and his marks in my body that I may attain to the resurrection from the dead . . . (40) and peace be with you. Amen.[a]

[a] The letter may have circulated independently, but our earliest extant copy is incorporated in the *Acts of Paul*. W. Schneemelcher, "The Acts of Paul," in *New Testament Apocrypha*, ed. W. Schneemelcher and Edgar Hennecke, trans. R. McL.Wilson (Philadelphia: Westminster Press, 1965), 2: 375-77.

---

in this letter was to underscore the authority of the original apostles and their teachings. The claim of Pauline authorship for this letter has been universally rejected since Eusebius.

A supposed letter of Paul to the Laodiceans appears in the Vulgate and other early Italian manuscripts. Although probably written originally in Greek, it is extant only in a Latin translation.[43] The Laodicean letter claims to be written by Paul, but it is a poorly executed forgery. The letter is comprised primarily of excerpts from canonical letters of Paul, mostly from Philippians. The pseudepigrapher likely drew his inspiration from Colossians 4:16, where Paul encourages his readers to read his letter to the Laodiceans. Since that letter no longer existed, the

---

[43] It is probably not the same letter mentioned by Marcion. We have no copies of Marcion's letter. Tertullian claimed Marcion's Laodicean letter was merely a butchered form of Ephesians. Moreover, it is also not likely to be Marcion's because it promotes none of Marcion's causes.

WHAT'S MORE . . .
Excerpts from Laodiceans

(1) Paul, an apostle not of men and not through man, but through Jesus Christ, to the brethren who are in Laodicea. . . . (9) And this will his mercy work in you, that you may have the same love and be of one mind. (10) Therefore, beloved, as you have heard in my presence, so hold fast and do in the fear of God, and eternal life will be your portion. (11) For it is God who works in you. . . . (18) The saints salute you. (19) The grace of the Lord Jesus Christ be with your spirit. (20) And see that this epistle is read to the Colossians and that of the Colossians among you.[a]

---

[a]Wilhelm Schneemelcher, "The Epistle to the Laodiceans," in *New Testament Apocrypha*, ed. E. Hennecke and W. Schneemelcher, trans. R. McL. Wilson (Philadelphia: Westminster Press, 1965), 2:131-32.

---

pseudepigrapher used the opportunity to cut and paste a letter together.

Near the end of the fourth century, we begin to find references to a collection of fourteen letters, supposedly the correspondence between Paul and the Roman philosopher Seneca. Although Seneca was in Rome during Paul's time, it is unlikely the two ever met, given Paul's vastly lower social status. This collection has eight letters supposedly from Paul to Seneca and six from Seneca to Paul. The letters imply Seneca had read to Nero some of Paul's canonical letters and that this began the dialogue between Paul and Seneca. While 3 Corinthians was accepted by a few church fathers (notably Hippolytus and Origen), and Laodiceans was received for a while by some Italian Christians, no early father argued for the authenticity of the Seneca correspondence,[44] which was apparently written during the second or third century.

The acceptance of the thirteen letters of Paul as authentic, the debated status of Hebrews, and the rejection of other purported letters of Paul were firmly established by the fourth century and can be seen in the Muratorian Canon. If the Muratorian Fragment is from the fourth century, then we have a rather consistent image of how Paul's letters were received in the two halves of the empire. At the Second Council of Carthage (A.D. 419), Hebrews was accepted in the West as Pauline as it had already been accepted in the eastern part of the Roman Empire.[45]

---

[44]Actually, Jerome (*De Viris Illustribus* 12) accepted them, but he is later than our discussion here.
[45]See F. F. Bruce, *The Canon of Scripture* (Downers Grove, Ill.: InterVarsity Press, 1988), p. 220.

SO WHAT?
Who Decides What's Scripture?

What difference does it make how Paul's letters were published or who used which ones? So what if some early church leaders gave their opinions about which letters to use? Whose advice should Christians follow? More significantly, why should any of their opinions be binding on us today? Should we not make our own decisions about which books to use? In actuality, many of us do, limiting the books we "use" to selected ones. When was the last time you heard a sermon from Paul's letter to Philemon? Nonetheless, it is a fair question to raise. Why do we consider our canon "closed"? May we vote again to allow a book "in" or vote one of our current books "out"?

This is not a hypothetical scenario. Currently several scholars are attempting that very thing, arguing the *Gospel of Peter* or the *Gospel of Thomas* should be accepted as reliable and authoritative for understanding the life of Jesus. Our students often ask us, "What if an archaeologist discovered Paul's letter to the Laodiceans? Should we accept it into the canon?" That's a fair question, although an unlikely scenario. Our answer would be "perhaps," if millions of Christians from all over the world read and used it for several hundred years and consistently believed God was speaking to them through it. As Americans, we are inclined to vote on it next week. The decision as to which letters were authoritative was not reached by a small group of church leaders meeting for a week in Turkey. They were reporting what their people had been doing for many years. In actuality, the churches voted. They voted every time they had to decide which books to recopy. It was not possible to have copies of everything. They made copies of the writings they deemed were authoritative and useful. God spoke to them through those letters. They might have said, "Sure, Polycarp's letter to the Philippians is good, but we like 1 John better."[a] As Americans, we are particularly susceptible to an argument based in individualism: "Why should someone else tell me what to accept?" Actually the question should be reversed. Why do we think we have a right to question a decision accepted by millions of Christians worldwide over two thousand years? Paul had a special caution for folks like us: "Did the word of God originate with you?" (1 Cor 14:36). Sometimes it is necessary to question the "establishment," as Martin Luther did; however, the verdict on even Luther's actions was determined by the church over an extended period of time.

---

[a]Note, as Westerners, we tend to think in either-or categories. Polycarp's letter is *either* okay to use *or* it is not. Ancients (and most of today's world) tend to think in terms of *degree*. First John is *better.*

The eight noncanonical letters claiming to be Paul's were rejected as forgeries.

CONCLUSION

Ancient church writers connected authenticity with authority. Modern writers have attempted to separate the two, arguing a letter might be a forgery and yet still authoritative in the life of the church. It is difficult to maintain letters as pseudonymous and yet retain them as authoritative. The euphemistic "innocent apostolic pseudepigrapha" seems unsubstantiated. If some canonical letters of Paul are pseudonymous, that is, forgeries, then they were likely written to deceive the readers into thinking Paul was the author. To argue this was their motive (and they were apparently successful for nearly two thousand years) places more confidence in modern scholarship and less confidence in the ancients than we see as justified. In light of ancient letter-writing techniques, something the ancients were more familiar with than we are, there are logical explanations for the variations among the letters of Paul. We do not see sufficient grounds for disputing the authenticity of the thirteen canonical letters of Paul.

Many of us prefer the viewpoint of the early church fathers: authority should be connected to authenticity. We want to read only the genuine letters of Paul and not forgeries. Which letters we read makes a difference. Why? Because like the early church we believe we are doing more than simply reading someone else's mail. Indeed, for two thousand years Christians have read the letters of Paul as if they were reading the word of God. We believe Paul's letters addressed to Galatians and Romans, Timothy and Titus, were written to our churches and leaders as well.

READ MORE ABOUT IT

DPL Articles:

"Apocryphal Pauline Literature," pp. 35-37, by R. J. Bauckham.

"Canon," pp. 85-91, by A. G. Patzia.

"Paul in Early Church Tradition," pp. 692-95, by J. R. Michaels.

Murphy-O'Connor, Jerome. *Paul the Letter Writer: His World, His Options, His Skills* (Collegeville, Minn.: Liturgical, 1995), pp. 114-30.

Patzia, Arthur G. *The Making of the New Testament: Origin, Collection, Text and Canon* (Downers Grove, Ill.: InterVarsity Press, 1995), pp. 80-87.

Porter, Stanley E. "When and How Was the Pauline Canon Compiled? An Assessment of Theories," in *The Pauline Canon,* ed. S. Porter (Leiden: Brill, 2004), pp. 95-127.

12

Paul's Letters to *Our* Churches

OBVIOUSLY, WE CANNOT GIVE A FULL TREATMENT of Paul's influence on the church. But it might be helpful to hit a few of the highlights—to see how Paul's letters have informed the theological ruminations of Christian preachers, teachers and writers through the ages. Other than Jesus, Paul has been the most influential thinker in the church's history.

PAUL READ THROUGH THE AGES

The early church. Paul's influence was felt even in the century after his death. As was the case during his lifetime, Paul became a battleground for the early church even as the New Testament canon was forming. The Gnostics loved Paul. Expressions such as "the likeness of sinful flesh" (Rom 8:3), "what the Spirit desires is opposed to the flesh" (Gal 5:17) and "it is raised a spiritual body" (1 Cor 15:44) were pressed into the service of Gnostic teachers who argued Christ was not a man, bodily existence is evil, and salvation comes by renewing the mind. Irenaeus (c. A.D. 180) countered these "heresies" not by dismissing Paul but rather by referencing him, using passages like Ephesians 1:3-9; 4:10, Philippians 2:10-11 and 1 Corinthians 15:50-57, to prove that Christ was a man—the second Adam—who reversed the curse of the first Adam. By his obedient life and death, Jesus proved to be the one and only Son of God when he was raised from the dead.[1]

Origen (c. A.D. 210) believed that one day God would redeem all creatures (even the devil and his angels) due to the comprehensive work of Christ. Using

---

[1] Irenaeus *Against Heresies* 9.3; 10.1-3.

SO WHAT?
Why Listen to Old Interpreters?

Why does it matter what previous generations of Christians thought? Shouldn't we just read and interpret the letters for ourselves? While there is value in reading texts for ourselves, Paul also reminded the Corinthians they were part of a community: "Did the word of God originate with you? Or are you the only ones it has reached?" (1 Cor 14:36). Paul's letters should not be read and interpreted only within the grid of current Western thought. Isn't it interesting that when you read an article or a book about "Paul and his interpreters," it nearly always begins with the Enlightenment? It is no wonder we have a Westernized Paul. Not only should we see how other contemporary (non-Western) Christians are reading a text, but also how the church through the ages has received Paul's letters.

Paul's statements that "one man's act of righteousness leads to justification and life for all" (Rom 5:18), that "all will be made alive in Christ" (1 Cor 15:22) and that "God was pleased to reconcile to himself all things" (Col 1:20), Origen seemed to "open a window toward universalism."[2] For him, Paul's insistence upon human belief and the irrepressible grace of God set aside any notion that individuals are predestined to be damned to eternal punishment.[3]

The doctrine of original sin was developed by Augustine (c. 400) based on Paul's argument in Romans 5:12-21. Augustine interpreted the phrase "so death spread to all men" to mean that Adam's sin was passed down biologically to all humanity. All die because all have been born with the guilt of Adam's sin. All humans sin because all share in the fallen Adamic nature.[4] This is why, according to Augustine's reading of Paul, salvation is by grace alone. Humanity cannot earn God's favor; salvation is a gift of God through Jesus Christ, who was born of a virgin (Paul never mentioned this) and lived a sinless life. Christ died on the cross, therefore, as a substitute for sinners who deserved the wrath of God. So, even though Irenaeus used the Gospel of John more than anything else in his fight "against heresies," he also used Paul to counter the Gnostics' use of Paul. Later,

---

[2]Mark Reasoner, *Romans in Full Circle: A History of Interpretation* (Louisville, Ky.: Westminster John Knox, 2005), p. 56.
[3]Origen *On First Principles* 1.6.
[4]Augustine *On the Merits and Remissions of Sin* 14.

Origen and Augustine quoted Paul with the same authority as the Gospels. In fact, by the time of Augustine, a preference for Paul's writings begins to appear.

The Scholastics and the Reformers. More philosopher than theologian, Thomas Aquinas (c. 1250) is considered the father of "natural theology."[5] Aquinas believed that much of what can be known about God is discovered in creation. Relying upon Aristotle as much as Paul, Aquinas thought that anyone with eyes to see and ears to hear could learn about the "invisible" attributes of God because his "divine nature" is "seen through the things he has made" (Rom 1:20).[6] This is why pagans know so much about God; the powers of observation and the gift of reason can make God's existence knowable through rational proofs, for example, the cosmological argument. And yet reason does not eclipse what can be known only by faith, which is why God's special revelation, his Word, is still needed for unregenerate humanity. The Scholastics did not make heavy use of any New Testament writer, but they did use Paul as much or more than the others. Paul was moving into the heyday of his influence in Christian thinking.

Martin Luther and John Calvin (c. 1530) are the progenitors of what is commonly called Protestant theology, and these Reformers relied heavily upon Paul for much of their thinking. In fact, in may be safe to say that, without Paul, there would be no "Calvinism," no "Lutheran theology." Breaking away from the traditions of the Catholic Church, Luther seized on the forensic metaphors Paul used to describe the significance of Christ's death. The question for Luther was, "How can a sinner—even a person who strives to live righteously and yet is still guilty before the bar of God's justice—receive the righteousness that comes from God?" The answer is found in Paul's letter to the Romans: only in Christ's sacrifice can a believer find such divine justification (Rom 3:21-26). "The very fact that Christ suffered for us, and through His suffering became a propitiation for us, proves that we are (by nature) unrighteous, and that we for whom He became a propitiation, must obtain our righteousness solely from God" by faith in Christ.[7] Therefore "justification by faith" became the centerpiece of Lutheranism and the interpretive key for reading Paul's letters. Many today still consider justification by faith to be the center of Paul's theology.

Calvin used the Pauline terms *election* and *predestination* to describe how God's

---

[5]We have an awkward problem here. We three authors have steadily complained of Westernized readings of Paul; yet here we jump from Augustine to Aquinas. This chapter should also examine how Paul was read in North African, Coptic and Eastern Orthdox traditions. Alas, we are limited by our training. Perhaps in a future edition we can add a non-Western author.

[6]Thomas Aquinas *Summa Theologica* 1.12.12-13.

[7]Martin Luther, *Commentary on the Epistle to Romans*, trans. J. Theodore Mueller (Grand Rapids: Zondervan, 1954), p. 62.

grace operates to justify sinners. Since "there is no one who is righteous, not even one" (Rom 3:10), it is up to God to have mercy and save some. Christ's atoning work is the means by which sinners are made righteous. But Calvin saw God the Father and God the Holy Spirit at work in the redemption of believers as well. In his foreknowledge, God the Father knew that Adam would sin, so he chose to save certain individuals (election) and planned for them to go to heaven (predestination) by sending his Spirit to convict them of their sin at the hour of his choosing, enabling these sinners to believe the gospel and be saved from eternal damnation. Calvin acknowledged that God's selection of certain individuals for heaven seems arbitrary, but Paul provided Calvin an answer: God "has mercy on whomever he chooses, and he hardens the heart of whomever he chooses" (Rom 9:18).[8] Faith is a gift from God that leads to righteousness so that no man can boast they have been justified by their own works (Eph 2:8-9). At least among Protestants, Paul's letters became the heart and soul of the gospel.

Pietism and the modern missionary movement. If Paul's teachings were the heart of the gospel, shouldn't Paul's heart for the nations not teach us as well? In some parts of Europe, Calvinism stifled missions. It was reasoned that evangelism did not depend upon human effort because God "has mercy on whomever he chooses" (Rom 9:18). Others, however, began to notice how Paul himself dealt with the tension between God's sovereignty (Rom 9:18) and his missionary heart (Rom 10:1): how can they believe without hearing, and how can they hear unless someone is sent (Rom 10:14-15)? After hearing a sermon based on Paul's words, a cobbler (William Carey) was inspired to form a missionary society to take the gospel to distant lands. Other Christian groups (including the Anglican Church) followed Carey's lead and established their own mission-sending organizations, giving birth to the so-called modern missionary movement.[9]

Paul's insistence upon God's initiative and grace (Rom 11:28-36) did not keep him from immediately insisting upon holy living: "present your bodies as a living sacrifice, holy and acceptable to God" (Rom 12:1). John Wesley argued Paul never surrendered his appeal for holiness to the reasoning of election. According to Wesley, Paul taught that "circumcision of the heart" was the work of the Holy Spirit, enabling Christians to choose to live in perfect obedience to God. In fact, Wesley's sermons are saturated with quotations from Paul's letters, as the founder of "Methodism" explained what he meant by Christian perfection: a process of

---

[8] Calvin *Institutes* 3.23.5-6.
[9] The fact that missions became wed to Western colonial aggression does not diminish the motivations of the original missionaries.

sanctification whereby the Christian fulfills "all righteousness," growing in grace until the last day.[10] And what about those who don't live holy lives? Can they fall from grace? Wesley answered, "I am well assured they can; matter of fact puts this beyond dispute. Formerly we thought, one saved from sin could not fall; now we know the contrary."[11] The righteousness of God, therefore, depended ultimately on human free will—which is why Paul wrote letters.

Modernity. The dueling of passages of Paul against other passages of Paul led many scholars of the nineteenth century to treat Paul as if he were the antagonist of the first-century Jesus movement. "Liberal" scholarship cast Paul into the role of re-defining, redirecting or completely reinventing the religious reformation begun by Jesus of Nazareth. A number of observations led to this conclusion: (1) Paul was not a follower of the historical Jesus and rarely quoted his teaching, (2) Jesus directed his efforts primarily to the Jews, Paul to the Gentiles, (3) Jesus preached the kingdom of God, Paul preached Jesus, and (4) Jesus stressed ethics, Paul emphasized theology. Working from a Hegelian dialectical model (thesis vs. antithesis = synthesis), F. C. Baur (c. 1850) pit Peter (Jewish Christianity) against Paul (Gentile Christianity) in the unfolding history of the early church and lined up New Testament writings to reflect the tension: Matthew, James and Hebrews (Jewish) versus Romans, Gala-tians and Corinthians (Gentile). Acts (a second-century document, according to Baur) was supposed to represent the resolution of this conflict, a unified church car-rying out the missionary agenda of the resurrected Messiah—to the ends of the earth. William Wrede called Paul the "second founder" of Christianity because of the apostle's emphasis on experiencing the Spirit of Christ. Where Jesus had a "this-worldly" agenda, that is, helping the poor, Paul spiritualized the gospel and made Christ the object of faith. Under the influence of the Hellenistic mystery religions, Paul turns the prophet Jesus into the Lord of the cosmos. Wrede lamented that Paul's influence ultimately eclipsed Jesus' in the life and practice of the church.[12] Al-bert Schweitzer believed Jesus' apocalyptic mission to bring about the end of the world morphed into a "being-in-Christ" mysticism due to Paul's spiritual experi-ences. Paul's converts, therefore, were not taught to ask, "What would Jesus do?" In-stead, they were taught to imitate Paul: live in the Spirit.[13]

---

[10]John Wesley, *A Plain Account of Christian Perfection* (Grand Rapids: Christian Classics Ethereal Li-brary, 1999), pp. 3-16.

[11]Ibid., p. 44.

[12]William Wrede, *Paul*, trans. Edward Lummis (London: Philip Green, 1907), pp. 179-80.

[13]Albert Schweitzer, *Paul and His Interpreters,* trans. William Montgomery (London: A. & C. Black, 1912); and *The Mysticism of Paul the Apostle,* trans. William Montgomery (1930; reprint, New York: Seabury, 1968).

A "new orthodoxy" (neo-orthodoxy) emerged, in part, as a reaction to liberal theology's dependence upon these "historical" reconstructions as foundational for New Testament interpretation. Scholars like Karl Barth (c. 1920) and Rudolf Bultmann (c. 1930) were opposed to a "natural theology" derived from human reasoning and believed that theology begins with the revelation of God's Word. Influenced by the apostle Paul, Barth emphasized the primacy of preaching the word as the means by which hearers encounter the Word of God—Christ Jesus (see Rom 10:9-17). Many of Barth's theological emphases (justification by faith, the sinfulness of humanity, the "otherness" of God), like those of Luther, derived from his study of Paul's letter to the Romans. Unlike Luther, Barth saw the gospel of Christ as an apocalyptic event that reveals the eternal work of God for all humanity. Salvation is not merely a matter of individual faith. God has reclaimed "all things" through Christ. Since Christ existed before time, this all-encompassing revelation of God "makes history in the supreme sense."[14] Time and space cannot contain all that God has done through Christ. Indeed, history will eventually catch up with the apocalyptic reality of God's revelation through the crucified and risen Word. Those who hear the good news, as well as those who proclaim it, participate in the new creation of God in Christ.[15]

Like Barth, Bultmann claimed the proclamation of the kerygma is an apocalyptic event whereby listeners experience the cross and resurrection of Christ. Paul preached "Jesus Christ, and him crucified" (1 Cor 2:2). Encountering the risen Christ comes, then, only in the Christ-event of preaching the gospel. A significant difference, however, between Barth and Bultmann appears in the relationship between history and theology. Where Barth saw the revelation of Christ as a suprahistorical truth (theology) anchored within history via the cross and resurrection of Jesus, Bultmann believed that theology (dogma) does not depend upon history. In fact, to believe in the cross and resurrection of Jesus as historical fact would be a faith-plus-works kind of faith. One must come to believe in the resurrection as personally true, just as one comes to believe that the death of Jesus is redemptive. What mattered to Bultmann was the truth of the message—that resurrection faith is inspired by the proclamation of the gospel.[16] And so, like Barth, Bultmann was heavily indebted to Paul's theology and his emphasis both on gospel proclamation

---

[14]Karl Barth, *The Doctrine of the Word of God,* prolegomena to *Church Dogmatics, Being,* trans. G. W. Bromiley (Edinburgh: T & T Clark, 1975), 1.1:144.

[15]Karl Barth, *The Epistle to the Romans,* trans. Edwyn C. Hoskins (London: Oxford University Press, 1933), pp. 35-42.

[16]Rudolf Bultmann, "Kerygma and Myth," in *Kerygma and Myth: A Theological Debate,* ed. Hans-Werner Bartsch, trans. Reginald H. Fuller (London: SPCK, 1972), pp. 35-43.

and our response by grace through faith. "Faith comes from what is heard" (Rom 10:17).

Postmodernity. In the college classroom today, students are not driven by the questions that captured the imagination of enlightenment thinkers: authorship, textual transmission, history of religions, pre-Pauline traditions. Instead, they want to spend more time in matters of interpretation. "What difference does it make?" drives their inquiry. Yes, they want to know what it was like living in Paul's day. They also have great interest in reception history; how Paul's letters have been read through the ages is important to them. But they don't want to stop there. These postmoderns want to know why Paul's letters should matter to them. Description is not enough. Our students want to know if Paul can help us. We do too.

"AND WHEN THIS LETTER HAS BEEN READ AMONG YOU . . ."

Paul intended his letters to be used to encourage and instruct the church. So what does Paul have to say to us today? Some think the issues of our world have moved far beyond the persecutor-turned-apostle. Paul is dismissed as passé and his teaching as irrelevant to our situation. Others point out that human beings and their problems are essentially the same despite all our technological and sociological advances. For them Paul remains a clear commentator on the human condition and a divinely inspired source for living as kingdom citizens. We stand squarely with the latter camp. We value Paul's letters, his insights and his directives. The problem for us involves seeing the correlation between the problems Paul addressed in the churches of Corinth, Galatia and Macedonia and the issues facing the churches of America, Asia, Africa and Europe. Since Paul's advice for his churches remains God's Word for us now, Paul is worth reading and rereading individually and collectively. To illustrate our point, here are a few of the problems with which we think Paul could help us.

Prejudice. Our world labors under the weight of various kinds of prejudice. Moderns have erected walls of culture, race, economics and religion that seem insurmountable. Paul's world was divided by many of the same barriers that still plague us. In his day the Jew-Gentile divide seemed the most intractable. Paul's experience of the risen Jesus convinced him that a new creation was underway. In that emerging economy the factors that divide people from each other had been eclipsed by the cross of Jesus. His death and resurrection had created a world in which the racial, religious, sexual and social distinctions no longer matter. Paul experienced a unique call to deconstruct those barriers (Gal 3:26-28). He lived and taught a radical universality realized in the *ekklēsia* (Greek for "church"), a diverse community comprising the one body of Christ. United by God's actions in Christ and the Holy Spirit, Paul insisted that his followers maintain, proclaim and extend that unity in all areas of life. Unfortunately, modern believers continue to live and labor under the old economy characterized by separation, xenophobia and prejudice. When Paul spoke of a church that embraced all peoples, he did not mean a mere global unity composed of black churches, white churches, Hispanic churches, and so on. It is often observed that the Christian church remains the most segregated institution in the modern world. If this is true, it is because we have failed to hear Paul. We've silenced Paul's stern rebukes by saying, "Paul didn't mean that." Yet, he did. His gospel of the cosmic Christ, of universal salvation and of the unity of all believers exhibited in the Lord's Table provides the spiritual resources necessary to confront modern churches addicted to similarity. Christ-believers who erect, support or otherwise maintain racial, economic, and sexual segregation will find themselves immediately at odds with Paul and ultimately on the wrong side of God's justice.

Disunity. If what we said in the previous section is true, does Paul have anything to say about all the Christian denominations in the world today? First, we must reckon with the fact that Paul's churches were rocked with disunity (see particularly 1 Cor 1). There were factions, schisms, false teachings and personality "cults." Second, although Paul struggled against the disunity in his churches, he never anticipated the kind of denominational explosion experienced in the modern world, especially in the last three hundred years. Still, despite all the controversies he faced, his message was clear: there is one Lord, one faith, one baptism. There is ultimately one body of Christ, even as there any many members. At the parousia every knee will bow, every tongue confess that "Jesus is Lord"; and there is nothing to suggest that the coming kingdom will be divided into a Baptist section, a Presbyterian section, a Catholic section, an Orthodox section and so on. It makes for good jokes but bad theology. Historically and sociologically, denominations have functioned in various and important ways. But so many Christ-believers today find the denominational distinctives irrelevant that it has become commonplace to describe our day as "postdenominational." As an alternative to denominationalism and in response to Paul's teaching on unity, the emerging ecumenical movement insists churches should find common ground, first in their mission and second in their theologies. Yet denominational differences are reinforced in every generation as members are trained to read Scripture and live their theologies in their own particular ways.

So it is difficult for us to imagine that denominations will ever fade away. But

Paul today would insist that our theological and social distinctives must coexist within the broader, transcendent unity created by the One Spirit. Paul would want all believers to have the same mind, the mind of Christ, and to consider "the other" before they consider themselves (e.g., Phil 2:1-11). Anything else distorts the gospel, weakens the body and denies the Spirit.

SO WHAT?
Can't We All Just Belong to One Church?

This is a familiar question put to most college professors of religion. I usually respond, "We can. Come join my church." Inevitably, that's not what they intended. While most of us yearn for a unity in the body of Christ, we also expect that unity to look and sound like us, or at the very least to not espouse doctrines that seem to contradict our own. Must every Christian believe exactly like we do on every issue and interpret every passage the same way? Is it possible that we could sort out which doctrines are primary, secondary and even tertiary for our faith? Could we even come to some agreement as to what is the most important thing? Some might think such an exercise would cause even more division. We don't believe, though, that fractured Christianity is unavoidable. The students we see in our classes today offer us hope that the Christian church will experience more unity in the coming decades than any time in the last three hundred years.

Paul, ministry and politics. Christianity appears to dominate the religious landscape in the West. Even if Western culture is secular, most people who practice any faith practice some form of Christianity. So the default religion in the West is a secularized form of Christianity. Nonetheless, Christians today are empowered politically, economically, intellectually and socially in ways Paul could have never imagined. As a result, many moderns think that the way to extend the kingdom of Christ is to get involved in politics, business and academia and "to make our voice heard." In other words, Christian ministry involves trying to change society to make it more "Christian." From Paul's perspective that goal is suspect, and the tactics employed to create a Christian society are often sub-Christian.

As a Christ-believer, Paul belonged to a tiny minority of closely watched individuals and communities. He lived in constant and often uncomfortable tension with the "powers-that-be," often landing in prison, ultimately losing his life to Roman authorities. Paul believed that these earthly power structures (political, economic, social and religious) were animated by "principalities and powers," unseen and malevolent spiritual forces under the control of the devil. What God had done, then, was to invade the devil's domain ("the gates of hell") and to rescue (redeem) humanity from the dominion of the powers through the cross of Jesus. As God's apostle, Paul knew it was his calling—and subsequently the church's mission—to bear witness to God's actions. According to Paul's apocalyptic mindset, ministry does not consist of trying to change society (through whatever means); it consists of calling people who live in darkness from the sphere of Adam and the powers to the sphere of Christ and the church (e.g., 2 Cor 5:17-20; Col 1:13-14).[17] This is why Christ's kingdom and the Roman Empire were mutually exclusive. Indeed, Rome was threatened by Paul's gospel message; the apostle was advocating a lifestyle contrary to the Roman way of life. The colonists in Philippi knew what it meant; they accused Paul of "advocating customs that are not lawful for us as Romans to adopt or observe" (Acts 16:21). A man cannot serve two masters.

If we take Paul seriously, we will not look to the state for acceptance, recognition or assistance because it is part of the old order and is destined to pass away. Further, we will not insist that the state become what we are, that is, "Christian." In Paul's vernacular, we are citizens of heaven who declare unapologetically "Jesus is Lord" (not "Caesar is Lord"). Salvation, then, does not consist in redeeming the body-politic (a government cannot be saved); it involves calling people (the governed) into the body of Christ, inviting them to step out of darkness and into the glorious light of the gospel. Indeed, God's apocalyptic purpose leads ultimately to the transformation of the cosmos, but not until the old passes away. For Paul that transformation had already begun in the cross and resurrection of Jesus, and the church is "the first fruits" of that renewal. If we follow Paul's example, we will live in tension with the "powers-that-be," never at home in any place except the church. And the church today that is faithful to Paul's gospel will struggle against the culture that is constructed under the powers, especially because our allegiances belong to Christ and his kingdom. Until Christ comes, his body will manifest the kingdom of God in the world and provide a risky and often subversive way of life.

Poverty. Jesus said, "You always have the poor with you" (Jn 12:8), which Western Christians often interpret by adding mentally, "and therefore you can't do anything about it and shouldn't waste time trying." Paul felt otherwise. In his first

---

[17]E. Earle Ellis, *Pauline Theology: Ministry and Society* (Grand Rapids: Eerdmans, 1989), pp. 5-14.

letter, he noted the other Christian leaders "asked only one thing, that we remember the poor, which was actually what I was eager to do" (Gal 2:10). In many ways, the practice that most united Jewish and Gentile Christians was their common concern to help the poor. For that reason, Paul was hopeful for the relief offering. First and foremost then, we should allow Paul to quicken our concern for the economically oppressed, both in our own country and abroad. While we recognize Jesus' claim that poverty is chronic, he also asserted that those who lost all for the kingdom would receive a hundredfold (Mt 19:29). How is this possible? Because Jesus (and Paul) expects those of us who "have" to share with our Christian brothers and sisters who "have not" (2 Cor 8:13-14). Every Christian[18] homeless person is an indictment of our failure to fulfill the promise of Christ.

We can garner other lessons from Paul's handling of the relief offering. For example, he expected Christ-believers to give more than could be given at a single moment—no offerings of loose change or extra bills (1 Cor 16:2). Also, Paul wanted believers to give generously but also cheerfully and without any sense of compulsion (2 Cor 8:8-15). Finally, Paul expected ministers to guard their reputation when money was involved (2 Cor 8:16-23). Paul himself did not handle the offering, requesting each church that gave to select an honorable member to carry the offering to Jerusalem (and likewise to carry back a report of how the offering was used).

Sexuality, immorality and celibacy. Any honest appraisal of sexuality in Western society will conclude that the West is obsessed with sex. Advertisements, entertainment and the Internet have played the primary role in shaping sexual attitudes and practices in the last few decades. Seldom have other institutions risen to the challenge of providing an alternative view of what it means to be male and female. Properly read and interpreted, Paul offers us some much needed guidance.

Sexuality is an important part of what it means to be a human being made in the image and likeness of God. While God is not male or female, the masculine and feminine reflect aspects of God's nature and character.[19] Therefore, maleness and femaleness are rooted in creation and fundamental to who we are as human persons. Sexual ambiguity and homosexuality are distortions of the created order.

---

[18]At the very least, the point is that the Christian community should care for its own, but the commands of Christ probably indicate the Christian community is to care for the poor wherever they are.
[19]God creates the one man (i.e., "the human") in his own image. He then takes part from one to create the other, making male and female. Thus, the image of God is split between the genders. God is neither male nor female, but he is certainly not neuter. It might be more correct to say God is both. That is, we must look at both men and women to find the image of God. Some characteristics of God are found primarily in one gender or the other.

WHAT'S MORE . . .
What Makes One Married?

In our culture, a legally signed license properly filed in a government office makes one married. This creates a bit of a dilemma for Christians who like to think the wedding ceremony does that. We usually solve it by making it all happen on the same day. The couple registers at the court house and receives a license. The minister performs the ceremony and then signs and mails the license. As a minister, I had no trouble with this until I moved to Indonesia. They had a similar system, but it didn't work well off the main islands. I was visiting a small remote island. One afternoon, the government agent arrived to officially register licenses. He comes once every five years. According to Indonesian (and American) law, someone is not legally married without a license. What of these island couples who had church weddings and have been living together as husband and wife for years before this agent came? Does God care about this government license? We may be quick to say, "No, as long as they had the church marriage ceremony." But what of people married by a Justice of the Peace here in America? What makes one married? Paul cites the saying "The two shall be one flesh" (Eph 5:31). Marriage is certainly more than the signing of a license. It is a life-long, sacred covenant between husband and wife and God. But for Paul, marriage also centered on the act of consummation. Why do we Westerners not consider premarital sex to be the creation of a marriage? Is it because there was no marriage license?

As such they are both among the cause and the effect of God's wrath currently in the world (Rom 1:18-27). While Paul never distinguishes neatly between sexual orientation and practice (a modern disposition), he does connect lust, passion and act as the reason "God gave them up."

Marriage provides the context for sexual intercourse. Again, this is rooted in the goodness of creation as man and woman leave their parents, are joined together and the two become one (Eph 5:31). Of course, to "become one" means more than sexual unity, but Scripture clearly acknowledges the important role that healthy, holy sexual expression has in creating and maintaining marital oneness. God's will in all of life, including sexuality, is a growing holiness (sanctification) among all his people. Negatively, this means avoiding sexual immorality, including premarital and extramarital sex. Positively, this means learning to control our own sexual impulses and not exploiting our husbands or wives (1 Thess 4:1-8). Marital celibacy, according to Paul, should not be practiced except for short periods by mutual agreement. In fact, both husband and wife have reciprocal obligations to sexual satisfaction in marriage (1 Cor 7:1-6). Christian sexuality involves both giving and receiving: giving ourselves in a receiving way and receiving our spouses in a giving way.

Paul is well known as an advocate for remaining single. Single men and women, he points out, are free to serve the Lord, while the married have divided interests. Singles can devote themselves completely to holiness of body and spirit, while the married tend to worry about what their husbands or wives need and want. Although he did not insist that people remain single, he did promote it as a legitimate lifestyle for Christians (1 Cor 7:31-35). Today most Christian young people grow up and get married with hardly a nod to Paul's teachings on the subject. The "normal" thing is to marry. To remain single is to be unlucky in love or to be really "religious" (e.g., priests, monks, nuns). This, of course, is not what Paul meant. For him to be single was a legitimate choice made by gifted men and women so that they might devote themselves more completely to God's work for them. Rather than consider Paul's advice as odd and out of place, we ought to reckon that Paul may have been on to something after all. If we did, perhaps there would be fewer divorces and more devotion to Christ.

CONCLUSION

We celebrate that the word of the Lord has come to us also and not just to the Corinthians (cf. 1 Cor 14.36). Therefore, we also share the responsibility to pass it along to those who would have ears to hear what the Spirit is saying to the churches through the life and letters of Paul. This is a noble calling but also a risky business. Should we trust Paul? Paul was a disruptive force in his world. He pushed the church beyond the known and perhaps even comfortable constraints of Palestinian Jewish Christianity. If we are not careful, he might push us beyond our comfortable Western churches as well. Paul stood up for the truth of the gospel even it if meant standing up to Peter, the rock of the church (Gal 2:11). He stood firm to the end even as the executioner's blade removed his head. But taking a stance that moves against the grain of culture, even popular Christian culture, is not our forte. Paul's exhortation, "If it is possible, so far as it depends on you, live peaceably with all" (Rom 12:18), is certainly not telling us to take a stance against war, is it? Surely Paul didn't mean that. Paul wouldn't want us to take a position that is unpopular or against our other loyalties or culture or, God forbid, our desires. And yet, if we read the letters of Paul seriously, should we, like Christian in Borneo, be persuaded that children (even adult ones) should obey their parents, even in matters like choosing a spouse?

Throughout this book our goal has been to help serious readers of the New Testament rediscover Paul within his or her world and consider what the apostle to the Gentiles can say to our world. Hopefully we have accomplished that, even in a small way. As you can now appreciate, rediscovering Paul is not easy; but it is a journey worth taking. Perhaps the goal is too ambitious, maybe the best we can hope for is to have a better handle on Paul and his enduring message. Nonetheless, you are ready for the next step: imitate him.

Glossary

address, letter. The beginning section of an ancient letter, usually in the format: Sender to Recipient, Greetings

agonistic. Combative, competitive; term used by scholars to describe the culture of the first-century Mediterranean world

agora. Greek word for the public center of a town or city (Latin, forum); much like an older American "town square" with stores and local government offices

allusion. Stylistic device whereby the author refers indirectly or subtly to something outside the text (like a different text), and the hearers or readers are expected to make the connection (*see also* echo)

amanuensis. Scholarly term for an ancient secretary, someone who wrote down a letter or document on behalf of another

apocalyptic. From the Greek word *apocalypsis* meaning "revelation"; used by scholars to describe a worldview (because the world is so corrupt, God must reveal "hidden truth" to the faithful), a kind of literature (visions of another world in time and space) and an ideology (the justice of God will come at the end of the world, which will be swift and complete)

apostasy. From the Greek word *apostasia*, meaning "rebellion" or "abandonment"; in 2 Thessalonians 2:3 this Greek word is used to refer to the future rebellion against God prior to the second coming

asceticism. The practice of austerity and self-denial; punishing the body to liberate and/or purify the soul

autograph. Scholarly term meaning "in one's own handwriting" and usually referring to the original of a document; there are no surviving autographs of any book of the Bible

benefactor/beneficiary. In sociological terms, the one who gives (benefactor) and the one who receives (beneficiary) a benefit or gift; such gifts generally come with "strings attached" and create obligations between the beneficiary and the benefactor.

blasphemy. An act or claim that detracts from or insults the honor of God or things pertaining to God (e.g., temple, priests, law)

canon. In this context, the collection of ancient writings that came to be accepted as authentic Scripture and hence authoritative for Christianity

carrier, happenstance. Someone who "happened" to be going the right direction who was asked to transport an ancient letter

carrier, private. Someone, often a slave, who was sent to deliver an ancient letter to its recipient

catechesis. Elementary instruction in religious or doctrinal matters

challenge (for honor). Questioning another man's social worth in public

chiasm (also chiasmus). Stylistic device in which words or clauses are placed in a particular order (often leading to a center phrase) after which the words or clauses are listed in reverse order, forming a structure: A-B-C-B-A, (see, e.g., Rom 10:9-10)

Christology. Theological beliefs about the person and work of Jesus Christ

Christophany. A revelation or appearance of the resurrected Christ, such as Paul's experience of the risen Christ on the Damascus road (Acts 9)

Cicero (January 3, 106 B.C. – December 7, 43 B.C.). Roman statesman considered one of Rome's greatest orators and a prolific letter writer

clean/unclean. All things (including people) of the ancient Mediterranean world were classified as clean or unclean, either temporarily or permanently, due to religious and social convictions; it was unrelated to "sanitation" in a modern sense

codex (pl. codices). An ancient book formed by folding sheets of paper in half, as in the format of a modern book (versus a scroll or roll); *see* quire

collection. In this context, the process by which the letters of Paul were gathered together and "published" together as a group

corpus Paulinum. Latin term for the collection of Paul's letters, usually consisting of the thirteen "accepted" letters, although ancients often included Hebrews as a fourteenth and many modern scholars accept fewer as authentic

cosmic dualism. The view that reality consists of two separate worlds (visible and invisible, material and spiritual)

cruciform/cruciformity. Conformity to the crucified Christ, consisting of Spirit-empowered correspondence to the patterns of Christ's faithfulness to God and love for others displayed in his self-giving death

day of the Lord, the. In OT prophetic terms, a future day of God's intervention in the world that results in universal judgment and deliverance; Paul appropriates this expectation and transforms it into the day of the Lord Jesus Christ

deutero-Pauline letters. Letters attributed to Paul but thought by some scholars not to have been written by Paul

Diaspora. The dispersion of Jewish people into lands outside the traditional land of Israel; precipitated initially by catastrophic events such as the Babylonian exile (586 B.C.)

diatribe. Ancient rhetorical device, often including elements such as the author/ speaker answering the question of an imaginary opponent; some scholars see evidence of diatribe in Paul's writings, particularly Romans, while other scholars doubt whether the diatribe existed as an established rhetorical device

dictation, Greek. Taking slow dictation was a common technique in elementary education to learn writing; some ancient letter writers may have dictated slowly to a secretary, although most probably spoke more quickly and the secretary merely took notes; Greek shorthand writers existed in the time of Paul but their use was probably limited to the wealthy

dyadic personality. A culturally determined orientation in which group membership reveals one's personal identity

ecclesiology. Theological beliefs about the church

echo. Stylistic device referring indirectly or subtly to something outside the text (for example, a different text), where it is not clear if the user expects the hearers or readers to make the connection (*see also* allusion)

Epictetus (c. A.D. 55-135). Raised in Rome as a slave to a wealthy freedman of Nero, he studied Stoic philosophy; after exile by Emperor Domitian, he established a famed philosophical school; many see parallels between his preaching style and that of Paul

epistolary Paul. A modern term for the Paul that we see from his letters, sometimes denoting the elements of his life and teaching that can be gleaned exclusively from his letters

fl. (*floruit*, "flourishing"). This abbreviation is often used when the date of an ancient's birth or death is unknown; it usually indicates the date(s) of his/her major writings or activities

freedmen. Ex-slaves in the Greco-Roman world who either bought their freedom or were released by their owners

Gentile(s). (Singular) a non-Jewish person; (plural) a people group or nation other than the nation of Israel

Gnosticism. Second-century religion that mixed elements of Christian belief and

Hellenistic philosophy; known for a variety of "heretical" views of Christ (Christ was not human; Christ was an angel; Christ was a "power/spirit" that possessed the human Jesus at his baptism and left him before his crucifixion), Gnostics emphasized the acquiring of secret "knowledge" *(gnōsis)* as the means of salvation

Greek. In the context of this book, the common language *(lingua franca)* and culture of the eastern portion of the Roman Empire; *Koine* ("common") Greek and *Hellenistic Greek* are often used as synonyms for the period 300 B.C. to A.D. 300

greetings, letter. Refers both to the introductory words with which an ancient letter writer introduced himself to his readers and to the concluding words with which he said farewell

hapax legomena. Technical term (from Greek, meaning "written once") referring to a single occurrence of a word or phrase in a literary corpus

Hauptebriefe. German term meaning "chief letters"; a scholarly designation for what some consider to be the principal letters of Paul (Gal, Rom, 1-2 Cor); the expression has a rich and complex theological and historical usage, beginning in 1840 with F. C. Baur

health-wish. A common element of ancient letters; the sender wishes the recipient (and often his/her family) good health, often couched as a prayer to a specific god/dess; as a stereotypical part of ancient letters, it may or may not have indicated any real sentiment on the part of the sender

Hegelian dialectic. A philosophy of history, introduced by G. W. F. Hegel, that says change is predetermined because opponents will always question the status quo. Things as they are (thesis) never stay the same because opposition (antithesis) always arises, and the new status quo (synthesis), the result of compromise, will eventually be challenged by another opposing view

Hellenism. Ancient Greek culture; to *hellenize* means to adopt Greek culture and language

honor and shame. A person's claim to social worth, either recognized (honor) or denied (shame)

iconic worship. veneration of deity through images or representations

imaginary interlocutor. Rhetorical strategy whereby a speaker or writers addresses an imaginary conversation partner, often in order to raise and answer the objections of an audience

imperial cult. Worship of Caesar (dead or alive), the state religion of the Roman Empire

imperial provinces. Territories acquired by Roman military during the empire and ruled by prefects and procurators

incarnation. Literally "enfleshment"; the doctrine that in Jesus of Nazareth a divine, preexistent being became human

inclusio. A literary device consisting of similar words or phrases placed at the beginning and end of a section; working like "bookends" or "brackets," the inclusio provides theme, structure and coherency to the section

intertextuality. The various ways that a writer or community (e.g., Paul and his coworkers) quotes from, alludes to or otherwise appropriates a text (e.g., the Old Testament) in order to generate new meanings for a new audience

Judaizers. Individuals (whether Jewish or Gentile) who opposed Paul's gospel by insisting that non-Jews keep Jewish practices (e.g., circumcision, dietary regulations, sabbath observance) in order to participate in the people of God

kerygma. Greek word meaning "proclamation"; as used here, the content of the proclamation (what is said) rather than the act itself (how or where it is said)

Lukan Paul. A modern term for the Paul that we see from Luke's description (Acts), sometimes denoting the elements of his life and teaching that can be gleaned exclusively from Acts

manuscript. Technically, any document written by hand (as opposed to printed); the term is often used to refer to a hand-written copy of an ancient text

Marcion (c. 110-160). An early Christian heretic whose teachings are known primarily through the writings of his critics; he apparently made heavy use of some of Paul's letters

membranae. Latin term for "parchments," (for our purposes here) likely meaning "notebooks," writings prepared in a codex format rather than the more accepted (and official?) format of a scroll or roll, probably indicating writings for private use rather than public dissemination (see 2 Tim 4:13)

mystery religions. Indigenous fertility cults that combined local, folk religions with the myth of dying and rising gods bringing life to the land (vegetation cult) and to a woman's womb (human fertility cult)

notebooks, ancient. *See membranae*

Onesimus (d. c. 90-95). A slave of Philemon of Colossae; he is at least part of the reason Paul wrote his letter to Philemon

oracles. Divine messages, often forecasting events, delivered by prophets and seers

orthodoxy. Correct belief, thinking or opinion; doctrines and beliefs that conform to an established faith tradition

orthopraxy. Correct practice; behaviors (ethical, political, social, communal, liturgical) that conform to an established faith tradition

papyrus. The ancient equivalent of paper, made from the papyrus reed that grows along the banks of the Nile; the term is used in the plural (papyri) to refer to the oldest manuscript copies of the New Testament, which were written on papyrus

papyrus letter. Technically, any letter written on papyrus, but commonly used by scholars to refer to letters from around the New Testament period (300 B.C.–A.D. 300)

paranesis, paraenesis. Technically means "exhortation"; for our purposes here, it refers to a rhetorical method to persuade someone not to a new way of thinking but rather to appropriate actions or lifestyle

parousia. From the Greek word *parousia,* meaning "presence" or "appearance," referring to the second coming of Christ

Pastorals (or Pastoral Letters/Epistles). An old designation for 1-2 Timothy and Titus as a distinct group of Pauline letters; recently scholars have questioned if these three letters should be grouped together

paterfamilias. Latin word meaning "family father"; the male head of a Roman family whose members would include wife, children, children's wives, freedmen, slaves and clients

patrons and clients. Benefactor (primarily male, but sometimes female) and those dependent upon the benefactor (clients); clients were often called "friends" of the patron

Pharisees. Jewish sect consisting of rabbis and laymen who promoted holiness by subscribing to the purity code for priests; known for recognizing oral tradition as being equal to Scripture

Praetorian. Elite soldiers of the Roman Empire attached to the emperor

predestination. The conviction that God deals with creation according to a plan that he has determined beforehand; for Paul, God's predetermined goal is to sum up all things in Christ (Eph 1:10)

preexistence. The notion that a person or thing exists in heaven prior to entering history; most often associated with Christ

preformed traditions. A recent scholarly expression to indicate material (often hymn fragments, sayings, etc.) that was composed some time prior to the writing in which it is now found

procurators, prefects and proconsuls. Magistrates of the Roman Empire. *Proconsuls* were of senatorial rank and ruled senatorial and larger imperial provinces. *Prefects* were the governors of imperial provinces at the beginning of the empire. Later (first century A.D.), these rulers of equestrian rank (the order below senator) were called *procurators*

pseudonymous letter. A letter written under an alias, especially the name of a famous person

quire (Greek, *quaternion;* **Latin,** *quaternum***).** Originally a stack of four sheets of papyrus or parchment, which were stitched down the middle and folded in half, forming eight leaves and thus a sixteen-page book; *see* codex

rapture. An interpretation of final things that posits a return of the Lord Jesus to take away (or *rapture*, from the Latin *raptus*) Christ-believers from the earth, usually (depending on one's other theological commitments) prior to the great tribulation or immediately prior to the millennium

realized eschatology. The belief that the end of the world has already come, recognized as a spiritual reality

recension. A revision or edited version of a text

reconciliation. Relational metaphor for salvation; humanity's separation and estrangement from God is overcome through the cross of Christ

redemption. Metaphor for salvation, derived from the Hebrew Scriptures, whereby enslaved humanity is liberated from spiritual powers, sin and death

rhetoric. The art of persuasive speech in content, form, style and delivery

Sadducees. Jewish sect consisting of priests and aristocrats who promoted holiness by encouraging devotion to the Jewish temple; known for denying the authority of oral tradition and the resurrection of the dead

sanctification. The process by which anything or anyone is set apart for God; in regard to salvation, believers are made holy by the work of Christ and yet increase in holiness through obedient faith empowered by the Spirit

Scholastics. Theologians of the later medieval period who sought to explain Christian doctrine by using philosophical categories and methods

Semitism. For our purposes here, a grammatical feature shared by ancient Semitic languages, that show up in the Greek text, indicating the author (or at least that phrase) has been influenced by or translated from Hebrew or Aramaic

senatorial provinces. Territories acquired under the Roman republic, governed by proconsuls

Seneca. (also known as **Seneca the Younger,** c. 4 B.C.–A.D. 65) A Roman Stoic philosopher and prolific letter writer

Shema. Jewish confession of the oneness of God based upon Deuteronomy 6:4-9; recited in temple and synagogue liturgies

sophistry. The study of rhetoric that emphasized style and delivery over content

sophists. Professional teachers who founded schools to instruct students in the art of public persuasion

soteriology. Set of theological beliefs about the salvation of humanity

stichos **(pl.** *stichoi***).** A Greek word meaning "row" that refers to a line of written text, often about thirty-six characters in length; secretaries charged by the *stichos*

subscription. For our purposes here, the concluding section of an ancient letter, most commonly in official or legal documents, summarizing the letter's contents and written (if possible) in the handwriting of the sender as authentication

symbolic universe. A view, informed by theological and social beliefs, as to how the world works; also called a worldview

syncretism. The combination or fusion of different ideas and practices into one system

tachygraphist. A writer of shorthand

tongues. In this context, refers to the spiritual gift by which believers could speak in unknown languages (see 1 Cor 12—14)

typology. The strategy for discerning the correspondences, pattern, shape or structural affinity between two of God's acts; these may include his work through persons, events or institutions (e.g., the temple, sacrificial system)

universalism. The belief or doctrine that all people will ultimately be saved

vice. Moral failing or sin, often habitual; rooted in a person's character or nature (according to Paul)

virtue. A beneficial moral trait or quality; according to Paul, virtuous qualities are generated by the work of the Spirit through the new nature

Vulgate. An early Latin translation of the Bible (c. 405); written by Jerome in the literary Latin of the time, its name is derived from its description as *versio vulgata* ("translation made public")

wisdom. In Jewish tradition, the ability to live life well and to make the right decisions; wisdom is a gift from God

zeal. Intense focus or action devoted to an object (e.g., God, God's law, God's people, ancestral traditions); as a technical term, firm resolve and forceful resistance against anyone who compromises God's covenant or insults God

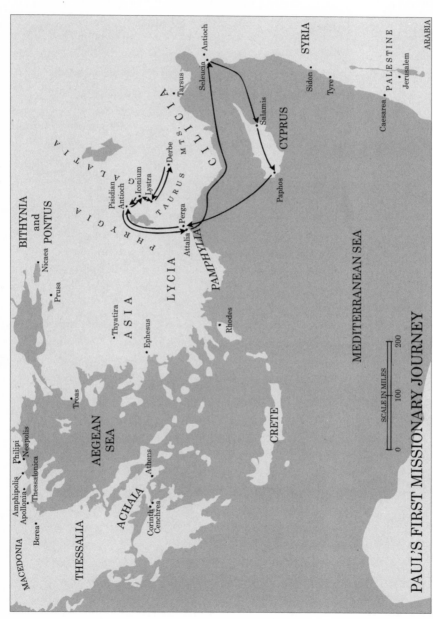

PAUL'S FIRST MISSIONARY JOURNEY

(Map created by Jordan M. Capes)

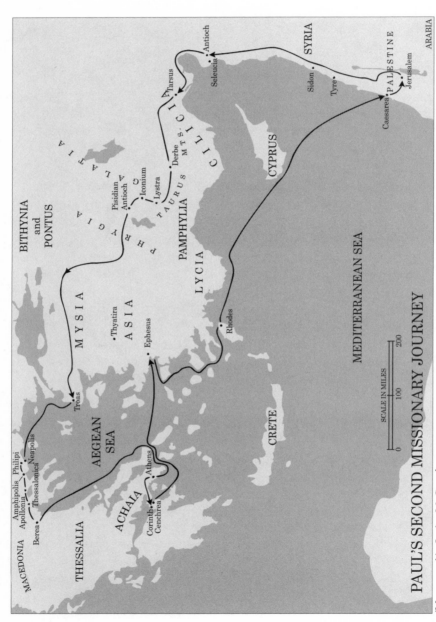

PAUL'S SECOND MISSIONARY JOURNEY

(Map created by Jordan M. Capes)

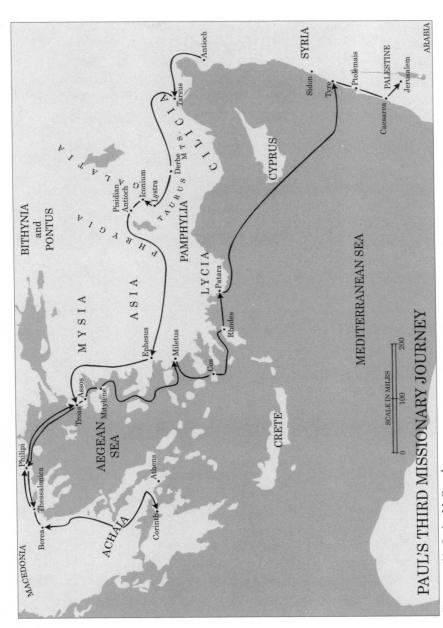

PAUL'S THIRD MISSIONARY JOURNEY

(Map created by Jordan M. Capes)

Bibliography

Aristotle. *The Poetics*, translated by W. H. Fyfe and W. R. Roberts. Loeb Classical Library. London: Heinemann; Cambridge, Mass.: Harvard University Press, 1953.

Arnold, Clinton E. *Ephesians: Power and Magic.* New York: Cambridge University Press, 1989.

————. *Powers of Darkness: Principalities and Powers in Paul's Letters.* Downers Grove, Ill.: InterVarsity Press, 1992.

Arrian. (See Epictetus.)

Augustine. *On the Merits and Remissions of Sin,* edited by John E. Rotelle; translated by Roland J. Teske. Hyde Park: New City, 1997.

Barclay, John M. G. *Jews in the Mediterranean Diaspora: From Alexander to Trajan (323 B.C.E.-117 C.E.).* Berkeley: University of California Press, 1996.

Barnett, Albert E. *Paul Becomes a Literary Influence.* Chicago: University of Chicago Press, 1941.

Barth, Karl. *The Doctrine of the Word of God.* Prolegomena to *Church Dogmatics, Being,* translated by G. W. Bromiley. Edinburgh: T & T Clark, 1975.

————. *The Epistle to the Romans,* translated by Edwyn C. Hoskins. London: Oxford University Press, 1933.

Barth, Markus. *Ephesians: Introduction, Translation and Commentary on Chapters 1—3.* Anchor Bible. New York: Doubleday, 1974.

Bauckham, Richard. *God Crucified: Monotheism and Christology in the New Testament.* Grand Rapids: Eerdmans, 1998.

Baur, Ferdinand Christian. *Kritische Untersuchung über die kanonischen Evangelien: ihre Verhältnisse zu Einander, ihre Character und Ursprung.* Tübingen: Fues, 1847.

Beker, J. Christiaan. *Paul the Apostle: The Triumph of God in Life and Thought.* Philadelphia: Fortress, 1980.

Bruce, F. F. *Paul: Apostle of the Heart Set Free.* Grand Rapids: Eerdmans, 1977.

―――. *The Canon of Scripture.* Downers Grove, Ill.: InterVarsity Press, 1988.

Bultmann, Rudolf. "Kerygma and Myth." In *Kerygma and Myth: A Theological Debate,* edited by Hans-Werner Bartsch; translated by Reginald H. Fuller. London: SPCK, 1972.

Calvin, John. *Institutes of the Christian Religion,* translated by Henry Beveridge. Grand Rapids: Eerdmans, 1979.

Capes, David B. "Adoption in the First Century." *Biblical Illustrator* 32, no. 1 (2005): 39.

―――. "The Lord's Table: Divine or Human Remembrance?" *Perspectives in Religious Studies* 30, no. 2 (2003): 199-209.

―――. *Old Testament Yahweh Texts in Paul's Christology.* Wissenschaftliche Untersuchungen zum Neuen Testament 2/47. Tübingen: J. C. B. Mohr, 1992.

―――. "Yahweh and His Messiah: Pauline Exegesis and the Divine Christ." *Horizons in Biblical Theology* 16, no 2 (1994): 121-43.

―――. "YHWH Texts and Monotheism in Paul's Christology." In *Early Jewish and Christian Monotheism,* edited by Loren Stuckenbruck and Wendy E. S. North. London: T & T Clark, 2004.

Carney, T. F. *The Shape of the Past: Models of Antiquity.* Lawrence, Kans.: Coronado Press, 1975.

Carson, D. A. "Pseudonymity and Pseudepigraphy." In *Dictionary of New Testament Background,* edited by Craig Evans and Stanley Porter. Downers Grove, Ill.: InterVarsity Press, 2004.

Cicero, Marcus Tullius. *Letters to Atticus [Epistulae ad Atticum],* edited and translated by Eric Otto Winsteadt. 3 vols. Loeb Classical Library Latin Series. Cambridge, Mass.: Harvard University Press, 1966-1970.

―――. *Letters to His Friends [Epistulae ad Familiares],* edited and translated by W. Glynn Williams. 3 vols. Loeb Classical Library Latin Series. Cambridge, Mass.: Harvard University Press, 1965-1972.

―――. *Letters to Quintus [Epistulae ad Quintum Fratrem], Brutus [ad Brutum]; Comment. Petit.; Ep. Ad Octav,* edited and translated by William Armistead Falconer. Enlarged ed. Loeb Classical Library Latin Series. Cambridge, Mass.: Harvard University Press, 1972.

Clement of Alexandria. *Clement of Alexandria,* translated by G. W. Butterworth. Loeb Classical Library. Cambridge, Mass.: Harvard University Press, 1939.

Danby, Herbert, trans. *The Mishnah*. Oxford: Oxford University Press, 1933.

Davies, W. D. *Paul and Rabbinic Judaism: Some Rabbinic Elements in Pauline Theology*. London: SPCK, 1948.

Deissmann, Adolf. *Light from the Ancient East: The New Testament Illustrated by Recently Discovered Texts of the Graeco-Roman World*, translated by Lionel R. M. Strachan. London: Hodder & Stoughton, 1912.

deSilva, David A. *Honor, Patronage, Kinship and Purity: Unlocking New Testament Culture*. Downers Grove, Ill.: InterVarsity Press, 2000.

Donfried, Karl P. *Paul, Thessalonians, and Early Christianity*. Grand Rapids: Eerdmans, 2002.

Donfried, Karl P., ed. *The Romans Debate*. Rev. ed. Peabody, Mass.: Hendrickson, 1991.

Duff, J. "P46 and the Pastorals: A Misleading Consensus?" *New Testament Studies* 44 (1998): 578-90.

Dunn, James D. G. *Romans*. 2 vols. Word Biblical Commentary. Dallas: Word, 1988.

———. *The Epistles to the Colossians and to Philemon*. Grand Rapids: Eerdmans, 1996.

———. *The Theology of Paul the Apostle*. Grand Rapids: Eerdmans, 1998.

———. *The Theology of Paul's Letter to the Galatians*. Cambridge: Cambridge University Press, 1993.

Ellis, E. Earle. *Paul's Use of the Old Testament*. Edinburgh: Oliver & Boyd, 1957.

———. *Pauline Theology: Ministry and Society*. Grand Rapids: Eerdmans, 1989.

———. *The Making of the New Testament Documents*. Leiden: Brill, 2002.

Engberg-Pedersen, Troels, ed. *Paul in His Hellenistic Context*. Minneapolis: Fortress, 1995.

Epictetus. *The Discourses as Reported by Arrian [Epicteti Dissertationes], The Manual and Fragments*, edited and translated by W. A. Oldfather. 2 vols. Loeb Classical Library, Greek Series. London: Heinemann; Cambridge, Mass.: Harvard University Press, 1925-28.

Esler, Philip F. *Conflict and Identity in Romans: The Social Setting of Paul's Letter*. Minneapolis: Fortress, 2003.

Fitzmyer, Joseph. *Pauline Theology: A Brief Sketch*. Englewood Cliffs, N.J.: Prentice-Hall, 1967.

Flint, Peter, ed. *The Bible at Qumran: Text, Shape, Interpretation*. Grand Rapids: Eerdmans, 2001.

Frederiksen, Paula. "Judaism, the Circumcision of Gentiles, and Apocalyptic

Hope: Another Look at Galatians 1 and 2." *Journal of Theological Studies* 42 (1991): 532-64.

Gamble, Harry. *Books and Readers in the Early Church: A History of Early Christian Texts.* New Haven, Conn.: Yale University Press, 1995.

―――. *New Testament Canon: Its Making and Meaning.* Guides to Biblical Scholarship, New Testament Series. Philadelphia: Fortress, 1985.

―――. *The Textual History of the Letter to the Romans: A Study in Textual and Literary Criticism.* SDS 42. Grand Rapids: Eerdmans, 1977.

―――. "Canon." In *The Anchor Bible Dictionary,* 1:837-61, edited by David Noel Freedman. 6 vols. New York: Doubleday, 1992.

Gaston, Lloyd. *Paul and the Torah.* Vancouver: University of British Columbia Press, 1987.

Gathercole, Simon J. *Where Is Boasting? Early Jewish Soteriology and Paul's Response in Romans 1—5.* Grand Rapids: Eerdmans, 2002.

Goodspeed, E. J. *An Introduction to the New Testament.* Chicago: University of Chicago Press, 1937.

―――. *The Meaning of Ephesians.* Chicago: University of Chicago Press, 1933.

Gorman, Michael J. *Apostle of the Crucified Lord: A Theological Introduction to Paul and His Letters.* Grand Rapids: Eerdmans, 2004.

―――. *Cruciformity: Paul's Narrative Spirituality of the Cross.* Grand Rapids: Eerdmans, 2001.

Grenfell, Bernard P., and Arthur S. Hunt, eds. *The Oxyrhynchus Papyri.* 51 vols. London: Oxford University Press, 1898-1951.

Guthrie, Donald. *New Testament Introduction.* Downers Grove, Ill.: InterVarsity Press, 1974.

Hahnemann, G. M. *The Muratorian Fragment and the Development of the Canon.* Oxford: Clarendon, 1992.

Harding, Mark. "Disputed and Undisputed Letters of Paul." In *The Pauline Canon,* edited by S. Porter. Leiden: Brill, 2004.

Hauerwas, Stanley. "The Sanctified Body: Why Perfection Does Not Require a Self." In *Embodied Holiness,* edited by S. M. Powell and M. E. Lodahl. Downers Grove, Ill.: InterVarsity Press, 1999.

Hays, Richard. *Echoes of Scripture in the Letters of Paul.* New Haven, Conn.: Yale University Press, 1989.

―――. *The Faith of Jesus Christ: An Investigation of the Narrative Substructure of Galatians 3:1—4:11.* Society of Biblical Literature Dissertation Series 56. Chico, Calif.: Scholars, 1983.

Hengel, Martin. *The Pre-Christian Paul.* In collaboration with Roland Deines, translated by John Bowden. London: SCM; Philadelphia: Trinity Press International, 1991.

Hock, Ronald. "Writing in the Greco-Roman World." *SBL Forum,* May 10, 2004. Online: <www.sbl-site.org/Article.aspx?ArticleID=264>.

Hoehner, Harold W. "Did Paul Write Galatians?" In *History and Exegesis: New Testament Essays in Honor of Dr. E. Earle Ellis for His Eightieth Birthday,* edited by Sang-Won (Aaron) Son. New York/London: T & T Clark, 2006.

Horsley, Richard A., ed. *Paul and Politics: Ekklesia, Israel, Imperium, Interpretation.* Harrisburg, Penn.: Trinity Press International, 2000.

Hurtado, Larry. *Lord Jesus Christ: Devotion to Jesus in Earliest Christianity.* Grand Rapids: Eerdmans, 2003.

Ignatius, "To the Magnesians." In *Apostolic Fathers,* translated by K. Lake. Vol. 1. Loeb Classical Library. Cambridge, Mass.: Harvard University Press, 1985.

Irenaeus. *Against Heresies,* translated by Dominic J. Unger. New York: Paulinist, 1992.

Jerome. *De viris illustribus.* Biblioteca Patristica. Firenze: Nardini Editore, 1988.

Jewett, Robert. *A Chronology of Paul's Life.* Philadelphia: Fortress, 1979.

———. *Romans.* Hermeneia. Minneapolis: Fortress, 2007.

———. *The Thessalonian Correspondence: Pauline Rhetoric and Millenarian Piety.* Philadelphia: Fortress, 1986.

Johnson, Luke Timothy. *The First and Second Letters to Timothy.* Anchor Bible 35a. New York: Doubleday, 2001.

Josephus. *Josephus,* edited by H. St. J. Thackeray et al. Loeb Classical Library. London: Heinemann; Cambridge, Mass.: Harvard University Press, 1943.

Käsemann, Ernst. "'The Righteousness of God' in Paul." In *New Testament Questions of Today,* pp. 168-93, translated by W. J. Montague. Philadelphia: Fortress, 1969.

Keener, Craig S. *Paul, Women and Wives: Marriage and Women's Ministry in the Letters of Paul.* Peabody, Mass.: Hendrickson, 1992.

Kim, Seyoon. *Paul and the New Perspective: Second Thoughts on the Origin of Paul's Gospel.* Grand Rapids: Eerdmans, 2002.

———. *The Origin of Paul's Gospel.* Grand Rapids: Eerdmans, 1982.

Klauck, Hans-Josef. *Ancient Letters and the New Testament.* Waco, Tex.: Baylor University Press, 2006.

Lincoln, Andrew T. *Ephesians.* Word Biblical Commentary 42. Dallas: Word, 1990.

Lincoln, Andrew T., and A. J. M. Wedderburn. *The Theology of the Later Pauline Letters.* Cambridge: Cambridge University Press, 1993.

Luther, Martin. *Commentary on the Epistle to the Romans,* translated by J. Theodore Mueller. Grand Rapids: Zondervan, 1954.

Malherbe, Abraham. "Ancient Epistolary Theorists." *Ohio Journal of Religious Studies* 5 (1977): 3-77.

Malina, Bruce J., and John J. Pilch. *Social-Science Commentary on the Letters of Paul.* Minneapolis: Fortress, 2006.

Marshall, I. Howard. *The Pastoral Epistles.* International Critical Commentary. Edinburgh: T & T Clark, 1999.

———. *New Testament Theology: Many Witnesses, One Gospel.* Downers Grove, Ill.: InterVarsity Press, 2004.

Martin, Ralph. *Reconciliation: A Study of Paul's Theology.* New Foundations Theological Library. Atlanta: John Knox Press, 1981.

Martyn, J. Louis. *Galatians.* Anchor Bible. New York: Doubleday, 1997.

———. *Theological Issues in the Letters of Paul.* Nashville: Abingdon, 1997.

McCready, Douglas. *He Came Down from Heaven: The Preexistence of Christ and the Christian Faith.* Downers Grove, Ill.: InterVarsity Press, 1995.

Metzger, Bruce M. *Manuscripts of the Greek Bible.* Oxford: Oxford University Press, 1981.

———. *The New Testament: Its Background, Growth and Content.* Nashville: Abingdon, 2003.

Metzger, Bruce M., and Bart D. Ehrman. *The Text of the New Testament: Its Transmission, Corruption, and Restoration.* New York: Oxford University Press, 2005.

Mitchell, Margaret. "New Testament Envoys in the Context of Greco-Roman Diplomatic and Epistolary Conventions." *Journal of Biblical Literature* 111 (1992): 641-62.

Mounce, William D. *Pastoral Epistles.* Word Biblical Commentary 46. Nashville: Thomas Nelson, 2000.

Mullins, Terence Y. "Formulas in New Testament Epistles." *Journal of Biblical Literature* 91 (1972): 380-90.

Munck, Johannes. *Paul and the Salvation of Mankind,* translated by Frank Clarke. Richmond, Va.: John Knox Press, 1959.

Murphy-O'Connor, Jerome. "Paul and Gallio." *Journal of Biblical Literature* 112 (1993): 315-17.

———. *Paul the Letter-Writer: His World, His Options, His Skills.* Good News Studies 41. Collegeville, Minn.: Liturgical, 1995.

Nanos, Mark D. *The Irony of Galatians: Paul's Letter in First-Century Context.* Minneapolis: Fortress, 2002.

Neusner, Jacob, ed. *The Mishnah,* translated by Jacob Neusner et al. New Haven, Conn.: Yale University Press, 1988.

Origen. *Contra Celsum,* translated by Henry Chadwick. Cambridge: Cambridge University Press, 1965.

———. *On First Principles,* translated by G. W. Butterworth. New York: Harper & Row, 1966.

Pate, Marvin, et al. *The Story of Israel: A Biblical Theology.* Downers Grove, Ill.: InterVarsity Press, 2004.

Perkins, Pheme. "Philippians: Theology for the Heavenly Politeuma." In *Pauline Theology,* edited by Jouette M. Bassler. Vol. 1. Minneapolis: Fortress, 1991.

Philo. *Philo,* edited by F. H. Colson et al. Loeb Classical Library. 10 vols. and 2 supps. London: Heinemann; Cambridge, Mass.: Harvard University Press, 1929-1962.

Polycarp. *Polycarp.* In *The Apostolic Fathers,* translated by K. Lake. Loeb Classical Library. Cambridge, Mass.: Harvard University Press, 1992.

Porter, Stanley E., ed. *The Pauline Canon.* Leiden: Brill, 2004.

Räisänen, Heikki. *Paul and the Law.* Minneapolis: Fortress, 1986.

Reasoner, Mark. *Romans in Full Circle: A History of Interpretation.* Louisville, Ky.: Westminster John Knox, 2005.

Reeves, Rodney R. "'To Be or Not to Be?' That Is Not the Question: Paul's Choice in Philippians 1:22." *Perspectives in Religious Studies* 19 (1992): 273-89.

Richards, E. Randolph. *Paul and First-Century Letter Writing: Secretaries, Composition and Collection.* Downers Grove, Ill.: InterVarsity Press, 2004.

———. *The Secretary in the Letters of Paul.* Wissenschaftliche Untersuchungen zum Neuen Testament 2/42. Tübingen: Mohr/Siebeck, 1991.

———. "The Codex and the Early Collection of Paul's Letters." *Bulletin for Biblical Research* 8 (1998): 151-66.

Riesner, Rainer. *Paul's Early Period: Chronology, Mission Strategy, Theology,* translated by Doug Stott. Grand Rapids: Eerdmans, 1998.

Sampley, J. Paul. *Paul in the Greco-Roman World: A Handbook.* Harrisburg, Penn.: Trinity Press International, 2003.

Sanders, E. P. *Paul and Palestinian Judaism: A Comparison of Patterns of Religion.* Philadelphia: Fortress, 1977.

———. *Paul, the Law, and the Jewish People.* Minneapolis: Fortress, 1983.

Schmithals, Walter. "On the Composition and Earliest Collection of the Major

Epistles of Paul." *Paul and the Gnostics,* translated by J. E. Steely. Nashville: Abingdon, 1972.

Schneemelcher, Wilhelm. "Paulus in der griechischen Kirche des zweiten Jahrhunderts." *Zeitschrift für Kirchengeschichte* 75 (1964): 1-20.

———. "The Acts of Paul." In *New Testament Apocrypha,* edited by Edgar Hennecke and Wilhelm Schneemelcher; translated by R. McL. Wilson. 2 vols. Philadelphia: Westminster Press, 1965.

———. "The Epistle to the Laodiceans." In *New Testament Apocrypha,* edited by Edgar Hennecke and Wilhelm Schneemelcher; translated by R. McL. Wilson. 2 vols. Philadelphia: Westminster Press, 1965.

Schweitzer, Albert. *Paul and His Interpreters,* translated by William Montgomery. London: A. & C. Black, 1912.

———. *The Mysticism of Paul the Apostle,* translated by William Montgomery. New York: Seabury, 1968.

Segal, Alan F. *Paul the Convert: The Apostolate and Apostasy of Saul the Pharisee.* New Haven, Conn.: Yale University Press, 1990.

———. *Life After Death: The History of the Afterlife in Western Religion.* New York: Doubleday, 2004.

Smith, Carl B. *No Longer Jews: The Search for Gnostic Origins.* Peabody, Mass.: Hendrickson, 2004.

Stendahl, Krister. "The Apostle Paul and the Introspective Conscience of the West." In *Paul Among Jews and Gentiles.* Philadelphia: Fortress, 1976.

Stowers, Stanley. "Friends and Enemies in the Politics of Heaven." In *Pauline Theology,* edited by Jouette M. Bassler. Vol. 1. Minneapolis: Fortress, 1991.

Suetonius. *Suetonius,* translated by J. C. Rolfe. 2 vols. Loeb Classical Library. London: Heinemann; Cambridge, Mass.: Harvard University Press, 1939-1944.

Talbert, Charles H. *Reading Acts: A Literary and Theological Commentary on the Acts of the Apostles.* New York: Crossroad, 1997.

Tertullian. *Adversus Marcionem,* edited and translated by Ernest Evans. Oxford Early Christian Texts. Oxford: Clarendon, 1972.

Thackeray, H. St. J., et al., eds. *Josephus.* 10 vols. Loeb Classical Library. London: Heinemann; Cambridge, Mass.: Harvard University Press, 1926-1965.

Thomas Aquinas. *Summa Theologica,* edited by Thomas Gilby. Garden City: Image Books, 1969.

Trobisch, David. *Paul's Letter Collection: Tracing the Origins.* Minneapolis: Fortress, 1994.

Tyrell, R. Y., and L. C. Purser. *The Correspondance of M. Tullius Cicero.* Dublin: Hodges & Figgis, 1915.

Ulrich, E. C. "The Qumran Biblical Scrolls—The Scriptures of Late Second Temple Judaism." In *The Dead Sea Scrolls in Their Historical Context,* edited by T. H. Lim. Edinburgh: T & T Clark, 2000.

Walker, William. "Acts and the Pauline Corpus Reconsidered." In *The Pauline Writings,* edited by S. Porter and C. Evans. The Biblical Seminar 34. Sheffield, U.K.: Sheffield Academic, 1995.

Walsh, Brian J., and Sylvia C. Keesmaat. *Colossians Remixed: Subverting the Empire.* Downers Grove, Ill.: InterVarsity Press, 2004.

Walters, James C. "Paul, Adoption and Inheritance." In *Paul in the Greco-Roman World,* edited by J. P. Sampley. Harrisburg, Penn.: Trinity Press International, 2003.

Watson, Francis. *Paul and the Hermeneutics of Faith.* London: T & T Clark, 2004.

Wenham, David. *Paul and Jesus: The True Story.* Grand Rapids: Eerdmans, 2002.

Wesley, John. *A Plain Account of Christian Perfection.* Grand Rapids: Christian Classics Ethereal Library, 1999.

Westerholm, Stephen. *Perspectives Old and New on Paul: The "Lutheran" Paul and His Critics.* Grand Rapids: Eerdmans, 2004.

White, John Lee. "Introductory Formulae in the Body of the Pauline Letter." *Journal of Biblical Literature* 90 (1971): 91-97.

Wilder, Terry. *Pseudonymity, the New Testament, and Deception.* Lanham, Md.: University Press of America, 2004.

Wink, Walter. *Naming the Powers: The Language of Power in the New Testament.* Philadelphia: Fortress, 1984.

Winter, Bruce W. *After Paul Left Corinth: The Influence of Secular Ethics and Social Change.* Grand Rapids: Eerdmans, 2001.

———. *Seek the Welfare of the City: Christians as Benefactors and Citizens.* Grand Rapids: Eerdmans, 1994.

Winter, Bruce W., ed. *Book of Acts in Its First Century Setting.* 6 vols. Grand Rapids: Eerdmans, 1993-1995.

Witherington, Ben, III. *Conflict and Community in Corinth: A Socio-Rhetorical Commentary on 1 and 2 Corinthians.* Grand Rapids: Eerdmans, 1995.

———. *New Testament History: A Narrative Account.* Grand Rapids: Baker, 2001.

———. *The Acts of the Apostles: A Socio-Rhetorical Commentary.* Grand Rapids: Eerdmans, 1997.

———. *The Paul Quest: The Renewed Search for the Jew of Tarsus.* Downers Grove,

Ill.: InterVarsity Press, 1998.

Wrede, William. *Paul*, translated by Edward Lummis. London: Philip Green, 1907.

Wright, N. T. *The Climax of the Covenant: Christ and the Law in Pauline Theology.* Minneapolis: Fortress, 1992.

———. *The New Testament and the People of God.* Minneapolis: Fortress, 1992.

———. "Paul's Gospel and Caesar's Empire." In *Paul and Politics,* edited by Richard A. Horsley. Harrisburg, Penn.: Trinity Press International, 2000.

———. *What Saint Paul Really Said: Was Paul of Tarsus the Real Founder of Christianity?* Grand Rapids: Eerdmans, 1997.

Youtie, Herbert Chayyim, and John Garrett Winter, eds. *Papyri and Ostraca from Karanis.* Michigan Papyri 8. Ann Arbor: University of Michigan, 1951.

Zahn, Theodor. *Grundriss der Geschichte des Neutestamentlichen Kanons.* Leipzig: Deichert, 1904.

Zuntz, Günther. *The Text of the Epistles: A Disquisition upon the Corpus Paulinum.* Schweich Lectures, 1946. London: British Academy, 1953.

Author Index

Subject Index

Scripture Index